Potters at War
Stoke City 1939-47

DESERT ISLAND FOOTBALL HISTORIES

Potters at War

Stoke City 1939-47

Series Editor: Clive Leatherdale

Simon Lowe

DESERT ISLAND BOOKS

First published in 2004
by
DESERT ISLAND BOOKS LIMITED
89 Park Street, Westcliff-on-Sea, Essex SS0 7PD
United Kingdom
www.desertislandbooks.com

© 2004 Simon Lowe

The right of Simon Lowe to be identified as author of this work has been
asserted under The Copyright Designs and Patents Act 1988

British Library Cataloguing-in-Publication Data
A catalogue record for this book is available from the British Library

ISBN 1-874287-78-3

Printed in Great Britain
by
Biddles Ltd, King's Lynn

Photographs in this book are produced with the kind permission of
Julian Boodell, Anthony Brown, Dennis Herod, Roger Martin, EMPICS

~ CONTENTS ~

~ AUTHOR'S NOTE ~

I never could understand why Bob McGrory, Stoke's manager, sold his shining star just before Stoke's most important game in their history – a game which could see Stoke capture their first ever trophy, the League Championship. When Clive Leatherdale of Desert Island Books proposed this book to me, I felt this was an opportunity to get to the bottom of this mystery. I hope this book will go some way to helping fans understand this mystifying conundrum. Along the way I discovered how totally different wartime football was to the game we know and love today. Everything from the ball itself to players' conditions, kit and training has changed. This book attempts to allow the modern fan an insight into what it was like to play professional football during and just after the Second World War.

Not surprisingly, many of the facts in the wartime statistics section of this book have eluded my best efforts to track them down. Despite lengthy research at the offices of the Football League and in local newspaper libraries, the names of certain referees and goal-times were often never recorded. I hope this missing data will be completed, if not by myself then by others inspired by my continuing efforts. I also hope the reader accepts my explanation for the gaps that appear. I would not be happy 'guessing', in order to make the stats section seem complete, as other, less scrupulous authors might have been tempted to do.

I conducted interviews with many of the Stoke players of the period. I was just in time, as many are sadly no longer with us. It became clear from those interviews that there was something special about this team. Hard-man left-back Jock McCue would go misty-eyed at the remembrance of 'My boys, my boys'. Goalkeeper Dennis Herod says: 'They were tremendous days. We had bonding, camaraderie and the greatest life of simply playing for the love of the game.' The newspapers loved Stoke's brand of football, too, calling it 'classical football' and 'a lesson in how the game should be played'. This was Stoke's greatest ever team and we should cherish them and the barriers they had to cross simply to play a game of football.

Thank you to everyone who gave their time to spend happy hours reminiscing about that Golden Era. Thanks to Stoke City FC and especially Ian Bayley, the Financial Director, for allowing me to peruse the club's Minute Books; also to John Abberley, Rex Audley, Owen Bennion, Brian Calvert, Stan Clewlow, Dennis Herod, Roger Martin, David Marks, Frank Mountford, Gerald Pearson, Mick Penning, Martin Spinks, Huston Spratt, and Jim Westland Jnr.

I wrote much of this book with my daughter Evie, who was born in December 2003, upon my knee. Although she may have hindered rather than helped its progress, her cheery giggle and doe-eyed smile have often kept me going. Her mother, Kath, has earned my undying love and thanks for giving me Evie, not to mention encouragement and plentiful cups of coffee along the way.

SIMON LOWE

Stoke's bin goin' dine-bonk fer a wheyle
Larke a mon wot's given up th'ghost
It meekes thee wonder wot started th'rot
An' who fer put th'bleeme on most

Somewheer in them local teyms
Ther must bey a Matthews or Soo
Or Wilshaw, or Mowld or Franklin
Or mebbee a Mountford or two

So somebody 'ad better get crackin'
An' build a new teym up, an' then
In a seyson or two theen bey pleein'
In th'fost division aggen!

JABEZ, Potteries folk poet, 1990

~ INTRODUCTION ~

In a world without mobile phones, teletext and the internet, where newspapers, not television, were the medium of mass communication, football in the 1940s was unrecognisable to the modern day. From boots to ball, players' wages to stadia, nothing remains the same. In 1939 England had not yet bothered to enter the World Cup, the First Division was the top flight of English football, and players were tied to their clubs like low-paid serfs.

In today's era of highly marketed superstars on film-star wages, it is notable that Stoke City's major signing of the summer of 1939, Pat McMahon, earned £5 per week with a £10 signing on fee, while the manager's salary was £850 per annum. It was a time when clubs could take care of their supporters' misfortunes, too, on occasion. Stoke agreed that a Mr Dean, whose spectacles had been smashed by the ball whilst watching a first-team game, could have a new pair paid by the club, while Mr S Parry had his trousers – which he had ripped while leaving the ground – replaced without charge.

In 1939 Stoke City Football Club had one dominating personality – its manager, Bob McGrory. The gruff, bluff Scot had made a club record 511 appearances as a tough-tackling right-back before becoming manager in 1935. His managerial style was abrasive and his tenacious personality ensured that Stoke's players never rested on their laurels. He was not afraid to axe any player deemed not to be pulling his weight, or to give youngsters the chance to pull theirs. He ruled the roost with an iron fist. Amateur youngster Stan Clewlow remembers that 'McGrory to me was an unknown figure, never seen at training times. We called him Mr McGrory and we had total obedience to seniority.' The manager divided fans, too. While many believed him to be a solid club man, with good managerial nous, others were less convinced. Fan Rex Audley recalls: 'McGrory was mean, both in the way he treated his players and the way he paid them. I didn't think he was that good tactically, either.' But McGrory, despite being still a fledgling manager, had built a winning team.

Throughout the late 1930s, Stoke City boasted a collection of top quality players. Goalscoring centre-forward Freddie Steele had won England caps alongside his Stoke teammates – left-winger Joe Johnson and right-winger Stanley Matthews. Steele was known endearingly to fans as 'Nobby', due to his powerful heading ability, honed during countless hours of practice heading a ball tethered to a stanchion in the bowels of the Boothen End.

City's half-back line of Arthur Tutin, captain Arthur Turner and Frank Soo – the first player of Chinese descent to play League football – remains to this day the club's finest ever midfield combination. The side oozed goals. West Brom succumbed 10-3 in February 1937, while Derby suffered an 8-1 thrashing. Freddie Steele set a new club record for a season by scoring 33 goals in 1936-37, a record which still stands. In the previous campaign, Stoke had finished fourth with a club record top-flight points total of 47. The club was enjoying its halcyon era, no longer the butt of football wags' humour – its history littered with wooden spoons, relegations and, in 1908, extinction due to too few supporters to keep it alive. What the Potteries prided itself upon now was that most of its stars were home-grown, nurtured by the club from teenage hopefuls to top-flight professionals. Stoke had now earned the nickname the 'Arsenal of the North'. Given that Herbert Chapman's Gunners had recently won a hat-trick of League championships, this was no mean soubriquet.

City played in front of average crowds of 25,000. On Easter Monday 1937, Stoke's Victoria Ground – which had hosted football since 1878 – clicked an unprecedented 50,000 through its turnstiles for the visit of Arsenal. The Vic was a very different ground to that consigned to history when the club moved to the new Britannia Stadium in 1997. With barely any of the old stadium providing cover against the elements, in 1935 the Butler Street Stand was updated at a cost of £30,000. It boasted a wooden multi-gabled roof that ran three-quarters of its length. Its seating was raised behind a paddock, which had steps sunken beneath pitch level, giving a worm's eye view of the game. The rebuilding also saw the construction of an indoor training track under the corner of Stoke's 'Kop', known as the Boothen End, and a £1,200 investment in land adjacent to the stadium to create a sixteen-acre car park.

The Boothen End was a recently concreted bank behind the southerly goal, under which the covered River Trent flowed at its corner connection with the Butler Street Stand. The Boothen End had no cover at this time. Behind the other goal, the Town End was merely a shale bank, shored up by wooden joists and terraced only halfway up its 80ft height, which was typical of many such terraces around the country. The ground's main stand, the Boothen Stand, allowed Stoke's better-off supporters to sit and watch the action on flip-up wooden seats. At its southern corner, where it met the Boothen End, stood the club house, in which players changed before the match before entering the field of play near the corner flag. The directors box overhung the changing rooms, and was at that time a wooden, white-painted construction with a balcony for directors and players' wives. It served another purpose for the players – as a stage upon which to showboat their tricks to impress the directors or, indeed, young ladies. Supporter Bernard Audley once accused the young Stanley Matthews of indulging in exactly that kind of behaviour. Matthews, desperate to win a first-team place, admitted his guilt.

In the summer of 1931, Sir Francis Joseph had become club president and established Stoke as one of the most hospitable clubs in the League, priding himself on entertaining visiting club directors. For that purpose, above the changing rooms perched the white painted Directors Pavilion, or, as one fan, Owen Bennion, puts it, 'a glorified Pigeon-coop'. From here, the players' wives and families could oversee the game from the balcony. For opponents, the Victoria Ground had become an intimidating arena. Its seething crowds were situated close to the play and were, the Stoke players believed, worth a goal start. These ground improvements were rewarded when, on 18th November 1936, Stoke hosted an international fixture and a crowd of 47,882 cheered England to a 3-1 victory over (Northern) Ireland.

Although the facilities for spectators had been updated, those for the players had not. According to Stan Clewlow: 'Our changing rooms were a dungeon. In the middle was an anthracite stove which Freddie Steele had a chair in front of. The kit was washed and dried in the room, making it dank as well as dark.' Goalkeeper Dennis Herod remembers the players' bath in which they washed every day after training: 'It was made of tin and had silted up on the bottom. We used coal-tar soap to scrub down. Water got everywhere and the place was never dry.' The pitch, which perpetually suffered from the high water table caused by the nearby River Trent, wasn't much better. Stan Clewlow again: 'The playing surface was simply awful down the middle. The bounce of the ball wasn't true at all. I never played on a flat pitch or one with grass on after October. I used to go and look at flat pitches and dream of playing on them.'

However, all was not harmonious in Stoke's world. Tensions surfaced between manager McGrory and his star player, Stanley Matthews. The right-winger had shot to prominence when he scored a left-footed hat-trick as England defeated Czechoslovakia 5-4 at White Hart Lane in 1937. Elevated to god-like status amongst Stoke fans, Matthews developed into a devastating wide-man, capable of destroying his marker and supplying a stream of crosses. Centre-forward Freddie Steele relished this service and Matthews became the shining star of his generation. He boasted his own column in the *Sunday Express* and endorsed various consumer desirables, including 'Craven A' cigarettes, despite the fact he did not smoke.

Matthews had earned his stardom by dedication to his craft, which included a strict personal training regime. He would rise at 6am for rigorous exercises before travelling to the Vic to train with all the other players. Bizarrely, the didactic McGrory held a long-term grudge against his star.

As a tyro winger, Matthews had ousted the manager's former roommate from his playing days, inside-right Bobby Liddle, from Stoke's first team. It seemed that McGrory was determined to avenge this perceived injustice. Matthews provided the necessary provocation in the summer of 1937 by asking for the maximum signing-on fee of £650 – £150 more than was on offer from the board. Matthews believed a player of his calibre was worth it, but McGrory and Stoke blocked the rise and Matthews went three weeks unpaid in protest. Eventually, after much unseemly wrangling, Matthews re-signed when the directors agreed to increase the offers to senior players such as Johnson, Tutin, Turner, and himself. Matthews insisted the increase be back-dated, but it is not clear if he had his way. The matter was resolved, but the feelings it had aroused simmered away beneath the surface.

In February 1938 headlines screamed that Matthews wanted to leave the club. He and McGrory had come to verbal blows once again. Stoke's supporters were provoked into uproar. Seven eminent local industrialists called a protest meeting at the King's Hall in Stoke on Monday, 14th February. The packed meeting agreed unanimously that 'Matthews Must Not Go'. Claim and counter-claim flew back and forth in the papers. Matthews cited 'footballing reasons' as the basis for his request to be sold. For his part, the canny McGrory assured everyone that he worked harmoniously with Matthews and that he treated him the same as everyone else.

But that was the problem. Matthews was an enigmatic genius who felt he should be treated *differently* and rewarded for his ability. Despite a belated offer from Stoke's Chairman, Alderman Harry Booth, Matthews reiterated his demand to leave. Clearly there was more friction between the manager and his brightest star than met the eye. The board convened on 15th February and spent two hours discussing the situation. They decided to block Matthews' transfer request, which was a blow to the litany of clubs queuing up to whisk Stan away from the Victoria Ground – among them Everton, Derby, Leicester, Newcastle and Wolves. Matthews wrote to the local paper to express his thanks to those who were supporting him and an uneasy truce was forged. With no possibility of breaking the contract which bound him in chains to the club, Stan pledged to stay and do his best for Stoke City. There was no doubt though, that the undercurrent of discontent lingered.

The Matthews wrangle left its mark on Stoke's players, who began the 1938-39 season poorly, spending most of the autumn in the bottom four. City also had to contend with the loss of goalscorer Steele with a cruciate injury, caused by a collision with Charlton goalkeeper Sam Bartram. This caused Steele to miss almost half of Stoke's games. Manager McGrory wheeled out those whose performances had deteriorated. Full-back Charlie Scrimshaw, previously on the edge of England selection, moved to

Middlesbrough for £3,000. Deposed captain Turner, now 29, was despatched to Birmingham, and Tim Ward returned to Port Vale.

In September 1938, Prime Minister Neville Chamberlain stepped off a plane at Heston Aerodrome waving the new Anglo-German peace accord, which decreed that Germany, and its leader Adolf Hitler, had no more territorial claims in Europe. 'I believe it is peace for our time,' Chamberlain declared. The next day Germany, as agreed in the accord, annexed the Sudetenland, which had been granted to Czechoslovakia by the Treaty of Versailles in 1919.

On the pitch, Stoke's players rallied, producing a run of form which brought five successive wins in January, with Freddie Steele bagging nine goals. He finished the season with 26, while Tommy Sale scored eighteen and left-winger Frank Baker ten, as Stoke continued their improved form to finish seventh. Stan Matthews was voted one of the four Footballers of the Year by Charlie Buchan's *News Chronicle Football Annual*.

As with most clubs of the era, Stoke played a rigid WM formation, whereby the inside-forwards hung back to act as attacking midfielders behind the centre-forward, whose job it was to score goals. The two wingers, whose task was simply to feed the centre-forward, formed the outer points of the W. The centre-half, since the change to the offside law in the 1920s, dropped deep into the back line to form a defence of three. Two defensive half-backs prowled the midfield, winning the ball and distributing it.

For Stoke, Syd Peppitt and George Antonio vied for the forward position inside Stan Matthews. On the other wing, Joe Johnson had been sold to West Brom and youngsters Alec Ormston and Frank Baker competed for his place. Inside them, 22-year-old Scot Jim Westland, a former Scottish schoolboy international, added some cultured passing to the general hurly-burly of Stoke's powerful forward line at inside-left. Considered by many fans to be one for the future, Westland was in line for a full Scottish cap, after being called up as a twelfth man (that is, reserve) by the Scottish selectors. Westland had persuaded a fellow Scottish schoolboy cap, left-half Jock Kirton, to come down from Aberdeen to join Stoke. Kirton had ousted the ageing Arthur Tutin from the half-back line, while Arthur Turner's replacement at centre-half was another youngster, Billy Mould. Behind the full-backs, Harry Brigham and Jack Tennant, Stoke's last line of defence was North-Easterner Norman Wilkinson, dependable if unspectacular. Squad players included veteran forwards Patsy Gallacher, Bobby Liddle and Tommy Sale, reserve right-winger George Mountford, half-back Clem Smith, and the elder brother of Jim Westland – Doug, the reserve goalkeeper.

Even in 1939, there were those who believed that football inhabited some parallel universe, but sometimes it had to live in the real world too.

Hitler's troops swallowed up the rump of Czechoslovakia in March, whereupon Chamberlain pledged that Britain would defend Poland, Hitler's next likely target. Stoke City had intended to spend the summer touring Poland and Germany, although the board had informed one host club, SV Hamburg, that 'we will receive consideration guided by the international situation.' Now, Stoke had little option but to cancel the proposed tour as the Continent slid to wards war.

The future of organised football in Britain was even called into question. As happened at many other clubs, numerous Stoke players joined the Territorial Army and other national service organisations, such as the War Reserve Police, throughout the course of the 1938-39 season. Despite the determination of some to believe otherwise, war was now inevitable.

The war would disrupt the routines of players and spectators. For several years past, after every Stoke home game, Stan Matthews would spend the evening in his father-in-law's pub, the Jolly Potters in Hartshill, reliving the match during a few rounds of his favourite card game, Solo. No longer would City's pre-match entertainment be provided by the 'S Heath and Son' works band. And the practice of the *Evening Sentinel*'s sports reporter of dispatching a pigeon – with a note of the half-time score affixed to a ring around its leg – to the paper's offices in Hanley was terminated by the installation of telephones in the press area in the main stand. When football emerged from the war in 1945 it would be unrecognisable from its pre-war state. What would the effect of the conflict be on Stoke City FC?

## CHAPTER ONE

~ 1939-40 ~
'Stan, t'way I see it, yon 'Itler fella is an evil little twat.'

Professional footballers across the country reported back to their clubs in the high summer of 1939 amidst a surreal atmosphere, with few truly believing they would be seriously affected by the worsening political situation. Cocooned from the reality of Britain's decision to stand up to Hitler, should he choose to invade Poland, many still believed, as did much of the population, in Prime Minister Neville Chamberlain's promise of 'Peace for our time'.

Among Stoke City's congregation were the club's only two close-season additions to their professional ranks – goalkeeper Patrick McMahon from Wrexham, and eighteen-year-old local centre-back Eric Hampson. For years, under both Mather and McGrory, Stoke had pursued a policy of routinely signing up reams of local amateurs, purely to stop other clubs creaming talent from under their nose. The junior clubs which provided the players benefited by receiving a donation from Stoke of around £10 in recognition of their involvement in developing the player. Hampson was one of the few to graduate through those ranks to sign as a pro.

McGrory had placed two players on the transfer list. Arthur Griffiths, an inside-forward, found himself at the bottom of the pecking order for a position described by Stoke as 'overstaffed' in the Football League transfer book. Signed for £1,250 from Rochdale in November 1938, injury had restricted Griffiths to just four first-team games. Despite this, Stoke placed a tag of £750 on the 26-year-old's head. Also unwanted, centre-half Billy Moore was listed at an asking price of £150. Aged 25, Moore's undistinguished Stoke career featured just two first-team appearances, during an injury crisis in March 1938, which resulted in thrashings at Charlton and Arsenal.

Missing from the ranks of McGrory's men were eight players who had joined HM forces during the summer in answer to a recruitment drive. It was during military training that Stoke's first 'wartime' casualties occurred. Territorial Army volunteers Freddie Steele and Jack Challinor both picked up knee injuries during a 41st Anti-Aircraft Battalion training camp at Newark-on-Trent. Challinor strained his knee ligaments, while Steele developed fluid on the knee from which a cartilage had been removed a season earlier. Stoke made representations to the TA authorities to have the pair, and Steele in particular, released from duty so the club could take care of them. But as Steele and Challinor were fit enough for Army duty, if not football, they were expected to remain to complete their training until 13th August. Existing members of the military – George Antonio, Norman Wilkinson, Jim and Doug Westland, Jock Kirton and Tom Brawley – also found themselves precluded from playing in Stoke's first public practice match on Saturday, 12th August.

When City finally gained Steele's release, Dr A P Spark, the club's Medical Officer, arranged for him to enter a Birmingham nursing home, where an orthopaedic specialist performed a second cartilage operation at 7.45am on Thursday, 10th August. When it emerged that the injuries to Steele and Challinor had occurred during boxing bouts, rather than military manoeuvres, McGrory's apoplexy was matched only by his growing selection difficulties. At short notice, five other players – Billy Mould, Syd Peppitt, Frank Baker, Alec Ormston and Alf Massey – were mobilised with their TA unit of the 61st North Midland Field regiment near Swansea. As the *Sentinel* tersely observed: 'with the club's professional playing staff numbering only 31, the selection of two teams for the practice game is likely to present something of a problem.'

Stoke's first public practice lined up like this – Red & Whites: McMahon, Brigham, Tennant, Soo, Bamber, Wordley, Matthews, Smith, Sale, Gallacher, Poulton – Blue & Whites: Martin, Tutin, Oldham, Hampson, Franklin, Fursland, Mountford G, Bowyer, Mountford F, Liddle, Adams (amateur trialist). Gallacher's opener, Sale's thunderbolt and Smith's hat-trick put the Reds five up by the interval. Half-time changes allowed Cairns, Ashley and Kinson a run out, while the forward lines swapped sides. Youngster Atkins, from Summerbank, replaced the injured George Mountford and he, and Frank Mountford, scored as the youngsters notched two against their young compatriots' defence.

Due to the absence of so many players, the club arranged a second practice on Tuesday, 15th. On a balmy, close evening, the youngsters took the limelight during a 5-4 win for the first team, six of whom had only returned from duty overnight. For the first time ever in a Stoke match, numbered jerseys were used, with Stanley Matthews sporting No 7. This led to small boys running around Stoke with '7' roughly stitched to their shirts and thence the birth of the football replica shirt industry.

The innovation was not Stoke's, but stemmed from the Football League, whose AGM decided henceforth that all players should be numbered to allow easy identification. The decision led to protests around the country that numbers might be alright for horses and greyhounds, but not for human beings. The same AGM had seen Derby County's proposal that promotion and relegation be increased from two to four clubs defeated by 28 votes to 21.

Stoke's reserve side, packed with seventeen-year-olds, performed creditably over the two practice games. Four of those lads would form the backbone of City's championship challenge in 1946-47 – Neil Franklin, Frank and George Mountford, and Frank Bowyer. When 29-year-old Norman Wilkinson was withdrawn at half-time from the first-team goal in favour of McMahon, it seemed McGrory was calling time on the keeper's Stoke career. But McMahon did not impress either, and the manager handed Doug Westland the jersey for the Football League Jubilee Fund match at home to Wolves. This was Stoke's only pre-season 'friendly', as modern fans would recognise it. The Fund celebrated the League's 50th anniversary, encouraged young players, equipped others for occupations after retirement, and assisted incapacitated former players. It was intended to raise £100,000, but after twelve months of fund-raising matches only £35,000 had been banked.

As with many of the Jubilee fund-raisers, a disappointing crowd of 6,000 turned up at the Victoria Ground. McGrory's selection options were further reduced when Frank Baker reported with feet blistered by his Army boots. The 'crowd' saw Dickie Dorsett score a hat-trick as Wolves raced into a four-goal lead. Between Stoke's posts, Westland had one of those games when nothing went right. This was his chance to stake a claim for the first-team jersey. Tommy Sale scored twice as Stoke rallied, with Smith and Gallacher wasting opportunities to snatch an unlikely draw. Stoke lost 2-4 and Westland was dropped for City's first League game.

On Wednesday, 23rd August, Germany and the Soviet Union shook the world by announcing the signing of a non-aggression pact. The following day Prime Minister Chamberlain warned the House of Commons that Britain was in 'imminent peril of war'. The Football League chose to bury its head in the sand: 'Unless the crisis takes a turn for the worse we are carrying on as usual, so Saturday's matches will take place.' One wonders what could have been 'worse' than two aggressive world powers joining forces against Britain? But across the country, clubs prepared as best they could for the new season, even though up to two thirds of their squads were missing. Belatedly yielding to the inevitable, the FA waived its Rule 33, which stated: 'no player serving in his Majesty's Forces can be registered as a professional footballer.'

On the Thursday, with neither of his understudies having staked a serious claim for his place, goalkeeper Wilkinson was named as part of Saturday's starting eleven, but the following day – along with Kirton, both Westlands, Challinor, Antonio and Brawley – he was called up into full-time service as Britain increased preparations for the inevitable conflict. It was a case of crisis management for McGrory, who lost his two first-choice goalkeepers, plus senior left-back, left-half and inside-left. At least he still had his captain, the dependable Frank Soo, ever present in the past two seasons. Better news arrived on the fitness of international centre-forward Freddie Steele. He left his nursing home the day before the season started, expecting to start training within two weeks.

The morning of Saturday, 26th August 1939 dawned bright and fresh. As football commenced a season that surely could not finish, German forces massed on the border with Poland. At the Victoria Ground, Sir Francis Joseph, the Stoke Club President and local MP, visited the dressing rooms to give a pep talk to his team, reserving a special word for junior goalkeeper Patrick McMahon, who had been thrust into the spotlight due to Wilkinson and Westland's unavailability. To cover the weakened left flank, McGrory switched Soo to left-half, played Tennant at left-back and Gallacher at inside-left.

3.15pm was the traditional kick-off time at Stoke. This allowed workers to finish their shift at 3pm and rush to the Victoria Ground. Public houses also closed at 3, giving an extra incentive to dash off to the match. This meant that a paltry crowd at kick-off might double fifteen minutes into the game. Some 16,000 eventually arrived on that first day, nearly 9,000 down on the previous season's average. It was by far the lowest opening day crowd at Stoke since their return to the top flight in 1933.

But despite the surreal atmosphere surrounding the opening day, some things did not change. The comforting familiarity of Stanley Matthews running Charlton's full-back James Oakes ragged dovetailed with Billy Mould performing like 'a stag in defence'. Stoke's 4-0 victory at least alleviated some of the deepening political gloom. Yet, just two days later, Stoke lost their long unbeaten home sequence, 1-2 to Bolton, in a subdued performance which reflected the mood of the nation. McGrory was in an unforgiving mood, and gave his forlorn troops a tongue-lashing when he had them assembled, shame-faced, back in the dressing room. War or no war, McGrory demanded maximum effort at all times. Both Bolton's goals had stemmed from individual errors. Keeper McMahon dropped a cross for Rothwell to slot the winner, and the exasperated McGrory began the search for a replacement custodian.

Around dawn on Friday, 1st September, Germany invaded Poland, their Panzer tanks smashing aside Poland's antiquated cavalry. Parliament prepared for imminent war by voting unanimously that the Armed Forces be allowed to call up men aged 18-41. Able-bodied footballers clearly became prime candidates and many of Stoke's squad responded by signing up for TA service. Britain also began the evacuation of three million children between the ages of three and thirteen from inner cities to rural areas. Despite its industrial nature, Stoke-on-Trent was deemed not to be a prime German target, as there was little heavy or armament industry in the

Potteries. While 30,000 children from Manchester were pouring into north Staffordshire, what was left of the Stoke City squad travelled to Middlesbrough by coach rather than the usual train.

Aside from those players who had rejoined their units, Massey had injured a leg against Bolton, so McGrory summoned 33-year-old Arthur Tutin for his first senior appearance for a year. Stoke's depleted team began the game at pointless Middlesbrough raggedly, but Tommy Sale's two second-half goals earned a rare point at Ayresome Park. The long journey home saw the team coach cross the Pennines through a lashing storm without headlights – with blackout regulations now in force, only sidelights were permissible. The tortuous journey lasted ten hours, the coach not reaching Stoke until 4am on Sunday, 3rd September. At 11 that morning Chamberlain's grave voice on the radio announced that Britain was at war with Germany. In footballing terms, Stoke were left with just three professionals – Brigham, Liddle and Sale. Twenty-two Territorial Army players found themselves thrust into full-time service. Several others, including McMahon (who joined Wrexham) and Tennant (Liverpool), returned to their home towns to assist the war effort, joining local TA units.

With the Government fearful that large sporting crowds would form attractive targets for German bombers, all sporting activity was halted forthwith. On 8th September the Football League announced that competition would be suspended for the season. Players would retain their club registration and would return to their clubs at the end of the conflict, according to Clause 4 of their contracts. Clubs were only liable to pay wages up to 6th September, although players who had joined up before 9th September received an extra 30 shillings for that week.

The average professional footballer's understanding of the political crisis in Europe can be summed up in a tale told by Stanley Matthews. Prior to the infamous international match in Germany in 1938, won by England 6-3, in which the England team were requested by the FA to give a Nazi salute, Matthews and England teammate Bert Sproston of Leeds had ventured into Berlin to sample local café life. The customers suddenly rushed to the window to glimpse a convoy supposedly carrying Hitler. Sproston was less than impressed by this show of dedication to the Führer. 'Stan,' he whispered, 'I've not 'ad much of an education and I know now't about politics and t'like. All I knows is football. But t'way I see it yon 'Itler fella is an evil little twat.'

On 9th September, the British Government, in what these days would be called 'spin', justified their decision to ration food in these alarmist terms: 'The idea behind rationing is very important. It does not imply any scarcity of food at all but the Government has to be responsible in the artificial conditions of war for the distribution of food right up to its final consumption, to make sure everyone gets his fair share.'

Given that industrial priorities were now diverted to the production of tanks, planes, guns and ammunition, grumblings about the Government intensified when people rightly began suspecting that food was about to become scarce. To add to their woes, blackouts meant stumbling through dark streets ripe for crime, leading to the oft-heard cry from Air Raid wardens – 'Put that light out'. When shops sold out of black fabric, householders simply painted their windows black. Posters urged the general populace to save, dig, work, buy war bonds, not travel or waste, nor spread rumours – all in the name of victory.

Football was seen by the Government as a vital means of sustaining the morale of workers forced to grind out munitions and fuel on long shifts while suffering the vagaries of food rationing. And it wasn't just the playing of the sport which kept spirits up. The War Office accepted that sport was so important to society that it renamed an entire class of naval ships after football clubs. *HMS Stoke City* was sequestered from its owner in September 1939. She was a corvette-like trawler that worked on contraband control between Iceland and the UK. Other similar vessels included *HMS Grimsby Town, Notts County, Huddersfield,* and *Arsenal.*

While those footballers who joined the Armed Forces were held up as heroes, it was inevitable that organised football would be allowed to carry on in some guise, and on 9th September the FA received the go-ahead to return. Stoke's chairman, Alderman Harry Booth, announced: 'We feel that it will be a good thing for the public generally if football in some form or another be resumed. Stoke are ready at once to support any arrangements made by the FA and Football League.'

The Victoria Ground's first wartime match was between two local military units. Not surprisingly, the side featuring Stoke first-teamers Peppitt, Mould, Ormston, Massey and Baker won 16-1. While preparations for an official War League took shape, a series of hastily arranged friendlies was played. A 50-mile travel limit was set, all matches had to be approved by the local police, and those clubs still attracting larger crowds had an all-ticket limit of 15,000 imposed. Football was not allowed to interfere with National Service, and Stoke had to negotiate with Army units to obtain players for their first friendly against Coventry. Bob McGrory succeeded in acquiring the services of nineteen of the club's 64 players. Admission prices remained at two shillings for the Boothen and Butler Stands, with the paddocks and corners at 1s 6d. 'Soldiers and Boys' paid sixpence. Just over 4,500 – well under the official limit, which had been set at 8,000 – made it to the Victoria Ground to see Stoke win 3-1. The following week Stoke took on neighbours Port Vale and won 3-2.

As Warsaw burned in late September, the newspapers maintained the official line that the Allies were fighting back, but it was bravado. In truth, Britain was a country in turmoil as it adjusted to the twin torments of rationing and blackout. Blackout times were printed in bold on the front of every newspaper. Any lights showing drew hostile crowds who would throw stones at windows to get them put out. In the darkness cars often collided and a Fenton man died when he stepped in front of a blacked-out bus. Secrecy was all. The authorities constantly reminded the public that 'Careless talk costs lives' and 'Walls have ears'.

This secrecy even applied to football. If players could not play due to military service, it was simply stated that they were 'unavailable' – their whereabouts were not to be disclosed. Stan Matthews was amongst those players keen to assist his country. He sought work but, as a footballer without a trade, he found few offers: 'I tried for many jobs, but when I was asked what experience I had, my chances were nil. I went straight into football from school and had never learned any trade.'

There was no star treatment for the stellar name of English football. Matthews eventually went to work in a local brass foundry making shells, which at least kept him in the Potteries. But as his Saturday shift finished too late for him to travel for Stoke's away games, Matthews sought permission to earn his match fee playing for Port Vale on alternate weekends. This was denied by Stoke's board who, churlishly – given the necessities of the time – reasoned that Matthews was their star attraction and no one else should benefit from him.

Instead, they sought his early Saturday release from his employers, which was refused in this time of emergency, so for a while Stan sat idle on Saturday afternoons whenever Stoke played outside the immediate vicinity. Matthews was not the only one missing when Stoke travelled to The Hawthorns. A team containing just four first-choice players collapsed 0-6 to Second Division West Brom. The following weekend a stronger Stoke side fared rather better, drawing 2-2 at home with a full-strength Manchester United.

Convening at Crewe on 2nd October, the Football League finalised plans for the War League. Even though travel restrictions had, by now, been relaxed to distances which could be covered there and back in one day, League Secretary Fred Howarth introduced a series of eight regional leagues with clubs grouped geographically regardless of pre-war status. Six of the 88 existing League clubs (they were not expanded to 92 until 1950) opted out – Aston Villa, Derby County, Exeter City, Gateshead, Ipswich and Southampton. Stoke were placed in the Western League, which comprised twelve clubs. League tables would be compiled as normal, but there would be no trophies or bonus payments. In the Potteries, minds harked back to the Great War and Stoke's championship triumph of 1917-18, when the team won 22 of their 30 games.

On the last weekend of friendlies before the new league commenced, Birmingham City fielded two sides simultaneously. One of them lost 0-1

at Wolves, while the other, containing several Aston Villa players searching
for somewhere to play, went down 2-3 at Stoke. The authorities almost
doubled the limit on the Victoria Ground's capacity to 15,000 and Stoke
announced that season tickets remained valid. Players' fees were set at £2
per match, although that was soon reduced to 30 shillings by order of the
FA.

This decision was at the heart of a pay dispute between the Players'
Union and Football League, with the former demanding that the League
give immediate consideration to increasing wages to £2 per match with a
ten-shilling bonus for a win and five shillings for a draw. The dispute fes-
tered below the surface as the war ran its course. Those players in military
service, or who returned to their home town to work towards the war
effort, were allowed to guest for clubs near where they lived or were stationed. Permission from that player's actual club had to be sought, but it
was only rarely denied – Matthews being an exception. Not surprisingly,
those clubs in garrison towns, such as Aldershot and Northampton, found
a rich vein of talent on their doorstep.

When Stoke played a friendly against Nottingham Forest late in the season, they faced an opposing back line comprised entirely of their own
players – Doug Westland, Jack Challinor and Tom Brawley – while George
Antonio and Jock Kirton also appeared for Forest during the season. Stoke
granted permission for Patsy Gallacher to play for Carlisle. Once recovered
from his knee operation, Freddie Steele guested twice for Notts County
and Norman Wilkinson six times. Jim Westland, Kirton, Challinor and
Antonio were permitted to play for Redditch, Doug Westland and Brawley
for Bromsgrove, and Massey for Stafford Rangers. Brawley later returned
to Scotland to resume his former employment as a brassworker. His
employers secured his release from Army service and he was granted permission by Stoke to guest for Kilmarnock.

Despite the unavailability of so many players, McGrory maintained that
he would only rarely use 'guests': 'I intend playing the regular members of
the club for as long as possible. It is the only fair thing for the available
players. Moreover if and when first team vacancies occur, Stoke have
splendid reserves in Franklin, Mountford, Hampson and Bowyer. These
young players are ready for promotion at any time.'

Stoke were not alone in preferring to use youngsters. Preston, Wolves
and Spurs also chose to think long-term. For Stoke, one problem position
was resolved, however, by exploiting the guest system. Stoke's goalkeeping
situation only took a turn for the better when McGrory – who had been
spared having to publicly drop McMahon when the player moved back to
Wrexham – secured former Stoke goalkeeper Doug 'Dai' Jones. Jones had
been offloaded to Carlisle, to the ire of supporters, just four months earlier, but had returned to the Potteries on war work. Ironically, given his

acrimonious departure from the club, Jones would spend most of the season playing for Stoke.

On 21st October 1939, Stoke City began their campaign in the Western Regional League disappointingly. They found themselves 1-4 down at Everton after 50 minutes. But, setting the tone for his exploits throughout the War, Tommy Sale then intervened. He bagged a hat-trick, which included a penalty and the equaliser three minutes from the end of a 4-4 draw.

Stan Matthews' unavailability for Stoke's away games dented attendances and opposing clubs' directors publicly mourned the absence of 'Magic Matthews'. On top of which, Stan was in high demand for representative games: he was selected some 30 times over the season, reducing his availability to Stoke yet more. The intention of these representative fixtures was to spread morale-boosting football to all parts of the country. The first such game, at Everton on 4th November, saw the Football League XI draw 3-3 with an all-British XI. Proceeds from the 15,000 spectators went to the Red Cross.

Matthews' numerous absences allowed reserve inside-right Syd Peppitt to claim a regular place. He took advantage and, by moving inside when Matthews was available, struck up a strong partnership with Stan. A sharp finisher, Peppitt bagged eighteen goals in the season, to end up second highest scorer. Matthews described him as 'never a classy inside-forward, but he was a grafter with an eye for goal and every team needs a player like that in its side'.

Dennis Herod, however, recalls the cynical side of the manager's relationship with Peppitt: 'McGrory was a shrewd Scotsman. He would always put Stan Matthews into the announced team so that it would put 3.000 or 4,000 on the gate. But Stan was quite injury prone and when he was not able to play they wouldn't announce the team changes until five minutes before kick-off. Well, the crowd felt terribly let down and you should have heard them boo. And of course they would boo Stan's replacement for not being Stan Matthews and that, more often than not, would be Syd Peppitt. It must have been incredibly demoralising. Time and again it happened and this for me was appalling treatment by McGrory of a young player who could really have made something of himself. I complained to Bob McGrory about it, but you couldn't say anything to him. What he said went. Anyway Syd never became much more than a bit part player, when he could have been so much more.'

Peppitt had distinctively large ears, a receding hairline and a seemingly perpetually furrowed brow, perhaps reflecting his concern at how his manager treated him. At just twenty years old, however, Peppitt soon found himself called up and he would make scant few appearances for his club throughout the war.

As football was not among the exempt occupations, such as mining or steel-working, which would protect a man from being called into military service, several of Stoke's players found work in jobs which would allow them to continue playing for the club. Tommy Sale joined the engineering department of Michelin, who also employed Frank Soo and Harry Brigham. Trainer Hubert Nuttall and his assistant Harry Pearson found positions in the local civil defence, while Peter Jackson, Stoke's assistant manager, enrolled in the Police Reserve Section.

Others found work, but further afield. Inside-forward Patsy Gallacher returned to Sunderland, where he had spent a decade playing for the Rokerites. He would never play for Stoke again. Arthur Tutin and Clem Smith found employment in Crewe and would be available only occasionally. George Mountford returned to Kidderminster and scored regularly for the Birmingham League club. Wallace Poulton, a young winger, returned home to Birmingham to be offered a job with a local electrical plant, but only on condition that he had Stoke's permission to play with their works team in the Birmingham League.

The War League reacquainted clubs which had not met for many years. Hence on 4th November, while Matthews represented the Football League at Everton, Stoke renewed rivalry with Wrexham for the first time since 1927. Wrexham used seven guests, including Stoke's Pat McMahon in goal, and drew 4-4.

On 12th November, Stoke registered on professional terms Neil Franklin, Frank Bowyer, Jock McCue, Ted Wordley and Frank Mountford. The pay was £1 10s 2d per week. McGrory revealed his masterplan: 'If this war lasts three years we'll be fielding a team drawn from within a seven-mile radius of Stoke.' Based on the club's philosophy of encouraging local talent, and given the travel restrictions on players, it was to prove a sound strategy.

In mid-October Stoke had signed seventeen-year-old 'B' team player Len Howell on professional forms. In January 1940, seventeen-year-old inside-forward Frank Bowyer made a goalscoring debut at Manchester United. Others later offered terms included Jock McCue, Bill Kinson, Bill Gould and Stanley Harrison, all members of the 'B' team. McGrory's vision belied that of many clubs, who exploited the guest system to lure the best players who happened to be close by on any given date. McGrory's policy allowed Stoke's young team to knit together and gain experience which would have been denied them in peacetime.

McGrory realised, though, that a team in nappies needed one or two old heads. He brought his old mate, Bobby Liddle, back into the side at the age of 31, to fill in at inside-forward or on the wing. Liddle's tricky play and incisive passing created many goalscoring opportunities for his fellow forwards, and he even managed to net four times himself. The Geordie had a permanent broad smile on his face and brought a sense of humour to the dressing room.

Despite his commitment, McGrory took advantage of those experienced players whose wartime work brought them back to their native Potteries. He tempted the likes of Jack Griffiths, the Manchester United defender, while Eric Hayward – the Blackpool and ex-Vale half-back – and Jack Smith, who had recently transferred from Vale to Chelsea, also returned to the area. Middlesbrough defender Charlie Scrimshaw, who McGrory had sold in October 1938, returned to the Potteries as a war reserve constable and later went into the licensing trade at Smallthorne. He answered McGrory's call to assist his old club at left-back and buttressed the defence with his experience, playing a further nine games as Stoke's defence tightened considerably.

Stanley Matthews was not selected for the first Wartime international on 11th November 1939, a 1-1 draw with Wales in Cardiff. Following that below-par performance, the selectors issued their usual response – 'send for Matthews'. Reinstated for the following week's return match, he assisted England to recover from 0-2 down at half-time to win 3-2 at Wrexham. That performance ensured Matthews retained his place for the final three international matches of the season.

Two weeks later England beat Scotland 2-1 at Newcastle, with Stan crossing for Lawton and Clifton to head England's goals. Jock Dodds replied and Raich Carter missed an England penalty on 85 minutes. The 25,000 crowd raised £2,071 for the Red Cross. The game was marred by a three-car pile-up in Wath-on-Dearne, involving Manchester City's Sam Barkas and Eric Brook, who were on their way to take part. Brook's injuries were so bad he never played again. Two Newcastle players were called upon to fill the breach. Consequently, a Scot, Tommy Pearson – nephew of Harry Pearson, Stoke's assistant trainer – made his international debut *against* his native country. He would later earn a Scotland cap.

Although Stoke's board were irritated by being regularly denied the services of their star player, their hands were tied. Matthews was part of 'the war effort'. His appearances at grounds around the country brought a little excitement to a population suffering the psychological torments of the Phoney War. Britain was bracing itself for Hitler's response to the British Expeditionary Force, currently reinforcing France's border with Germany. Against this broader picture, any football club denying permission for their players to represent their country was severely dealt with. Everton received a heavy fine for insisting that Joe Mercer play for them, rather than allow him to appear, as selected, for England.

After four games, Stoke sat atop the formative league, averaging four goals per game. On 18th November, Dai Jones saved his second penalty of the season, this time from Manchester City's Percival, which preserved

Stoke's unbeaten record in a 1-1 draw. A 2-0 win over Chester followed, but City's first loss came at Crewe on 2nd December, after Stoke had taken an early lead. Crewe's offside tactics thwarted Stoke's forwards and the home side scored three times in fourteen second-half minutes to win. Stoke remained on top, however, by virtue of Manchester City's improbable 6-6 draw with Stockport.

The first indication that Stoke had serious title pretensions came when defeating Liverpool 3-1. At left-back, Liverpool had the Stoke player Jack Tennant, who was tormented by Matthews, while at right-back, Cooper failed to deal with Ormston's wing threat. Eric Hampson had a memorable day. Required to make his first-team debut, due to the illness of Alf Massey, Hampson had to be taxied from his home in Goldenhill after finishing a hard shift at work. For their part, Liverpool's players had a much-delayed journey and barely had time for a snack at Stoke station before kick-off. As their manager, George Kay, declared: 'Players are putting up surprisingly good shows in football.' Sale clinched the points with an overhead kick to take his tally to eleven goals in eight league games, seventeen in all. Sale's hotshot shooting was straight, often at the goalkeeper, but so powerful that he also netted his fair share of deflections.

Stoke's win allowed them to reach the Christmas break in fourth place, with eleven points from eight games, one point behind Manchester United, Everton, and Manchester City.

In mid-December British warships finally tracked down the German 'pocket' battleship *Admiral Graf Spee*, crippling her in the harbour of the Uruguayan capital, Montevideo. At home, a month's gap in league fixtures allowed a respite to play friendlies. Stoke fared badly in four games, their only win being 2-1 over Sheffield Wednesday, who had not won a game all season. Bolton's Indian sign over City at the Victoria Ground, which had seen them end Stoke's year-long unblemished home record in the Football League, continued with a 5-1 win on Boxing Day. Thanks in large part to Jack Hurst's hat-trick, Bolton inflicted City's first wartime home defeat. The size of the defeat was mitigated by Stoke fielding novices Harold Glover, Jock McCue and Neil Franklin, as McGrory persevered with his policy of blooding youngsters.

The friendly at Lincoln on 23rd December fell victim to a heavy snow-fall just before kick-off. City had spent two hours travelling to Sincil Bank and claimed their guarantee of £35, otherwise they would never have undertaken the journey. Instead, they had to settle for £7 expenses in lieu of their guarantee, although Lincoln tried to wriggle out of even that outlay. The return journey took from 3.15pm to 10.30pm as the team's bus ploughed through Pennine snowdrifts.

Stoke's last game of 1939, at Bury, proved to be one of the most astonishing in which any Stoke team has been involved. Who would have thought at half-time, with the score at 1-1, that it would end 7-6 to Bury, yield three hat-tricks – Sale for Stoke, and Dougal and Burdett for Bury – five goals in a six-minute spell, and another five in eight minutes, plus a last-minute winner?

On New Year's Day 1940, Stoke President Sir Francis Joseph wrote to the chairmen of the other 21 First Division clubs, toasting the health of the King prior to City's first home match – against Tranmere – of the New Year. In his letter he remarked on the differences between pre-war football – when up to one million played or watched the game each week – and the deserted grounds which now posed growing financial problems for clubs. Joseph asked clubs not to forget that once the war was over, football would be needed as never before.

On matchday, Joseph used a specially-made pottery Loving Cup to toast the King with visiting Tranmere directors. This ceremony survives to this day, and is performed at the first Stoke home game of each calendar year. But on the Victoria Ground's terraces, a mere 714 spectators turned up to see City's 1-0 win.

Concerned for their finances, Stoke, in common with many other clubs, submitted a plan for the future of wartime football. All agreed that the divisions needed to be expanded. With too few attractive fixtures on offer, due to regional restrictions and being deprived of star players, several clubs indicated that they were no longer viable and would shut down at the end of the season. Stoke needed gates of between 4,000 and 5,000, but the average was just 2,500. The club was hit by a change in work practices in the Potteries, so that many shifts now ended at 4.30pm, too late to allow workers to see Stoke play. Clubs' financial hardships were hardly helped by the 'crushingly heavy' 30 per cent Entertainment Tax imposed on their takings, which the Government steadfastly refused to reduce.

Stoke Chairman Harry Booth's plan envisaged clubs being rearranged into six larger regional leagues, rather than the eight at present, with a new cup competition to run from March. Either way, matters could not continue. As if to confirm his fears about crowds staying away, fewer than 3,000 attended Stoke's next game, at Old Trafford. Despite leading 3-0, City's confidence was shattered when Manchester United scored twice in three minutes – the second goal being a clear handball by Butt, guesting from Blackburn. Sale then fluffed a gilt-edged chance at 3-3 before a late Jones goal handed United both points.

The young men of Stoke City FC had to accept the harsh realities of life. Working for a living meant more than kicking a ball around. Britain was put on 'short rations' on 8th January 1940. To try to ensure equality of food distribution, butter, sugar, bacon and ham could, from now on, only be bought using coupons from ration books. The War Budget implemented a tax on cigarettes, which now cost 8½d per packet. Footballers attached to military units were identified as potential PT Instructors and the FA supplied lecture materials to encourage keep-fit regimes amongst troops. Having completed his training course and taught several sessions, PT Instructor Alf Massey found himself promoted to sergeant in early February 1940. Guest player Jack Griffiths had already joined the RAF as a PT Instructor and switched his services to his new 'guest' club, Fulham. As a contribution to the war effort, all this reflected well on football. But players such as Syd Peppitt, who attended physical training courses for his unit, found his availability to play for his club severely reduced.

One problem facing players and spectators was the ban on newspapers and radio from giving weather reports. So when winter hit hard in February, many travelled fruitlessly. On 3rd February, for example, only one match was played. In the coldest winter since 1894-95, a combination of freezing temperatures and the consequences of food rationing contributed to hundreds of deaths. Stoke's only match in this month-long freeze was a 1-0 win over Everton, which finally offered proof that City could defend. Billy Mould and Charlie Scrimshaw were prominent in repelling attacks, and Wilkinson – making only his fourth appearance since the war started – had little to do. Sale bundled Toffees' keeper Ted Sagar into the back of the net with the kind of challenge which would earn a yellow card these days. Curiously, the clampdown on indiscriminate shoulder charging had already begun: in the summer of 1939 the FA inserted into Law 12 – which dealt with shoulder charging – the phrase 'within playing distance of the ball', whatever that might mean. This amendment took two decades to catch on. One Stoke match report describes this new 'obstruction' rule as being 'far too easy to infringe'. Referees did not understand the laws either. Often penalties were given for offences which should only have resulted in an indirect free-kick.

City won their first six home league games, but had yet to win away until, on 24th February, in a rare appearance, Syd Peppitt scored four second-half goals at Stockport in a 5-1 win. Tommy Sale's goalscoring feats had brought him into national focus. In early March he was selected as a replacement for England centre-forward Tommy Lawton, whose Army duties denied him a place alongside Stan Matthews for a Football League XI, in another contest designed to raise money for the Red Cross. While Sale and Matthews scored a goal apiece in a 4-4 draw at Bradford, Stoke defeated Wrexham, who included City inside-forward George Antonio in their forward line. In Sale's absence, Freddie Steele made his comeback from knee injury, playing his first game since 6th May 1939. After recovering from cartilage surgery, Steele had rejoined his unit. He was now home on Army leave and, had he not been required by Stoke, would have been requested to guest for Notts County in the Nottingham derby. Steele scored Stoke's third goal, chesting the ball down and rifling it into the far corner. In ten appearances for Stoke, Steele banged in ten goals. With other matches postponed, City went top. 1st Stoke P 13 Pts 19; 2nd Liverpool 12 17; 3rd Everton 12 17; 4th Manchester United 12 16.

The following week saw a bizarre episode involving shirts. Stoke travelled to the now defunct New Brighton's Rake Lane Ground in Wallasey. The home team played in maroon and white stripes, so Stoke donned their change kit of blue and white stripes. Referee A Smith, however, ruled that so many stripes confused everybody, so Stoke were asked to wear the home side's second kit of all-maroon. The sea of maroon appeared to particularly affect Stoke, who lost 1-3, all three home goals scored by former Aston Villa and England international veteran Pongo Waring. His second goal came from a high cross dropped into the net by Doug Westland. McGrory's patience snapped and the Scotsman never played a competitive match for Stoke again.

For the visit of Manchester City, Stoke welcomed Matthews back from the Football League XI fundraisers. Jim Westland and Clem Smith, for once, were also available. Stoke won 2-1 in a thrilling finish which saw Sale cut through the defence to beat Swift at close quarters. The following Saturday, Sale's last-minute effort was ruled out for a foul which would have given Stoke both points at Chester. But the 3-3 draw kept Stoke level with Manchester United at the top.

With Matthews once again poached by the Football League, City thrashed Port Vale 5-1 on Easter Monday. Sale had two shots turned into his own goal by Vale's Harry Griffiths, and had another disallowed before notching the fifth. The following Saturday, 30th March, Matthews turned out in Scotland for Glasgow Rangers in an attempt to boost morale and production. He did so well in the Gers' Scottish Cup semi-final against Patsy Gallacher's Morton that the Ibrox club wanted him to stay and assist them as long as possible, with a particular eye on the final.

A touchy situation was avoided when Stan was selected to play for England against Wales on 13th April. It was now that the bitter dispute between Matthews and McGrory, player and manager, started to take root. If Matthews was prepared to travel up to Glasgow for a game, why wasn't he prepared to play for Stoke? On the same day that Stan helped Rangers reach their final, a 1-1 draw with Crewe ended Stoke's 100 per cent home league record. Former Stoke skipper Arthur Turner returned as a guest to haunt his old team with a succession of tackles and goal-line clearances for the Railwaymen.

Before the Crewe game, Stoke finally secured the signature of one of the hottest properties in Potteries junior football. Frank Mountford was a sporting prodigy who had been recommended for England schoolboy honours at thirteen and won the Burslem Under-14 sprint championship in every event from 80 to 440 yards. He had joined Stoke's youth side, known as City Old boys, which normally featured 14-16 year olds, at the age of twelve, in 1935. Boyish and babyfaced in his youth, Frank had by now grown to 5ft 9in, weighed 10st 7lbs, and had developed into a centre-forward with an appetite for goals. He stepped up into the 'B' team in 1938 and terrorised defences by scoring 72 goals in thirty matches. The press dubbed him 'the new Freddie Steele', no mean tribute. McGrory was not often moved to soliloquy, but he admitted that only Sale's 'wholehearted form' kept Mountford out of the Regional League side.

Stoke thrust professional forms in front of Mountford with almost unseemly haste on his seventeenth birthday, the minimum age for turning professional. At the end of the season, Mountford led Stoke City 'B' to victory in the Sentinel Football Shield. In the semi-final they defeated Trent Vale United 4-2, with Frank bagging two bullet headers. In goal for Trent Vale that day was another seventeen-year-old, Dennis Herod, who so impressed the watching McGrory with his springing saves that he too joined the ranks of local talent destined for Stoke, along with left-winger Stan Clewlow.

In mid-April, with Doug Jones joining the RAF, Stoke finally managed to gain the release of Norman Wilkinson from the Army – on condition that he continued to work in the colliery in Tantobie, Durham. Such a restriction meant Wilkinson was rarely available, and McGrory was forced to shuffle his goalkeepers around for the rest of the season, keeping his fingers crossed that one would be available each week. With four games remaining, Stoke travelled to Anfield needing a victory to maintain their slim chance of winning the league. Seventeen-year-old Pat Bridges debuted in goal as a late change for Jones.

Another new RAF man, Stanley Matthews, found that his posting at a unit near Blackpool allowed him to play in almost all of Stoke's remaining games, home or away. Jock Kirton, home on leave, and Soo, returning from injury, meant that Stoke travelled to Anfield with a stronger than usual away side. Liverpool netted first through Jack Balmer's twenty-yarder which cannoned in off the bar. Steele nodded in Matthews' centre before lady luck shone on Stoke. Balmer struck the inside of the post. Kirton cleared the rebound to Bobby Liddle, who sent Peppitt in on goal. Peppitt drew out Liverpool keeper Riley before rolling the ball into the corner. Stoke's 2-1 victory placed them in pole position, although their fate still lay in others' hands. The placings read: 1st Stoke P 19 Pts 27; 2nd Manchester United 17 26; 3rd Everton 18 22; 4th Liverpool 17 22.

Following proposals by several clubs, the season was extended into June to allow time for a national cup competition. The War Cup began with two rounds of regional qualifiers played over two legs, following the format already adopted in Scotland. The North and South would each pro-vide one team for the final, to be played at Wembley. The entire 137 games of the cup competition would be condensed into nine weeks. As the cup took precedence over those league fixtures postponed due to the big freeze, Stoke's championship hopes were left dangling. They now had to squeeze in three remaining games amidst the cup matches. In the first round, City were paired with New Brighton, who had already caused Stoke problems in the league. City, though, survived thanks to a Freddie Steele second-half hat-trick in a 4-1 first-leg win. The return saw Stoke field an unchanged side – one of the few occasions this proved possible in these transient times.

In round two Stoke came up against Barrow, who had caused a sensation by beating Liverpool 4-1 over two legs, including a 2-1 win at Anfield. When Stoke's directors arrived at Barrow for the first game, they were greeted by their enthusiastic counterparts telling them that this was the greatest day in Barrow's history. A record home gate of 11,870 and receipts of £610 stood testament to that fact. Liverpool had only attracted 5,963. Undoubtedly, the huge attendance was down to the Matthews effect. Stoke won thanks to Steele's brace in the first game and a 6-1 romp in the return leg. These results carried City into the last sixteen, four teams having progressed from each of the four regions.

Amidst the cup rounds, Stoke had to fit in their outstanding league matches. Between the two Barrow games they won 2-1 at Port Vale to keep up the pressure. On 10th May Neville Chamberlain handed over to Winston Churchill as Prime Minister. Churchill rushed through the Emergency Powers Act, giving the Government unprecedented authority over every citizen. The following Monday, Whit Monday, 13th May – normally a national holiday which Churchill now cancelled – Stoke travelled to Tranmere, knowing that a win would give them a great chance to seal up the league. But Stoke lacked Steele and Matthews, who had not returned from a representative game at the weekend.

Steele's absence allowed Bob McGrory to give a debut to Frank Mountford. His faith was repaid by a crisp Mountford header within five minutes. But City's youngsters succumbed to continual harassment by Tranmere's forwards and Stoke slumped 1-5 to a team destined to finish well adrift at the bottom. It seemed the league title had slipped away, but when Stoke players picked up their papers the next day they found that Manchester United had lost at Wrexham.

Still in with a shout of winning the league, Stoke also fancied themselves in the cup. They travelled to Goodison Park in the third round, where 9,000 saw a tense match. Sale missed a good chance when clean through, but Ted Sagar blocked and then saved Sale's point-blank header. Stoke conceded a late penalty for a foul on Stevenson, which Lawton converted for a 1-0 win to send Everton into the quarter-finals. The players perked up when news reached the dressing room that both their league rivals had slipped up. Manchester United had been thrashed 0-6 at New Brighton, while Liverpool had crashed 0-4 at Chester. Stoke just needed to win their final game to clinch the championship.

The day after the arrest of the fascist sympathiser Sir Oswald Mosley, Stoke took on Manchester United. McGrory's pleas to secure the services of Kirton and Steele from their respective regiments failed, so Massey played at right-half with Sale at centre-forward. Charlton's Potteries-born full-back, John Oakes, who had played against Stoke for Port Vale two weeks earlier, found himself fielded by McGrory at left-back.

But Stoke's difficulties were nothing compared to those of United, who struggled to raise any sort of team and even sought a cancellation on the morning of the game. The Football League insisted the match went ahead. The Manchester party arrived late, delaying the kick-off. United's trump card, however, was having acquired the services of Burdett and Dougal, the deadly duo who had grabbed a hat-trick apiece for Bury in the 7-6 win at Christmas.

The fifteen-minute delay to kick-off played on Stoke's nerves and they began sluggishly. Burdett fired an early warning shot narrowly over, and then found himself clear with just Jones to beat, burying a low shot into the corner. The goal stung City into action. With Matthews and Ormston in forceful mood, Peppitt drove a first-time shot into the roof of the net. Right on half-time, Ormston followed up Sale's blocked shot to put City into the lead. Against the run of play, Syd Peppitt extended Stoke's lead with a running header, only for United to rally, Burdett netting a simple knockdown by Pearson. But time had run out. Stoke, having won 3-2, finished as champions.

There was very little celebration. No lap of the pitch. No reception at the King's Hall. No special issue of the *Sentinel*. Stoke had waited years to actually win something, only to achieve the feat in the same week that Hitler – having already taken Denmark and Norway, completed his invasion of the Low Countries. The people of Stoke-on-Trent, as across Britain, could not have cared less about a distraction such as football at such a time.

To honour a commitment given after an earlier postponement during the big freeze, Stoke played a final friendly against Rochdale on 8th June, winning 3-2. The late date meant this result has been omitted from previous histories of Stoke City. It was the only game which full-back Harry Brigham missed all season – a distinction he shared with centre-half Billy Mould.

At 6.30pm that night, BBC Radio broadcast the first War Cup final, between West Ham and Blackburn. The crowd's cheering of Sam Small's winning goal for the Hammers rankled amongst those in the huge flotilla of boats in the Channel. Their radios were tuned to the BBC for news, while they grimly fished bodies of British soldiers out of the water at the end of Operation Dynamo, the four-day evacuation from the beaches of Dunkirk. The 'miracle of deliverance' of 335,000 soldiers had given way to a realisation that 'at long last the country understands that we are fighting for our lives'. Less than a week later, on 14th June, German troops marched down the Champs Elysees in Paris. It would not be easy, but somehow life had to go on.

## CHAPTER TWO

~ 1940-41 ~

'A football equation without answer'

British football changed for the worse during the dark days of early 1940. Throughout the 1930s, crowds had become used to an exciting brand of play, encompassing speed, gung-ho attack and tough-tackling with no quarter given. Even if this image was coloured by rose-tinted nostalgia, there is no doubting that, by comparison, spectators in 1940 found the far younger wartime teams unable to match their pre-war counterparts. By and large, those stars who remained to play with their clubs shone brightly amidst the mediocrity around them.

This was hardly the fault of the players. Increasing austerity greatly reduced stamina levels among them and hardly encouraged spectators through the turnstiles. A survey by the government agency Mass Observation found attendances had shrunk by 65 per cent of their pre-war levels. Consequently, the first few years of the war proved financially disastrous for many clubs. Of the 60 which presented accounts in 1940, only five reported a profit. The FA itself lost £13,337.

By the summer of 1940, Stoke had lost the services of eight of the team which had played the final Football League game of 1938-39. Of the three who still were available, two – Stan Matthews and Frank Soo – travelled regularly to play from their RAF barracks near Blackpool. But their availability was vastly reduced once the Luftwaffe began its bombing campaigns across the country. Among the club's pre-war first-choice players, only 26-year-old right-back Harry Brigham was available throughout the whole of the next, 1940-41 season. Brigham, who had joined Stoke from Frickley Colliery in the mid-1930s, was a Selby-born Yorkshire man. Tough as old boots, his defensive style focused on tackling opponents and winning the ball. At 5ft 7in, Brigham provided solidity and kept things simple. Whenever he found himself with the ball at his feet he would look up and belt long balls for the forwards to chase. Dennis Herod remembers: 'Harry had a terrific right foot, but he was self-centred and didn't much bother with anyone else in the side.' Supporter Owen Bennion recalls: 'There was a man who stood by us on the Boothen End and he had it in for Harry, only he never got his name right. He always called him Bingham. It would be "Come on Bingham" and "Bingham this and Bingham that", which made us laugh.'

Other peacetime players found football was ruled out for a variety of reasons. Charlie Scrimshaw had entered the licensing trade and found it impossible to combine his business with playing for Stoke. James Oakes sidelined himself for the entire 1940-41 season to recover from a foot injury. On the other hand, Arthur Griffiths, though still on Stoke's books, found himself surplus to requirements, although no offers matching his £750 price tag arrived at McGrory's door. Griffiths would not make a Stoke appearance all season. Given the paucity of experienced players available, Griffiths's absence begs the question: what had he done to get on the wrong side of his notoriously tetchy manager? This conundrum has no satisfactory answer. A dearth of football officials ensured that every qualified referee was mobilised to keep organised soccer going. Requiring spectacles was no longer a barrier to their appointment, which provided a guide to the advanced age of some men in black. Naturally, this brought chuckles from the terraces, even though it deprived spectators of one of their favourite jokes.

The summer brought news of the death of the first, and last, Stoke footballer in the war. Gunner Francis Carpenter of Rocester was killed in action at Dunkirk. He had signed as a professional for Stoke as an inside-forward, then transferred to Burton Albion and on to Manchester United, where he had been a reserve-team player at the outbreak of war. During his military service he had captained Artillery football teams. More fortunate was former Stoke amateur forward Albert Mullard, who had since joined Walsall, and was captured on Crete. He spent four years incarcerated as a PoW before being liberated in 1944.

Just seventeen players reported for duty at the Victoria Ground for the start of pre-season training on 13th August 1940 under the supervision of groundsman Harry Loffill – one of only three non-playing members of staff retained, with even Secretary Tom Hancock released. Training, pre-season or otherwise, consisted of track and gym work and did not exactly tax the players. Stan Clewlow recalls: 'No one ever coached us like they do today. We never kicked a ball in training. We'd walk along the short side of the pitch and then run the long side and do about six trips round.'

The dark age was beginning to end, however, and Stoke's board even discussed employing a trained masseur. Massage was something that Stanley Matthews in particular had become interested in. The lax training regime allowed youngsters Dennis Herod and Neil Franklin plenty of opportunity to slope off to the bookies. Both had become hooked on gambling, particularly on horses. Franklin, however, proved to be by far the luckier, or better, of the two. Over a period of ten years he amassed a small fortune in winnings. In the public practice match, the Blue & Whites (reserves) drew 3-3 with the Red & Whites (first team). With receipts donated to aid the British Red Cross and the Spitfire Fund, all of the club's available professionals played some part, along with a number of local amateurs.

With only 68 clubs still active, and competing in just two leagues, Stoke switched to the South (B) section. The league concept this season constituted a departure for domestic football. Instead of a conventional season, Stoke would play as many games as they could arrange against opponents from their 'B' section – comprising Midlands clubs. Then the entire championship, including the Southern clubs from the 'A' section, would be determined on goal-average (goals scored divided by goals conceded). A minimum of sixteen games would have to be played to qualify. Most clubs arranged fixtures so that they would play back-to-back games one Saturday after another. Good news for the players arrived when payments returned to £2 per game. Fixtures were compiled until the end of the calendar year, 1940, at which time arrangements for the second half of the season would be reviewed.

Given that almost his entire first-team squad had been wrenched from his grasp, McGrory re-stated his aim that in three years he would have 'a team comprising players drawn from a seven mile radius of the club'. He had already blooded Neil Franklin and the two Franks, Mountford and Bowyer. Six further youngsters staked their claims early in 1940-41 – Pat Bridges, Bill Kinson, Stan Glover, John McCue, Ted Wordley, Fred Basnett and Stan Harrison – each of whom looked a good prospect. Stoke's policy was consistent: McGrory would choose the club's own players before resorting to guests. This was a radical departure from the way most clubs were thinking. Many needed to grab every player within travelling distance simply to field a full side, especially away from home. Often a club's matchday programme – little more than a printed, one-sided sheet of paper – would carry the words A N Other or A G Player (a guest player) against one or more positions on the team sheet. Fulham even came up with S O Else (someone else). The only positive news for clubs struggling to field teams was that stringent travel restrictions curtailed the number of representative games luring star players away.

Stoke's season began with three wins and a narrow defeat in the first four games. On opening day, while Stoke's first choice centre-forward, Freddie Steele, scored for Sheffield United against Rotherham, McGrory proved that City might not miss 'Nobby's' services too greatly, as his replacement, Frank Mountford, notched his first hat-trick for the club. His victims, a Notts County side composed entirely of guest players, were trounced 4-1. Mountford's inspired form, scoring in his first five games as a professional, allowed 30-year-old Tommy Sale to revert to his favoured inside-left position. The pair formed a keen partnership which brought 50 goals between them over the season. For the return game at Meadow Lane the following Saturday, Stoke welcomed back Kirton, Mould and Steele, who, as first choice, replaced Mountford. Their units' camps near Nottingham allowed McGrory to secure all three leave to play. City raced into a two-goal lead, but unfamiliarity in defence between players who probably hadn't even seen each other for the best part of a year helped Stoke slide to a 2-3 defeat.

Throughout the late summer the skies of southern England echoed to the dogfights of the Battle of Britain. Mass German raids began on 8th August. According to contemporary press reports, in the first ten days alone, the RAF shot down 694 Luftwaffe Focke-Wulf, Messerschmitt and Junkers planes, while losing just 150 of their own. The Spitfire, designed by Stoke-on-Trent engineer Reginald Mitchell, now earned its place in aviation history. Churchill would later immortalise the RAF: 'Never in the field of human conflict was so much owed by so many to so few.'

On the football season's opening day, 88 enemy aircraft were reported downed, while the newspapers kept a running total of enemy casualties in bold letters on their front pages to boost flagging morale. In the event of air-raid sirens during a game, the Ministry for Home Security instructed that the match should be suspended until 'raiders passed' was sounded. Spectators should take refuge in the stadium, rather than leave it. If no suitable cover was available, then the match was to be abandoned. While Stoke's game at Mansfield on 14th September passed off without a hitch, many southern games that day were interrupted by air-raid warnings. Brentford versus Charlton was suspended after twenty minutes and again after 70, while Southampton and Bournemouth had their kick-off delayed by two hours. Over the season, the scores of many unfinished games were allowed to stand. Buckingham Palace's Royal Chapel took a hit, and so did already fragile public morale. Spectators at the Victoria Ground, however, would be safer. The Boothen End was now an official air-raid shelter, housing up to 400.

Mansfield arrived late for their return game after having difficulty raising a team. John Hubbard, who had played at centre-forward the previous week, spent the whole game in goal in place of regular goalie J Downham. The Stags held out until half-time and had a penalty saved by City's Bridges when 0-1 down, but eventually perished 0-5. They also had a shot whereby the ball ended up in Stoke's goal, but it had been wide of the mark and served only to indicate the deteriorating state of the nets. After four games, seventh-placed Stoke had a good goal-average of 2.33.

One of six junior professionals in the team that faced Leicester, 21-year-old Stan Glover, debuted on account of Harry Brigham's ankle injury. Stoke's board, encouraged by McGrory's intransigence, continued to be less than generous in releasing their star players. They refused to permit Freddie Steele to play against them for Leicester, who had already fielded him once without Stoke's permission.

This, ostensibly, seems fair enough. Modern day football has provided numerous examples of players not being allowed to appear against their own clubs whilst on loan. Otherwise they were sure to play a blinder. Leicester, however, by dint of Football League rules, had Steele under *their* jurisdiction. They had secured the player's release from the Army for this particular game and, in turn, refused to allow Steele to play for his own club Stoke. With the two clubs locked in dispute, Steele was sidelined as they battled out a 3-3 draw.

No such problems beset Stoke's non-stars. McGrory wanted to keep them fit and match-sharp for those occasions when they became available. In mid-September Stoke received a telegram from Liverpool manager George Kay seeking permission to play 'Massey of Stoke'. Permission was granted and Massey duly played, but Kay was unimpressed with his temporary acquisition – 'he has more enthusiasm than ability.' This was hardly surprising, as it was revealed that this was not Alf Massey, PT Instructor and First Division half-back, but E J Massey, a man from the Potteries who had one trial with Stoke and was summarily discarded.

Similarly, Glentoran asked Stoke for permission to 'borrow' Mould, who was billeted nearby, but Stoke replied that their Billy Mould was in England, not Ireland, and some cheeky chappie's bluff was exposed. As happened week in, week out across the country, Stoke often faced teams containing at least one of their own players. Some actually fielded more of Stoke's pre-war first-teamers than City themselves, such were the vagaries of obtaining players' release. George Antonio, for example, guested seven times over the season for Nottingham Forest, scoring three goals. His acquaintance with the City Ground would, in fact, last for the duration of the war. Jack Challinor also played thirteen times for Forest and Jock Kirton fourteen times. Both played alongside Antonio, who scored Forest's late equaliser as Stoke drew 3-3 in Nottingham on 26th October.

But Stoke put their 'teammates' in their place during the return game the following weekend, hammering them 5-0 in front of a crowd of just 714, the smallest yet at the Victoria Ground in wartime football. The puny crowds presented no obstacle to the military sequestering the Butler Street Stand for use for the remainder of the war, although belatedly a rent payable to the club of £200 per annum softened the blow. The club also assisted the war effort by allowing the 'B' team pitch to be cultivated for growing potatoes, charging £7 for allowing it to be ploughed.

A/C 1361317 Stanley Matthews was 25 and in the prime of his career. He would be past 30 by the time the war ended. The good news was that his genius would not go completely wasted. On arrival at his RAF unit near Blackpool, his Commanding Officer informed Stan that War Office policy allowed footballers to assist the war effort by continuing to play as and when circumstances allowed. This would provide entertainment and a diversion for both troops and civilians. Naturally this delighted Stan, who became a Stoke regular again until injury struck him down in the home game against West Brom in mid-October. Matthews' NCO (non-commissioned officer) was QPR player Ivor Powell, who would win eight Welsh caps after the war. Powell proved to be something of a disciplinarian, ensuring that he licked his recruits into shape. He needn't have worried about one of them. Matthews continued his own regime of rising at 6am and training on the beach, undergoing a rigorous routine of sprints and shuttle runs before being subjected to Powell's square-bashing routine.

One of the characteristics which marked Stanley Matthews out as a footballing giant was his ability, throughout his career, to constantly look for ways to improve his game and learn new tricks. He eagerly watched other top players of all nationalities, hoping to pick up something which he could put into practice himself. Matthews' initial method of beating a full-back had developed early on in his career and it revolutionised wing-play: 'Instead of waiting for the left-back to approach me, I would make a beeline for him. That would surprise him for a start and he wouldn't know what on earth I was intending to do. Once on top of him, I'd put into operation the body swerve I'd cultivated. That was throwing my body in one direction, then when the player had committed himself, swerving away in the other.' This one, simple, devastating trick condemned countless full-backs to an early footballing grave.

Following his left-footed hat-trick against Czechoslovakia at White Hart Lane in December 1937, Matthews had become the darling of English football. That performance resulted in autograph requests pouring in at a rate of 200 per day, and the cost of replying ate considerably into Matthews' wages. When he began to receive queries on subjects as diverse as politics and birth control, it became obvious that the Matthews personality cult had reached deep into the country's psyche.

Matthews' style then shifted from fast-paced goalscoring winger to the creator supreme, focused on dribbling, taking on a full-back in a series of duels and driving him into the ground mentally as well as physically. This allowed Matthews, as the game wore on, to provide a stream of lethal crosses and cutbacks from the deadball line. In this way, Stan reasoned, he could best provide his team with the best result of his individual skills.

A quotation in *Picture Post*, then Britain's biggest selling magazine, neatly encapsulated his qualities as 'a football equation without answer'. Eric Simpson wrote in the *Daily Mail*: 'Matthews, with football magic in his feet, and the Stoke club, who have a reputation for being exciting and entertaining opponents have been missed by the supporters of the Manchester and Liverpool clubs, among others in the North since this two-section season started. My hint to the Northern Clubs who are now thinking about making their own fixtures for next year is place Stoke on their list … I have no doubt that Stoke City too would benefit by trekking north occasionally. In the present grouping they are a border club.'

Underlining this point, Stoke's match at Prenton Park was billed as 'Tranmere v Stoke City (with Stanley Matthews, England's star right-winger)'. The game ended 2-2, with Frank Mountford scoring both in the first of several Inter-League matches which filled blank Saturdays. These games were included in the goal-average calculations to decide each league championship.

The rampant Matthews was now part and parcel of a settled forward line. Following a 5-0 home win over Birmingham, Stoke (2.00) stood equal second, level on goal-average with Millwall, 0.37 behind leaders Arsenal. Mountford's second hat-trick – one rising volley, one low drive and one cross-shot – hoisted him to second in the country's top scorers list on 16th November. Playing inside him, Frank Bowyer's scheming provided many chances for teammates, although he notched ten goals himself along the way. At West Brom, Bowyer half-volleyed a rebound for a last-minute winner, but in the return Stoke lost their first home game of the season. An early ankle injury, due to a bad foul, curtailed Matthews' involvement and he did not reappear after the interval. Two quick second-half goals, the first a rebound off 'Ginger' Richardson's knee, killed off Stoke. During a lull in the game one wag, referring to a further increase in Entertainment Tax, urged on Stoke's team: 'Come on lads. Let's have that extra penny's worth.'

The Football League took until November to arrange fixtures for the second half of the season. After initially considering the Scottish model, where a league which finished early in the New Year was followed by a cup played initially on a mini-league basis, they opted for simpler cup competitions. There would be one national and several regional cups, played on a home and away basis, with results also counting towards the League. This recipe did not find favour with many clubs, who considered it too complicated a formula, and several openly displayed their dislike. London clubs demanded, and won, the right to organise their own cup competition as they were not permitted to travel around the South. A fresh system would have to be found for next season. Better news arrived when, in October 1940, the Ministry of Food granted clubs permits to sell refreshments. Previously, no catering had been allowed. This relaxation finally allowed the FA to grant permission to allow refreshments for players taking part in matches.

Stoke bade farewell to two important alumni during the season. On 30th November, Arthur Sherwin, former Stoke Chairman, died following a long illness. His involvement in the club, lasting over 50 years, began when, aged twelve, Sherwin had acted as runner between the Copeland Arms Hotel and the ground in the days when both teams used it as a changing room. As a reward, he was allowed into games for free. Having become a season-ticket holder from the age of fourteen, Sherwin in due course founded Sherwin's Printers in Hanley. His successful business saw him invited onto the board in April 1915, when Stoke were on the brink of returning to the Football League, having folded in 1908. Sherwin was chairman from July 1924 until July 1936, when he resigned due to ill-health, succeeded by current incumbent Harry Booth. The second loss was Alf Edge, an inside-forward who had played in Stoke's first ever Football League game in 1888. Edge died aged 76 on 19th April 1941.

Deterred from attacking London, the Luftwaffe's focus switched to provincial industrial cities. Birmingham, Sheffield and Manchester found themselves under attack from up to 400 bombers per night. Stoke-on-Trent also became a target. Like Coventry, which saw its cathedral destroyed by aerial attack on 30th November, Stoke took its fair share of hits, mainly aimed at Shelton Bar, a huge steelworks involved in the production of tanks and warships. In these circumstances, a complete black-out became all the more vital. The dark caused an early end to one Stoke youngster's career. Whilst training on the Victoria Ground's running track around the pitch, Derek Parton, an amateur, slipped and fell onto an iron stanchion which pierced his leg. Dr A P Spark also fell victim to the black-out. With German bombers overhead, he was about to set off for his medical post when two air-raid wardens, Long and Shaw, saw his tail-light uncovered. The pair dragged the doctor from the car, which he was reversing out of the drive, and delivered 'a cruel and abominable assault'. The case went to court with Spark recovering damages.

The two games against Cardiff in early December proved pivotal to Stoke's fortunes. The Bluebirds' board questioned whether their team should bother to travel to Stoke as they always lost money on away games. In an effort to ensure that the fixture went ahead, City's directors dangled the 'promise' of bringing Stan Matthews with them for the return game. Stoke beat Cardiff 5-1, to stand seventh in the table, but Matthews could not be released from his unit in time to make the following week's journey to South Wales, instead guesting for Wrexham at Crewe. City also lacked Frank Mountford, who had strained lateral tendons in the home win and without him they slumped to a 0-4 defeat. Mountford returned after missing just the one game, but he did not carry the same threat and would only score seven further goals that season.

Stoke's increasingly young side began to suffer. Most notably, the goal-keeping situation once more lurched towards crisis. Seventeen-year-old Pat Bridges endured a nightmare month. As Stoke sank 2-6 at Birmingham, Bridges copped the blame for three of the goals. It did not help his cause that the five-goal Birmingham hero, Trigg, was a left-back before the war. Bridges let one under his body, dropped Jones's shot for Trigg to complete a hat-trick inside half an hour, and repeated the ricket for Craven to score Birmingham's sixth.

On Christmas Day the increasingly unsteady Bridges gift-wrapped a goal for Mansfield and never looked confident thereafter. Although Bridges shouldered the blame for the 2-7 defeat, in truth Stoke's team had weakened considerably, even since the start of the season. They now lacked Soo, Matthews was injured, while Liddle and Frank Mountford carried knocks which curtailed their effectiveness. Although still capable of scoring classy goals – Mountford ran 50 yards to wallop in Franklin's pass for a Stoke consolation – the youngsters naturally struggled to keep up with the rigours of a full season in the rough-house world of professional football. The defence in particular was showing alarming signs of tiredness and naivety. City conceded 23 goals in just four games around Christmas, plunging down the goal-average league table like the proverbial stone.

Had Bridges not been Stoke's only professional custodian, McGrory would surely have dropped him sooner, but his misfortune proved the making of an even younger goalkeeper. Dennis Herod had played for Hanley High School Under-14s, along with future Stoke players Alan Martin, Alec Humphreys and Dennis Wilshaw, who would make his name as a striker with Wolves and England. Herod initially played outside-right and scored eighteen goals in one season to Wilshaw's fourteen. But when he progressed to the school's first XI, it lacked a goalkeeper and, despite being only 5ft 9in tall, he ended up between the sticks where he made his name in local football.

Now seventeen, Herod, still an amateur, made his debut at Walsall on 28th December 1940. City scored first but fell away as Wolves' Johnny Hancocks ran riot for a Saddlers team much bolstered by guests. Luton's Edward Vinall notched a hat-trick and hit the bar. But the barrage thrown at him allowed Herod to shine. He was rewarded with an ovation at the end by the home spectators, voted man of the match, and received the accolade of 'best junior goalkeeper for several seasons'. 'Herod handles a ball cleanly and confidently but his best asset is a well-developed sense of positional play,' glowed the *Sentinel*.

Herod had his work cut out, though. Further heavy hammerings followed at Mansfield 1-6, Walsall 3-7 and Northampton 0-7, as the crisis of confidence amongst City's youngsters worsened. At Northampton, Herod's blushes were spared as Norman Wilkinson – finally released by his Army unit after McGrory's increasingly frenzied representations – made one of two rare appearances in goal. But Herod's displays ensured that Stoke thrust a pen into his hand to sign pro. In fact, Stoke's 3-7 hammering at Walsall only materialised after Herod damaged his shoulder in a typically brave challenge. An X-ray revealed no fracture, but severe bruising.

In his comeback game at home to West Brom, Herod dived headlong at the feet of Baggies' 'Ginger' Richardson to prevent a goal, but the collision saw him being confined to bed for a week.

Such heroism endeared him to Stoke's fans instantly. Here was a boy whose appetite for the game matched theirs. His courage was aided by his agility, which allowed him to rush out to challenge oncoming forwards and make flying saves. His bravery, which he now acknowledges as 'somewhere between the rash and the stupid', would inspire his defensive colleagues and demoralise opposing forwards. Blessed with a bellowing pair of lungs, with which he thundered orders to his defence, Herod was king. 'King Herod' in fact to the fans, although he preferred the nickname the players gave him, 'the Cat'.

After carrying a groin injury for several weeks, Frank Soo felt it worsen in January, leaving the team further bereft of experience. Surgery at the North Staffs Royal Infirmary proved necessary and Soo did not recover in time to play again that season. Sale and Steele, on his few appearances, captained the team in his absence.

Matthews' ankle injury proved nigglesome in more ways than one. Now wearing a plaster cast, Stan, while visiting relatives in Glasgow, met with representatives of Airdrieonians to discuss the possibility of playing for them, but due to the injury nothing initially came of it. Stan then dropped the bombshell of securing employment in Glasgow, effectively asking for a transfer to Airdrie. Pre-war talk had seen him valued in the region of £15,000, which if carried through would have exceeded Bryn Jones's record transfer from Wolves to Arsenal for £14,000 in August 1938.

Stoke initially claimed to be 'without information', other than the press stories, about Matthews' intentions. An application for a temporary transfer for the duration of the war with no fee involved was eventually received and Stoke's directors met Mr Richardson, the Airdrie chairman, on 6th March, after which they requested clarification from the authorities about Matthews' military position. The likelihood was that Stan would leave, but Stoke were also concerned about insurance for their star turn, given Matthews' continuing injury worries. A figure of £10,000 was bandied around. The previous season he had been insured for £5,000 for the one match he played in the Scottish Cup.

As Airdrie got cold feet at the size of the insurance premium, Hamilton Academicals threw a spanner in the works, announcing that they had got their man and that Stan would face Albion Rovers the following day. Stoke knew nothing of this turn of events, and neither, it seemed, did Matthews. Airdrie eventually got Stoke's blessing to sign Matthews for the remainder of the season, leaving a belligerent Hamilton threatening to take their case 'elsewhere'. For ten days the contract with Airdrie went unsigned. They then dispatched a telegram to Stoke which read: 'Regret we cannot now utilise the services of Matthews.' Stoke's directors resolved in future to bar Matthews from appearing for any Scottish club. The whole affair left a bad taste in the mouth of McGrory, who chalked another notch of grievance against Stan's name.

The war was going through a desperate phase for Britain and morale was very important. It could swing wildly. Dark was the mood when Amy Johnson's aircraft ditched in the Thames Estuary, while it brightened again once Tobruk in Libya fell to British troops. Football became a stimulating, therapeutic pastime, although the fortunes of Stoke City could barely compare to the visit of King George and Queen Elizabeth to Stoke-on-Trent on Valentine's Day.

Cup competition provided little respite from City's horror run. For the visit to Filbert Street in the Midland Cup, McGrory cobbled together a reasonably experienced side on paper, with Jock Kirton and Jack Challinor released especially for the game. But returning soldiers could not fit in with teammates they barely recognised and, after an even first half, Stoke sank to a 2-6 defeat.

It was the same story when Freddie Steele and Alf Massey made rare appearances in the return leg. Massey's role as PT Instructor effectively precluded him from turning out for Stoke. This would be one of only two appearances this season, and he only managed three spasmodically over the next three years. Ostensibly the war had ended his football career at the age of 24. Approaching Stoke, the Foxes' coach driver lost his way and Leicester arrived late, getting off to an even slower start when Frank Mountford surfed two tackles to rifle home, but eventually Leicester ran out 5-3 winners. Curiously, the cup served a dual purpose. The score at the end of 90 minutes counted as the league result, but for knock-out purposes games would extend to extra-time if necessary to determine who progressed to the next round. Stoke did not need another 30 minutes to know they had been summarily dispatched 5-11 on aggregate, with their goal-average taking yet another hit.

While nineteen-year-old Potteries-born Bob Dunkley – a former outside-left with Huddersfield – arrived back in Stoke for employment and was given 'B' team trial in early January, news of City players' fortunes elsewhere continued to filter through. Doug Westland had been promoted to sergeant and was recommended for a commission. His brother, Jim, also became a sergeant. Tom Brawley wrote to McGrory in February 1941 complaining that his work in a ship-building yard in Glasgow left him 'with little time for football'. Syd Peppitt had plenty of time. He bagged four goals whilst guesting for Middlesbrough in an 8-2 win over Bradford on 11th January.

Stoke bid adieu to players headed for military service at an alarming rate. Neil Franklin, along with Eric Hampson, opted to join the RAF in mid-February. The loss of Franklin, in particular, only worsened Stoke's defensive woes, as he had matured into a skilful and commanding defender. In early March, goalkeeper Pat Bridges and tyro winger Dunkley headed for the Royal Navy. In mid-April, 'B' team right-winger Wally Gould joined the Army. By this time Stoke had twenty players in the full-time forces. Desperate for cover, McGrory utilised Manchester United full-back Harry Griffiths – serving in the Stoke Police Force alongside former Stoke club secretary Tom Hancock – as emergency cover for the War League cup-tie at Mansfield. But neither Griffiths, playing out of position at centre-half, nor Dai Jones, pressed into service in Herod's place, could prevent Stoke's porous defence from shipping six goals. Mansfield showed the benefit of having a settled side, having called on just fourteen players throughout the whole season.

Griffiths' shift pattern meant he could not even provide a short-term answer. Billy Mould wed in late February, with his 'best man' Harry Meakin, who also served as a gunner in the Royal Artillery. Mould spent one day of his honeymoon leave playing at centre-half in the second leg at home to Mansfield. Mrs Mould's reaction to this is not recorded. Mould's appearance at least allowed Stoke to keep a clean sheet and win the game 2-0, City's first victory since 7th December. But, despite that, Stoke bowed out 3-6 on aggregate.

In an effort to bolster the defence, McGrory acquired the services of his gargantuan former captain and centre-half, Arthur Turner, who had been sold to Birmingham in November 1938. Introduced as a direct replacement for Neil Franklin, Turner's first match, a 1-1 draw at home to Walsall on 1st March, promised better things. But Stoke would secure only two more victories in the remainder of the season.

One of those proved to be Pyrrhic. On 29th March, Nottingham Forest turned up at the Victoria Ground four players short. Forest manager Billy Walker sought out Stoke's George Antonio and Norwich's Harry Ware from the crowd. In addition, McGrory loaned him Curtis, a left-winger from Lincoln City, who, by rights, should have debuted for Stoke. Forest's eleventh man was Walker himself, playing for the first time in two seasons. Walker had no kit, but McGrory loaned him his own boots, which he had kept in his manager's office ever since he hung them up six years earlier. The match kicked off twenty minutes late and, not surprisingly, Stoke won easily.

On Easter Monday, Stoke boldly fielded two sides simultaneously, at Wrexham and Northampton. As an aggregate of two goals for, and twelve against told, it proved a dismal failure. Stoke's resources were meagre enough without this suicidal scheduling. The supposed first team, bolstered by the on-leave Wilkinson, Steele and Kirton, lost 0-7 at Northampton. They were not helped by Bill Kinson's concussion from heading the ball away under the Cobblers' persistent assaults. Morale hit rock bottom. Stoke won just one of the last seven matches, avenging that thrashing by defeating Northampton 2-1. Fred Basnett celebrated his signing professional forms for Stoke by scoring his first goal in that game – for Northampton. Not an own-goal, but wearing their strip. Northampton were just the latest team who turned up short.

City finished 25th out of the 34 teams in the South Regional League with a goal-average of 0.791. Frank Mountford's 29 league goals made him the club's leading scorer, ahead of Tommy Sale on 21. Elsewhere, a Hunt class Minesweeper, *HMS Stoke*, named after the city, sank following a raid by German aircraft on 7th May 1941 trying to relieve the ANZAC force besieged by Rommel at Tobruk. As the war continued to swing Germany's way, football provided only a minor diversion. At a Stoke board meeting on Tuesday, 3rd June, McGrory revealed that of his 54 retained players, including 45 professionals, nearly half were unavailable for selection, with a further ten available only occasionally.

The club had its own question to answer. Could it carry on? Dark as Stoke City's fortunes looked, Britain's looked far worse.

## CHAPTER THREE

~ 1941-42 ~

'We were more or less like slaves'

The summer of 1941 marked a gradual change in the course of the war. 'V' now stood for victory, thanks to Churchill's famous two-fingered salute. The RAF had warded off the threat of the Luftwaffe over England, and British bombers were now delivering their deadly cargo to German cities. For his part, Hitler had revoked the Pact of Steel with the Soviet Union and unleashed a massive assault on his temporary ally. The opening of a second front redirected crucial German resources, allowing Britain the breathing space to rebuild her forces.

Everyday life in Britain became ever more austere. The Government introduced clothing rationing, with some families opting to use food coupons to pay for something to wear. Two years of war meant that some women now used beetroot juice for lipstick and soot for eye-liner. As for Stoke's increasingly threadbare kit – or what remained after much of it had been donated to the forces – after three years of use it was barely serviceable. The pitch, too, had long forgotten the sight of grass. The club struggled to find the money and time to re-seed it, on account of its almost constant use.

The city of Stoke-on-Trent had by now become ravaged by a new problem – unemployment. The Government had instructed that the 200 or so potteries operating in the area be 'concentrated' into just 90 firms, with the result that numerous companies closed for the duration of the war. Although many workers found jobs in factories whose men had been called up, others did not, causing more hardship. The city did have one lucky escape, though. It benefited from its relative obscurity when Hitler, angered by the RAF's destruction of Lübeck, apparently ordered the Luftwaffe to destroy all the British cities named in the Baedecker Guide. While Norwich, Coventry and Bristol suffered badly, Stoke escaped almost unscathed.

Everyone involved in football – including the administrators – accepted that wartime soccer had become too complicated and thus had begun to lose its lustre. So it came as no surprise when the Football League restored its competitions to a more straightforward set-up. For 1941-42 the country was split into North and South leagues, with games played only against close neighbours to alleviate travelling difficulties. To the relief of all concerned, the league championship returned to the traditional points system. In the event, however, points average (points earned divided by games played) was used to determine placings in the second half of the season, as some clubs played many more games than others. Stoke now joined the League North.

Less welcome news arrived in the form of another increase in Entertainment Tax, which caused Stoke's admission prices to rise by three-pence to 1s 4d. With Bob McGrory now running the administrative side of Stoke City single-handedly, he received permission from the FA to represent the club at the meetings of the various leagues in which it competed. The FA's Rule 37 stated that former professionals should not act in such capacities. That honour had previously been reserved for clubs' chairmen or secretaries.

During the summer of 1941 Stoke played against Ipstones, a local village side in North Staffordshire, to raise funds for the trawler *Stoke City*. Its skipper Jack Evans visited the club to give his personal thanks. Ipstones set up a general 'Comforts Fund' for the crews of such trawlers.

As the new season approached, Stoke's playing resources became further stretched. George Mountford had joined the RAF and turned out for Blackpool alongside Stan Matthews, while Frank Soo had begun his rehabilitation from surgery back in January by appearing for Newcastle. Eric Hampson, unavailable in any case due to his posting, cracked his ribs during an RAF boxing match and took three months to recover, while guest full-back Charlie Scrimshaw announced his retirement from football following a motorcycling accident during the summer. Stanley Matthews continued to turn out for his adopted Blackpool and scored direct from a corner in the second minute at Stockport on 20th September. McGrory noted that Soo, billeted at the same RAF base as Matthews, at least made the effort to travel to Stoke to play for his own club whenever he could. Matthews made no such effort, chalking up another black spot against his name in McGrory's book.

Despite these problems, McGrory ensured that the board agreed with the decision that the club continue to operate. He argued in the crucial meeting that, after the war was over, City would have a head-start over rivals, as his talented youngsters would have played together for a good many years. Equally, McGrory recognised that no youngster could develop if a run as bad as the spring's – just three wins since Christmas – continued. He drafted in two 'guests' in the half-back line in the form of Bolton's experienced right-half Lol Hamlett, who would miss only three games over the season, and Northampton's left-half, Edwin Blunt, who would appear twenty times over the season. The pair offered continuity, experience and stability, protecting Stoke's young rearguard, plus improved service to the front players.

The best news McGrory could have hoped for arrived from centre-half Billy Mould. Having made just three appearances, due to military commitments the previous season, Mould now became available to Stoke on a regular basis, bridging the gap left in Stoke's fragile defence by Neil Franklin joining the RAF. Franklin appeared in the Blackpool Services team which swept all before them in the Lancashire Combination, alongside Sheffield Wednesday's Dave Russell and Blackburn's Harry McShane. The team was under the supervision of former Huddersfield centre-forward, and now Franklin's sergeant, Willie McFadyen.

McGrory's reconstructed team began the new season in a whirlwind, with goals raining in from all angles, starting with eight against Everton on the opening day. Tommy Sale's early brace was followed by young left-winger Fred Basnett's second-half hat-trick. Despite a 1-3 defeat in the return at Goodison, when Herod saved a penalty but could not stop Cook netting the rebound, City's flying start gathered momentum. The team notched five wins in the first eight games, scoring 35 goals in the process. In a ding-dong battle, which saw Stoke lead 2-0 before slipping 2-3 behind, City claimed the scalp of unbeaten leaders Chester. Dennis Herod saved another spot-kick to set the seal on a 4-3 victory at Sealand Road. He had developed a system: 'Whenever we had a penalty awarded against us I always used to leave it as long as I could before getting back into my goal, just to see if the nerves started to play on the taker. Then I left a bigger space on my right than on my left as my right was my best side and more often than not they'd put it there and I could at least have a chance of saving it.' With or without Herod, this was now an altogether different, more resilient Stoke than had been exposed in the first, miserable half of the year.

On 4th October Stanley Matthews starred for England v Scotland at Wembley in a 2-0 win. Despite not having played for Stoke in a year, he was listed in the programme as Matthews (Stoke City). The BBC radio commentary informed eager listeners how Matthews systematically destroyed highly-rated Scottish left-back Andy Beattie. After the game one Scottish supporter was heard to mutter, 'They ought to tie his legs together,' while the English press eulogised Stan. *The News Chronicle* claimed 'Matthews' artistry with the ball placed him on a pedestal,' and *The Times* paid tribute by saying, 'He has the astonishing ability to not only beat his man, but the touchline as well.' The two nations would meet twice more during the season, with Matthews tormenting the massed Scots defence on each occasion. England won 3-0 and then lost a titanic struggle at Hampden 4-5.

On such occasions the BBC radio commentary team and the press had Britain's morale uppermost in their minds when reporting Matthews' dazzling performances. But the headlines gave Stoke's fans a glimpse of what they were missing and McGrory a reminder that Matthews remained the most loved player in the country.

With Britain now seeking to recruit into service every fit and able man up to the age of 46, those players who for one reason or another did not answer their country's call scrambled to find a 'protected job'. As few able-bodied men remained available for work, those players soon found suitable occupations to keep them out of military service and able to play football on Saturdays.

These routes out of conventional soldiering led to questions being asked in Parliament about players being too easily excused proper military duties. Even those players who did join up could not escape cynicism. It was claimed that they were too easily absorbed into the Physical Training (PT) Corps, thus avoiding service in the more hazardous units. Although star footballers often were given preferential treatment, the truth was that less-famous footballers did give their lives serving their country. Bolton, whose captain Harry Goslin died in the Middle East, and Liverpool, in particular, were hit heavily by deaths among their players.

After the war, public opinion held that footballers, tersely referred to as 'D-Day Dodgers', generally had an easy time of it. In fact many had simply contributed to the war effort by using their existing skills, namely as an athlete, to become ready-made PT instructors, working to keep Britain's forces fit for action. Somebody had to do it, so it made sense to use professionals. The game also raised thousands of pounds for the Red Cross from the various representative matches over the course of the conflict, which helped to lift flagging morale, especially in the dark days of 1940 and 1941. Later, those same players helped cement good relationships between the forces and Britain's allies.

Indeed, avoidance of military service was sometimes not all that it was cracked up to be. 'Reserved Occupations' included the arduous, but vital, tasks of mining, farming and steelwork – none of which could be said to present an easy life. Dennis Herod and Frank Mountford, two of Stoke's young stars, found work at White and Collins' foundry, alongside one of the club's older heads, Bobby Liddle.

Herod became an apprentice coalmaker, shaping black sand into moulds and tipping in molten steel to make valves and engine parts for Britain's fleet. Each ten-hour shift would end with Stoke's first-choice goalkeeper covered head to foot in soot, having toiled in temperatures up to 40 degrees Fahrenheit. 'It was bloody awful. After working until six o'clock I would dash down to training where everyone would laugh at me as my feet and legs were black. They had this running joke that I never washed my feet!' In more than one sense Stoke City benefited from their players being engaged in such activities. Not only did City retain their services on a regular basis, but they kept physically fit. Plus they turned up to play their football with renewed passion for the game as they relished the release from a week's toil.

On the pitch, confidence hit a high after City's youngsters hammered Wrexham 7-1 away. Syd Peppitt had a hand in six goals, but somehow ended the game as the only forward not to score. The match provided an example of the minor difficulties of wartime football. Both sides were handicapped by long grass which had not been cut due to the restriction on petrol supplies. To mow the Racecourse Ground's pitch required three gallons of petrol and the club's allocation would only allow it to be cut twice a month.

Fuel rationing also hit bus travel as the authorities restricted journeys to under 40 miles. More and more clubs had shunned the vagaries of rail timetables, which often extended journeys by two or three hours, in favour of relying on buses. The new restriction meant players struggled to gain release from work early enough on a Saturday in time to travel. Stoke, for example, travelled to New Brighton by train, departing two hours earlier than usual (and returning later), which caused Bobby Liddle and Tommy Sale to miss the trip. As it happened, the pair went down with influenza and would have been unfit anyway. Freddie Steele, home on leave, netted one and Frank Mountford – fully recovered from a tendon strain – two, in City's 5-3 win.

In the return, Tommy Sale, fully recovered, bagged his fourth hat-trick of the season in a 4-0 win. Now nearing 32, Sale's career as a centre-forward – which seemed to have been heading for the doldrums before the outbreak of war – had been rejuvenated by it. Sale revelled in the space and time allowed by wartime defences and hit a rich vein of form which has never been matched before or since by any Stoke player. Owen Bennion remembers: 'Tommy was a very left-footed player. His shooting from distance was phenomenal. He was a real hard man too and had a cauliflower ear.'

Sale's second treble of the season had come as Stoke lost to the odd goal in seven at Maine Road in early October. For once, Herod could do nothing about the hotly disputed late penalty which decided the game. That leant all the more spice to the following week's return match, which Manchester's own hat-trick hero, Sam Barkas, missed as he could not get off work in time. Ernest Bevin, Minister for Labour and National Services, greeted both teams before the kick-off and saw Stoke romp to a 5-0 revenge win. Bowyer, Basnett and Blunt pulled the visiting defence apart, enabling Sale to net a second successive treble, becoming in the process only the second Stoke player (after Freddie Steele) to achieve back-to-back hat-tricks in 30 years.

But Sale was just warming up. His treble against New Brighton proved to be the first in a run which saw Sale hit four hat-tricks in successive matches, a club record never since threatened, bringing his personal tally to 26 goals in nine games. His pace and ferocious shooting, particularly from his left boot, meant that, by Christmas, Sale had already banged in 34 goals, including eight hat-tricks, to head the national list of goalscorers. Thoughts turned towards the possibility that he might overtake Dixie Dean's record of 60 goals in a season, and maybe earn a call up for England. The reality was that Sale stood at least fourth in line for the England No 9 shirt, behind Lawton, Welsh and Rowley, but for the veteran to be mentioned in such despatches proves that his form was being taken seriously by those who mattered.

But this was no one-man team. On the last Saturday of November, Herod saved yet another penalty, this time at Tranmere, with City 4-2 ahead. His team went on to win 7-2, in the process becoming the highest scorers away from home in the country, moving into seventh place in the League North, five points behind leaders Blackpool. City's defence had developed a welcome mean streak, conceding just five goals in five games in December, while 26 flew in at the other end. And it wasn't just Big Tom Sale who frightened the daylights out of opposing defences. In scoring Stoke's third goal in the 4-3 home win over Liverpool on Christmas Day, Fred Basnett took his tally to fourteen for the season. This left him just one behind the club goalscoring record for a winger – fifteen – achieved twice in the 1930s by Joe Johnson.

Small and slight, Basnett had dark, broody eyes and slicked-back dark hair. He was too slim to survive the hurly-burly of forward play at the top level, but in wartime he became a top-notch player, blessed with bundles of energy, cutting in off the left wing to score with fierce drives with his natural right foot. Such was his impact on the team that supporter Rex Audley recalls Bob McGrory describing Basnett over a drink or two in the Talbot Hotel, Hanley, as 'a bloody freak'. Basnett's pursuit of the club record, however, came to an anticlimactic halt when he joined the RAF in late December.

The Basnett family continued a presence at the Victoria Ground, however, as younger brother Albert – often referred to as AE while his elder brother was known as A (for Alfred) – signed amateur forms and impressed on the right wing in the reserves. Meanwhile, reserve left-back George Oldham, having been transferred with his unit to Ireland, received permission to play for Derry City in the (Northern) Irish League. Goalkeeper Doug Westland, relocated to his native Scotland, was given permission to play for Raith Rovers. McGrory's relentless accumulation of local talent continued as half-back Ted Wordley and forward John Sellars – son of former Stoke half-back Harry Sellars – both signed as professionals in October 1941. Sellars celebrated his introduction by scoring a hat-trick for the reserves.

For the first time in the War, the BBC chose to broadcast second-half radio commentary of the Potters' home game against Stockport, on 13th December, which at the very least sustained interest in Sale's run of hat-tricks. This was Stoke's first fixture since the Japanese attacks on Pearl Harbour, which embroiled the United States in what now became a truly global conflict. These were sombre days in the course of the war and the British public craved any sort of feel-good story. Sale's quest for a fifth successive hat-trick served the purpose.

Accordingly, kick-off at Stoke was moved forwards from 3.15 to 2.45pm to fit into the BBC's schedule. Listeners heard Raymond Glendenning describe Stockport put up quite a fight, literally. Frank Mountford damaged a shoulder in a bruising battle with County's Culling, but exacted revenge by scoring a belter with his right foot, even though he was a relative passenger on the wing. Stoke's fiercely contested 3-1 win ended with Rigby, County's keeper, departing injured after a penalty-box melée. Right-half Titterington pulled on the gloves for the last ten minutes and succeeded in keeping Sale from adding to his one first-half goal.

Two games against Liverpool over Christmas further tested the mettle of Stoke's youngsters. Despite Sale's penalty being saved by Hobson, City drew at Anfield, albeit against a side weakened by Fagan and Dorsett not turning up. Gutteridge only arrived after kick-off and Eastham had recently left hospital following ankle surgery.

Although home on leave, for once Freddie Steele passed up the chance to assist Stoke for the return at the Victoria Ground on Christmas Day. He had a prior engagement as best man at his sister's wedding. Other players amongst the new wartime record 8,000 crowd were the on-leave Stanley Matthews, Alf Massey and Bert Mitchell. These veterans could not fail to have been impressed by the young protégés in the Stoke side, for City won a titanic game 4-3 after trailing 0-2 at the interval. Stoke concluded the first half of the League season in fifth place, just three points behind leaders Blackpool.

Christmas brought news of some of their 36 colleagues serving in the military. Eric Longland sent greetings from his posting in Iceland, while Eric Hampson, now recovered from his broken ribs, received permission to play for Fulham while stationed near London. The 5th North Staffordshire regiment's team – which now boasted Stoke's Norman Wilkinson, Jack Challinor, Jock Kirton, George Antonio, Jim Westland and Freddie Steele – sent news of their phenomenal progress in the Army Cup. Their first two games resulted in 15-0 and 15-1 victories, with Steele, now promoted to the rank of sergeant, scoring ten and then six, before cracking in an astonishing seventeen goals in his side's 24-0 victory in the next match. So good was this team deemed to be that, later in the season, they took on Derby at the Baseball Ground and won 4-1, with Steele scoring three. These reminders of the talent of which Stoke were deprived, merely served to confirm that McGrory's policy could be the making of the club.

Stoke's reserves, average age 16½, matched their senior colleagues' feats by winning successive games 3-0, 7-2, 16-0, and 13-1. The storming run featured twelve goals by amateur left-winger Stan Clewlow, including two hauls of four. Right-footed, due to a lack of genuine left-footers available to play outside-left, Clewlow often cut inside to unleash right-footed shots on goal: 'I used to think if I hadn't scored twice in a game I'd played badly. Plus I got a reputation for goal-hanging. Once, this ref said to me "You're here again, Stanley, waiting for snips".'

His form earned Clewlow a first-team call up for Stoke's opening War League Cup game at Walsall, replacing regular winger Fred Basnett, who had tweaked his ankle. On the trip to Fellows Park, the City players sprang a surprise by presenting McGrory with a Christmas gift of a box of his favourite cigars. The whip-round was organised by the on-leave Freddie Steele and suggests a strong bond between McGrory and his personal star, Steele. McGrory consistently prized Steele's dedication, work ethic and motivation of teammates, higher than the more obvious talents of Magic Matthews, the fans' favourite.

City's 4-1 win at Walsall started like a dream for the young debutant, Clewlow, whose day job as a junior clerk at Lloyd's Bank allowed him time to pursue his first love, football. After spending the first five minutes of the game in a daze, thinking 'I've no right to be here', Walsall goalkeeper Biddlestone parried Liddle's shot. Scampering in at the far post to score was Clewlow: 'I headed it back into the goal from three yards with the keeper prone on the floor. It was the easiest goal I ever scored in my life.'

Clewlow, however, being an amateur, never earned a penny from the game. 'I earned £1 a week at the bank and Stoke used to give me expenses,' he recalls, 'but even then they'd quibble over the bus fare.' In the return game, City ran riot, scoring eight times, with Sale banging in six, although he did not have it all his own way. His penalty, given for handball by Male, was saved full-length by Biddlestone.

With nine wins and a draw in their unbeaten run since November, Stoke looked favourites to fill one of the sixteen places available to northern clubs to progress to the last 32 of the Cup.

1942 started gloomily in Stoke-on-Trent. At 7.50am on the morning of 1st January, an explosion, described by the *Sentinel* as 'of serious character', ripped through the Seven Feet Banbury Seam of No 4 Pit, Sneyd Colliery, Burslem. The pit had been regarded as one of the new breed, efficient to the modern degree. Fifty-seven men, some mere boys of fifteen, perished. Only 64-year-old Robert Gibbons, tending an engine at the top of the seam, survived the blast. Lord Mayor Alderman H W McBrine set up a

Relief Fund to help the victims' families, which by 16th January had grown to £13,555 and eventually closed at £28,136 in June. Stoke sought FA permission to play a representative game against an FA XI in aid of the disaster fund, similar to that which Stoke had played against Rangers following the Holditch Colliery disaster in 1938, but the FA rejected the application due to 'present commitments of the Association', although they did donate £250 from their coffers. Sneyd Colliery somehow returned to full production just four days after the disaster, but the grim task of removing all the bodies took over a week. Victims' funerals continued throughout the following month.

City's unbeaten run came to an abrupt end in the War Cup match at the Hawthorns on 10th January. McGrory's weekly battle to persuade the military authorities that players should be released seemed to have borne fruit for this tough-looking fixture. But Steele and Kirton, now stationed in 'a more distant part of the country', 'failed to arrive'. They had been called at the last minute to represent their regimental team at York. In their absence, Fred Basnett was pressed into emergency service, despite not being fit and, after Blunt twisted his knee early on, Stoke found themselves with two passengers. West Brom cruised to a 4-0 win, 'declaring' early in the second half after talismanic centre-forward 'Ginger' Richardson bagged his 300th career goal. That milestone summed up Stoke's day. Herod's poor goal-kick landed perfectly for Ginger to volley it straight back. Herod, however, compounded his error by diving too early. He missed the ball completely, allowing it to bobble in.

For the return match, Steele and Kirton did turn up – just. The pair separately hitch-hiked to Stoke through the generosity of lorry drivers and motorists. Kirton arrived 30 minutes before kick-off and Steele five. Thus strengthened, Stoke won 2-1. Not knowing who might turn up to play each week frayed not only McGrory's nerves, but the fans' too. Supporter Owen Bennion remembers: 'You never knew who was actually going to be playing. One day I turned up at the ground to see a young lad running towards us excitedly shouting "Soo's here. Soo's here!" It was always so thrilling to see the likes of Soo, Matthews and Steele when they could make it back to play and if word got around it could add a lot to the gate at the last minute.'

The teenage Owen rarely missed watching a home game during Stoke's war years, cycling the twelve miles with pals Basil Aitken and Tony Evans from his home in the market town of Eccleshall to the Victoria Ground and paying tuppence to have his bike 'looked after' at a house in Lonsdale Street, opposite the Victoria hotel: 'A lot of people cycled in those days due to fuel rationing and the lady kept an eye on quite a few bikes while we watched the match. We'd always stand in the same place, behind the goal at the Boothen End, behind the middle centre rail. Believe me the fans were just as passionate and as vocal about winning in those days. We'd sing

"Stoke City, Stoke City, We are the Champions!" During the winter, we'd cycle home with a cover over the lamps on our bikes so as not to break the blackout.'

On the way home, Owen freewheeled downhill from the village of Swynnerton back to Eccleshall, passing on the way the huge Royal Ordinance factory concealed in the backwoods at Swynnerton. Camouflaged by a black and green painted roof, the factory churned out thousands of rounds of ammunition every day. In an effort to retain its anonymity, the authorities built several fake barns visible from the air to act as decoys. Many of these met with the Luftwaffe's bombs, but the deception worked and the factory remained intact, manufacturing millions of bullets with 'Swynnerton' famously stamped on their base.

Another way in which North Staffordshire played its part in the war was honoured when the actor/director Leslie Howard began filming the biopic of Stoke-on-Trent engineer Reginald Mitchell, 'The First of the Few'. In 1933, after a visit to Germany had convinced him of the need for a fighter plane to deter the rise of Nazism, Mitchell had designed the first Spitfire, which played such a major role in the Battle of Britain. Mitchell never lived to see his creation in combat, as he contracted cancer and died in June 1937 at the age of 42. The film proved enormously popular on its release later in 1942, although the modern eye perceives a large dollop of melodrama in the painting of Mitchell as a tortured and ailing genius and Germany and Italy as evil foes.

If Mitchell's story provided drama, then the tale of four gentlemen of Stoke City – Peppitt, Ormston, Mould and Baker – offered high farce. Before Christmas the four had been informed that if they transferred to the 53rd Welsh Infantry Division they would be stationed at nearby Meir, thus remaining available to play for Stoke most Saturdays. The quartet duly joined up, but within weeks found themselves shipped off to serve in Northern Ireland. McGrory had lost another four players for the foreseeable future. At least Neil Franklin had become available again, after completing his initial RAF training, to replace Mould at centre-half. The Ireland Four however, found solace, and some small hero-worship, by turning out regularly for Linfield. Three of them – Ormston, Baker and Peppitt – all scored on 10th January. The Linfield secretary wrote to Bob McGrory: 'our spectators have taken a great fancy to your players, who apart from their football ability are real gentlemen and a credit to the Stoke club. We are lucky to have them in our side.' One can only imagine McGrory's private response.

Although the German 16th Army was now encircled by Soviet forces at Leningrad, events in the Far East looked bleak. Japanese forces swept through Malaya, threatening the British stronghold of Singapore. The newspapers were full of the usual bravado. On 9th February the Singapore situation was 'well in hand with severe Japanese losses'. Six days later, on Sunday 15th February, Singapore had fallen with 130,000 Allied soldiers captured. According to newspaper reports, the Army put up terrific resistance, 'fighting to the last', but the truth was that General Percival had misjudged Japanese capabilities, expecting them to attack by sea, when they had actually come through the jungle. He also failed to realise that the Japanese supply lines were stretched to the limit, and that Japanese forces were outnumbered by three to one. As a result of these misjudgements, Singapore fell in a matter of minutes. Among the minor consequences of its capitulation was a dearth of football bladders, rubber no longer being available. Leather was also restricted, meaning balls had to be used many times, not just once for each first-team match.

Stoke's season threatened to fizzle out amidst the continuing player absences and a run of bad luck. A weakened City team, owing to Steele and Kirton representing the Northern Command and Soo playing for the RAF, pressed hard throughout the second half of a fierce encounter in Nottingham. Forest's Astley nodded Bert Mitchell's header off the line before Stoke had a goal disallowed for Basnett being offside, a decision which provoked a rare show of dissent for these times. In a goalmouth scramble Beaumont scored Forest's winner with the last kick of the game after Herod had denied Crooks and Starling. The manner of defeat seemed to crush Stoke's morale, which had served the team well all season. In the return match, City again found goalkeeper Rutherford almost unbeatable, and England international Jack Bowers, playing his first game in domestic football for over a year, scored twice in Forest's 3-1 win.

At least Tommy Sale was still scoring. At home to Bolton on Valentine's Day, Stoke won 3-1 thanks to Sale's tenth hat-trick of the season. He might legitimately have claimed eleven, as he had bagged six goals – a 'double' hat-trick – against Walsall. Even so, he had overtaken the previous record of nine set by Middlesbrough's George Camsell in 1926-27 and equalled by Dixie Dean of Everton in 1928-29. Sale had now scored 46 goals in 22 games. Surely he would break Dean's record of 60.

More immediately, Stoke were now struggling to qualify for the War Cup proper. City's visit to Chesterfield on 14th March did not go well. Already lacking one full-back, Harry Brigham, through injury, Stoke lost the other, Jock McCue, when he failed to make it to Saltergate from his unit. Lol Hamlett switched to right-back, with Edwin Blunt, still recovering from injury, turning out in the half-back line. Once again it wasn't Stoke's day. Herod punched Miller's shot against the back of Blunt's head and watched in horror as it rebounded in. Harley rammed in the Spireites' second goal through a ruck of players before Kirton struck the angle of post and bar and Liddle headed the rebound wide. Sale did at least win and score a penalty, but Stoke could not claw back an equaliser. They now needed a point from their final game at Burnden Park. Fred Basnett's goal, which equalled Johnson's club record, earned a draw, but Stoke had only sneaked through when qualification had seemed a formality.

Qualification brought another episode in the unfolding mini-drama of club versus Matthews. Having assisted Blackpool as a guest throughout the season, striking up a goal-laden partnership with Scottish international forward Jock Dodds – whose seasonal tally eventually reached 65 in just 30 games – Matthews did not expect to be disturbed from his routine. However, as no player could play for more than one club in the Cup, being Cup-tied as normal thereafter, Stoke wished to utilise Matthews for 'his' club. He effectively refused, hiding behind a smokescreen of RAF travel restrictions. In truth, he evidently loved life in and around Blackpool, and his heart was there, no longer in the Potteries. Blackpool was, after all, a better place to bring up children than smog-bound Stoke.

Without Stan, McGrory had to be satisfied with the services of Eric Hayward, the Blackpool and former Port Vale half-back who had been working in North Staffordshire and training at the Vic in a reciprocal arrangement with Matthews. Ironically, Stoke's first game in the second stage of the League North, which commenced after the cup qualification matches, was at Blackpool. Before kick-off the Tangerines were presented with the trophy for topping the table after the first half of the season. They then celebrated by thrashing Stoke, with Matthews setting up Jock Dodds for two goals of his hat-trick.

The draw for the first round proper of the War League Cup paired Stoke with West Brom. The two legs would be played over the Easter weekend. This allowed City to utilise the service of some of their Army players. Thus Jim Westland played his first games for Stoke in over two years, although they would be his only appearances of the season. On Easter Saturday, City rediscovered their form as Sale notched his 50th of the season, a typically rasping left-footed drive. Stoke went 5-0 ahead and looked to be cruising, particularly after Albion's Shaw crashed a penalty for handball against the bar. But a rousing finale saw the Baggies net three times in the last twelve minutes to force themselves back into the tie. Stoke's morale had taken another hit.

On Easter Monday, Sale's drive sent City in level 1-1 at half-time and Herod's flying saves from Richardson, Elliott and McKennon seemed to have kept City two goals to the good. But Herod, under a heavy challenge, was beaten by Elliott's cross-cum-shot, and that sparked an Albion scoring spree. A brace from McKennon inside three minutes, the first another disputed penalty, put the Baggies ahead as City's youngsters sank to a 1-6 defeat. The gate of 13,864 brought in £840 gross, breaking the previous wartime record attendance at the Hawthorns of 8,000, or so, on the last occasion Stoke had visited.

Mentally drained from squandering their five-goal lead, Stoke struggled through the rest of the season, finding goals hard to come by. Walsall, whom Stoke had thrashed twice just three months earlier, snatched a 1-0 victory at Fellows Park and then had the temerity to win 3-2 at the Vic. The previously rampant Sale lost confidence and now found himself hitting the bar from three yards out, saw penalties saved, and even missed routine one-on-ones with goalkeepers – everything, in fact, except score.

Over in Northern Ireland, 'the Stoke Four' all played as Linfield won the Irish Cup final on 18th April, 3-1 against Glentoran. Mould, Peppitt and Baker were also picked to represent the Irish League. Stoke gave Eric Hampson permission to guest for Dundee United, and he helped them thrash Rangers 8-1 on the same day. RAF man Emlyn Williams, a young half-back from Preston, debuted as a guest for Stoke at Chester on 25th April. He had come close to joining Stoke six years previously when playing for Burton Town, but Barnsley beat McGrory to his signature and Williams was later transferred to Preston for £2,500. His introduction to life at Stoke started badly when the team arrived at Chester railway station in good time, but found no transport to convey them to Sealand Road on the outskirts of the city. The players had to walk the two miles, arriving well after the appointed kick-off time. It came as no surprise when Chester scored early on, but Stoke stormed back to secure a 4-1 half-time lead which they clung on to. City's cause was helped when Chester's right-half Howarth was sent off and later fined £5 plus a one month suspension for 'improper conduct'. Due to illness, Stoke Vice-Chairman J H Walton failed to attend, and thus missed his first wartime match.

For their part, the 'B' team completed 21 matches without defeat, winning every trophy in sight. So superior were they that in the Sentinel Shield quarter-final they played with just eight men after three missed the bus due to work commitments. It mattered little as, with Fred Basnett in goal, they still won 11-7 at Cheadle. Johnny Sellars caught the eye by scoring eight goals in a forward line numbering just three players.

Harry Brigham's season-worth of solid performances saw him picked to represent the Football League against the Western Command at Molineux on 2nd May – his first such call-up. Also earning honours was Frank Soo, picked in an experimental half-back line, alongside Everton's Britton and Coventry's Mason, to represent England against Wales at Cardiff on 9th May. It had taken his posting to London and subsequent appearances for Millwall to bring him to the selectors' notice. With Matthews at outside-right, Stoke had two players in the England team, even though Matthews had not played for Stoke all season and Soo just eleven times. Wales won 1-0, thanks to Lucas's twentieth-minute shot.

That same day, Stoke travelled by train to Preston with Stan Clewlow amongst their number for a rare first-team start: 'When we arrived at

Preston station we had to walk to the ground. I think all the first-teamers knew what was coming, so they all set off sharpish while I was left behind and had to help carry the skip containing all our kit. I'd already done a morning's work and by the time the game started I was knackered. I touched the ball about five times all game but we still won 2-1.'

Two weeks later came the ignominy of Stoke's heaviest defeat of wartime football – a 0-10 hammering at Northampton in late May. The Cobblers regularly fielded a strong line-up, which over the course of the season had included Stoke's own Freddie Steele and ex-Potter Harry Ware. On this occasion Joe Fagan, Gilbert Alsop and Harold Shepherdson were notable inclusions among a team of eleven guests. Everything went wrong for Stoke. Herod was penalised for 'carrying', or taking too many steps, with the ball, and Ware back-heeled it for Dearson to open the scoring from the ensuing indirect free-kick. Stan Glover put past his own keeper in a mix up, to spark a spell of four goals in six minutes. Six opposition players got their names on the scoresheet, including a brace from Harry Ware. Stoke enjoyed a small revenge by defeating the Cobblers 3-2 at the Vic on the final day of the season, but Harry Brigham summed up Stoke's season by missing a penalty in the closing seconds.

At the end of every season, in peacetime or war, each club announced its retained list of players. Stanley Matthews was, of course, amongst Stoke's 55 retained players, but he must surely by now have been hankering after a move to his adopted Blackpool. There was certainly no love lost between club and player: 'You would get a letter saying "Dear Mr Matthews, we've decided to retain you for the following year, your wage is so-and-so." Or they would say "We are sorry you are on offer for a free transfer." We had no say. We were more or less like slaves in those days. I had asked for a transfer one year before the war. I was turned down, so the club held you. You were tied. You couldn't do anything about it.'

Matthews' Blackpool won the overall League North title, while Stoke, shorn of their entire pre-war first-choice team, finished sixteenth in the second round of league games. The season, though, promised much for Stoke's future, despite the sour note to its ending. It marked the first real sign of progress, particularly after the previous season's debacle. McGrory now needed to work on toughening up his raw youthful recruits.

Tommy Sale finished second, behind Blackpool's Dodds, in the national scoring charts with 56 goals from 37 games, as Stoke recorded 116 in 39 matches. Although the record books show Sale's club record as eleven hat-tricks, he often claimed the true total was twelve, although only two came after his double hat-trick haul at Walsall on the first weekend in January.

Sale's purple patch can be viewed in two different lights One view is that, had the war not happened, a team like Stoke, featuring not only Sale, but also devastating forwards such as Matthews and Steele, plus half-backs

Soo and Mould, mixed up with young talent like Herod and Franklin, would have pressed hard for honours. Indeed, Stoke City Football Club may have been denied a fabulously successful era by the intervention of the Second World War. Alternatively, one could argue that achievements such as Sale's could only have happened in wartime football. As Tommy's previous best seasonal total of 24 had come back in 1935, how could this ageing striker have scored regularly in a truly competitive First Division? The argument is endlessly circular and can never be resolved.

Back in 1942, Bob McGrory had plenty of other conundrums with which to toy over the summer break. Why, for the second successive campaign, had Stoke fallen apart in the final four months of the season? Were there any more young stars ascending into Stoke's firmament? And had Stanley Matthews played his last game for Stoke City?

## CHAPTER FOUR

~ 1942-43 ~

'We used to call him "Chopper" because no one got past him'

The US Airforce landed in Britain in the summer of 1942 with a mission to bomb Germany into the ground. The influx of American GIs no doubt contributed to record profits for breweries as the sizzling summer brought victory in the Battle of Midway against the Japanese Pacific fleet. The Soviet Union withstood a renewed Nazi offensive before beginning to turn the tide. In North Africa the Desert Rats halted the advance of Rommel's Eighth Army. Meanwhile, the RAF's carpet bombing of the industrial Rühr set about smashing the heart of the German war machine. Despite these successes, the tide of war had not turned as much as some had hoped. With British citizens suffering severe food and fuel hardship, Winston Churchill had to survive a vote of censure on 2nd July after a two-day Parliamentary debate over his leadership.

The FA's AGM tabled the first plans for post-war football, although talk of including leading Scottish clubs in a post-war British League proved a non-starter. £36 was optimistically splashed out on a Victory Cup. For the coming 1942-43 season, a smaller Western Division was added to the usual North and South, with each organised around two series of league competitions, plus a cup. Stoke remained one of the more southerly teams in the League North, although they faced the added enticement of games against Aston Villa, who had returned to competitive football for the first time since the outbreak of war.

At the club's AGM at Stoke Town Hall on 1st July, Stoke's Chairman Harry Booth announced that, despite a slight increase in gate receipts, the club reported a loss on the 1941-42 season of £901 19s 8d after tax. McGrory's insistence on the club playing on, for the overriding purpose of developing his young fledglings in readiness for post-war football, was costing the club dear, but with a credit balance of £12,561 2s 1d, Stoke were still financially in the black. With the outcome of the war still in the balance, it was difficult to predict how the future of the game would be affected. Booth expressed his concern that 'several more seasons like the previous one could damage Stoke's finances severely'. But the directors decided that: 'so long as the Government permit reasonable facilities for wartime football, Stoke City FC will continue to play its part in providing sport as attractive as possible in North Staffordshire.'

Stoke returned to training in mid-August, shorn of the services of yet more young players, as Ted Wordley, Bill Kinson and Roy Brown had all joined up. Among the starry-eyed teenagers signed by the club that summer was Alec Humphreys, a seventeen-year-old goalkeeper from Kidsgrove, who started an association with Stoke City which continues into the 21st century. He later became a director during the glory years of the 1970s and his son, Keith is, as of 2004, a director of the club.

Three practice games were arranged for the week of 17th-22nd August, with all profits from the public practice match on Saturday 22nd donated to the 'Lidice shall Live' fund. The story of Lidice, a Czech village ten miles outside Prague, had become something of a *cause célèbre* in North Staffordshire. On 27th May 1942, Reinhard Heydrich, the Nazi *Reichsprotektor* of Czechoslovakia, had been badly wounded in a grenade attack on his car near Prague by Czech partisans, acting on behalf of the Czech government-in-exile, who had hatched their plans in a refugee camp at Penley just outside Stoke-on-Trent. On 4th June, Heydrich died, whereupon Hitler ordered the indiscriminate execution of thousands of Czechs. At dawn on 10th June, all the residents of Lidice were taken from their homes and shot in batches of ten at a time. By late afternoon, 192 men and boys and 71 women had been executed. The SS then razed the village and expunged the name of Lidice from all official records. Thousands of pounds were raised in Stoke-on-Trent in an effort to aid the rebuilding of a community whose story touched the hearts of the people of the Potteries and became a symbol of hatred of Nazism.

Happier times awaited some of Stoke's players. Neil Franklin married Vera Goodwin just before the season started, with Dennis Herod's wife as bridesmaid. Vera's honeymoon began by watching her new husband play in Stoke's opening fixture of the season. She saw a rejuvenated Tommy Sale bang in another hat-trick. Opponents Crewe could be forgiven for appearing so rusty, as they had disbanded in 1941-42 and effectively fielded a scratch team.

Not so good news arrived of Jack Challinor, whose recurring knee problems – which had begun in that Army boxing bout in 1939 – returned. His knee gave way ten minutes into the new season whilst playing for Notts County.

Stoke's refreshed youngsters began the season with five wins from six games. But this time it was the turn of the defence to impress, conceding just four goals in the five games they won. Experienced guest half-back Lol Hamlett, a Bolton player born and bred in the Potteries, had added solidity and organisation to Stoke's youthful rearguard. And that was not the only way by which Hamlett tended his flock. Arch prankster, gambler and all-round tomfooler Dennis Herod recalls: 'Lol Hamlett was a lovely person. In the midst of this bunch of uncouth, rough lads, was this lay preacher who, because he tried to live by his beliefs, would never swear. But he commanded respect. In fact we respected him so much that, despite the fact he would only say "flipping" or "flopping", he carried such respect that he didn't have the Michael taken out of him at all. In fact he had a wicked sense of humour actually. After the war he asked me to read a sermon during a service for soldier players and when I got there I found he had chosen one for me to read about the sins of gambling!' With slicked-back light brown hair above a kindly smiling face, Hamlett's classy use of the ball kept Stoke's attack moving forward, while his tenacious tackling set an example to his young protégés as to the level of commitment needed to succeed.

None took this to heart as deeply as left-back John, or Jock, McCue, who had by now become a regular name on McGrory's team-sheet. McCue, starting a sequence that would see him miss only one more game during the war, would go on to make more appearances in a Stoke shirt (672) than anyone before or since, although as so many were made during the war, he stands only second in League appearances to the Stoke legend of the 1960s and 70s, Eric Skeels, with 542. A lanky full-back, McCue was famed for the ferocity of his tackling. Modern fans should think Stuart Pearce in his most bullish mood, and you might be about halfway there. McCue looked as psychopathic as Pearce, too. Blond crew-cut army hair topped a lean, angular face, the focus of which was his nose, broken so many times throughout his career that it seemed to bend several different ways at once. But the most telling attribute of this bulldog's make-up were his wild, staring eyes that betrayed McCue's total focus on doing his job of stopping the opposition. Through the use of a judicious kick or two at opposing wingers, McCue induced fear, respect and loathing in opponents in equal measures.

Wolves' Dennis Wilshaw recalls: 'His [McCue's] tackling was never the fairest and I tended to keep away from that part of the field when I played against him. Once I began to play with him after moving to Stoke, I could see that I would much rather have him on my side!' Frank Mountford chuckles: 'We used to call him "Chopper" because no one got past him. Or if they did, they were lucky!' Thus McCue earned the moniker 'Chopper', well before Chelsea's infamous Ron Harris had even been born.

Stan Matthews took time out in his autobiography, *The Way It Was*, to defend McCue's physical style in his understated way by claiming 'High velocity tackling. He was never a dirty player'. McCue, though maybe not considered dirty, simply did everything in his power to ensure his opponent did not get past him. A more revealing description from the war years heralded McCue as the 'poor man's Wilf Copping'. Copping was the

Arsenal and England destroyer of the 1930s, whose sole job in Herbert Chapman's triple title-winning side was to stop the opposition playing. Off the pitch, McCue was morose and quiet and never got involved too much in socialising. Frank Mountford remembers McCue as a 'loner', and 'a blunt man, very much in the mould of Bob McGrory'. Mind you, the seemingly steely emotionless McCue never forgot his teammates of the 1940s. When interviewed about his time at Stoke, the grey eyes misted over slightly as he cracked a smile: 'Those local lads will always stay with me. Excellent it was. I can't get them out of my system.'

Despite his reputation, in a football sense, Jock brought more to the Stoke team than merely destruction. Dennis Herod recalls McCue's professionalism: 'Jock McCue was a total fitness fanatic, who trained and played hard,' and Jock's distribution often allowed Stoke's left wing, staffed by Baker, Ormston or Liddle, to operate at its most fluid best. Although he did often simply whack the ball clear to see it fortuitously turn into an accurate long pass, the naturally left-footed McCue could also legitimately pass precisely over distance. Indeed, during late 1942, at the age of twenty, McCue was regarded as Stoke's 'best product of the wartime years'. This epithet should not be taken lightly given the other starlets in his company.

One of those young stars, Dennis Herod, had come to the end of his tether. Tired of toiling in White and Collins's furnace room, Herod opted out of his personal hell in favour of joining up, having come to the conclusion that: 'it sounded rather glamorous to join up and anyway anything had to be better than that.' He joined the 44th Royal Tank Regiment, undergoing basic training at Bovington, Royal Army Corps base in Hampshire. Dennis still found time to keep his football going, however. He trained with Southampton and guested for Aldershot under manager Bill McCracken, who also had Stoke's inside-forward Patsy Gallacher available to him. As Aldershot was the home of the Army Physical Training Corps, the pair played alongside a bevy of footballing greats of the era – Stan Cullis, Wilf Copping, Tommy Lawton, Cliff Britton, and future England trainer Harold Shepherdson amongst them. Herod produced another in his long line of penalty saves on his debut in a 3-2 win. So, by the time Stoke travelled to Crewe, they had lost one established player, but had regained newly-wed Neil Franklin, whose transfer to Hereford to undertake a PT instructor's course kept him readily available to Stoke.

Meanwhile Frank Soo, originally down to play for Everton, answered Stoke's call and played in City's 2-1 win – although this meant he had to catch a 3.15am train on Sunday morning and cycle eighteen miles to get back to his unit in time for *reveille* at 0730 hours.

Herod's departure left a gaping hole behind the established defence. Efforts continued, as they had for three years or so, to secure the services of Norman Wilkinson, but again came to no avail. Port Vale keeper Arthur

Jepson, whose club had closed for the duration, due to dire finances, offered his services. But Jepson, whose summer employment was as a Nottinghamshire County cricketer, failed to turn up for the home game with Wolves, the one match for which he was selected. Reserve goalkeeper Fred Sherratt played four games before McGrory brought in Phil Bates, a professional with considerable pre-war Midland League experience with Shrewsbury. Bates, having been promised release from his Army duties on a regular basis, made the first-team jersey his own for most of that season. Jepson turned to Nottingham Forest instead, but McGrory would remember his offer and it was not the last Stoke fans would hear of this talented footballer-cricketer.

On 12th September, as Stoke met Wolves for the first time in wartime football, Billy Mould and Syd Peppitt represented the 'Army in Ireland' against a touring Army XI, which featured the Wanderers' Jimmy Mullen. George Oldham also joined Linfield, having been transferred to Northern Ireland with his unit. This brought to five the number of Stoke players representing the Belfast club, and together they helped establish a new Irish League record for an unbeaten start to the season. One Linfield fan was so moved by what he saw that he wrote to Stoke to describe Billy Mould as 'the best centre-half I have ever seen in football'.

Against Wolves, Tommy Sale missed a penalty, firing straight at Sidlow from the spot. Frank Bowyer missed two open goals to add to City's woes as Dennis Westcott bagged a hat-trick of headers. Stoke sneaked a 1-0 win in the return game, albeit against a weakened Wolves side, while in the next home game, Harry Brigham – the previous season's failed penalty-taker – became the latest to miss from the spot. He drove his kick against the post at 0-0 during Stoke's 5-2 win over Derby, and compounded his error by driving the rebound into the net to give away an indirect free-kick. That result was no mean feat as Derby, despite competing in their first season of wartime football after closing for three years, boasted a 100 per cent record and a goal difference of 16-2. Frank Soo rounded off the scoring by finally netting the first penalty of Stoke's season, from their third award.

Frank Baker transferred from Ireland back to England at the end of September, travelling through the night to reach the Victoria Ground for that match against Derby. But Baker arrived unannounced and, for once, both clubs had full teams, so he had to be content with watching Stoke canter to victory. Baker did get a game the following week when Stoke won 1-0 at Derby, crossing in the eighth minute for Sale's goal. Alongside Baker, Stoke fielded Alec Ormston, who had also returned from Ireland, but Ormston strained his groin and spent three-quarters of the game limping out on the wing. Consequently, under heavy onslaught from Derby, Stoke survived the woodwork being hit twice and Bates saved Nicholas's second-half penalty to cling on. It would, however, be Ormston's only appearance in a Stoke shirt this season, and one of just four for Baker, as new post-ings took them away from the Midlands and eventually abroad. After seven games Stoke stood fifth in the table, on ten points, two behind Blackpool who boasted a 100 per cent record. The good start mirrored those of the previous two seasons. Had McGrory's youngsters matured enough to maintain their improvement over the whole campaign?

A run of three defeats suggested that they had not. Stoke's first wartime game at Birmingham's bomb-damaged St Andrews ended in defeat. Despite Bates keeping out goalbound efforts by Dearson and Pearson, Acquroff scored Birmingham's winner three minutes from time. Stoke's penalty jinx continued in the return at the Vic, when Birmingham and England's goalkeeper Gil Merrick saved Soo's spot-kick as Stoke slid to a 1-3 defeat.

Tommy Sale converted Stoke's next spot-kick, given for handball on the goal-line, to secure a 1-0 win over Aston Villa. A 5-1 thrashing of West Brom featured two debut goals from the younger of the Basnett brothers, Bert. He coolly rounded Kinsell to score past Adams for his first. But that game proved a one-off and Stoke's malfunctioning attack, with the previ-ously prolific Sale losing his pace and presence, struggled to carry any sig-nificant threat to opposing defences. Fans, and no doubt manager McGrory, yearned for the likes of Steele, Peppitt, Ormston, Matthews and Baker.

Another of City's absentee attackers was inside-right George Antonio, who had played just once for the club since the beginning of the war and would not appear again for Stoke until October 1945. Antonio was an enigma to Potteries folk. On his day, he could be brilliant. His incisive, crisp passing could release his wing partner, Matthews, while his audacious shooting – such as the chip which deceived Billy Light for the tenth of Stoke's goals in City's record 10-3 victory over West Brom in February 1937 – marked him out as a future star. But Antonio had a flaw in his make up, which meant he blew hot and cold to the eternal chagrin of Stoke's supporters and manager. His inconsistency saw him in and out of Stoke's team, while his penchant for vanishing for long stretches during bad games irked some of City's ever-present boo-boys. Owen Bennion recalls: 'George was a very tricky player on his day and he often played with his head but he made mistakes and people could get on his back, especially when his job basically was to give the ball to Matthews. My father loved him, but I wasn't so keen.'

Small and chunky, with flowing dark hair and a broad face, George's real surname was Antonio, under which he had to be registered with the FA, but he would later play under his adoptive parents' surname, Rowlands. Despite being born of Italian parents, before the war George had come close to becoming a Welsh international. However, a few days before his scheduled international debut, it was discovered that the English-Welsh border in fact looped around the farmhouse at Larkhall in which George had been born. It was, in fact, in England and made him ineligible to play for Wales. In any case, Antonio would not be playing for anyone for the rest of this season. While guesting for Notts County, as he had for much of the war, he developed fluid on the knee which kept him out of football for six months.

On 21st November the Victoria Ground hosted its first wartime 'Big Match', a representative fundraiser between an FA XI and the RAF. For this special occasion, the Butler Street Stand, still requisitioned by the War Office as a storage depot – as had happened to many sports stands around the country – was reopened for the first time. Invited guests numbered more than 200, while many of the huge 23,358 crowd – a wartime record attendance at the Vic (which would not be exceeded) – came to see 'our Stan' make his first home appearance since 21st December 1940. Matthews lined up for the RAF, alongside Frank Soo, Hardwick (Middlesbrough), Dodds (Blackpool), and Hapgood (Arsenal). The FA XI featured Bacuzzi (Fulham), Mercer (Everton), Finney (Preston), Liddell (Liverpool), and Westcott (Wolves) amongst many other contemporary stars. The FA XI won 4-3, thanks to goals from Broome, Liddell, Goulden, and a late winner from Joe Mercer. The RAF scored through Dodds twice and Frank Soo, who headed in a Matthews corner, flicked on by Dodds to set the crowd alight. Watching with no small interest was Bob McGrory, ostensibly present to represent the club and chaperone Stanley Rous, the Secretary of the FA. The following day Rous called to congratulate the club for the support shown to football in the Potteries. Receipts raised £2,214 for RAF charities.

While McGrory was otherwise engaged at the Vic, his own team took the field at Wrexham. It was the first occasion McGrory had not super-vised his team in person while at the club. It looked as though the Potters would suffer, as Muir netted in the first minute for the Welshmen, but now the wisdom of McGrory's youth policy began to bear fruit. Bill Caton bagged his first senior goal with a shot in off the post, while Fred Basnett and Frank Mountford also got on the scoresheet. City won 4-2 with some 'clever play' and several 'three-pronged moves' admired in the *Sentinel*'s match report of the game. Stoke now embarked upon a long unbeaten run which extended beyond Christmas, the third successive season they had timed such a successful winning run in this way. Could the winning ways continue, enabling the team to make an impression in both league and War Cup?

As Christmas approached, tales reached Potteries folk of how football raised spirits in PoW camps overseas. Hugh Irving, organiser of the North Staffs Prisoners War Comforts Fund, reported a communication from

Stalag 20A which stated that a league with ten teams had been instituted
by inmates using sporting kit donated by the citizens of Stoke-on-Trent.
Company Sergeant-Major Smith wrote: 'I am no Bob McGrory or Stanley
Matthews, but on the whole we fellows do play a wonderful game. It keeps
us fit and cheerful.'

Football played an integral part in numerous stories from the war, none
more moving than that which emerged from newly liberated Kiev in the
Ukraine. During the German occupation, members of the famous
Dynamo club had taken on and beaten several German forces teams,
including one sprinkled with professional footballers. Dynamo's success
caused such a furore that the German authorities arrested each member of
their team and consigned them to the concentration camp at Babi Yar, just
outside the city, where several met their deaths. The legend of that
Dynamo Kiev team lives on today in the form of a memorial outside the
Republican Stadium in Kiev. It is dedicated to the players who defied the
Nazis through sporting endeavour, bringing hope to millions that one day
they might be free again.

Back home, Tommy Sale was injured at Wrexham, forcing McGrory to
rearrange his forward line. George Mountford was now increasingly available from his base in Kidderminster, while namesake Frank, who up to this
point had been used on the left wing, returned to centre-forward. The
switch worked. Stoke's potent strikeforce ran riot, scoring 25 goals in six
games, starting with the 6-1 hammering of Crewe. When fit again, Sale
could not force his way back into the attack, although his availability invari-
ably guaranteed him a game. He settled in at left-half, replacing the injured
and unavailable Frank Soo for the rest of the season. Sale still contributed
the odd goal to City's cause, although he missed yet another penalty when
Crewe's Poskett saved his second-half effort.

Stoke's defence, described as 'outstanding', saw Franklin and McCue
receive special mentions. Harry Brigham's form was rewarded with another representative appearance for the Football League. But it was the forwards who took most of the plaudits. By now, Frank Bowyer's role in
Stoke's incisive attacking had become key. The twenty-year-old's form
rocketed him to the forefront the club's future hopes, his partnership with
Frank Mountford yielding 38 goals over the season.

Born at Chesterton, Staffordshire on 10th April 1922, Bowyer had
joined Stoke's ground staff at the age of fifteen in June 1937. He signed
professional forms in July 1939 after playing for both Hanley and Stoke-
on-Trent Schoolboys whilst attending Birches Head Catholic School. A
placid character on and off the field, Bowyer's shy smile hid a burning passion for the game of football. At 5ft 10in he was relatively tall for an
inside-forward, but his skills lay in his twinkling feet, a deft passing ability,
and a rasping shot with either foot.

In particular, Bowyer's jet-propelled right foot often had supporters behind the goal ducking as the net ballooned towards the terraces. Frank Mountford remembers Bowyer as 'a wonderful volleyer of a ball. His goals always seemed to be sweetly timed on the half-volley and I thought personally that he was the best inside forward I ever saw.' Fan Rex Audley remembers: 'Bowyer was a sensation, a tremendous player. He was well-balanced when he volleyed and had thighs like tree-trunks. I know, because I used to live in the same village as the Stoke trainer Harry Pearson and he told me how big they were when he had to massage them.' Fellow youth-team player, and later *Sentinel* Sports Editor, Peter Buxton, recalls Bowyer's distribution skills: 'Frank could hit a long pass as accurately as any player in the game.' Bowyer had one other distinguishing feature – huge ears. He combed his jet black hair across into a quiff which fell over his right temple, but it could not hide his huge buckets, which made him the butt of many a friendly joke from his teammates and some less pleasant abuse from opposing supporters.

But it was as a creative force that Bowyer excelled. Often when Stoke indulged in bouts of heavy scoring during the war, the scheming and industry of Bowyer lay at their heart. He did not always receive the recognition he deserved from the critics, simply because he did not always get on the scoresheet. Of the seven goals that flew into Walsall's net on the Saturday before Christmas 1942, Bowyer could be credited for creating four, but his name does not appear amongst Stoke's scorers. This season he did weigh in with his fair share, contributing nineteen goals, a good return for what would be described these days as an attacking midfielder.

Stoke's coruscating winning run, which ended with a 2-2 draw at Walsall on Christmas Day, propelled them to the summit of the Southern Section of the League North. They finished with 25 points to Derby's 24, in sixth place overall in the War League North. As a token of their respect for this small achievement, Stoke's players gifted Bob McGrory a box of his favourite cigars for Christmas, with Sale, the senior pro, making the presentation. Christmas greetings arrived from Doug Westland, who had received a commission and was *en route* for service overseas, Frank Soo, now playing for Chelsea, and Freddie Steele from Doncaster.

Meanwhile, forgetting the previous Scottish debacle, Stoke granted Stanley Matthews permission to play for Greenock Morton while on leave in Scotland over the holiday period visiting his in-laws. As Stoke commenced a War League Cup campaign, of which much was expected, Crewe collapsed to a second successive 6-1 whipping just two weeks after their first. The on-leave Dennis Herod missed out on that match as he had injured his hand playing for Aldershot on Christmas Day.

Eleven games without defeat, but now Stoke faced a severe test when Aston Villa – the last team to topple them – came to town. A battle royal ensued and Stoke won 1-0 – as they had in the League – thanks to a strange goal. Frank Bowyer and George Mountford appeared to strike the ball simultaneously, following a half-cleared corner, with Bowyer eventually claiming credit for the goal. After three games, City sat atop the 52 teams searching for qualification, ahead of fellow unbeaten sides Manchester City, Chesterfield, and Coventry. For the return match, despite Jock Kirton being in the Potteries on leave, McGrory kept faith with his young charges and refused to change a winning team. The youngsters had to be given their heads at some time, and McGrory chose this as the right time. Villa, however, gained revenge by ending Stoke's twelve-game unbeaten run with a 3-0 win. Frank Mountford suffered a knock to the face early on, while Bates had an off-day in Stoke's goal.

Once again Stoke appeared to wilt with the turn of the year. In the next match, at Wolves, Stoke allowed Billy Wright to record a hat-trick as a stand-in centre-forward. Wright capitalised on Harry Brigham's absence in Yorkshire, grieving for his deceased father. Wright's haul included an injury-time equaliser, after Frank Bowyer's 90th-minute trademark volley appeared to have handed City victory. Given that Wright only managed sixteen goals in 541 appearances in his long peacetime career, his hat-trick is as good an indication as any that wartime football did not quite come up to scratch. In fact, Wright's third goal was vehemently disputed by the Stoke players, who held up the final moments of the game with their continuing protests to referee Bryan. Say what you like about the quality, the players still cared desperately about winning.

Despite the upturn in Allied fortunes, the war tightened its grip on the public still further in the winter of 1942-43, with clothing, petrol and food all increasingly scarce. Dennis Herod was spared the worst. His wife, Joyce, had a family-owned shop, Moseley Stores on Lonsdale Street, 500 yards from the Victoria Ground, which still exists today under different ownership. Says Herod: 'Joyce's Mum would be making cups of tea for the players from 9am until they went home after lunch. I was lucky though because they always had plenty of eggs and bacon for me to have. Bob McGrory used to pop in for his 10 Prize Cop cigarettes too.'

Not everyone was so fortunate, as food shortages bit hard. In early February 1943, while Churchill launched the Dig for Victory campaign to encourage folk to grow their own, people found many different ways of putting food on the table. A poacher from Chesterton, Sid Cumberbatch, reared rabbits illegally in his back garden. To reduce the risk of being caught, he press-ganged local children from the council estate on which he lived to each look after one of the fluffy bunnies. Peter Cotton takes up the story:

'Old Sid got us to look after the rabbits and we used to raid the big council bins where everyone dumped their household waste to find food for them. The bins were supposed to go to the Hospital to feed the pigs which were reared there to feed the patients, but we found all sorts to feed our bunnies with. Every so often Sid would tell us that our rabbit had died. In fact he was killing them, selling them or eating them himself and then giving us another one to look after for him! I didn't realise what was going on. He also reared pigs without a licence – you were supposed to have a licence during the war – and he'd hide them in the garage to make sure no one saw them. But the community spirit was wonderful. If Sid caught a rabbit he would often give it to my Mum who would cook it and share it out. My Mum was renowned as the local helper. She would ensure that everyone helped each other out. She was also the person who laid out those who had died. I always knew someone had snuffed it when our back gate was taken off its hinges as it was used to lay out all the dead people from our estate!'

Footballers kept pigs too. Frank Bowyer, whose common sense marked him out amongst Stoke City's happy-go-lucky, fun-loving young brigade, eschewed a lifestyle of carousing and betting in favour of a settled home, doting wife and pigs. His teammate in the 1950s, Johnny King, recalls: 'Frank was shrewd and he'd had this sideline going for years, selling his pigs to local butchers. He did very nicely.'

This habit began during the war when the pigs brought many a hearty meal to the Bowyer table, although surely not to anyone else's, as illicit meat became the subject of much censure. Some prosecutions followed in Stoke-on-Trent as butchers sold meat from 'unlawful sources' under the counter. Often it would not be fit for human consumption and caused the person who devoured it untold pain.

In response to worsening public health, not helped by the lack of fresh fruit, the Government instigated the Beveridge Report, which would produce the blueprint for the future Welfare State. For the proposed original contribution of 4s 3d per person per week, it would bring to the population a comprehensive compulsory insurance policy from cradle to grave.

Back on the pitch, Bowyer scored twice in the 2-1 home win over Walsall. One of these, as Stoke's fourth penalty taker of the season, came from the spot. But Roy Micklewright had an unhappy debut at centre-half as Walsall won 4-1 at Fellows Park with Nicholls bagging a hat-trick. Micklewright's luck did not improve the following Saturday when he returned to the 'B' team and sustained a fractured nose in a collision with an opponent.

McGrory decided that young keeper Bates was now making too many mistakes. For some time, the manager had sought to utilise Don Bilton from Wolves. Bilton, who was being kept out of Wolves' first team by Cyril Sidlow, had attracted McGrory after Herod's departure at the start of the season, but there were problems with his availability. Now, however, Major

Buckley, Wolves' manager, permitted Bilton to play for Stoke and his experience improved Stoke's defence.

Fortunately, given Stoke's poor run, other results had left them just needing two points from their games against Derby to qualify for the first round proper. Bilton's saves earned successive clean sheets as Stoke defeated Derby 4-0 at home and 1-0 away to earn a tie against Chester in the last 32. Maybe the youngsters had, after all, learned to keep their run going to the end of the season. A Derby fan who witnessed City's win at the Baseball Ground felt moved to write to McGrory: 'I am taking the liberty of writing to tell you how much I enjoyed the football played by Stoke against our team last week. It was a pleasure to see such a fine sporting young side in action and I hope to have the treat of seeing Stoke play again. I wish you all success in the Cup.'

For the visit to Chester in the first leg of the first round, McGrory had Freddie Steele available, but opted once again to stick to his settled side, which was unchanged for three successive matches for one of only three occasions during the war. The decision was repaid with a 3-2 win against a side packed with five guest players imported specially for the occasion. Stoke had placed Preston's Fairbrother on standby to play if Bilton was not released by Wolves. In the event, Fairbrother – the Scottish international keeper – turned out for Chester, alongside Arsenal's Leslie Compton, Birmingham's Hughes, and Charlton's Welsh. In the second leg, shorn of most of their guests, Chester succumbed to a 5-2 defeat at the Vic, thanks to two early goals and a Frank Bowyer brace.

The cup draw now pitted Stoke against Aston Villa, provoking a huge surge of interest for the first, home leg. A sense of expectation hung in the air. Long queues at the turnstiles led the *Sentinel* to claim 'It's just like the old times'. Over 18,000, the largest crowd to watch Stoke at home thus far in wartime, soon found those hopes dashed as Villa, who had knocked out Cup holders Wolves in the first round, stamped their influence on the game. A Stoke side, weakened through injury to the extent that reserve centre-half Roy Brown played on the left wing, gave a good account of themselves, but, at the end of an even first half, Villa's Edwards skipped past McCue, who lost his footing, and centred for Davis to nod home at the far post. After surviving an all-out Stoke assault early in the second half, Villa finished the job when Brigham handled Davis's shot. Houghton converted the penalty and Davis later made it three. Bowyer's late consolation could not stop Aston Villa becoming only the second team, after Birmingham, to win at the Vic this season.

The second leg, despite being effectively dead, attracted a crowd of 22,921, the best home attendance for Villa in wartime and the best away for Stoke. With Soo and Franklin away, playing for the RAF, Stoke once more sought the services of Arthur Turner. However, he could not be released, so Lol Hamlett filled in at centre-half. By now Frank Mountford, injured in the first game, also looked jaded. He had been rested occasionally, but had failed to recover his spark. He now wasted a one-on-one with Wakeman, which, had he scored, would have put Stoke back in contention. Alas, Edwards burst past Hamlett to net, while Houghton's deflected shot saw Villa home and dry, 5-1 on aggregate. Despite his slip in the first leg, Jock McCue proved to be Stoke's outstanding player of the tie, to the point that Villa Chairman, Mr Normansell, approached his Stoke counterpart with a view to a post-war transfer, offering a kind of early pre-contract agreement of the type which is in vogue today. The Stoke board, who had not come this far with McGrory's youth policy to toss away all their good work, unanimously rejected Villa's advances.

The wind having been taking out of their sails by an early cup defeat for the third season in a row, Stoke played a series of relatively meaningless league games and treated them as such. In distant parts, the war was now turning in the Allied direction, perhaps decisively. Monty's Eighth Army smashed through Rommel's Panzer lines at Gabes in Tunisia, opening up a bridgehead for troops to pour through and begin to take control of North Africa. The Potteries mobilised to fundraise during 'Wings for Victory' week which began on 10th April. Opened by the Chief of Fighter Command, £1,801,950 – the cost of over 370 Spitfires – was raised for the RAF through exhibitions, parades and over £1,500 raised by the club during the home game against Notts County. McGrory chose that game to blood seventeen-year-old Emmanuel (Manny) Foster, a goalkeeper signed from local amateurs Mow Cop. Foster kept goal steadily, impressing particularly at Derby during City's 1-2 defeat. With Dennis Herod currently manning the 17lb gun of his tank in North Africa, who knew what Foster's opportunities after the war might be?

Stoke's finest, Stanley Matthews, now promoted to the rank of corporal, continued to turn on the style for England – starring in a 4-0 win at Hampden Park on 17th April – and for Blackpool, who knocked league leaders Manchester City out of the cup at the quarter-final stage. The *Manchester Guardian* lauded Matthews' performance in that match to the skies: 'Rarely has one man so dominated a cup-tie. Matthews is the Joe Davis [a famous snooker player] of the football world. His command of the ball is absolute. Players advance towards him with the air of victims ordained to succumb.'

Blackpool, helped by a run of 35 unbeaten home matches, and Jock Dodds' 47 goals from 31 games, retained the League North title and lifted the War Cup, recovering from two goals down to defeat Arsenal, Stan's other guest club, 4-2. Matthews considered this the best team in which he had played and there was little doubt that his hankering for a transfer to the Golden Mile was growing by the day.

On 12th April 1943 former Stoke full-back Arthur Beachill died aged just 37. He had complained of feeling unwell whilst working in the Foundry at Messrs Robert Hyde and Son Ltd, and was walking home when he collapsed and died in Fletcher Road. During 1932-33 Beachill had helped Stoke establish a club record for the fewest goals conceded in one season – 39. Beachill – a native of Monk Bretton, Yorkshire – had been discovered playing for Frickley Colliery in September 1926. He made 128 appearances for Stoke over five seasons from 1929, winning the Second Division title in 1932-33, before being transferred to Millwall in 1934. His death was popularly attributed to 'overstrain', a rising complaint amongst men working feverishly towards their patriotic duty, despite feeling unwell. Beachill, in fact, had suffered from bronchitis, believed to have stemmed from his career as a professional footballer, which gives an insight into the conditions in which players performed in the 1930s.

Citing the cause of death as 'coronary thrombosis', during evidence at the inquest Dr Dathan told the coroner that that Beachill probably would not have noticed anything more than a persistent cold. Work in a foundry would have been unsuitable for a man in his condition and no doubt contributed to his early demise.

Another former Stoke player to pass away was Fred Johnson, on 14th May. Aged 65, Johnson had played 196 games for the club as a right-winger from 1892 to 1903, scoring twenty goals. He later became licensee at the Saracen's Head in Stoke.

By 20th April, with the threat of German invasion of these islands long gone, the Government gave the go-ahead for the country's church bells to be rung again in celebration of God, and not as a warning of air raid or invasion.

On the pitch, a 1-4 home defeat by Wolves showed Stoke's youngsters how far they still needed to go to match the best. At least that hammering spurred them on to beat Leicester twice in their final two games. McGrory allowed Bobby Liddle to play for the struggling Foxes at Filbert Street, in favour of fielding younger players himself. Then, in the return, McGrory leant Leicester three players to complete a full eleven. Although City had been just three points behind leaders Manchester City and Liverpool with five games left, they slumped to finish tenth after the second series of league games.

The season proved more successful from a financial point of view, thanks to a huge improvement in attendances. Sixty-one players, a record, were retained, 44 of whom were locally born. On 15th May Stoke took a virtual first team to play Wrexham in a previously unrecorded friendly to raise funds for local hospitals. McGrory blooded young goalkeeper Edgar Podmore in this game and it was his dazzling performance in a 2-1 win that saw him gain a regular place for the beginning of the following season.

By the end of the 1942-43 season, the FA's plans for post-war football were well advanced. Interestingly, administrators of the time constantly refer to the war period having returned to football its spirit, perspective, and the joy of playing simply for the game's sake. This, they would endeavour to retain after the war. Stoke's youngsters had plenty of spirit, but still had to build the stamina to last them a full, gruelling season, even at wartime level. If the end of the war heralded a quick return to full-time football, then Stoke might not have made as much ground as McGrory had planned. Could he swing things the following season?

CHAPTER FIVE

~ 1943-44 ~
'Staffordshire folk are keen on sport, but they are also keen on perfection'

The summer of 1943 saw Axis forces across Europe and North Africa forced on to the defensive, and in many cases in retreat. The German surrender in North Africa in late May was followed by an Allied invasion of Sicily on 23rd July. In Germany, Hamburg in particular suffered terrible bomb damage in early August, and in the Soviet Union the tide of battle had turned decisively. Sicily fell on 16th August and by early September Allied forces had landed on the toe of Italy. Within days Mussolini had been deposed and fled into hiding. Resistance in southern Europe now came solely from retreating German troops.

Over the summer, Stoke learned that Harry Cope, a former 'B' team player, had been invalided out of active service after losing his sight fighting in North Africa. Closer to home, re-elected City Chairman Harry Booth fell ill, although details are sketchy as to exactly what form his illness took. Whatever it was, he recuperated by taking the waters and long walks in Buxton, although he did not return to his desk until December and remained unwell throughout the season.

The Football League increased players' fees by ten shillings per match, although the ban on all forms of bonuses remained in place. The Government was hardly in a frivolous mood either, refusing any reduction in the crippling 33 per cent Entertainment Tax, which hit football clubs' finances so heavily.

Following his success in Stoke's final match of the previous season at Wrexham, Edgar Podmore now signed professional forms. Podmore, from Fenton, had been playing for prominent local works side Teddy Toy SC, where McGrory stole him from under the nose of Bury. In the public trial n 21st August, Podmore's Blue & Whites (fielding the first-choice attack) defeated the Red & Whites (first-choice defence) 4-1. The result indicated City's weaknesses might lie in defence. With Frank Soo unlikely to be available – he was posted to southern England, where he guested for Reading and Brentford – McGrory conferred the captaincy on Tommy Sale.

News of Stoke players scattered to the winds filtered back throughout the season. Eric Hampson, now serving with Frank Baker in the Middle

East, wrote home and discussed footballing activity within his regiment. He complained about hard pitches and the heat taking its toll. Ted Wordley had better cause to moan about the hard pitch on which he broke his wrist in a fall whilst playing in Iceland. Bert Mitchell wrote from Ceylon to boast of his display for the RAF Command's 5-0 win over the Army Command. In Scotland, Tom Brawley was earning rave reviews as Dumbarton ran Rangers close at the top of the Scottish League, while in Northern Ireland full-back George Oldham transferred his services from Linfield to Glenavon. Freddie Steele turned out for both Doncaster and Barnsley, while Massey, Ormston and Peppitt all helped out Millwall during the season. But the news was not always good. Ormston's return to Stoke was hindered when he injured an ankle playing for the Lions in early September.

At the start of the campaign, Neil Franklin – temporarily posted to Weston-Super-Mare to undertake a flight mechanics' course – had to travel to Aberaman in the Rhondda valley, simply to get a game of football. He appeared on a few occasions alongside Blackpool's Willie Buchan. Franklin did, however, win selection for the RAF's representative side, often also featuring Soo and Matthews. Franklin excelled in matches against other arms of the services to the extent that newspaper gossip had him down as a certainty to replace Wolves' Stan Cullis as England's centre-half. The *News Chronicle*'s Arthur Shrive wrote: 'Franklin is undoubtedly the finest young centre-half-back in the country, and it cannot be long before the FA selectors recognise his merit.'

Meanwhile, Stoke's board had become so disillusioned with Stanley Matthews' lack of determination to play for his own club that they made a public announcement on 13th August to that effect. They pointed out that he had played several games in Scotland, but not once for Stoke in the past two seasons. They went so far as to write to him, making their displeasure clear. It must be remembered that, with Bob McGrory now fulfilling the dual role of secretary-manager, he attended every board meeting and wielded considerable influence. Gossip-mongers already had Matthews' post-war transfer to his new home-town of Blackpool down as a certainty. The likelihood of Stan ever again wearing Stoke's red and white seemed remote.

So Stoke's youngsters, once again, enjoyed plenty of opportunity to learn from the school of hard knocks. Two opening defeats by Aston Villa showed that if they did not shake off the malaise which had struck the players since the cup defeat by the same team six months previously, the season would prove to be one of long struggle. With his major worry now finding a replacement for Neil Franklin, McGrory went against his principles for the first time, opting to bring in a star guest player. He acquired the services of Glasgow Rangers' captain and centre-half Jock Simpson, posted by the RAF to South Cheshire. McGrory also coveted Black, the Hearts centre-forward, but he opted to guest for Crewe rather than Stoke.

But Simpson's recruitment did not bring any improvement to Stoke's predicament. In particular, his part in a 1-2 loss at Crewe, where he marked Black, was described indignantly by the *Sentinel* as 'indefensible' and McGrory soon terminated the player's involvement. Three defeats in succession marked the club's worst start to a season since 1912. Even Jock McCue, 'Mr Consistency', came in for heavy criticism for his lacklustre displays. Perhaps believing the maxim 'form is temporary, but class is permanent', Aston Villa persisted with their pursuit of McCue. Mind you, at least Villa abided by the rules. Wolves found themselves up before an FA commission, accused by Stoke of making a 'wrongful approach' to an unnamed junior player. Director David Duddell and McGrory testified to this effect on behalf of Stoke at the commission at Crewe on Tuesday 5th October 1943. Unfortunately, the board minutes do not identify the player or reveal the outcome.

The return match with Crewe, at Stoke, gave McGrory grounds for hope. Two late goals saw Stoke win 4-2 to register their first victory of the season. Stoke then beat Derby 5-1 at the Vic, with a flurry of late goals, partly assisted by Rams' keeper Townsend's broken finger. Better co-ordination and increased steadiness in defence was noted by the *Sentinel*, mostly attributed to the return of Mould and Franklin to the side.

Meanwhile, an accompanying improvement in attack laid the basis for back-to-back wins over equally youthful Wolves, with Stoke's 2-1 win at Molineux their first in ten years. Syd Peppitt's return provided added firepower, and George Mountford impressed on the right wing with his speed, dashing approach play, and crosses, which created numerous chances. Mountford's form, including notching a few goals – a knack which Stanley Matthews notoriously lacked – prompted some impishly-minded folk to wonder whether Stoke needed Matthews to return from his Lancashire exile after all.

Injury and unavailability of key players, such as Frank Mountford, Brigham, Franklin, Mould and Hamlett – who had the misfortune to have a finger amputated after an accident at work – precipitated an inconsistent spell. With the Allies building up their forces in Britain in readiness for an invasion of Europe, football clubs across the country eagerly anticipated the return of their players from overseas postings. Everyone knew the invasion was coming and resources were diverted away from the Italian campaign to prepare for it. Often, however, a player's promised release was delayed for several weeks. In Billy Mould's case, his availability proved sporadic until late-October, when his return coincided with a pronounced upturn in Stoke's form. Mould's absences generally occurred when he failed to keep to his matchday routine. That meant a 6am departure from his Army unit near London, train travel to Stoke, generally arriving twenty minutes before kick-off, then a return journey to arrive back at his base around 3am.

Neil Franklin, however, relished the long journeys. By now stationed at RAF Helmswell in Lincolnshire, Franklin's normal post-match routine saw him catch the 'stopping train' across the Pennines to arrive in Lincoln after midnight, whereupon he would cycle the twelve miles back to camp. He maintained: 'I found that did me more good than all the physical jerks. Cycling is one of the best exercises there is.' Mind you, Franklin did apply to the board for some funds to assist him in paying for a taxi to and from his post to Lincoln station, so he was not always so keen on the added exercise.

Franklin and Mould had become vital to Stoke's defensive solidity and thus good form. Having two such talents in the same squad left McGrory with a problem, although admittedly of the kind which managers like. Who to select at centre-half? At the moment, McGrory conferred that honour to the more senior Mould, with Franklin appearing at right-half, unless Mould proved to be unavailable, in which case Franklin was handed the centre-half shirt and performed like a man determined to hang on to it. McGrory's plan to develop a squad capable of invigorating itself through healthy competition, with young players forcing senior colleagues to play at the top of their game, was never better illustrated.

At 5ft 9½in and 11st, Mould wore a shy smile on his moon-shaped face. His high balding forehead, topped with brown curly hair, and stocky build gave him a look reminiscent – save for the hair colour – of future England captain Billy Wright. Despite his boyish, soft good looks, Mould was made of stern stuff. Dennis Herod recalls: 'Billy was dour and determined, physical, careful and mean – and he was the same off the field.' Mould's playing style was that of the classic physical centre-half of the 1930s. He crunched into tackles and paid attention to clearing his lines. Don Whiston, a young fan at the time, believes 'Billy Mould was the finest kicker of a ball I have ever seen. He was so clean in his clearances and he had a lovely balance while making tackles.' Mould's importance to the Stoke side went further than his own play. He quietly imbued those around him with his own will of steel.

With Frank Mountford still struggling with injury, and Tommy Sale lacking the pace to play at centre-forward, McGrory needed a goalscorer. Centre-forward John Jackson, who had been given a couple of sniffs of first-team action the previous season, had scored ten goals in four 'B' team games. Jackson, however, failed to justify his promotion, finding the net just once, against Wolves, at the end of the season.

Centre-half Roy Shufflebotham made his debut in a 0-3 defeat at West Brom, enduring a barrage of first-half Baggies pressure which saw Stoke fortunate to concede just three. Roy's nerves were not helped by the sight of many Albion fans evacuating the ground well before the end, knowing that Stoke were being toyed with. Shufflebotham had only signed as a pro a fortnight beforehand, but had no chance to set the record straight as he was called up to the Army within a week.

As neither Jackson nor Shufflebotham successfully bridged the gap between the reserves and first team, clearly the promised return of Freddie Steele and Alec Ormston could not come quickly enough. A 1-4 reverse at Wrexham saw McGrory lose patience with the increasingly erratic Podmore, even though George Mountford's early head injury reduced City to ten men. Mountford was hospitalised, and ensuing influenza kept him out of the side for two months.

But while Steele and Peppitt were home on leave, Stoke turned on the style. Revenge by 7-3 was wreaked on Wrexham, followed by a 5-0 thrashing of Crewe. But the two stars' departure caused Stoke's form to dip again over the Christmas period, and City finished 34th out of 50 at the conclusion of the first set of fixtures in the league championship. This was hardly the improvement that McGrory was anticipating.

Stoke's 2-4 defeat at Walsall on the Saturday before Christmas provided a memorable moment for amateur outside-left Stan Clewlow. Called into the team as a late replacement for the injured Tommy Sale, Clewlow found himself playing at inside-left: 'Bert Williams was in Walsall's goal, and after the war he went on to star for Wolves and England, but on this occasion, Bert misjudged a cross. It hit the bar, came out to me and I headed it in.' It was a rare starring moment for young Clewlow, who readily admits that he was lucky to play at a higher level during the war only because of the absence of senior players: 'I don't think I'd have got in anyone's reserve side today. I don't think any of us would.' Crowds, however, didn't make any allowances: 'I remember playing one game and I wasn't having a great match and because I played on the wing I could hear people in the crowd. This bloke shouted at me "Hey, Clewlow, buy a programme – you're playing".'

Stan Clewlow also recalls the horrendous state of City's training kit, which was now wearing perilously thin: 'Our training gear looked at least twenty years old and because it was kept in the dank changing rooms, it was ringing wet through. Then we had to go out and train in it. We lived our whole lives soaked to the skin. We wore that same kit all year round and when you came into the side you simply got handed someone else's redundant kit which probably had socks with no soles in. The match day kit wasn't much better. Stoke may have played in red and white, but the stripes got paler and paler.'

City's final game of 1943, the first of what looked a tough qualifying programme for the War League Cup, saw Manny Foster forced off the

Molineux pitch for fifteen minutes through injury, with Jack Griffiths deputising in goal. Griffiths, and the second largest away crowd to watch Stoke in wartime – 19,951 – saw Wolves' McLean crash a drive against his goalpost. But Stoke survived and a trademark Tommy Sale free-kick – following thunderous strikes against West Brom and Crewe – earned a point. It might have been two, as Wolves did not equalise until four minutes from the end, through Spanish teenage winger Aldecoa.

While that point was considered a bonus, on account of Wolves' strong form, what happened at the Vic when Wanderers visited on New Year's Day was little short of sensational. Being a holiday fixture, City had Freddie Steele, Frank Soo and Jock Kirton all available for rare appearances, while Wolves could also boast a dangerous addition to their side in the shape of centre-forward Dennis Westcott. Despite falling behind to an early Billy Wright goal, Stoke ran riot, with Steele scoring six goals, three with his head and three with his right foot. His 'double hat-trick' emulated Tommy Sale's achievement of 1941-42, and the two players remain the only ones ever to have bagged six goals in Stoke's colours. To complete the rout, Sale netted a penalty and tapped in after Sidlow half-saved Steele's cross-shot, while Bobby Liddle scored a one-on-one. The final score was 9-3. J T Stevenson, Staffordshire's representative on the FA, campaigned to have Steele selected again for England. Freddie had won six pre-war England caps, scoring eight goals. Now, despite his vastly reduced availability, he managed to score as prolifically as ever. In just nine games for Stoke this season he notched twenty goals.

For the next match – the visit of another of Stoke's *bête noires*, Aston Villa – McGrory surprisingly made eight changes to that winning team, although half were enforced due to unavailability. One unforced alteration saw the reappearance of Stanley Matthews in Stoke colours. Not having worn them since 21st December 1940, Stan, home on leave, at last made himself available for the rest of January 1944 and made three appearances. Could the fact that Stoke had just thrashed one of the strongest sides in the country 9-3 have influenced that decision, when on all previous home leaves over the past three years Stan had not made himself available? Was McGrory secretly hoping that the maestro would fall flat on his face? Both must have known the huge expectation and interest Matthews' appearance would provoke. Indeed, the kick-off had to be delayed due to the weight of spectators at the turnstiles. In the end, 16,492 made it into the ground, setting a new best home wartime attendance for Stoke.

The wing wizard did not disappoint, producing a dazzling display to delight his public. Time and again Villa's left-back, Cummings, warily shepherded him towards the touchline, only for Stan to twinkle to the byline and produce a series of crosses. Cummings resorted to trying to kick Matthews out of the game, but Stan was irresistible. He twice set up

Peppitt for tap-ins, was felled for a penalty, and then, having left Cummings on the seat of his pants, floated over a perfect centre for Sale to head ferociously home – and that was all before half-time in what ended as a 6-3 Stoke victory.

Matthews' return, albeit brief, motivated other far-flung players to ensure they became part of Stoke's resurgence. Mould, Ormston and Peppitt, although all were selected to play for Millwall, due to the proximity of their barracks to London, preferred a twenty-hour return trip to assist their own club and play alongside the maestro. A 2-0 win at Villa Park, Stoke's first there since 1934, completed City's first ever double over Aston Villa, in front of the largest attendance for any English club during the season – 32,000. Fan Rex Audley remembers the crush: 'at New Street station I was carried off my feet and up the stairs as the crowds moved off towards the ground.'

The lure of Matthews extended the length and breadth of the country. Another long-forgotten Stoke hero duly made a telling return to the team. Jock Kirton scored four minutes into the Villa game, while Alec Ormston's journey proved not in vain. He scored the late clincher, although his goal provoked a demonstration amongst some of the crowd who claimed that the ball had entered the net via the side netting.

The next prodigal son to return was Norman Wilkinson, whose job as a collier had taken him back to his native County Durham. He had been assisting both Nottingham clubs and Sheffield Wednesday this season. Wilkinson had the misfortune of timing his arrival with Matthews being unable to travel to Stoke's next match at Birmingham City. A subdued performance resulted in a 1-4 defeat, two of the goals being put down to Wilkinson's handling errors.

Nearly 20,000, another Stoke wartime record crowd, paying £1,558, saw the return match with Birmingham, in which Matthews made his last appearance before his leave ended. Steele and Sale rolled back the years to produce a display which depended less on Matthews' crosses and more on power and pace through the middle. In sum, those three victories created, in the words of the *Sentinel*, 'more sporting enthusiasm in North Staffordshire than probably any previous period in wartime football.' Neil Franklin later explained the huge upsurge of interest from fans when Matthews appeared in Stoke: 'Staffordshire folk are keen on sport, but they are also keen on perfection.' To reiterate the point, Stoke's next, Stan-less, home gate numbered just 3,982.

With so many experienced first-teamers populating the side, Stoke's young breed sought other turf to tread. Frank Mountford had impressed Derby's director George Robshaw so much in scoring twice in Stoke's 5-2 victory at the Vic that he persuaded Frank to guest at the Baseball Ground. Mountford, with Frank Bowyer and Harry Brigham, guested for Derby against Sheffield Wednesday, with the two Franks both scoring in a 4-1 win. Mountford had become somewhat aggrieved because he was still being treated as a reserve to Sale and Steele, whenever they were both available and, fed up, he agreed to don Derby's colours.

This was, of course, all part of McGrory's plan to foster competition in his squad, and the ploy worked a treat. At Derby, Mountford played between Raich Carter and Peter Doherty. It was a wonderful footballing education for the young man and he took full advantage. Another Stoke starlet, Frank Bowyer, played at inside-right, but fell foul of the legendary arrogance of England international inside-forward Raich Carter: 'I played the ball straight to him, Carter controlled it, stopped and then kicked it out of play over the touchline! He shouted at me "You, play it in front of me. I want it two yards in front of me, not to my feet".'

The pragmatic Mountford discovered another bonus for playing for the Rams. Derby paid him more than Stoke did, added to which his aunt lived in Derby so he could stay for free and be well up on the deal. There was talk of a permanent move, but when push came to shove Mountford did not want to up sticks and leave his marital home, so he remained with Stoke.

That was not the only vital decision Mountford took which affected the fortunes of his future career. The goalscoring young buck had begun to suffer regular injuries brought on by the rough attentions of uncompromising defenders. He had become fed up with being kicked from pillar to post: 'I loved playing at centre-forward when I was younger, but when I played professionally and found out what it was all about I wanted to play in defence, where I could kick people rather than get kicked. My mother was all for it!'

With McGrory's assistance, over the rest of the season Mountford successfully converted into a right-half, revealing unexpected determination and ferocious tackling. His speciality was the sliding tackle, which, on the muddy Victoria Ground, would begin with a leap into the air, continue as he careered towards his intended target, and result in ball and man, or one or the other, being claimed with a rousing cheer from the terraces. Frank credited McGrory for initiating the switch: 'He spotted right-half was my true position. He knows my game inside out.'

Derby's interest in Stoke did not end there. Their directors not only expressed a keen interest in Stoke's youth policy, but, with their manager, George Jobey, having been suspended for life by the FA for paying illegal bonuses to players since 1925, the Derby board plumped for Bob McGrory as their preferred replacement. McGrory, though, would have none of their advances, and was determined instead to see through the job he had started at Stoke. Later in the season he also turned down an opportunity to join Wolves.

In response, Stoke rained in 24 goals in five successive victories as the previously problematic qualifying fixtures were made to look a mockery. First, Walsall were brushed aside by an aggregate of 7-1, and then West Brom suffered an 8-2 humiliation at the Hawthorns, with Steele bagging another four goals. A closer game at the Vic saw the Baggies restore some pride, but City won 5-4, despite Steele having a penalty saved by keeper Heath. Stoke finished atop the qualifying group, while West Brom failed to qualify for the competition proper for the only occasion in the war. City's odds for the War Cup had shortened from 50-1 down to 8-1 by the time the draw for the last 32 paired Stoke with the one team they had cause to fear – Aston Villa.

Despite the previous season's second-round exit at the hands of Villa, back-to-back victories for Stoke over their adversaries in the past two months left McGrory in no doubt that City could, and probably should, win this tie. So confident were they that the board permitted Matthews, Antonio and Challinor to guest for other clubs in the competition proper, and thus render themselves cup-tied if Stoke should have need of them.

The agreement with Blackpool saw Matthews swapped for half-back Eric Hayward, but Hayward pulled a muscle the day before the game and could not play. Over 11,000 excited fans witnessed an afternoon which provided plenty of drama. After the teams swapped early goals, Villa took what seemed like a decisive two-goal lead. Broome raced through to beat Foster and then Houghton followed up O'Donnell's shot after Foster had only parried. City hit back gamely. Steele burst through and was felled, whereupon Sale dispatched the penalty. Then Steele headed powerfully home to level matters. Right on half-time Peppitt was tripped and Sale again lashed the spot-kick home to send City into the break 4-3 up. But Villa proved their class as they turned the game once more on its head, scoring twice in two minutes through Houghton and then Broome's close-range finish. The excitement did not end there. Despite having the injured Peppitt as a passenger for the last half-hour, Stoke took the game to Villa. Try as City might they could not force an equaliser.

With a match like that as the first leg, who knew what could happen in the second? Having lost at home, Stoke may have been long odds, but they certainly weren't out of the tie. The build-up to the second leg was over-shadowed by the death in action of Bob McGrory's son, Corporal Robert McGrory, of the Argyle and Sutherland Highlanders. Flowers and mes-sages of condolence flooded the Stoke club offices and McGrory issued a public 'Thank you' to all well-wishers. Dennis Herod recalls: 'I was abroad then so I don't remember that happening, but I do know that Bob McGrory was a very private man. He kept his family well away from foot-ball. I think I met his son once, but his family never came to see the games. I never saw his wife.'

One must remember – at a time when so many lost sons, fathers and husbands – that, sad though it was, the loss of another did not inspire the outpouring of sympathy that would attend such a loss today. McGrory's personal grief did not stop him leading his team into battle at Villa Park. Crucially of course, Stoke did not have Matthews, Kirton or Steele at their disposal. Just before half-time, Frank Mountford, still suffering a crisis of confidence when pressed into service up front, missed an easy tap in from two yards which would have levelled the scores on aggregate.

Instead, City suffered a mortal blow moments later when Massey tore a muscle in his side. He could not continue and Villa took full control. Houghton fired in from the edge of the area and then dispatched a penalty for a foul by Brigham. Broome's late goal set the seal on Villa's win. They went on to win the cup, defeating Blackpool, Matthews and all, 5-4 in the final.

Allied air-raids over Germany now reached new levels of intensity. On 19th January 2,300 tons of bombs rained down on Berlin in the space of half an hour, bringing the total to 17,000 tons in two months. The Allied air assault was chipping away at the strength of industrial Germany, weakening its productivity and hindering its war capability, all with a view to the planned invasion of northern France. Indeed, Dennis Herod's unit was pulled out of Italy and he was sent to Scotland for training prior to the planned invasion.

In Italy, all eyes were on the besieged Monte Casino, towering over the Rome-Naples highway, which entrenched German forces turned into one of the bitterest land battles of the war. On 18th March news arrived from the area that Stoke's twenty-year-old reserve half-back Bill Caton had been taken captured. On the field, prior to his call up, Caton's prodigious long throw, which could reach the penalty spot from near the halfway line, had kept him in contention for a first-team spot, despite his modest talent with the ball at his feet. He would not recover sufficiently from his injuries to figure in Stoke's plans until November 1947.

Stoke again provided several players for the season's internationals, although none played much for the club. Frank Soo and Stanley Matthews contributed to England's 8-3 destruction of Wales at Wembley on 25th September. That game threw up another bizarre wartime anomaly when Stan Mortensen, Blackpool's English inside-forward, made his international debut – for Wales. He came on as an unofficial substitute for the injured Ivor Powell, but went on to win 26 caps for his own country, England.

Stanley Matthews even got on the scoresheet as England again scored eight, this time hammering Scotland 8-0 at Maine Road on 16th October. His teammates, appreciative of Stan's part in building a 6-0 lead, tried to set him up for a goal. When Tommy Lawton, whose ten-minute hat-trick had been carved out by Matthews, teed up one chance, goal-shy Stanley miscued. The ball fell to Lawton, who promptly scored his fourth. The crowd bayed for a Matthews goal. At the death, Stan embarked upon a silky run from the halfway line, waltzed round a succession of Scottish defenders and to frenzied excitement rounded keeper Joe Crozier to score. The crowd erupted and the legend of Matthews, destroyer of the Scots, was cemented for all time.

Scotland were slain again, 6-2 at Wembley, on 19th February when Matthews faced his nominal teammate Jock Kirton. Jock, appearing at left-half, became the first Stoke player to win a Scottish cap since Billy Maxwell back in 1898. For the trip to Hampden on 22nd April, Soo and Matthews turned out in front of 133,000, the largest gate anywhere in the British Isles during the whole War. England won 3-2. Frank Butler of the *Daily Express* called this team 'England's best since 1907'.

There were sound reasons for England's success. Firstly, players of quality abounded. The Matthews/Raich Carter wing partnership was untouchable on its day as the two players capitalised on the understanding already established as regulars in the RAF side. In goal, England boasted a redoubtable custodian in Manchester City's Frank Swift. No less important, England's internationals played together much more than during peacetime football. The squad developed more of a team mentality and the selectors, deprived of many options to tinker, left the side well alone. The result – 27 goals scored in five wins out of five.

On 11th March Stoke hosted a Services Charities fundraiser between an FA XI and the Army. Seats, priced five shillings and 3s 6d, sold out in advance for a chance to see so many of City's own. Wilkinson, Challinor, Soo, Matthews and Steele appeared for the FA XI, with Frank Swift, Stan Cullis, Joe Mercer and Tommy Lawton playing for the Army. The match was billed as a duel of the potential England centre-forwards – Lawton versus Steele. Freddie Steele laid his claim first, scoring just after half-time, but Lawton shortly headed in from close range. Both, however, found themselves overshadowed by West Bromwich Albion right-winger Billy Elliott's hat-trick, completed after 55 minutes, as the Army won 5-2. Another new wartime record attendance for the ground of 23,542, paid £2,919 for the privilege.

With the public's greater appetite for one-off, or cup matches, Stoke City backed a proposal by the Birmingham County FA to stage a Midland Cup, in order to prolong an otherwise dead season. The competition featured ten clubs, with ties being played on a home and away basis. Results also doubled for League North purposes. Having reached the War Cup competition proper, Stoke went straight into the hat for the last eight and came out paired with Derby. Trailing to Harrison's header, and having escaped further damage when the same player also hit the inside of the post, City turned their opening game at the Baseball Ground on its head.

Sale set up Peppitt to lob over Swindin – a goalkeeping guest from Arsenal – and two minutes later Steele latched onto Peppitt's pass to lash into the net. Frank Bowyer's volley, which rocketed in off the underside of the bar, must have stung opponents who had taken him to their hearts during his brief sojourn at the Baseball Ground not two months before. That goal effectively killed the tie, and a 1-1 draw in the home leg saw Stoke through to face West Brom, who had defeated Walsall, in the semi-final. Stoke attempted to secure Matthews' services for the tie but failed. They also lacked Mould, Peppitt, Ormston, Wilkinson and Steele, causing Bill Pointon – in only his second appearance in the first team – to be included at inside-left.

Stoke drew first blood when Sale lashed in a rebound after Bowyer's drive hit the bar. Elliott levelled for Albion three minutes later, as City's defence stood still expecting an offside flag. City had the edge throughout the second half, with Sale failing to capitalise on a great opportunity when he shot straight at Heath. A draw was a commendable result in the circumstances, but without Bowyer, out with influenza, and the injured Fred Basnett, Stoke travelled to the Hawthorns more in hope than expectation. City began the match gamely, with Stan Clewlow, in for Basnett, causing problems on the left wing. After twelve minutes Clewlow chased a long pass and forced Southam to turn an attempted back-pass past his own keeper to hand Stoke an early lead. Elliott tapped home after Foster had spilled Richardson's shot, but City should have regained the lead when Peppitt beat the offside trap but fired straight at Heath. West Brom took advantage and Heaselgrave and Richardson both scored. Albion went on to play the winners of Nottingham Forest v Northampton in the final, which Forest won 4-3 on aggregate.

The losers of the semi-final had agreed to play Wolves in what would be the last two games of the season. Tommy Sale missed a second-half penalty as Stoke drew the home game. With another drastically weakened side, City then lost 1-2 at Molineux, mitigated by losing Liddle early on due to a head injury and seeing Sale blast against the angle of post and bar. The better form over the second section of the season saw Stoke improve on their 34th out of 50 after the first set of fixtures. They stood sixth in early April before finishing thirteenth overall. Tommy Sale finished as the club's leading scorer with 30 goals in 39 games.

At their AGM on 28th June, for the first time since war began, Stoke announced a profit of £4,266 9s 10d on the season. The directors had learned an important lesson: Matthews equalled money. He might wish for a transfer to the Lancashire seaside, but now it would be over the dead bodies of the board. The healthier balance sheet allowed the board to reward McGrory with a £300 bonus. Groundsman Harry Loffill, now the club's only other non-playing employee, received just £5.

But if the club was considerably better off, some of its players were not. Freddie Steele made an application to the board for financial assistance while his wife was having her third child. He was on three months compassionate leave from the forces and would not receive any pay during that time. The board gifted him £40 to tide him over. There was more expense to be outlaid on keeping the ground from falling apart. The Military's occupation of the Butler Street Stand had caused broken glass and the need for repainting, although the Army agreed to reimburse the club to the tune of £600.

Mysteriously, in the board minutes of 7th June 1944, the directors agreed to fund the cost of rebuilding the boundary wall behind the Town End of the ground. This had formed what was known as Selwyn Passage, now demolished by what was described as 'bomb-damage'. None of the present author's researches has disclosed that a bomb landed on or near the Victoria Ground at any point during the war. Nor does any contemporary issue of the *Sentinel* record such an event. The bombing, if in fact it took place, has been erased from every record, bar the club minutes. It seems unlikely that the Luftwaffe had targeted the Victoria Ground, but perhaps a bomber attempting to hit Shelton Bar or flying south from Manchester jettisoned its payload. As the Victoria Ground lay close to the main railway line from Stoke to Stafford, and planes often navigated by following railways, this seems the most likely explanation. It is also likely that the bomb did not land directly on the ground itself, but in or around Butler Street, which backed onto that corner of the ground.

The speed and hush-hush nature of the repairs clearly reflected the desire of the authorities to keep potentially morale-damaging news from leaking out. The rebuilding cost amounted to £750 and all those in the know took their secret to the grave. The club also agreed to donate some barriers and railings free of charge to the War Department, where they could be melted down to assist preparations for the Normandy Landings. The Allied invasion would change the course of the war, but for the clubs whose barriers had gone, it left a legacy akin to a ticking time-bomb.

## Chapter Six

~ 1944-45 ~

'Any lout can knock a man off a ball, but it takes a footballer to take a ball off an opponent'

6th June 1944. Daybreak on D-Day. Allied troops, massed in landing craft off the Normandy coast, storm ashore to be met by a hail of shells and bullets. Amidst the cacophony of the Longest Day, the Americans lost 2,000 men on Omaha beach alone. One GI who survived later said: 'When the door swung open I became a visitor to hell.' Further down the coast, British forces, swarming onto Gold, Juno and Sword beaches, lost ten per cent of their total wartime casualties. By dusk, a foothold on French soil had been won with 150,000 men safely ashore. To paraphrase Winston Churchill, they fought on the beaches, then in the forests and in the streets with a steely determination to rid the world of the terror of Fascism. The months of detailed preparation, which the Allies had put in, paid off handsomely. German forces, expecting the invasion to come further east along the northern coast of France, did not have sufficient strength to withstand the whirlwind of co-ordinated attacks from sea and air.

Stoke's reserve centre-half, Jack Bamber, was amongst the British troops who landed at Sword beach on D-Day. He survived the hail of bullets as his landing craft spewed forth its human contents, and his beach was secured by nightfall. Bamber was not heard of again until he despatched news to the club of his well-being in October.

Goalkeeper, Dennis Herod, arrived in Normandy on D-Day plus one, crossed the Channel on a flat-bottomed tank-carrying craft, which slap-bottomed on the beach and dispatched his Sherman tank to engage the enemy. Herod saw plenty of action over the summer: 'Our commander was Lieutenant Beetham. He had a great tactical mind. One day we were camouflaged on a hill, overlooking a grassy valley and saw four Panzers travelling in a line. Beetham got us to take them out from back to front, so that the tanks at the head of the convoy did not know what was happening and had no warning.' Despite his admiration for the skills of his commanding officer, Herod was no war-monger himself: 'We didn't *want* to kill Germans, we just wanted to go home, but we understood that we had to do this and we got on with our job. When people are bonded together like that and your lives depend on each other, the kind of camaraderie you have is fantastic. We lived every moment as if it was our last. Our attitude was "If you don't get killed today, it'll be tomorrow".' Throughout his active military service, Herod received support from one particular member of Stoke's wartime squad: 'Lol Hamlett, the lay preacher amongst the team, had taken a kind of fatherly shine to me and he used to write me regular letters wishing me all the best. He was a real Christian.'

On 7th August 1944, Herod's tank took a direct hit from an enemy anti-tank gun. The Sherman exploded, killing the driver, while two other crew members suffered severe wounds to the eye and leg. Dennis got lucky. He escaped relatively unscathed, bar a fractured jaw, which, for a goalkeeper, was not as important as, say, a hand. This time, however, it was a missile and not a forward's boot inflicting the damage. Shipped back to Britain, Herod first received treatment at Manchester Hospital and then rehabilitated at Trentham Park on the south edge of the Potteries, a major centre for rest and recuperation of injured frontline troops.

Herod made the most of his enforced lay-off, taking plenty of physical exercise, but ensuring that his re-hab lasted as long as possible: 'I'd done my time. I was in no hurry to get out.' Dennis successfully got himself re-classified from category A1, fit to fight abroad, to category B1, fit to serve, but not fight abroad. He remained in the Army, but garrisoned close to Stoke so he could return to playing football two months into the new season.

Recuperating alongside Herod at Trentham was pre-war Stoke halfback Harry Ware, who had been wounded while serving in the infantry. Ware, too, remained in England and became the new manager of Northwich Victoria. Nor was Herod the only current Stoke footballer to be invalided out of front line duties in Normandy. Centre-half Billy Mould received shrapnel wounds to his leg, when his unit came under attack from a bomber. These injuries proved more serious than Herod's, and Mould did not recover sufficiently to play for his club until the following March. Jock Kirton, also serving in France, sent a communication to the club playing down reports that he had been wounded in the arm.

With the Third Reich crumbling before the Allied onslaught, certain aspects of life at home started to return to something resembling normality. On 8th August the Victoria Ground played host to a £100 handicap sprint contest, similar to the famous pre-war Powderhall Sprints. The event attracted three former Powderhall winners, plus Liverpool's James Harley, Burnley's Chatburn, and Newcastle's Jackie Milburn. Local man J Hill won the final, pipping Milburn to the tape.

The next event at the Vic was Stoke's public practice match, for which the teams read like a reserve versus youth game. So much so, that Tommy Sale, now nearly 35, managed to plunder four goals as the Reds beat the Blues 7-1. The goalkeeping position still gave Bob McGrory grave cause for concern. Youngster Edgar Podmore was not yet ready to be Stoke's front-line keeper for the whole season. Breaking with his usual policy, but understandably, given his lack of other options, McGrory offered Aston Villa's Cooper a trial. Cooper's RAF service, however, barred him from playing. The good news for McGrory was that Dennis Herod, part way through his recuperation, paid a visit to the ground to show off his war wounds during the week prior to the season's start.

The day after Allied troops entered Paris, Stoke City began their latest campaign poorly, with a 0-4 thrashing by cup winners Aston Villa. With the war having swung so definitively in favour of the Allies, 25,000 rejoiced in the opening of a new football season and saw Stoke's mix-and-match side crumble under a prolonged second-half assault. Two days later Maidenek in Poland became the first Nazi extermination camp to be liberated by advancing Soviet troops.

Stoke won three of their next four games, including a 5-0 thrashing of Northampton and a 2-0 home win over much-admired Wolves. That match saw Stan Matthews' first appearance of the season for his club. He was specifically released by his RAF commander in time to make the trip to Stoke as the game would raise funds for the Reginald Mitchell Memorial Fund. Following that result, Stoke embarked upon a run of five games without a win. This inconsistency led to City being dubbed 'a team of two moods' – capable of attacking flair or stale play.

Lack of availability of key players bit just as hard now, with so many serving abroad, as it had done at any point in the war. McGrory's determination to carry through his youth policy, however, can be judged by the fact that, after the first four games, Stoke were the only club in the country to have exclusively used their own players. Every other club had resorted to guests, sometimes to the extent that guests provided most of the team. Stoke fans clamoured for the immediate use of guest players to bolster City's side. Clearly frustrated that his masterplan had not yet begun to bear fruit, in late October McGrory issued a statement defending the policy – '1: The policy has been operated for five years of wartime football with successful results. 2: Guest-players, who might be of service to Stoke, are difficult to secure, having regard to the position of North Staffordshire in relation to the Armed Forces personnel.'

Determined though he was to justify his philosophy of the entire war, McGrory could not allow progress or morale to be hindered by blind adherence. He dropped Podmore after a poor performance in the 1-4 defeat at Wolves in September, replacing him with Arsenal's international goalkeeper, George Marks, for two matches. Marks plugged the gap until Herod returned from his facial injury.

Stoke's team for the goalless draw with Birmingham still contained ten players who had graduated through the youth ranks. City's main problem,

however, lay in attack. Scoring-chances consistently went begging. Freddie
Steele's form had slumped to an all-time low due to a bout of flu that he
could not shake off. Even when fit, Steele and Sale swapped their centre
and inside-forward positions in an attempt to freshen things up. The team's
plight moved the *Sentinel*'s correspondent, 'Potter', to bemoan City's forwards for being 'goal-shy to almost an irritating extent'.

Left-winger Wallace Poulton began the season promisingly, scoring
three times in the first five games. But his overall contribution to City's
attack left much to be desired in 'Potter's' eyes and also in those of his
manager. McGrory's problem, however, was who to play instead, especially once Poulton had been called to arms in November. Effectively, Stoke
were forced to staff the No 11 position with any fit player available. Thus
Jackson, Sale, Sellars, Howshall, Tommy Pearson, Newcastle's Scottish
international – who just happened to be the nephew of Stoke trainer,
Harry Pearson – and Williams, guesting from Aberdeen, all played out of
position wide on the left before Fred Basnett became available again in
February. One natural left-winger, who almost fitted the bill, was eighteen-
year-old reserve John Mannion. His story, which has become a kind of
urban myth in the Potteries, was one of the most remarkable which came
to light during research for this book.

During the 1930s an area of Hanley, in the centre of Stoke-on-Trent,
had become inhabited by Irish immigrants and was nicknamed 'the Irish
Free State'. The immigrants sought work and for the large part found it in
one of the numerous pits in the area. One such family was the Mangans.
The youngest of the nine Mangan children, John, proved to be a fine junior footballer and soon attracted the interest of Stoke manager Bob
McGrory. Some who saw him play compared John's pace over ten yards to
the legendary Matthews. Mangan could also dribble a bit and so was an
exciting prospect, especially as he was predominantly left-footed. In an era
when individual skill was still deemed to be paramount to this 'foreign idea'
of teamwork, the thought of unearthing another Matthews caused some
excitement. Seventeen-year-old John, however, was a shy lad and many
times McGrory knocked on the door of the family home to persuade his
father that he should encourage his talented son to play for Stoke City.

The slender and gaunt John Mangan made his Stoke debut against West
Brom and played five games, starring in the home win over Coventry,
when his speed and mazy dribble earned a penalty, before he scored his
first goal for the club. A month after his debut, the club received an official letter which effectively ended John's professional football career almost
as soon as it had started. Mangan's surname was pronounced with a soft
'g', so it sounded like Mannion, as in the case of the famous Wilf
Mannion. Crucially, John had actually been registered under that spelling –
Mannion – rather than the correct spelling of Mangan.

At that time the Football League took a particularly dim view of players attempting to play under assumed names, especially in view of the official guest system, which meant that almost anyone could play for any team without resorting to false names.

Stoke replied to the Football League that the registration form, which had been filled in on John's behalf, amounted to nothing more than a spelling mistake, but the League would have none of it. John Mangan was suspended *sine die* from any further participation in professional football – a shocking punishment for such a minor indiscretion.

In researching this story, your author came across a member of Mangan's family, Mick Penning, who provided numerous details about John's life. Mick had delved deeper into John's past and discovered that his birth certificate similarly misspelled his name – 'Mannion' instead of 'Mangan' – so the ban and curtailment of a promising football career was all for nothing. Following his departure from professional football, John returned to working down the local pit, where his life fell apart amidst heavy drinking. Poignantly, Mangan's last ever game of football was at the Victoria Ground, where he played in the Sentinel Cup final for Eastwood Hanley, a notable local amateur football team. His team lost 0-6 and as he walked away from the Vic in the rain he threw his boots over the wall of St Peter's Church, telling his teammates 'I've had enough'. He was 32 – a prodigious talent wasted.

By September the Low Countries had been liberated. As the Germans fought to delay the Allied advance into Germany, the North Staffordshire Regiment became embroiled in the major battle at Arnhem. Detailed to take three bridges which would give the Allies control of the Lower Rhine, the initial assault and parachute drop behind enemy lines turned into an Allied disaster. Of the original 10,000 troops, only 2,400 returned, but the setback was only temporary. By 20th October, the first German town, Aachen, fell to the Allies.

Stoke suffered another wartime casualty in Belgium. Scottish inside-left Jim Westland rode a motorbike as part of his military duties with the 5th North Staffords. One morning he was involved in an accident and as the machine landed on top of him the clutch pedal pierced his knee. It took Westland nearly eighteen months to recover. Even then, the young man, who had so nearly won a pre-war Scottish cap, found that his ability had become restricted and he knew he would never play top-level football again.

Strangely for a man who came so close to winning international honours, Westland was a reluctant footballer. He had grown up in a tenement building in Aberdeen within a working-class family who could not afford for the academically bright Jim to go to college. Instead he was sent to work. Fortunately, his talent as a footballer meant he did not have to go down a pit, or toil in a shipyard. The fact that his own career was now effectively ended by his knee injury fostered a jaundiced view of a footballer's lot. His experience, which had denied him the opportunity to fulfil his potential, meant he refused to allow his own son – also Jim, also talented – to become a professional. Jim senior's knee caused him endless trouble throughout the rest of his life as a publican in Newcastle-under-Lyme. Nowadays, the problem could probably have been treated and he would have been able to continue playing. Instead, his knee suffered occasional flare-ups and he needed a cast to reduce the inflammation.

On 21st October 1944, Dennis Herod returned to play his first game for Stoke since being invalided out of active service. He relished the freedom to live the life of a professional footballer: 'Freddie Steele was a pisstaker. He made training a pleasure. I was proud to be his scapegoat. I was so pale he called me "a bottle of milk with shoes on". The club recommended that I drink Guinness [a black beer prescribed by many doctors during the war years due to its high iron content] but I didn't drink. My vice was gambling and there was plenty of that too. Could one have a better life?'

After the rigours of military service, Herod appreciated the easy life that footballers led: 'Training was an absolute joke compared to modern standards. Bobby Liddle was hopeless. We all pleased ourselves. It was a rest home. There was no discipline. He'd tell us to do 30 laps of the Victoria Ground and I would jump over the wall halfway through and have a fag.' Often Herod and Franklin would abscond from the regular run to Trentham, which Stoke used in pre-season training, to have tea and toast in the Monica Café and catch a bus back to the ground. Even for those with more dedication, the club's training barely sufficed. Stanley Matthews recalls: 'They used to say, "Well, if you have too much ball, you're gonna be tired on the Saturday." Of course you had those leather balls. Mud and water put an extra 3lbs or so on the ball. If it was a very sludgy, muddy ground, they'd play with a Tugite ball because it wouldn't gather so much mud. And of course we had those very big toe-capped boots.'

Of course, training was merely a distraction from the main event of the week, Saturday's game, but there was always a question in the back of every player's mind – would I be in the team? Dennis Herod recalls: 'The routine on a Friday was training in the morning, which was only five or six short sprints anyway, then the teamsheet would go up outside the dressing rooms and we'd all see who was playing in which teams. Then we would have to queue up for our wages, which were paid in brown paper envelopes filled with cash from the office, knowing what the teams were. Sometimes the atmosphere could be a bit difficult.' Typical of Herod's bravery, he broke his finger diving at a forward's feet in the 1-1 draw at Birmingham and, true to policy, instead of trying to persuade Arsenal's Marks to return in goal as a guest, McGrory threw in young Manny Foster to plug the gap while Herod recovered.

Only when tyro inside-right Frank Bowyer returned did City's attack begin to click. The improvement began slowly, with a 3-2 win over West Brom, Stoke's first win away from home. But a 5-0 thrashing of Coventry served notice that Stoke had returned to something like top form. City also scored five in their next two games, home and away against Leicester. Soon the improvement had blossomed into a run of just three defeats in the next thirteen games. Eight of these were won, including six in a row from 2nd December. Tommy Sale was prolific once again. He bagged thirteen goals in seven games. Even Stan Matthews was playing his part. His scintillating form prompted Stoke to recover from 1-2 down to defeat Leicester 5-2 at home. Matthews had a 'roving commission to expose big gaps in the visitors' defence and provide numerous scoring opportunities'. Stan also scored twice to 'popular acclaim'. Perhaps, after all, he could be persuaded that his footballing future lay with his own club rather than Blackpool, if he could expect this level of adulation.

November saw the first Potteries derbies for five years, on account of Port Vale's decision to close down because of financial difficulties. There was great excitement at the prospect. Manchester United defender Jack Griffiths guested for Vale against his former Stoke colleagues and turned up fifteen minutes late, causing the kick-off to be delayed. Bowyer gave City the lead early in the second half, following 'a skilful triangular move between Matthews, Sale and Steele', and Bowyer's second clinched the game for Stoke. The gate had been expected to set a new wartime record for a home Stoke match, but fell just short. With the end of the war in sight, Stoke began the process of re-engaging staff. On 1st December 1944, trainer Harry Pearson was appointed to work on the groundstaff for £4 per week.

Stoke ended the first period of the league in eleventh position and with their best performance, a 4-2 home win over Derby, who would finish runners-up. The Christmas period brought a series of representative games. Stan Matthews was not averse to using his celebrity to help him out of a sticky situation. He and teammate Jock Dodds needed to get to Elland Road for an RAF v Army game on Boxing Day. They arrived at Leeds railway station five minutes before kick-off, where they were confronted by a large taxi queue. They rushed to the front shouting 'Footballers! We've got to get to the ground in five minutes'. It worked. The pair changed into their kit in the taxi and arrived as nine men saluted the national anthem. They still lost!

Elsewhere, news arrived of the happy reunion of three Stoke players in Florence. Playing for the Royal Marines in an international match, Ted Wordley found his changing room invaded by well-wishers Frank Baker and Eric Hampson. New Year saw McGrory take three days leave, heading for Scotland for his first Hogmanay in twelve years.

Stoke began the War League Cup qualifying competition with a 2-0 home win over Wolves. 'Potter' made his admiration known for Stoke's half-back line of Frank Mountford, Neil Franklin and John Jackson, which had been 'proving its worth and has become the backbone of the side'. Stoke benefited from Matthews' extended leave, due to the illness of his father, Jack, who had undergone surgery from which he would not recover. The loss of his father, of course, would give Stan yet another reason to sever his ties to Stoke. Frank Soo, too, became available after he was posted to Staffordshire, but his favoured position of right-half was occupied by a player in the classic McGrory mould – Frank Mountford. This forced Soo to play in a number of positions, filling in where necessary. Soo, remember, was a current England international, and he soon became frustrated at his cavalier treatment. Rumours abounded of a possible transfer to Leicester, managed by his former boss at Stoke, Tom Mather.

The Victoria Ground in these times presented an intimidating edifice for visiting teams. On the exterior of the main wooden Boothen Stand a huge red and white sign declared 'Stoke City Football Club'. A smaller sign over a narrow door pointed the way for players. The walls of the corridor that led to the tunnel and onto the pitch were adorned with photographs of players and games from the club's history.

But it is the dressing rooms which contrast most starkly with the facilities provided for the modern player. The 'home' dressing room had an old anthracite stove in the middle of the floor. Its stovepipe rose up, belching fumes through the flu in the roof. The huge communal bath was heated from below by a coal fire and sported a dirty tide-mark eighteen inches up its sides. At its bottom sat enough silt to clog the Nile Delta. Dennis Herod remembers: 'It was a good habitat for cockroaches, but we had no complaints. We had a hut with a snooker table in it behind the Boothen End. We all played, but I was no good. We had tournaments with handicaps.'

After training the humid dressing room would be left in a mess, with old socks, bandage strips and clumps of soil adorning the floor for the juniors to clean up. Their duties also included filling the huge grey metal teapot, that seemed to date from the previous World War. An equally battered metal tray held cups from which the players drank their post-training tea. Stan Clewlow recalls: 'If you think the home dressing room was bad, we sure made the visitors' one hell. Groundsman Harry Loffill and his son Bert would put damp coke in their dressing room.' Mind you, the board were well aware of the wretched state of these facilities. In December 1944, director E Henshall was asked to ensure that the groundstaff 'strip the tiles from the baths and make them sound for holding water', while the manager was asked to 'get the spouting repaired on the dressing room'.

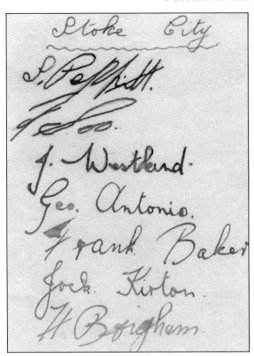

A collection of signatures from the 1938-39 Stoke City team

In the early years of the war, pre-season training rarely saw more than a handful of players available for Stoke

Stoke City Football Club Ltd. (1908)

SATURDAY, JANUARY, 17th, 1942

STOKE   CITY

RIGHT WING]   [LEFT WING

Herod

Brigham (2)   Glover (3)

Hamlett (4)   Franklin (5)   Kirton (6)

Liddle (7)   Bowyer (8)   Sale (9)   Steele (10)   Basnett (11)

Referee: Linesmen :
Mr. E. V. Gough   ▪   J. Bridgett
                                                                  S. Chatfield

Johnson (7) Evans (8) Richardson (9) McKennan (10) Elliott (11)

McNab (4)   Edwards (5)   Sankey (6)

Shaw (2)   Bassett (3)

Merrick

LEFT WING]   [RIGHT WING

WEST   BROMWICH   ALBION

A one-page team-sheet served as the programme throughout the war. Stoke won this
War League Cup-tie 2-1. Albion goalkeeper Merrick's name appears upside down

Dennis Herod
plunges in
typical style to
save at the feet
of Blackpool's
Stan Mortensen

Pre-war goalkeeper Norman
Wilkinson played just 18 games for
Stoke during the conflict, while
serving his country as a miner and
then in the Army

BILLY
MOULD
(Stoke City)

Stoke City team group in the summer of 1939

Stanley Matthews in action for country and club

The players relax after training in 1947

Stoke repel a Blackpool attack in this FA Cup-tie from March 1949.
Note the supporting struts of the old Boothen Stand

STOKE CITY FOOTBALL CLUB (1908) Ltd.

SATURDAY, MARCH 4, 1944

STOKE CITY

Right Wing   [Left Wing

WILKINSON

KINSON (2)   McCUE (3)

FRANKLIN (4)   MOULD (5)   MOUNTFORD F. (6)

MOUNTFORD G. (7)   STEELE (9)   ORMSTON (11)

PEPPITT (8)   SALE (10)

Referee :   :::   Linesmen .
G. TODDS   ::::   F. H. BRYAN
                   ::::   A. T. IVES

STARLING (10)   EDWARDS (8)

HOUGHTON (11)   O'DONNELL (9)   BROOME (7)

IVERSON (6)   CALLAGHAN (5)   MASSEY (4)

CUMMINGS (3)   POTTS (2)

WAKEMAN

ASTON VILLA

Left Wing]   Right Wing

Kick-off—3.15

Printed by Citz Times Ltd. 51-55. Liverpool-road. Stoke

In this thrilling Cup-tie, Stoke
lost 4-5 to Aston Villa after
leading 4-3 at half-time

Dennis Herod is beaten by a penalty at Fratton Park

Stoke's two Franks
– Soo and Baker –
who played at left-half
and inside-left
respectively

Stoke City Football Club Ltd. (1908)

SATURDAY, MAY 17th, 1941
STOKE CITY

RIGHT WING]   [LEFT WING

Herod

Brigham (2)   Glover (3)

Franklin (4)   Turner (5)   Harrison (6)

Basnett (7) Bowyer (8) Steele (9) Sale (10) Mitchell (11)

Referee:—   Linesmen:—
S. Chatfield, Hanley.   ●   H. J. Lees.
                              J. Stevenson.

Collinridge (11) Jones (10) Milligan (9) Hunt (8) Crooks (7)

Pringle (6)   Nicholas (5)   Hartley (4)

Pitt (3)   Milburn (2)

Middleton

LEFT WING]   [RIGHT WING

CHESTERFIELD

K I C K - O F F———3.15 p.m.

For this 2-2 draw, Chesterfield's side is notable for the number of guest players. They include Sheffield United's Collinridge [sic], Derby's Crooks, and Leeds' Milburn

Newcastle was never a happy hunting ground for Stoke. Here Dennis Herod hangs his head as the Toon's ninth goal flies past him in September 1945

Two of the old men of
Stoke. Bobby Liddle's
career was extended by the
war, but Arthur Tutin saw
his ended by the conflict

ROBERT LIDDLE,
Stoke City F C.

The Football League record book shows the second half of the 1946-47 season

	H	*Dec*	7	*Blackpool*	4	1	2	45	30	24
	A		14	*Brentford*	-	-	1	45	30	25
	H		21	*Blackburn Rovers*	2	1	2	47	31	27
	H		26	*Liverpool*	-	2	-	47	33	27
	A		26	*Liverpool*	-	1	-	47	34	27
	A		26	*Charlton Athletic*	3	1	2	50	35	29
	H	*Jan*	4	*Middlesbrough*	-	3	-	50	38	29
	A		18	*Derby County*	5	-	2	55	38	31
	H	*Feb*	1	*Preston North End*	1	1	1	56	39	32
	A		8	*Manchester United*	6	1	2	62	40	34
	H		15	*Chelsea*	3	1	2	65	41	36
	H		22	*Arsenal*	-	3	-	65	44	36
	A	*Mar*	1	*Wolverhampton W.*	1	1	1	66	45	37
	H		22	*Portsmouth*	2	2	1	68	47	38
A			29	*Everton*	5	2	2	73	49	40
A	*April*		4	*Grimsby Town*	3	-	2	76	49	42
H			5	*Huddersfield Town*	3	-	2	79	49	44
H			7	*Grimsby Town*	2	-	2	81	49	46
A			12	*Blackpool.*	3	1	2	84	50	48
H			19	*Brentford*	2	-	2	86	50	50
A			26	*Blackburn Rovers*	2	1	2	88	51	52
A	*May*		3	*Leeds United*	-	-	1	88	51	53
H			17	*Sunderland*	1	-	2	89	51	55
A	*June*		14	*Sheffield United*	1	2	-	90	53	55

The Club's last annual day out before Herr Hitler put an end to this ritual

Alec Ormston,
Stoke's hump-backed
left-winger, scored
21 goals in 1946-47

Future Foreign Secretary Ernest Bevin greets skipper Neil Franklin before Stoke thrashed Manchester City 5-0, helped by a Tommy Sale hat-trick in October 1941

The team which remained at the Vic after the failure to secure the title, bereft of Matthews, sold, and Steele, whose career was ended by injury

STOKE CITY FOOTBALL TEAM

Back Row (left to right): J. Sellars, F. Mountford, C. Watkin, D. Herod, N. Franklin, J. McCue.
Front Row: G. Mountford, F. Bowyer, S. Peppitt, W. Caton, A. Ormston.

George Mountford (centre) shares a joke at a press conference,
but Freddie Steele (second right) does not appear to share it

Stoke's exotic duo, Frank Soo of Chinese descent,
and, right, George Antonio, of Italian extraction

Herod watches Blackpool's McIntosh (No 11) fire over the bar under a heavy challenge by Harry Brigham (No 2). Stoke won this match 6-3 in March 1946

Stanley Matthews
dons his RAF jersey
ready for wartime
action in 1943

FRANK
BOWYER.
(STOKE)

G. MOUNTFORD
STOKE CITY

George Mountford, whose inspired form caused a rumpus when McGrory chose not to select the fit-again Matthews in October 1946

The war saw the first Potteries derbies for a decade. In this match just 800 spectators saw George Mountford score four as Stoke won 6-0

NOTES

We were beaten 2-0 by Aston Villa at Villa Park on Saturday in the Midland Cup. We travelled with a one goal advantage, but conditions suited the bigger Villa team. Our forwards could not get going. Once again Franklin was the star defender. He was ably supported by Watkin, Kirton, and Frank Mountford.

v v v v

Basnett, playing inside left for Crewe Alexandra on Saturday, scored the first of the home team's goals.

v v v v

Kirton, still on extended leave from the Continent, again appears in our team this afternoon.

v v v v

The duel between Tom Sale and Harry Griffiths, the Vale centre half, should be interesting—a meeting of old friends. Griffiths was playing exceptionally well for the Vale until he was injured in the match against Crewe on Christmas Day in Hanley.

v v v v

Our club is to support a proposal, to be submitted to a meeting in Manchester on May 7th, to revive the Central League.

v v v v

A charity match will be played against an R.A.F. XI at Tern Hill on Wednesday.

v v v v

Our "B" team play the final of the North Staffordshire League Cup against Alton Amateurs on the Port Vale ground on Tuesday night.

Printed by "City Times" Ltd. Stoke-on-Trent.

Stoke City Football Club (1908) Ltd.

Official Programme

SATURDAY, MAY 5th, 1945

Price Twopence.

STOKE CITY NOTES
By G.T. WRITER

This afternoon we meet our neighbours, Port Vale, for the fifth time this season. From our four previous meetings we have obtained six points. The season na. now been extended to May 25th, so we have three further matches to fix up in addition to the one this afternoon. A suggestion that a Staffordshire Senior Cup competition be played between ourselves, Port Vale, West Brom, and Birmingham, was not favoured by the Southern clubs, and has fallen through.

v v v v

Matthews and Franklin are playing for England this afternoon against Wales.

v v v v

A circular from the Football Association arrived at the Victoria Ground yesterday morning. It stated that clubs would be permitted to arrange matches, as part of peace celebrations, on the two public holidays announced by the Government, if these come before the end of the season on May 25th. It is possible that, if V.E. Day comes during the season, local "derby" matches will be fixed up with Port Vale.

Neil Franklin in 1949, as graceful in training as he was in action for Stoke and England

Stanley Matthews in action for the Royal Air Force in 1943

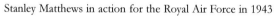

McGrory's tyros crouch in front of their elder statesmen.
From the left: Bowyer, Herod, Malkin, Brown, Sellars and Meakin

The once-familiar gasometer behind the barrel-shaped Butler Street Stand
was demolished in the 1950s

Herod clutches the ball to quell a Manchester City attack in September 1945

STOKE CITY FOOTBALL CLUB (1903) Ltd.

SATURDAY, MARCH 13th, 1943

STOKE CITY

Right Wing]   [Left Wing

BILTON

BRIGHAM (2)   McCUE (3)

HAMLETT (4)   FRANKLIN (5)   SALE (6)

MOUNTFORD (G.) (7) MOUNTFORD (F.) (9) BASNETT (11)

BOWYER (8)   LIDDLE (10)

Referee :   ::::   Linesmen :
G. L. ICLIFFE   :::   G. A. A. LINNELL
                       ::::   W. H. CLINTON

IDDON
SHARP (10)   ASTBURY (8)

McINTOSH (11)   COMPTON (9)   BREMNER (7)

BOOTH (6)   WILLIAMS (5)   CLARKE (4)

McNEIL (3)   HUGHES (2)

SHORTT

Left Wing]   [Right Wing

CHESTER

Kick-off—3.15

Stoke won this War League
Cup-tie against Chester 5-2

F. STEELE

W. MOULD
STOKE-CITY.F.C.

Freddie Steele lashed 43 goals in
44 matches for Stoke City in 1945-46

Billy Mould won many admirers for his
centre-half performances before the war

McGrory and Matthews were once team-mates, as in this 1933 team group

STOKE CITY

Back Row (left to right)—Sellars, Turner, Lewis, M'Grory, Spencer, and Tutin.
Front Row—Matthews, Liddle, Sale, Davies, and Johnson.

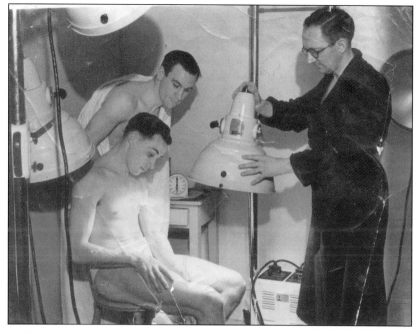

Dennis Herod receives innovative heat treatment for a muscle injury from trainer
Hubert Nuttall. Neil Franklin takes a keen interest

Liverpool attack at the Vic on Christmas Day 1946. Stoke won 2-1,
but Liverpool would have the last laugh

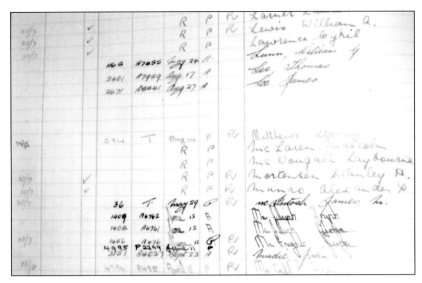

The Football League record book displays
Stanley Matthews' transfer to Blackpool in May 1947

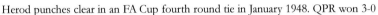

Herod punches clear in an FA Cup fourth round tie in January 1948. QPR won 3-0

Jock McCue, Stoke's hard-man left-back. Not many managed to get past him

Of these 1939 autographs, only four players remained at the club by 1947

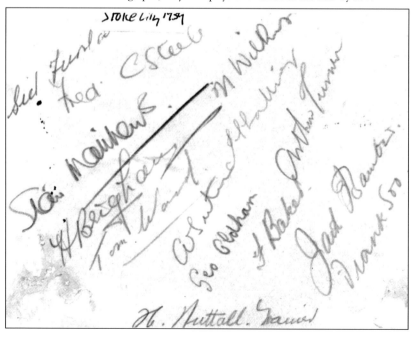

Herod punches clear at Highbury, but Stoke lost 0-1, thanks to Dr Kevin O'Flanagan's corkscrew shot in October 1946

Herod foils Manchester City on this occasion but Stoke lost 2-5 in September 1945

A record wartime crowd at the Vic of 23,358 saw this star-studded representative game

Spurs' Ludford heads a late equaliser as Stoke drew 2-2 at White Hart Lane
in the FA Cup third round in January 1947

Stoke's two right-wingers, George Mountford and Stanley Matthews,
share a joke in Matthews' hotel in Blackpool

Neil Franklin rose
to captain Stoke,
play in 10 wartime
internationals, and
set a new record of
27 consecutive
England caps

Stoke goalkeeper Norman Wilkinson grabs the ball, watched by John McCue
and skipper Arthur Turner at Highbury in March 1938. Stoke lost 0-4

Frank Soo points a jocular finger at Alec Ormston

Franklin and Herod with tomato juice and coke.
Neither player drank, but both enjoyed another vice – gambling

Stoke City were renowned for the club's family atmosphere

George Mountford poses
before Stoke's 5-2 victory at
Chelsea in October 1946

McGrory shows off his new-look 1947-48 team, but the club never recovered from the
twin blows of losing the league championship and the world's most famous footballer

Club skipper Jock Kirton's contract for the second half of the 1945-46 season

THE FOOTBALL LEAGUE, Ltd.

Extract from Agreement between *Stoke City* Club

and *John Kirton* professional player.

Period of Engagement *Jan. 12th 46.* to *May 4th 46.*

Wages £ *7 : — : —* weekly from *Jan 10th 46.* to *May 4th 46*

£ *: :* weekly from *——* to *——*

Other Special Clause: *£9. per week when playing in the first team.*

(Signed) *R Mcevoy* . Secretary.

Jan. 12th 46. Date

Previous Service with League Clubs (including Scottish and Irish) : —

Club and Season

Stoke City from. Nov. 1935.

(Signed) *J. Kirton* Player.

REGULATION 36 "In the case of a professional player, a certified copy of or extract from the Agreement must also be forwarded to the League Secretary on the form provided."

17 JAN 1946

Mould, Ormston, Herod and Baker feel the icy cold in City's threadbare wartime kit

The players board the coach before travelling to Sheffield United for
the most important league game in the club's history

Stoke lost this FA Cup-tie 2-3 at
Sheffield United, but won 4-3 on
aggregate (January 1946)

Stanley Matthews
(Stoke)

Frank Baker formed an
incisive partnership with
Alec Ormston on the left
wing, which yielded 27
goals in 1946-47

Among McGrory's tyros, the young Frank Bowyer (front row, second left) made his
debut at Manchester United in January 1940

Sheffield United Football Club Ltd.

Directors : A. J. Platt (Chairman), Coun. G. E. Marlow, J.P. (Vice-Chairman), *E. S. Atkin, F. R. Atkin, T. S. Carter, E. R. Davy, *F. Copestake, B. W. Doncaster, *Coun. E. S. Graham, J.P. (Lord Mayor of Sheffield), *R. Lawrence, *A. Laver, *L. Lewis, *H. Stokes, L. N. Stubbs, R. Macro Wilson, *H. Blacow Yates, F.R.C.S.

* Football Committee.

LEAGUE—DIVISION I

UNITED versus STOKE CITY

SATURDAY, 14th JUNE, 1947.   Kick-off 3 p.m.

EDITORIAL

THE end of the season 1946-47 at last. It has been a long drawn-out affair, but it is finishing today on a more exciting note than had been thought a few weeks ago. For on the result of this game between United and Stoke the destination of the Football League Championship Trophy depends.

If Stoke defeat United, then they become League Champions for the first time in their history by virtue of a superior goal average. If they drop a point, then Liverpool become the Champions. Liverpool enjoyed Championship triumphs in 1921-22 and 1922-23.

Merseyside enthusiasts will await with anxiety the verdict. Some will have made the journey to Sheffield to see the struggle.

Stoke have had many ups and downs at one time or another and have played in all four sections of the League—First Division, Second Division, Northern and Southern Sections.

OUR HANDICAP.

It is unfortunate that two of our stalwarts, Jimmy Hagan and Fred Furniss are unable to play against Stoke. Jimmy damaged his knee in the match with Charlton a fortnight ago and developed fluid on it, and last Saturday against Arsenal, Fred fell heavily after colliding with Lewis, Arsenal centre-forward, and fractured his left collar bone.

But Stoke will find United are no easy meat for all that. They realise that, of course. They have not forgotten our Cup duels of the past two seasons, especially that second "leg" game last year. It is not to be expected that today's game will be such a terrific struggle as that one was. It will never be forgotten by those who saw it.

Well, here's to a fine finale to the season ! The passing of a season is not without its tinge of sadness, marking as it does the passing of Time, and reminding us of those good sportsmen who are no longer with us and whom we shall long miss. However, it is the way of the world.

SHORT BREAK.

Turn over the page and let us look at the brighter things. United have performed better than some may have expected in this their first season in the First Division following the promotion success of 1938-39 and the war. The team had changed a good deal during the interval.

Young players introduced had not had First Division experience and there might have been failure.

With a bit of luck United would have finished among the top four, and at one time it looked as though we were booked for Wembley. Perhaps we took too much for granted or expected too much of the "boys". In any case it doesn't matter now.

In another six weeks or so we shall open another season and have fresh opportunities ; fresh fields to conquer. It rather takes your breath to think that the interval between this season and the next is so short.

Everyone hopes that the season will never again have to be extended until the middle of June. You can have too much of a good thing. The appetite becomes jaded.

The players will have to make the most of their summer vacation. One imagines them saying " We shall ! "

LOOKING BACK

While you are waiting for the teams to come out, glance at the record of the season's

Sheffield United's programme notes for the critical last match

No footage or stills exist of Stoke's catastrophic defeat at Sheffield United in June 1947.
Here are the teams in action at Bramall Lane in the FA Cup a year earlier

FIXTURES FOR 1946-47

FIRST TEAM (League, Division 1).   RESERVE TEAM (Central League).

DATE	DAY	OPPONENTS	G'ND	F	A	DATE	DAY	OPPONENTS	G'ND	F	A
1946						**1946**					
Aug. 31	S	LIVERPOOL	h	0	1	Aug. 31	S	Leeds United	a	1	6
Sept. 4	W	Preston North End	a	2	1	Sept. 2	M	BURNLEY	h	3	0
7	S	Leeds United	a	2	2	7	S	WEST BROM. ALB.	h	0	1
9	M					10	Tu	Burnley	a	2	2
14	S	GRIMSBY TOWN	h	1	1	16	M	BOLTON WANDERERS	a	1	0
21	S	Charlton Athletic	h	1	1	21	S	BIRMINGHAM CITY	h	3	0
28	S	MIDDLESBROUGH	a	0	3	28	S	Stoke City	a	0	5
Oct. 5	S	Stoke City	h	0	3						
12	S	MANCHESTER UNITED.	h	2	2	Oct. 5	S	MANCHESTER UNITED.	h	2	3
19	S	Blackburn Rovers	a	0	2	12	S	Blackburn Rovers	a	1	3
26	S	DERBY COUNTY	h	3	2	19	S	MANCHESTER CITY	h	0	8
Nov. 2	S	Arsenal	a	1	1	26	S	Derby County	a	3	5
	M	NORRKOEPING (Sweden)F				Nov. 2	S	ASTON VILLA	h	1	1
9	S	BLACKPOOL	a	4	1	9	S	Chesterfield	a	1	1
16	S	Wolverhampton Wanderers	a	1	3	16	S	WOLVERHAMPTON W.	h	2	1
23	S	SUNDERLAND	h			23	S	Huddersfield Town	a	0	4
30	S	Aston Villa	a	0	2	30	S	EVERTON	h	0	4
Dec. 14	S	Everton	a	2	2	Dec. 7	S	Bury	a	4	1
21	S	HUDDERSFIELD TOWN.	h	2	1	14	S	BLACKPOOL	h	6	1
25	W	BRENTFORD	h	0	1	21	S	Sheffield Wednesday	a	3	3
26	Th	Brentford (11 a.m.)	a	1	2	26	Th	Preston North End	a	3	3
28	S	Liverpool	a	1	1	28	S	LEEDS UNITED.	h	3	3
1947						**1947**					
Jan. 4	S	LEEDS UNITED.	h	6	2	Jan. 1	W	SHEFFIELD WED.	h	0	
11	S	CARLISLE..Cup (3rd Rd.)	h	3	0	4	S	West Bromwich Albion	a	1	4
18	S	Grimsby Town	a	1	2	11	S	Liverpool	h	1	3
25	S	Wolverham'ton Cup(4th Rd)	h		2	18	S	NEWCASTLE UNITED.	h	2	1
29	W	do. de. replay				25	S	LIVERPOOL	a	3	3
Feb. 1	S	Middlesbrough	a	1	0	Feb. 1	S	STOKE CITY	h	4	3
8	S	Stoke City F.A.Cup (5th Rd)	h	1	0	8	S	Manchester United	a	0	4
22	S	BLACKBURN ROVERS.	h	0	1	22	S	Manchester City	a	1	4
Mar. 1	S	NEWCASTLE UNITED F.A. Cup (6th Round).	h	0	2	Mar. 22	S	Wolverhampton Wanderers	h	0	2
15	S	Blackpool	a	2	4	29	S	HUDDERSFIELD TOWN.	h	4	1
22	S	WOLVERHAMPTON W.	h	2	0	April 5	S	Everton	a	3	0
29	S	Sunderland	a	1	2	12	S	BURY	h	5	1
April 4	F	Bolton Wanderers	a	2	3	19	S	Blackpool	a	0	1
5	S	ASTON VILLA	h	1	2	26	S	NORTON WOODSEATS	h	2	1
7	M	BOLTON WANDERERS	h	4	2	May 3	S	DERBY COUNTY	h	1	1
12	S	Portsmouth	a	0	0	10	S	Birmingham City	a	1	2
19	S	EVERTON	h	2	0	17	S	CHESTERFIELD	h	2	2
26	S	Huddersfield Town	a	1	J	24	S				
May 3	S	Chelsea	h			31	S	BLACKBURN ROVERS	a	1	1
10	S	PORTSMOUTH	h	3	1	June 7	S	Aston Villa	a	0	3
17	S	Derby County	a	2	3						
24	S	PRESTON N.E.	h	3	2						
26	WM	Manchester United	a	2	6						
31	S	CHARLTON ATH.	h	1	3						
June 7	S	ARSENAL	h	2	1						
14	S	STOKE CITY	h								

Sheffield United's fixtures in their programme, the first team on the left, showing their bad form prior to playing Stoke in June 1947

The front cover of the programme from June 1947, when Stoke went so close to winning their first ever League championship

Freddie Steele (left) blasts the ball past Arsenal's George Swindin, but wide of the post, as Stoke lose 0-1 at Highbury in October 1946

Although it may not have seemed so at the time, one of the most damaging wartime losses Stoke suffered was Frank Bowyer's call-up into the Army in January 1945. Bowyer had matured into Stoke's prime playmaker and also notched his fair share of goals. Stationed in Northern Ireland, Bowyer assisted Linfield, but without his incessant prompting Stoke's forward line spluttered. The player had become popular with Stoke's fans, too. Donald Lawton remembers meeting Bowyer in the Globe Café in Newcastle one lunchtime, before a home game. Bowyer, once he realised that Mr Lawton was heading for the game, refused to allow him to pay the 2s 6d for his meal, stumping up the requisite cash – despite earning only £12 per week himself. Stoke's fans had become excited at the prospect of a post-war right-wing combination of Bowyer and Matthews. Until now, the perfect pairing had eluded Stoke throughout Matthews' time at the club. It was not to be. Bowyer and Matthews played in the same Stoke eleven on fewer than two dozen occasions, and just once post-1945.

Snow forced the cancellation of all Stoke's games between 13th and 27th January. On 20th, McGrory and his players arrived at Crewe to find the referee, J Brown of Ormskirk, and about 200 prospective spectators 'walking' the snowbound pitch. Stoke, having travelled, wanted to play, but Crewe's directors considered the conditions dangerous. A 'verbal altercation' occurred when the referee chose to call the game off. The respective directors retreated to the Gresty Road boardroom, but Crewe could not be persuaded and McGrory stalked off in a huff, telling his players, who were ready to start, to change back again. When the thaw eventually arrived, Tommy Sale completed 300 career goals by netting Stoke's second in the 3-2 win at Chester on 3rd February, although that statistic includes 182 wartime goals.

That same day, Neil Franklin made his international debut for England against Scotland at Villa Park. The son of a Shelton gasworker, Franklin was the seventh of eight children and the sixth of seven sons. He played his early football as an inside-forward for Stoke boys, under the tutelage of Arthur Tams, a schoolteacher at Cannon Street School, Hanley, and earned a schoolboy international trial. Franklin impressed in the game, but found himself overshadowed by the skills of fifteen-year-old Len Shackleton. Stoke converted Franklin to centre-half when he joined the groundstaff as a sixteen-year-old, playing him in the third team alongside Dennis Herod, John McCue, Frank Mountford and Frank Bowyer. His selection for the national team followed several appearances for the FA XIs, in the most recent of which, on 20th January, he had scored a rare goal.

Franklin joined Frank Soo and Stanley Matthews in the England side as, for only the second time, Stoke provided three players for the national team. England defeated Scotland 3-2 in front of 66,000 spectators, who paid a new wartime record £17,799 to see the contest. Franklin's debut went reasonably well, although he found himself 'drawn in' by Jock Dodds immediately prior to Scotland's first goal, scored by Delaney. *The Times* noted that 'Franklin is not afraid to go through with the ball and start attacking movements. But he generally kept Dodds quiet, no mean task.' While under consideration by the selectors, Franklin had come under scrutiny from Wolves' director Mr A H Oakley. Oakley's position as a member of the FA international selection committee allowed him to run the rule over Stoke's rising star as a potential transfer target. Oakley denied the rumours about an impending Wolves swoop, but there was no doubt that another of City's young talents was in demand.

Franklin oozed class. Amongst his many qualities were his reading of the game and ability to carry the ball out of defence and provide an extra midfielder, much as Alan Hansen would do for Liverpool in the 1980s. Not the tallest of defenders, in this era of brutal, granite 'stoppers' – such as Wolves' Billy Wright, Rangers and Scotland's Georgie Wood, and Arsenal's Herb Roberts – Franklin's timing and aerial ability allowed his 5ft 11in frame to launch into prodigious leaps. Most famously, his tackling would be timed to such perfection that legend has it he would often leave the pitch after 90 minutes with perfectly white shorts, an incredible feat given the infamously boggy Victoria Ground pitch.

Sometimes, the only visible sign that Franklin had been involved in a game of football was a circle of mud on his forehead, planted by the ball. Andy Cunningham of the *Sunday Express* wrote: 'Franklin does not believe in giving the ball the big boot. He uses it intelligently and with a gliding header or a slick ground pass to his wing-halves initiates as many attacks for his side as any of the old-time classical pivots did when the defensive duties were less onerous. His timing and accuracy in the air or on the ground stamp him as outstanding among the dominating players of recent years.'

Just like Stan Matthews, Franklin's ice-cool temperament marked him out. He would never retaliate when fouled. Instead, he would pick himself up, dust himself down and cast a glance at his attacker as if to say, "Are you having such a bad game that you have to resort to that?" In Stoke's first game of 1946-47, Franklin indulged in a ding-dong battle with Charlton's Bill Robinson. Eventually, after Robinson's umpteenth naughty tackle, the referee took him aside, only for Neil to walk past saying, 'Be lenient with him ref. His last term's report showed some improvement.'

Franklin always accepted that football was part of the entertainment industry. He was determined to give Stoke's fans full value for money and they loved him for that. But this same carefree approach to his football brought Franklin into conflict with his manager. McGrory was often to be seen, smoke spouting from ears, jumping with rage on the bench as Franklin cleared danger, not by aimlessly hacking the ball into touch, but by trapping the ball on his goal-line and dribbling his way out of trouble. Along the way, he might play a one-two inside his own penalty area, or throw an outrageous dummy to his own goalkeeper before waltzing upfield to deliver a pass to his wingers. Franklin's bosom buddy was keeper Dennis Herod.

As Franklin recalled in his 1956 autobiography *Soccer at Home and Abroad*: 'Not only did we get on well together on the field, but we were great friends off the field. Which, of course, helped considerably in our partnership in defence, because there is nothing better than perfect understanding between centre-half and goalkeeper. Once, though, this understanding broke down. We were playing Derby County and Dennis cleared the ball with a hefty punt. The force was there, but the direction was lacking, and the ball struck me a terrific blow on the back of the head. For a second Dennis was panic-stricken. No, not about my health, but about the ball, which rebounded towards the net. Fortunately for him it went into the side netting for a corner-kick and all the sympathy I got from Dennis was "Why don't you keep your big head out of the way?"'

With a run of five successive victories, including heavy wins over Chester and Port Vale, twice, Stoke confirmed their qualification for the War Cup proper. There is no doubt that the backing of their manager helped Stoke's youngster's confidence to blossom. With many clubs having fallen by the wayside, City received offers from numerous players to provide guest assistance, including three England internationals – George Hardwick of Middlesbrough, Robert Brown of Charlton and Leslie Smith of Brentford. Curiously, each of these three had played alongside Franklin on his England debut. Being members of the RAF, this trio had been posted to the Midlands for three weeks and had offered their services to Stoke via fellow England international Frank Soo.

But McGrory refused to drop his fledglings in favour of guests, however eminent, even for a few weeks. He had previously rejected the offer of Arsenal's future England full-back, Laurie Scott, choosing to stick with his defence which had been doing so well. On 22nd March, the directors backed their manager by voting to turn down Crewe's application for the transfer of Johnny Sellars and Fred Basnett. McGrory's success in convincing his talented youngsters to stay to fight for their place once senior players returned from overseas was a major coup. Good news also arrived from the west coast. For the first time, Stan Matthews agreed to play in the cup's knockout stages for his own club rather than for Blackpool. Stoke's directors felt they were winning that particular battle.

But City's cup campaign was blighted by the selection of players for representative duty. For their final qualifying game, against Crewe on 10th March, City lost Franklin, Matthews and Soo to the RAF team which took on the Army. Stoke lost 1-3. The following week, the FA picked Matthews and Franklin to tour Belgium for five days from 22nd March. McGrory vainly wrote to Stanley Rous, the Secretary of the FA, requesting that at least one or other of these stars be left available to Stoke.

In fact, that tour cost Stoke doubly. Matthews injured an ankle playing against the Red Devils in Bruges and was out of action for a month, and that would seriously affect the remainder of Stoke's campaign.

Franklin, for his part, played alongside future Manchester United manager Matt Busby, then Liverpool's right-half and captain. Busby gave Franklin a piece of advice which he would always heed: 'Just remember Neil, keep playing football at all times and you'll never go far wrong.' Franklin described his own footballing philosophy: 'To me football is a game to be played with the head. I also include the grey matter which we are all supposed to have inside our heads. If you have nothing more than physical strength then you can never hope to be a success at soccer. Any lout can knock a man off a ball, but it takes a footballer to take a ball off an opponent and then beat others, either by dribbling or by passing the ball correctly.'

Leading Aircraftman Frank Soo departed with the next FA tour to Belgium, from 21st-22nd April, and Jock Kirton joined them along with other players serving in the Low Countries. Frustratingly for McGrory, Soo did not even play. As so often in wartime, bad news for one individual was offset by good news for another. Kirton was granted extended leave to nurse his ailing wife, and took the opportunity to play for Stoke in each of the last eleven games.

Stoke's first-round cup opponents, Bury, had a 100 per cent record in qualifying and maintained it with a guest-assisted 3-2 win in the first leg. The Shakers scored three goals in the opening twenty minutes, among them a penalty for hands against Mould. Stoke battled back gamely. Steele rounded Bradshaw to net and then delivered a classic hanging header. In the return game, Sale's first-half rocket put Stoke level on aggregate, before late goals by Basnett and George Mountford sealed a 5-3 aggregate win.

In the second round, Stoke faced opponents of different class – Manchester United. On paper, Stoke's side, boasting four internationals, seemed strong. But one of these, Soo, reported unfit. Another, Stan Matthews, defied his ankle injury to play, against the wishes of club doctor A P Spark. City began well and played 'their best football for many weeks' for the first twenty minutes. Steele had two headers saved by Crompton, but Matthews' injury rendered him mostly ineffective. Disaster struck on the half-hour. Frank Mountford injured his groin in a thunderous tackle and hobbled out of harm's way on the left wing thereafter. Against nine fit men, United took charge and scored six goals with City managing just one, and that an own-goal.

Shorn of three of their England players for the return, Stoke submitted again – this time 1-4. Tommy Sale had a penalty, given for a foul on Fred Basnett, saved by Crompton. On the same day, England – with Franklin, Soo and Matthews in their ranks – thrashed Scotland 6-1, a result which still ranks as Scotland's heaviest defeat at Hampden Park. Before the kick-off the vast 133,000 observed a minute's silence for the recently deceased American President, Franklin D Roosevelt.

In between the two ties with Manchester United, on 10th April, Frank Soo submitted a transfer request. He was no longer prepared to play second fiddle to Frank Mountford in the right-half berth. The directors invited Soo to their next board meeting, to be held on 6th June, to 'air his grievances', but Soo would not attend. The *Sentinel* published a letter signed by six supporters siding with Soo: 'We do not think the treatment meted out to this player is in accordance with the services he has rendered to the club. We trust the difficulties will be overcome and that we shall see the player filling his rightful position, right-half, and in this wish we feel that we are by no means alone.' But McGrory stuck to his guns, preferring the derring-do and potential longevity of 22-year-old Frank Mountford to the silky skills of 31-year-old international Soo.

Defeat in the War League Cup saw Stoke enter the Midland Cup, where they were paired with Aston Villa. Stoke won the first leg despite being without their England trio. John Jackson ran 30 yards before belting in a drive for the only goal. But even with the internationals back in the side, Stoke lost 0-2 at Villa Park to go out 1-2 on aggregate.

On 29th April, Benito Mussolini and his mistress, Clara Petacci, were shot by Italian Partisans and their corpses strung up in Milan's Piazza Loretto. On 1st May, the Soviets marched into Berlin to discover that Adolf Hitler had taken his own life. General Alfred Jodl signed Germany's surrender on 7th May. In Britain, the VE (Victory in Europe) celebrations lasted two long and loud days, and 8th May was declared a public holiday. Suddenly, the drabness and privation of the past six years were forgotten in a blaze of flags, fireworks and floodlights. Stoke and Port Vale celebrated by staging another match. Stoke won 4-2 to clinch the Staffordshire Victory Cup.

Even international footballers were allowed to rejoice. News of the surrender reached England's players at the Great Western Hotel in London, where they were preparing to travel to Cardiff to play Wales the following day. The team enjoyed what Neil Franklin recalled as a 'tremendous celebration, and I remember the hotel floodlights being switched on immediately. We claim to have been the first people to switch on the floodlighting!' England won 3-2 at Ninian Park, thanks to a Raich Carter hat-trick. To continue the victory celebrations, which lasted from 12th-19th May, Soo, Franklin and Matthews toured Scotland with an RAF team which included Bill Shankly, Jock Dodds and Stan Mortensen. On 26th May England drew 2-2 with France at Wembley, with French goalkeeper Da Rui saving Leslie Smith's penalty.

With hostilities over, players returned to their clubs in dribs and drabs. It was not always good news. Reserve centre-half Billy Moore returned to Stoke, although having been on the 'for sale' list for five years he soon left again. Moore joined Notts County as trainer, later moving to Aston Villa, where he acted as trainer for the 1957 FA Cup-winning side. Later he managed Walsall, winning the Saddlers consecutive promotions from Division Four to Two in 1960 and 1961. Villa's board renewed their enquiries about Stoke's left-back, Jock McCue. No sooner was that request turned down than Villa moved for City's reserve left-back Cyril Watkin. Watkin had impressed when standing in for McCue, who had been posted to train troops in Cornwall. Villa, however, received another curt rejection. McGrory was not about to undo the good work of the entire war by offloading his talented youngsters.

Stoke had plenty of positives on the pitch. During May alone, City netted nineteen times in five games, the majority coming from players not considered as prime goalscoring material – including George Mountford, John Jackson, and Johnny Sellars. Stoke were ending the war in fine fettle, with McGrory's masterplan now coming to fruition. Tommy Sale's war ended in a blaze of glory. At the age of 35, and firmly in the twilight of his goal-laden career, he banged in 34 goals in 40 games. George Mountford finished second highest scorer with fifteen. On 11th July, at their AGM at the Town Hall, Stoke reported a healthy profit of £2,778 12s 4d for the season. Stoke City Football Club had survived the war in a relatively healthy state. Would McGrory's policy allow them to take advantage and be amongst the honours for the first time in their history?

CHAPTER SEVEN

1945-46
'I knew those people hadn't fainted.
I knew they were dead.'

Over the summer of 1945 General Election fever dominated talk around the Potteries, with most expressing the widely held view that Conservative Prime Minister Churchill – commanding a Parliamentary majority of over 100 – would comfortably win. On 5th July, however, a massive turnout of 76 per cent handed Labour leader Clement Attlee a mandate to govern with an even bigger majority of 146. The Allies had fallen out even in their moment of victory, creating a web of international suspicion and intrigue which would shape international affairs for the next 40 years. In the Far East, the war with Japan was brought to a rapid conclusion by the dropping of American atomic/nuclear bombs on Hiroshima and Nagasaki. Japanese Emperor Hirohito officially surrendered on 14th August, sparking another celebration, Victory in Japan, VJ-Day. Overall the Second World War had cost some 55 million lives around the globe, of which over 600,000 were British.

Given that these momentous developments in the summer of 1945 spanned what would in ordinary circumstances be the British close season, the Football League was left with unsufficient time to organise the coming 1945-46 campaign on anything other than makeshift lines. This would be a transitional season, but problems of transportation and player availability would hit many clubs no less severely than in wartime.

Consequently, First and Second Division clubs were split between North and South Divisions, with the River Trent being used as the dividing line. As demobilised players returned to their clubs, the League was forced to impose a limit of six guest players per match per club, and that number was reduced to three by 3rd November.

Stoke City had little to worry about on that score. McGrory's youthful team now had up to six years' experience playing together. Unlike the League, the FA Cup was reinstated at once, given breathing space by not having to kick into action until January 1946. It would, however, for one peacetime season only, retain the two-leg format of the War Cup as part of the transition, and, intriguingly, there would still be no medals for winners and runners-up.

Those demobbed from the military returned home to discover mass unemployment, war-damaged homes and often, infidelity, causing heartbreak and anxiety. On top of that, Britain was still gripped by serious food shortages. By providing healthy escapism, football had never been so vital to the life of a troubled country, as attendances, up by 40 per cent on the previous season, proved. Hungry for the passion of competitive sport, crowds flocked through the turnstiles of every club across the land. Dennis Herod recalls: 'Football during the war years hadn't been half as competitive without all those players and so, when the war had ended, crowds flocked to see us play. It was joyous. Families were being reunited, there was a confidence and it seemed as if the birds were constantly singing. They were tremendous days. And we professionals got something wonderful out of the game that the modern millionaires never have. We had bonding, camaraderie and the greatest life of simply playing for the love of the game.'

The fabric of the country, from a male perspective at least, seemed only to be held together by the ritual of 'going to the match'. Those seasons of post-war boom left a lasting legacy. Many of the modern fans' pre-match routines, meeting places and watering holes took root in those turbulent years. It was not just in Britain that crowds went mad for football. During the summer Neil Franklin and Frank Soo played for an FA XI in Berne and Zurich to celebrate the Swiss FA's jubilee, with crowds of 45,000 and 33,000 setting records for both venues.

Stoke aimed to bounce back to 'business as usual'. Chairman Harry Booth said he expected the club's soldier-players to be demobbed by November, but it did not quite work out as he had hoped. It took Frank Bowyer two years to be released, in which time he made just four appearances for Stoke. Although Frank Baker arrived back in Britain in mid-September after three years' service abroad, he did not play for Stoke until February. Alf Massey did not return at all to peacetime football, a leg injury sustained whilst in the Army forcing him to terminate his career.

Others made it back home against all the odds. Stoke's players had already mourned the death in action of gunner Harry Meakin, and so were understandably wide-eyed when he reported back, fit as a fiddle, for pre-season training – complete with a Military Medal. As the papers insensitively explained, 'a man bearing the same name, from the same town, unwittingly caused the confusion.'

Manager Bob McGrory signed a new five-year contract, on the same terms of £850 per annum, while Vic Shaw, who had assisted the club on an honorary basis as trainer throughout the hostilities, was invited to stay on permanently. Hubert Nuttall returned to duty as first-team coach, while Bobby Liddle, McGrory's best friend, replaced Harry Pearson as reserve-team coach. Prior to the outbreak of war, Pearson had served the club in this capacity for twenty years. He had served in the North Staffordshire Ambulance Service throughout the war and his dismissal came as a complete shock to him.

McGrory predicted a bright season ahead, and that Stoke's left-wing partnership of Ormston and Baker would become the talk of the land. City began the season in the right vein. In a VJ Day fixture played on the afternoon of 17th Friday August, Stoke walloped Port Vale 6-0 at the Vic. Three thousand saw Fred Basnett bag a hat-trick, while Steele, Sellars and Sale completed the rout.

Stoke's attendances immediately shot up to around the pre-war figure, although over the course of the season the discerning Stoke public often stayed away from matches against opposition considered unworthy. Hence, amongst Stoke's early home games, fewer than 7,000 bothered to turn up to watch uninspiring Leeds, while three times as many were attracted by Newcastle.

Above all, Stoke fans yearned to see their stars wearing the famous red and white stripes. If news spread that Matthews, described by that season's *Athletic News Annual* as 'unequalled as an artist or a crowd-magnet', had made it back from Blackpool to play, then the gate could double simply by word of mouth alone. On the Matthews issue, Stoke's directors started to put their foot down, forcing Blackpool to make a separate application each time they wished to use him. In fact, Stoke became more obstructive throughout the season as Stan's legitimate reasons for not playing for his own club grew fewer and fewer. The public drooled over the prospects of Stoke's rising fortunes, as the likes of Matthews, Freddie Steele and Jock Kirton slotted in alongside City's young bucks. Four wins from the first five games hinted that McGrory's youth policy had indeed paid off. Life was good. Stan was back in a Stoke shirt, Nobby was banging in the goals, and Hitler was dead.

Beneath the expression of feverish excitement, however, lay churning discontent, both at Stoke and within football in general. The vitality of the sport as the nation's favourite entertainment led directly to clubs realising fortunes from their gate money. The players, being no mugs, quickly realised that, while clubs' bank balances might be stacking up, they, the performers, earned nothing more than a breadline wage. Indeed, their £4 per week had not risen since 1939. The clubs cited the Government's increase in the dreaded Entertainment Tax to 45 per cent as the prime reason for not increasing players' pay, but the Players' Union undertook to redress the situation. The season continued under the growing threat of strike action by militant footballers determined to extract a fairer deal from their employers.

Of no less concern to the Union was the problem of those older players, whose contracts had been suspended in 1939, who now returned to claim continuation of employment. In Stoke's case, goalkeeper Norman Wilkinson had worked as a collier in his native Durham for most of the war, before serving with the Army in France, and was therefore scarcely available to play for Stoke. He returned to the Vic after being demobbed on 26th October to find himself unwanted. Not only had he reached the advanced age of 35, but Wilkinson had lost two stones in weight. He had also received a facial injury which left him with a twisted mouth, not to mention losing most of his teeth. At first sight, or on second for that matter, he hardly looked like a professional athlete, added to which Stoke City now had three younger goalkeepers on their books, each with first-team experience.

The board minutes show a resolve to 'get Wilkinson off our books at a reasonable figure'. Wilkinson, however, was not prepared to go quietly and took Stoke City to task, determined to enforce the rule that those players who had served would get their jobs back. The club had little choice but to back down and Wilkinson was eventually re-engaged.

There was dissent, too, from two other veterans. Harry Brigham and Tommy Sale both asserted their right to re-engagement on full-time pre-war terms. The board minutes state: 'it would have been more patriotic if they had taken the part-time jobs found for them.' Former club secretary Tom Hancock was less fortunate. As he had been made redundant in 1942, he did not qualify to return to his former employment. Instead the assistant secretary from before the war, Bill Williams, returned from military service to become club secretary, removing from McGrory's neck the administrative burden he had borne for several years.

Having been demobbed from the RAF, Stanley Matthews chose to keep his family in Blackpool. He cherished the resort's bracing sea air and the long sands where his four-mile run and shuttle sprints each morning could be undertaken in relative privacy. In October 1945, Stan put down even firmer roots when buying a small hotel in a sheltered crescent in South Shore. He ran the hotel personally, exploiting his famous name to attract custom. Later in the season Matthews attempted to reopen the sports outfitters in Stoke which he had run before the war, but faced problems with restricted supplies.

McGrory viewed all this as a major irritation. He believed that Stan could not concentrate fully on playing football with all this extraneous nonsense carrying on. Matthews would need to tread carefully lest he incur the wrath of his manager.

The youngsters were not necessarily happy either. Neil Franklin was worried at being deposed from his first-team shirt by Billy Mould, when the senior player returned from military service, and asked permission to play for Port Vale on 3rd September. His request was rejected by Stoke's board. Meanwhile, the club captain at the start of the war, Frank Soo, still aggrieved about being asked to play at inside-forward, declared at a board meeting on 5th September that going on the transfer list was in 'the best interests of himself and the club'. In response, the directors urged him to reconsider, believing his reasons for wanting away 'unfounded'.

Former Stoke manager Tom Mather, now in charge at Leicester, monitored the situation and cheekily applied for permission to play Soo as a guest, while he remained in limbo at Stoke. Not only was the request denied, Stoke's board determined not to allow Soo to guest for any other League club, obliging him to play for non-league Shrewsbury to keep match fit.

Interest in the player now came from Blackpool, Manchester United and Newcastle, who were all reported to have offered £4,000. Stoke held out for £5,000. Bizarrely, given his club difficulties, Soo – along with Franklin and Matthews – was selected for international duty in Northern Ireland that week. The trip did not go well. After being delayed for eight hours, the players' train derailed at Lambrigg near Kendall, fortunately without casualties. England won 1-0 in Belfast, but by the time Soo returned, Stoke's board had agreed a sale and on 27th September Soo transferred to Leicester for a fee of £4,600. The sum was made up of a down payment of £3,000 with the balance due on 1st January 1946. A popular player, and current England international no less, had been shunted off because he had fallen out with the manager. McGrory's marker had been laid down.

Despite the early promise shown, the first few months of the new season saw Stoke's squad affected by the same ills that had shorn them of their stars throughout the conflict. Those still in the services failed to gain regular release, while injury struck Freddie Steele once more, leaving Frank Mountford as a reluctant centre-forward. The perennial problem of City's inside-forwards gave most cause for concern. Frank Bowyer's absences left George Mountford playing at inside-right, while George Antonio suffered one of his fitful spells at inside-left, resulting in Tommy Sale being thrown back into the forward line. Stoke's defence might have conceded the fewest goals in the League North in its first six games, but up front the forwards either bagged a hatful or fired blanks. In response, McGrory sought to sign the prolific Micky Fenton of Middlesbrough and pencilled him in to guest against Manchester United as a trial. In the event, Fenton could not travel to Stoke and McGrory's interest cooled.

Inevitably, the absences took their toll. Stoke travelled to Newcastle searching for the win which would put them joint top of the league, alongside early leaders Chesterfield. The biggest crowd of the day saw the country's meanest defence taken apart by one of the country's hottest striking properties – United's Albert Stubbins. He gave reserve centre-half Stuart Cowden a torrid time, bagging five goals, including a first-half hat-trick.

After half-time Stoke tried to counter Stubbins' threat by swapping Cowden with Jock Kirton. It made no difference. Kirton damaged knee ligaments and 1-3 at the break became 1-9, Stoke's second heaviest defeat ever.

Dennis Herod, despite being flattened by Stubbins early on, remembers the drubbing all too well: 'I hated Newcastle, and Spurs. I always had either a nightmare or got injured. And that Jackie Milburn frightened me to death. It became a mind thing. When we lost 1-9 at Newcastle, I just kept shouting at everyone to give the ball to Stan. At least it would relieve some pressure. It didn't work though! That was a bitter experience for our team.' It later emerged that the President of the Australian FA had journeyed to St James' Park to watch Herod and McCue, with a view to inviting them to play exhibition matches to promote football in Australia. Herod recalls: 'Yes. He never followed up his interest after that – Sam Bartram of Charlton and Sheffield United's Burgin went instead!'

Just as during the war, however, a hearty thrashing one week could be countered in the following week's return. Stoke's 3-1 home win over Newcastle could be viewed as just one of those anomalies but, critically, Franklin returned to action and snuffed out Stubbins' threat. Two Fred Basnett headers set the seal on a comprehensive win, and the *Sentinel* described City's revenge as a 'triumph of real distinction'.

The rumblings between McGrory and his star turn Matthews surfaced again when Stan failed to turn up for the kick-off of Stoke's fixture at Hillsborough on 13th October. Matthews arrived at half-time, 'handicapped by starting out late on his journey from Blackpool.' This hardly endeared him to McGrory, who probably would have dropped Stan to set an example, and to create a storm in the process. But Matthews was due to miss Stoke's next two games anyway. The dispute simmered along for now. Minus Matthews and Franklin, both playing for England in a 0-1 defeat by Wales at the Hawthorns, Stoke's third successive away defeat followed at Huddersfield. Frustration was setting in: 'the referee was seen through the mist to speak to a Stoke player after [Huddersfield's] Waller went down holding his face.'

Stoke had slipped down to mid-table, but as their absent stars returned, performances picked up. Huddersfield received a 2-6 beating and leaders Chesterfield – who had conceded just five goals in twelve previous games – left Stoke on the wrong end of a 1-6 thrashing, inspired by Matthews. Following a 4-0 defeat of Barnsley, Stoke had risen back to third place in the league, just two points off the leaders.

Freddie Steele scored successive hat-tricks, providing Stoke fans with a reminder of what they had been missing. If Stan was City's brightest light, Steele was Stoke's folk hero. His goalscoring exploits became legendary even during his own playing career, to the point that his teammates idolised

him. Dennis Herod's glowing reminiscences illustrate the point: 'He was
the most complete footballer I ever saw. He could head, shoot with either
foot, bring others into play. Freddie never stopped telling jokes. You never
stopped laughing at the gags, from Monday morning until after the game
on a Saturday. I was the fall guy for many of his jokes as I was one of the
youngest. I loved it and felt privileged to be a part of the team. I learnt a
lot from playing with him. He had a heart like a lion and he played for the
team. The spirit he created in the dressing room was fantastic. We got on
famously.'

Amongst supporters, this hero-worship saw Freddie Steele dubbed
'Nobby', due to his prodigious heading ability. According to Owen
Bennion, 'Nobby had a way of leaping high and then just at the moment
of making contact with the ball he flicked his neck muscles sharply and the
ball seemed to fly off at high speed. I've never seen anyone head a ball as
cleanly as Nobby.' Surprisingly then, for a man so gifted in the air, Steele
was just 5ft 9in tall. He could bulldoze through opposing defences to
unleash powerful shots from either foot. In 1936-37 he had plundered five
hat-tricks in a total of 33 League goals, setting a new club record for a season which still stands today. He had won six pre-war caps, but lost out to
Tommy Lawton in the battle to be England's first-choice centre-forward.
Much as Steele was loved by the fans, he was also cherished by his manager, to the point that Freddie handed McGrory his own commemorative
medal awarded on the occasion of his first cap. The admiration was recip-
rocated. Just as mutual animosity characterised the relationship between
McGrory and Matthews, mutual respect between manager and Steele kept
Freddie incessantly striving to better himself and his team. Here was proof
that McGrory could handle stars – at least those who played the game by
his rules.

Surviving Nazi leaders were now about to stand trial at Nuremberg.
Despite the tension of the Cold War, the passion for football reached a
new peak during Dynamo Moscow's tour to Britain in November 1945.
They created a storm by drawing 3-3 at Chelsea in front of an unprecedented Stamford Bridge crowd of 85,000. The following day, Stoke were
among 35 clubs to submit frenzied applications to the FA to play the touring team. The Russians thrashed Cardiff 10-1 before facing an Arsenal side
packed with guests, including Stan Matthews. Matthews suggested to
Arsenal's manager, Tom Whittaker, that Neil Franklin play, but Bernard Joy
suddenly became available on leave, added to which the Dynamo management insisted that guest players only fill those positions where Arsenal did
not have a player available. The game went ahead in dense fog, which hid
the action from the watching 54,000 on White Hart Lane's terraces. Many
of the crowd had queued for nine hours to catch a glimpse of the now legendary Russians. The fog meant that most saw little of Dynamo's 4-3 win,

or George Drury's sending off for retaliating to some of the rough stuff the Russian defenders dished out.

Stoke had gained eight points from their last five matches of 1945 and only one club – Newcastle – had scored more goals. This set up City nicely for a good run in the FA Cup. They faced Burnley in round three and won the home leg 3-1, thanks to a Steele hat-trick. It could have been more. Basnett hit the underside of the bar and Matthews teed up Antonio, who missed a sitter. In the second leg at Turf Moor, Antonio went from villain to hero. Stoke conceded twice to bring the tie level before Antonio, sporting a gashed forehead from the icy first game, ignored not only his stitches to score a brave late winner, but also boils on his legs and hands, acquired from unhygienic Army accommodation.

Two days after the execution at Wandsworth prison of Lord Haw Haw, whose mocking radio broadcasts from Germany had irked his countrymen, the FA announced that, before the international against Belgium at Wembley on 19th January, they would honour Stan Matthews' 44th appearance for his country and his breaking of Eddie Hapgood's English caps record with a special presentation.

Stoke City, who on 1st January 'agreed not to entertain Blackpool's enquiry for the transfer of S Matthews', acknowledged Stan's feat by presenting him with a £75 silver tea service. The City of Stoke-on-Trent celebrated their favourite son's achievement through a presentation of £100 in Savings Certificates and an Illuminated Address. But Matthews nearly did not make his record-breaking appearance. He reported to London with influenza, contracted whilst on RAF night duty. England trainer Bill Voisey had to ply him with alcohol, a substance from which Matthews abstained, to get him back on his feet. Matthews sweated the flu out under the watchful eye of Voisey, who spent the night seated on a chair in Matthews' room. A subdued Stan played and England won 2-0.

The beleaguered McGrory soon found another problem on his hands, although this was of the kind that managers enjoy. With Billy Mould, along with Challinor, Ormston and Peppitt, expected to be demobbed imminently, the question arose of who would be Stoke's preferred centre-half. The *Sentinel* speculated that McGrory's penchant for young Franklin would make 'Mould's position when he returns a "poser". When he returns he will be behind Franklin in the number 5 shirt. The club may be interested in a transfer.' When he did return, Mould was most certainly not happy to play second fiddle, although his availability still remained restricted, as his demob date became ever more delayed.

For the fourth round FA Cup-tie with Sheffield United, leaders of the League North, the 1,566 bookable seats in the Boothen Stand sold rapidly. Named as captain in honour of his new England appearance record, the talismanic Matthews arrived at the Vic still hoarse from his bout of influenza. Stoke trainer Vic Shaw had just the remedy, popping a couple of pep-pills, of the type used by the Luftwaffe's bomber pilots on long-range raids over England. Later Matthews recalled: 'The pills worked so well I felt like "bombing" the Sheffield defence!' Stan inspired Stoke to a 2-0 win, but there was a price to pay for Matthews, however. The pills perked him up to such an extent that hours later he scuttled around his house re-arranging his kitchen cupboards in an attempt to make himself tired. That didn't work, so he went for a night-time jog, swept the carpets, had a bath and raked the garden of fallen leaves – all in his dressing gown – before finally falling asleep at 3am. Heaven knows what a modern random drug test would have discovered.

At Bramall Lane, Stoke killed off the tie by scoring twice in a minute through Antonio and Steele. An injury to Herod, saving at the feet of Rickett, livened up the tie as it occurred just before the interval. Herod was replaced between the posts by Jock Kirton. Despite Colin Collindridge's hat-trick for the Blades, City held on to reach the fifth round with a 4-3 aggregate win.

Neil Franklin injured an ankle in that Bramall Lane game. Stationed at nearby RAF Hemswell, his Medical Officer, Flight-Lieutenant Henderson, despatched him to Gainsborough Hospital for an X-Ray, which showed he had cracked an ankle bone. With the next round of the Cup against Sheffield Wednesday looming, Franklin asked the RAF to rush him into re-hab. They agreed, whereupon he took to his bed to ensure he rested his ankle. How that assisted his general fitness, is another matter.

Stoke were now putting out one team for the Cup and another for the league. McGrory accomplished this by trading the availability of key play-ers for Cup-ties, leaving them out for league matches in between. Cup-fever had truly come to Stoke. All reserve tickets for the fifth round, first leg against Sheffield Wednesday sold out in under a day. Bob McGrory had to run the gauntlet of an angry 2,000-strong crowd who had queued for hours but went home empty handed. Three inches of overnight rainfall produced the worst floods in North Staffordshire for 25 years, but the game nevertheless went ahead. On a Victoria Ground quagmire, Freddie Steele ran amok, powerfully converting two Matthews corners with a trademark flick of his bull-neck. In the return game, Wednesday could make no headway into Stoke's rugged defence and the game finished goal-less. One generous Stoke supporter, mindful of the need to keep his heroes' strength up in this time of food shortage, gifted two eggs apiece to the team which defeated Wednesday 'in the hope that they will do it again against Bolton'.

Everyone in the Potteries sensed this was the year. Hence, despite only having scored once in four games – and that a penalty – to drop into mid-table in the league, when Stoke avoided favourites Villa, and Derby and were paired with Bolton in the quarter-final, demand for tickets went through the roof. Stoke expected their record attendance – 51,373, set against Arsenal in 1937 – to be broken, but an Arctic weekend kept the attendance just short. Queues formed at 9.30am, with vendors doing a roaring trade in everything from rattles and handbells to fish and chips.

As 50,000 spectators crammed into the Victoria Ground for only the second time in its existence, the *Sentinel* reporter noted that 'Boys were passed down to the front to sit around the edge of the track as a crush is relieved'. The band of the Royal Marines struck up before kick-off and Billy Mould, recently demobbed, watched his teammates presented to the guest of honour, the Earl of Lichfield.

Once play commenced, Stoke pressed hard but found Bolton goal-keeper Stan Hanson in defiant mood. He twice denied Antonio with point-blank saves before pulling off a one-handed stop from George Mountford's header. Bolton's counter-attack saw former England international inside-forward Ray Westwood constantly threatening Herod's goal. Westwood scored once in each half, while the Wanderers' massed defence kept Steele at bay. At 0-2 the tie seemed all but over. Bolton left the Potteries mocking: 'Pull t'blinds dahn, yoan lost.' But City had Magic Matthews and still fancied their chances of making a game of things in the second leg at Bolton the following Saturday.

The morning of 9th March 1946 dawned fresh and bright, encouraging many fans who might otherwise have stayed away to converge on Burnden Park. Seventy thousand began queuing from 11am. Neil Franklin credits the hype surrounding the visit of Stan Matthews as another reason for the bumper crowd: 'This game had something else besides an interest to the two sets of supporters. With Ray Westwood on one side and Stanley Matthews on the other, the neutrals would be assured of some great football, so even though the neutrals might have thought a Bolton victory was a foregone conclusion, they decided to have their money's worth of class football from those two great artists.'

At that time the Burnden Stand, which ran along the length of the pitch, was still closed, sequestered for use as a Ministry of Food store. This necessitated spectators to pack the other three sides of the ground. Some areas were more popular than others and the Railway Embankment end, which rose up to meet the railway line that ran from Bolton to Bury, was a natural focal point. The 'terrace' was, much like Stoke's own Town End, little more than a shored up mass of rubble and earth with occasional flag-stone steps. In places, wooden barriers had replaced the steel girders which had gone to assist Britain's war effort. As the railway line itself passed close to one end of the embankment terrace, the public could only enter from the other side, causing further congestion at the turnstiles, where around 18,000 people tried to get in.

With kick-off fast approaching, the embankment terrace full and thousands still outside, the clamour built to a frenzy. Desperate to get in in time for the kick-off, fans took matters into their own hands. Hundreds threatened gatemen before vaulting turnstiles, while the Police pulled down many of those attempting to climb the fencing.

Chelsea manager Billy Birrell acknowledged at the time that crowds had short fuses: 'war has made everyone more aggressive ... The temper of soccer crowds has changed radically since the war ... The former Commando, for instance, when he comes along here and secures a good vantage point, refuses to move up, down, or along for anyone.'

As it was already full to overflowing, Burnden Park's Railway Embankment had become 'pretty strained' soon after 2pm, with those fainting – men as well as women and children – passed bodily down, 'sometimes roughly – it being no happy matter for those doing the handing down. Their sagging heads jerked perilously and frequently they disappeared entirely as though they had been allowed to drop to the ground.' Waiting ambulancemen were soon overwhelmed by the numbers of those needing attention.

At around 2.45, a twelve-year-old boy, panicked by the developing crush, pleaded with his father to go home. His dad, Norman Crook, picked the lock of the exit gates: 'in a desperate attempt to get out I tried some of my own keys and an ordinary screw key did the trick.' But the opened doors allowed a torrent of fans to gain access to an already dangerously crowded enclosure. Crook later recalled: 'When I turned round after exiting, I saw people jammed in the crush to get in.'

At 2.55 as the two teams emerged, the 60 police on duty – of which just fourteen patrolled the Railway Embankment – tried to stem the flood of spectators jostling for a view. Shirley Pilkington remembers: 'I was at the far end, the Great Lever End, and all I could see was the pressure of people coming down from the back of the embankment and we could obviously tell that there were problems but we didn't know the extent of the problems.' In fact, the sudden incursion at the top of the embankment caused a surge forward and two of the wooden crash barriers collapsed under the weight of numbers. The crowd swayed like corn in the breeze before hundreds lurched down the terraces towards the pitch. Harold Riley recalls vividly: 'it was like the waves of the sea, like when you are swimming sometimes and you feel the suction. It was like the release of a tidal force.' It became a general stampede. Spectators fell three or four on top of each other and were trodden underfoot as panic spread. A witness on the Railway Embankment itself recalled: 'I was lifted off my feet and flung on the heads of those in front. I saw people on the ground and others sweeping over them, but nothing could be done to keep the crowd back. I could see men being crushed to death against the barriers before they gave way.' 'It was a horrible scene,' blurted another witness. 'Arms and legs were sticking out at odd angles and most of them were significantly motionless. I shall never forget the sight.'

As those nearest the pitch began to jump the low wall to reach it, Neil Franklin found himself distracted from the game: 'Suddenly there appeared to be a mass invasion of the pitch near the corner flag at the Railway Embankment end. It seemed strange to see one side of the ground completely empty and the rest of the ground completely packed. But queer things happened during the war and just after it. As far as I could see the Railway Embankment was uncomfortably full of people and there was the usual depressing sight of the fainting and fainted being passed over the heads of the crowd.'

Like Franklin, most of those present assumed the stretchers were still bearing fainting cases. Bolton fan Bert Gregory recalls: 'The wife was getting a bit over-excited and I said "It's all right, it's only a crowd, they'll sort it out. There's room over there." She said 'Some of them people are injured'. They brought a lady on and laid her down at the back of the goal, on the grass verge, and she said "That woman's dead, I can tell, woman's instinct'. Dennis Herod, too, knew the fate of those being laid behind his goal: 'I'd served in North Africa, Italy and Normandy and I'd seen plenty of dead people. I knew those people hadn't fainted. I knew they were dead.' Supporter Audrey Nicholls remembers the horror: 'they were a ghastly colour, a colour that I'd never seen on a living person.' Soon the casualties spilling onto the sunken running track began to obstruct the linesman. As the bodies incurred onto the pitch, the police raced on to deal with what they at first believed to be a pitch invasion. Play was inevitably halted. As the players stood around in groups watching, two police horses attempted to restore order, while Bolton secretary-manager Walter Rowley appealed for calm. But as fast as the crowd receded at one point, it eddied at another and more casualties dropped from the terracing onto the pitch-side. The game clearly could not continue.

Referee George Dutton summoned the two captains, Harry Hubbick and Neil Franklin. Franklin recalled in his autobiography: 'He told us that some people had been injured and suggested that we leave the field until some sort of order had been restored. Both Harry and I thought it a sensible idea, so Mr Dutton, his two linesmen and the twenty-two players walked off the pitch and into the dressing-room. As we trooped off, we were loudly booed by some of the crowd. They had no idea that any accident had occurred. To them people had just fainted and that happens at almost every big game. Remarkably many of them were ignorant as to the real cause of the walk-off even at the end of the game.'

It was twelve minutes past three when the players left the pitch. Meanwhile, initial estimates from doctors put the death toll at 28. The dead were removed from the embankment corner and carried under the main stand. Stoke's club doctor, Dr A P Spark, was commended by the St John Ambulance workers for his assistance: 'The faces of many who had been thrown to the ground bore the marks of hobnailed boots with which they had been trampled, socks and stockings of men and women had been torn to pieces and they were all covered in dirt. A number of victims had been suffocated.' During the hold-up a goods train stopped at a signal overlooking the ground. Twenty or so spectators clambered aboard hoping for a view of the game. But then the signal changed and the train moved off, taking its new passengers with it.

In the bowels of the stand, the players remained blissfully unaware of what was happening. On the advice of Bolton's Chief Constable, the referee took the dramatic decision to resume playing. Stan Matthews remembers George Dutton appearing in the Stoke dressing room to announce that the game would continue: 'We stood up but my legs felt like lead. I didn't want to go back out. None of us did.' Those fans who knew the extent of the disaster wanted the game stopped too. As Frank Baker ran out of the tunnel, one of the Bolton fans grabbed his arm and angrily shouted ''Tis a crime to carry on'. The game restarted at 3.25pm with over a thousand spectators rehoused in the closed Burden Stand, and another thousand spread around the touchlines.

Unsurprisingly the match, played on a pitch now churned into a paddy field by stampeding feet and shrunk by fresh touchlines drawn inside the existing ones with sawdust, progressed with little appetite. The players simply went through the motions. Franklin: 'No longer was this a cup-tie in which Stoke City had to battle against a two-goal deficit. It was now just a mere formality that we completed ninety minutes and to hell with the result. No one wanted to score, let alone win. It was a blessed relief when Mr Dutton blew the final whistle.' The nearest anyone came to a goal was when Baker hit the bar, while Nat Lofthouse's shot stuck in the churned up mud on Herod's goalline.

The crush claimed 33 lives – more than had been killed in Bolton during the entire war – and left 520 injured in what was then the worst disaster English football had suffered. All the casualties occurred within ten square yards of the enclosure by the corner flag. Almost everyone in Bolton knew someone who had been bereaved. Peter Campbell went home for tea before finding his ex-Marine son and daughter were dead: 'Frederick had only been married five weeks and his wife should have been at the match with him but they missed each other in town.' Thomas Smith was another victim. He and his daughter got separated at the turnstiles and, finding the crowds so dense, she took refuge under the stand. She heard the news on the train home to Rochdale. A small boy hanging about would not leave without his father, Winston Finch, who was seen on the pitch with a mac over his face. Frank Judd had survived being a Royal Artillery gunner and three years as a PoW. Just demobbed, on Monday he was due to start work again. Stan Matthews captured the poignancy of such deaths: 'To survive a war, only to die at a football match sent a shiver running down the spine of nearly every one of us.'

Home Secretary Chuter Ede launched an official enquiry, which opened at Bolton's No 1 Court on 28th March, while the FA committee held a minute's silence before launching its own investigation. Bolton certainly knew what had caused the disaster. Bert Gregory worked for the club and when he arrived on Monday morning he was asked to perform a particularly grizzly duty: 'The manager said "Find a rope, Bert, will you, and rope that portion off". When I went there, there were belts, raincoats and hats and scarves, what a sight, so I roped it off. Later on I was detailed to pick up these two barriers. They were flattened to the floor and I took them away so that people wouldn't keep coming asking questions. I know where I put them, but they're gone now, of course. Later on the club renewed them, but they just got the joiner from the local colliery to come and he helped me put these barriers up again.'

Predictably, the FA buried their heads in the sand. Despite admitting that these events 'might easily happen on twenty or thirty other grounds in their present state', Stanley Rous, FA Secretary, defended football by claiming: 'Public safety has always been uppermost in the minds of those responsible for football crowds.' Clearly this was rubbish. Football had failed to heed a warning, which had come only weeks before, when a similar incident of gate-crashing occurred at Leeds. The FA even hosted international matches on grounds featuring the kind of embankment that had now proved fatal. Spectators watched February's England v Holland from Huddersfield's 'Kop' standing on 'broken bricks' or 'tightly folded newspapers' to find a vantage point on the 'steeply sloping, unterraced top half'.

Already, football's administrators were practiced in the art of saying 'something must be done by somebody, just as long as it doesn't have to be me'. Stoke donated £500 to the Bolton Disaster Relief Fund, launched by the Mayor of Bolton, which culminated in August's England v Scotland match. Its 10,853 gate enabled the FA to donate £14,259. Stan Matthews contributed £50 personally. The fund closed at £50,936, with £29,282 granted in lump sums to widows and ten shillings weekly to each child, at least one unborn, who had lost a parent.

On 6th July, R Moelwyn Hughes KC, chairman of the official enquiry, reported his findings on the cause of the disaster. The club and police came in for heavy criticism, while a glance at his 'sixth point' gives us an indication of how the Hillsborough disaster of 1989 might have been avoided had his advice been heeded:

'The siting of crush barriers allowed involuntary swaying of the crowd and meant that just a small addition to it would cause a massive problem. In an excited moment the crush began and, as it was not easy to move from one enclosure to another, people were penned into a death trap.'

In consequence, Hughes recommended the implementation of a safety certificate which would be granted on the basis of each enclosure being expertly examined according to a number of criteria. These included its maximum capacity, mechanical counting so that total admission should be known at any point, making unauthorised entry an offence in law and for legislation to be passed to enforce periodic inspection. Clubs soon complained that this was too draconian, a reaction after a one-off event and, unsurprisingly, that it would prove prohibitively expensive. Several chairmen also attempted to deflect blame from administrators by pointing the finger at 'hooligans', as would also happen after the Hillsborough disaster. The government dragged its feet over introducing legislation and failed to prioritise ground improvements as a matter of public safety.

The two clubs involved in the disaster, however, were at the vanguard of wanting to improve their own grounds. Even that proved difficult, despite Bolton's Secretary, Mr Banks, admitting that 'the cost would be willingly paid'. A visit from the police and the City of Stoke-on-Trent surveyor, indicated that Stoke needed to terrace the upper 40ft of the Town End, which until now had been nothing more than a shored up ruck of scree. Stoke also needed to replace 60 steel crush barriers which had been removed for war scrap metal. Stoke agreed to 'make every effort to have the Town End of the ground terraced before the opening of the season', with estimates already in place for the required 10,000 concrete slabs.

On 1st August, Stoke City, under the Ministry of Works scheme which approved such applications, requested a work order to undertake some £4,000 worth of ground improvements. The Ministry approved an outlay by Stoke of just £200, a pointless sum. Instead of being able to render an embankment – similar to that which had contributed to the disaster – safe, Stoke spent the allowed sum on new loudspeakers to assist crowd control. They replaced the existing system which the military had used to breaking point during its tenure. The work on the Town End was held in abeyance for over a year and the flagstones had to be stored underneath the embankment for the rest of the season before work could get under way the following summer, with Messrs Kirton, Brown and Mitchell helping to provide the labour.

With ground improvements too expensive for tight-wad chairmen, all-ticket matches became the preferred option. The theory ran that they offered a better solution as, by guaranteeing entry, the crush outside and the clamour to get in could be controlled. To test this, the FA Cup semi-finals became all-ticket, with restricted attendances well below capacity at their respective venues (10,000 below for Bolton v Charlton at Villa Park). There was no fairytale ending for the people of Bolton though, as a subdued Wanderers lost 0-2. Despite the tragedy, the nation's love for football was undiminished. It would take the remarkably similar events of Hillsborough 43 years later to finally force football to improve the housing of its paying spectators.

Despite Matthews missing a first-half penalty, awarded for handball by Vincent – which was tipped against the foot of the post – Stoke won their first match after the disaster 2-0 at Grimsby. A collection at the ground raised £51 for the Disaster fund. Before the visit of Blackpool the following Saturday, the Stoke crowd observed a tense minute's silence before launching into a tearful rendition of 'Abide With Me'. Stoke beat Blackpool 6-3, thanks to four more goals from Steele. This would be Stoke's last win for seven games, the team not being helped by niggling injuries to three key players. Matthews had strained a ligament, Franklin an ankle, and Baker pulled a leg muscle.

Shortly added to this list were Mould, victim of a leg injury picked up in training, and, at Burnley, Steele with a twisted ankle. Stoke lacked depth in attack to cover such a crisis and McGrory admitted: 'We need at least one or two experienced players to restore the balance. Good inside forwards are hard to come by but that will not deter us from making the effort.' McGrory attempted to address the problem by trying John Boothway, the Manchester City forward who had guested for Crewe throughout the war. He had blossomed into a fine player and bagged 39 goals over the season. Boothway did score on his only appearance as City started the game against Grimsby in a whirlwind, to go 4-0 up after 21 minutes. But Stoke then went off the boil and Boothway did not impress McGrory enough to justify competing for his signature. Stoke's deficiencies were made all the plainer as City conceded three first-half goals in a 1-4 reverse at Liverpool. It didn't help that Brigham belted a penalty – given for handball by Ramsden – straight at keeper Sidlow and then ballooned the rebound over the bar.

On 14th April, Freddie Steele became the next unsettled star to submit a transfer request: 'I made a suggestion to the club to be placed on the transfer list as I think a change might be in my own interests. I have received certain official assurances which I am thinking over before taking any further step.' McGrory's attitude to this turn of events is curious: 'There is no serious issue between Steele and the club and I am quite sure the position can be satisfactorily resolved.' It was, and Steele soon came off the list. Compare this with the fate of dissenter Soo, and McGrory's wrath at the ongoing Matthews saga, and it is easy to see why the finger can legitimately be pointed at the manager for having his favourites – a trait always likely to cause division and suspicion in a football dressing room.

Matthews himself was now so determined to leave that he even tried recommending John Lawler, Glentoran's outside-right, whom he had seen whilst in Ireland with England earlier in the season. A trip to Ireland soon gave McGrory the impression that the player was not as talented as Stan would have him believe.

Stoke's inconsistent run since the Burnden Park Disaster saw them finish thirteenth, although there was the promise of improved attacking play when all the first-choice forwards were fit. Freddie Steele, despite a season of injury and upset, bagged 43 goals, 35 in the league and eight in the FA Cup. But City's over-reliance on Steele was plain from the fact that George Mountford was the next highest scorer with just nine. 'A great deal remains to be done by the City before the "kick-off" next August,' opined the *Sentinel.*

On 4th May McGrory announced his retained list, with nine players handed free transfers. These included Bamber, Gallacher, Tutin and Tennant. As a cruel reminder that the war cost so many players so much from their careers, the Football League transfer book saw each man have the words 'Too Old' scribbled against his name. In July 1946 Stoke reported a healthy profit of £16,868 19s 4d for the season, prompting Chairman Booth to declare the position as 'the strongest in the history of the club'. Life was getting back to something resembling normality. The Football League had declared that the Leagues proper would begin again in August 1946 with the same sets of fixtures as had been drawn up for the aborted 1939-40 season. Stoke's two stands, which had been requisitioned for military use during the war, were returned fully to the club over the summer.

Now would come the acid test of all Stoke's planning, testing and perseverance with young players over the war years. Would McGrory be vindicated in pursuing his youth policy? Could he work with Matthews? And how would he resolve the Mould-Franklin conundrum at centre-half? The game was very much on.

## CHAPTER EIGHT

~ 1946-47 ~

'The British treat war like a sport and sport like a war'

Football prepared for its first full professional season in six years, against a backdrop of testing atomic bombs at Bikini Atoll in the Pacific. The A-bomb was seen as the 'end of all wars' by its proponents, who noted that despite the blast, goats still grazed on surrounding islands, while the aged US battleship *Nevada* remained afloat. The greatest threat to life would not emerge for another 30 or so years. Broadcasting by radio from Bikini, writer Norman Cousins cut straight to the chase: 'The real issue is not whether an atomic bomb can sink a battleship, but whether the peoples of the world can prevent an atomic war.'

In Britain, an unbearably hot summer led to serious water shortages. The Potteries saw residential supplies intermittent in many areas, which only added to the misery of ongoing food rationing. Then, on 27th July the skies cracked. That one day saw over half the normal month's rain. The consequent flooding hit the wheat crop particularly hard, bread was rationed, and bakeries found themselves under siege. In the Potteries, folk found their beloved oatcakes under threat. This local delicacy, made of milk and oats, and eaten hot off the griddle, had become a mainstay during the war, and to lose it now caused a furore in the *Sentinel*. The population was 'living near to the bone' with low resistance to disease and an increase in minor maladies, particularly to the skin and stomach.

Clothing was also an issue. While millions struggled to clothe themselves, several top football clubs – including Manchester United, whose Old Trafford home had also been rendered unusable by German bombs – appealed for clothing coupons to replace tattered kit. Exeter City were forced to change to red and white hooped shirts, as 'replacements for red and white vertical shirts are off the market'. Any thoughts that Stoke might have stolen a march on Exeter were dispelled by a glance at contemporary team photographs. They reveal Stoke's shirts full of undarned holes.

Over the summer months demobbed players returned to train with Stoke for the first time in years. Amongst the returning faces was Harry Sellars, father of tyro half-back Johnny Sellars and midfield mainstay of the Stoke side which won promotion to the First Division in 1932-33.

Sellars replaced Hubert Nuttall as first-team coach, Nuttall reverted to his duties as trainer, and Bobby Liddle remained reserve-team coach.

McGrory was confident that, with the benefits of full-time training – denied to players during the war – his side would blossom. After all, most of his players were in their prime. The *Sentinel's* 'Potter' correspondent declared his confidence in the 'wealth of talent' at the club: 'I am looking forward to one of their most successful seasons in their long history.' Not all of Stoke's fans felt as confident. At the AGM, supporters F Leigh and P Simpson enquired whether the board intended to spend Stoke's considerable profit on improving the team. Chairman Booth retorted: 'that would be a matter for boardroom discussion and this was neither the time nor the place to discuss such matters.' Twas ever thus.

Mr David Duddell, who had served as a director of the club for 30 years, died of natural causes just before the season began. Most of the team who resided locally attended his funeral on Friday, 16th August at Cross Street Methodist Church. The service included renditions of 'Fight the Good Fight' and the Cup final hymn 'Abide With Me'.

The following Wednesday saw the reinstatement of the annual Stoke City FC club outing after a lapse of seven years. A party numbering over 40 enjoyed a trip to the spa town of Buxton. The spacious grounds of the Pavilion Gardens were placed at the disposal of the team, who stretched their legs and enjoyed a warm, dry day. Bowling proved a popular pastime and on the day Freddie Steele and Hubert Nuttall beat Harry Pearson and Harry Meakin 15-14. Others played tennis and one or two joined in the afternoon tea dance. The England internationals amongst Stoke's squad had an extra spring in their step. The international selection panel had appointed a new team manager, Walter Winterbottom, but had retained control over team selection. Winterbottom requested that England's players assemble in advance of the season for training, with Buxton being chosen as the venue. While their teammates returned to Stoke, Stanley Matthews and Neil Franklin stayed behind to meet Winterbottom at the Spa Hotel.

A 6-1 win in torrential rain for Stoke's first team against the reserves in the public practice match boded well. The left-wing partnership of Baker and Ormston 'interchanged positions at will to allow Ormston to score the first goal following good work by Steele. One shot by Steele was so hard that Foster was forced to turn somersault to hold it.' George Mountford, deputising for Matthews – who chose not to travel from Blackpool to play – scored two goals which resulted from 'splendid opportunism'. New admission prices were announced. Entry to the open Town End cost 1s 3d and the covered Boothen End cost 1s 6d, while a seat in the Boothen Stand cost five shillings and a season ticket seven guineas (a guinea was 21 shillings).

Now that Stoke had most of their senior players back – including the entire pre-war front line – the youngsters, having been accustomed to playing in the first team, either had to face up to life in the reserves or seek pastures new. Stoke received a bid of £1,250 for winger Fred Basnett from Portsmouth's manager, Jack Tinn. Basnett, however, refused to go. Happy with his 'bungalow, and a job with his father-in-law, a nursery gardener', Fred simply craved 'a part-time engagement' and so preferred to join non-league Northwich Victoria for £250. On the same day, blond full-back George Oldham moved for £100 to Newport, where in the season's first month he would suffer the ignominy of a league record 0-13 defeat by Len Shackleton's Newcastle. Robert Dunkley was sold to Barrow, and Jim Westland – whose top-flight career was ended by his knee injury – to Mansfield for £750. Billy Mould, George Mountford, Syd Peppitt, Tommy Sale and Bert Mitchell all began the campaign in Stoke's reserves, lining up in a Central League fixture at Newcastle. Keeping his huge squad happy would clearly tax McGrory's managerial skills.

On Saturday, 31st August the sport-starved nation welcomed back League football. Over 900,000 spectators found themselves sardine-packed on terraces up and down the country on that day alone, with almost as many outside fighting to get in as there was inside, struggling to see. The figures set the tone for the whole season, which would see aggregate crowds exceed 35 million.

The weather dominated the entire campaign. That opening day carried primeval portents. The season began 'to the accompaniment of sunshine, thunder, lightning, floods and a roar from a total crowd of nearly a million'. The weather did not let up, turning pitches into glue-pot mudheaps, favouring those teams with tactics based on power rather than skill. Peace may have been restored among nations, but in the world of British football war now broke out. Tackling was violent, made more dangerous by the treacherous surfaces.

The imagery supplied by newspaper correspondents – chief providers of information for supporters, particularly when your team played away – bristled with echoes of war. Teams adopted 'blitzkrieg tactics', goals 'dive-bombed into the net', while tackles were 'heavy enough to buckle a submarine'. For many, the Saturday *Green 'Un* was the only way to find out what was going on. Thomas Taw, in his celebrated *Football's War & Peace: The Tumultuous Season of 1946-47,* stated 'phenomenal scenes' greeted the arrival of Saturday evening football papers. Newsboys were overwhelmed by swollen crowds – 'couldn't have been worse if we'd been giving away beer'. Newspaper sales were 50 per cent up on pre-war levels, although newsprint restrictions kept production low: 'I heard of one hostelry where on Saturday night last there were about fifty customers, all of whom had to share one *Green 'Un,* which was passed from one to the other.'

Local papers were passionately committed to their town and their club, and that pride was carried on to a national stage. Footballing failures were roundly condemned. Within the game, too, there was turmoil as Thomas Taw recounts: 'The clubs wanted a return to the past, to the disciplines and class relations of the Football League's first fifty years. The players remembered being "thrown out of their jobs" in 1939. The War had changed their lives. Now it was football's turn to change. And change must come, for the country was mad for football: "there is scarcely a home in the land wherein the game does not exert its sway".' The huge crowds meant huge profits for the clubs, but footballers still received scandalously low wages, forced to struggle on without adequate housing or enough food. As the season kicked off, the mood was black amongst pros. Football as yet had no peace conference.

Stoke began the season poorly. An opening draw against Charlton at the Vic was followed by three successive defeats. The *Sentinel*'s 'Potter' described the team's efforts as 'ragged and individualistic'. George Antonio had not found consistency playing away from the Victoria Ground during the war. Back in Stoke's colours, he played too deep and lacked grit in front of goal. McGrory dropped him after the first two matches, with George Mountford and Syd Peppitt contesting his place.

And worse followed as injuries began to pile up. First Matthews, following the previous season's injury plague, limped out of the home defeat by Bolton due to 'rough and ready tackling ... which received scant punishment'. Stanley then exacerbated the problem by tweaking his knee in training.

At Middlesbrough, home forward Andy Donaldson shoulder-charged Herod into the back of the net, allowing centre-forward Fenton to tap home. Referee Mortimer gave the goal, telling Herod – 'he barely touched you'. Dennis, concussed and feeling a large lump growing from his forehead, replied: 'Where did this come from then?' Herod made it through the 90 minutes, but then succumbed to the injury, spending a week in bed and contracting flu in the process. Syd Peppitt was also injured in that game, ricking his back just before half-time. The 8,000 who found themselves locked outside Ayresome Park for Boro's first home game since the war, saw the match turn into a personal shootout between two pre-war England centre-forwards – Micky Fenton and Freddie Steele. Fenton, who had also scored two and won a penalty in the corresponding fixture seven years earlier, won his personal duel 4-3, as Boro triumphed 5-4. With the game at 4-4, City's best two chances to win it fell to the limping Peppitt, but he missed both.

Stoke had just one point to show from four games – hardly championship form. The fans were agitated and McGrory, having expected a grand start, was caught off-guard. Supporters also expressed concern that

McGrory's tactics were outdated. A T Finney of Longton told the *Sentinel*: 'There is too much stress on feeding Matthews, whether he is free or not. Stoke's forwards are often too close to one another instead of being in open spaces where the ball can be given more easily.'

As any worthy manager would do, McGrory acted on his team's failings, but it was in defence that he perceived the problem. He dropped Harry Meakin and Manny Foster, whose nightmare in City's defeat at Bolton would prove to be his last first-team appearance for Stoke. In goal he brought in Arthur Jepson, signed from Port Vale for £3,750. Jepson had offered his services to Stoke back in 1942, after Herod had joined the Army, but had been unable to play through reasons of unavailability, and had eventually joined the RAF himself. Jepson was one of a number of sportsmen who played football in the winter and professional cricket during the summer. His county was Nottinghamshire – alongside Harold Larwood and Bill Voce – for whom he took 1,051 wickets with his right-arm fast-medium pace bowling in a career which lasted until 1959, when Jepson was in his 44th year. He then became a Test Umpire.

The portents of Jepson's arrival at Stoke were ominous. He signed on Friday the thirteenth and went straight into the revamped team to face Derby the following day. He proved a steady keeper, dominating his penalty area to good effect, but was quiet, especially when compared to Herod's constant bellowing. This led to occasional misunderstandings between Jepson and his defenders in the months to come. He also had a penchant for charging from his goal to claim the ball or confront oncoming forwards. This often worked well for him, but occasionally penalties ensued. In the modern era he would have risked red cards for denying clear goalscoring opportunities, but that sanction was not available to the referee in 1946. Despite helping Stoke to win their first game of the season, albeit shakily, against Derby, Jepson did not prove a hit with Stoke's fans. Owen Bennion remembers: 'We didn't hold Arthur Jepson in the highest regard. Firstly he had come from Port Vale. Then he made a few mistakes. We thought he made too many mistakes.'

Alec Ormston's late winner in that 3-2 defeat of the Rams transformed Stoke's season. It was followed two days later by a 5-2 crushing of fellow strugglers Leeds. Crucially, McGrory was now able to field a settled line-up. In addition to Jepson, left-back sergeant instructor Jock McCue returned from honeymoon after tying the knot as the season got under way. Now posted to Chilwell, between Nottingham and Derby, he replaced Meakin and added grit, solidity and experience to City's defence. The rejig at the back helped Stoke curb what had become a worrying tendency to concede and allowed the side to concentrate on what it did best – attack.

Neil Franklin had no doubts as to why Stoke's fortunes altered so dramatically: 'once the run starts, you get tremendous confidence and can do no wrong.' Dennis Herod agrees: 'Winning is a habit. The confidence grows and you carry the luck.' A six-game winning streak propelled Stoke up the league table and with it came the usual bout of superstitions that accompany such a run of form. A jet-black cat, nicknamed Blackie, which had wandered into Bob McGrory's office immediately prior to the winning run, soon featured heavily in the local press. One fan explained: 'I have been unemployed and have wanted a job as a gate steward at Stoke for a long time ... I went to see if there was any chance of a job. The cat followed me into the office, and stayed when I came away. I had been given the job at last, so I said "It's brought me luck. I'll let them keep it and see if it brings them any". They needed it – four games without a win. It did – six wins in succession.' Plus, in an effort to stop the rot, Bob McGrory had tried an innovative training technique based on Army PT, with the players swinging their legs and arms rhythmically to music relayed around the ground by loudspeakers. The players now believed this gave them an edge over their opponents.

George Mountford returned to the side during Stan Matthews' recovery from injury and was soon integral to Stoke's buoyant strikeforce. His direct, abrasive style, contrasted with that of Matthews, as Neil Franklin remembered: 'he covers miles of ground, looking tireless as a steam engine, a tribute to his evening's training after a day's work at the colliery.' Mountford clicked with Stoke's front line, which was by now running into form and City, prompted by George's quick thrusts and forays down the right, hit a purple patch.

But Mountford wasn't Stanley Matthews, and when league leaders Manchester United rolled into town, the fit-again Matthews replaced him on the right wing. Circumventing the problems of injury and the previous night's monsoon, which had engulfed North Staffordshire, Matthews produced a *tour de force* performance to ritually humiliate United's Billy McGlen – 'roars of laughter from the crowd as Manchester United's McGlen trailed Matthews like a big game hunter stalking a gazelle – and about as successfully.' Stoke led 3-0 after an hour, with all three crafted by Matthews, but the enraged United's 'vigorous tackles ... told their tale'. Stan limped out of the attack, the following week's international, and Stoke's team for another month. His game relied on cat-like balance and jet-propelled acceleration and he could not perform to anything like his best whilst injured. He rehabilitated in Blackpool, as treatment for such injuries amounted to little more than rest and recuperation. Surgery was not an option.

Other players, however, grew accustomed to playing through injuries. Frank Mountford and Harry Brigham were both injured early in the season, but carried on despite the knocks. Frank's committed approach in particular often meant he required the services of Stoke's trainer, Bobby Liddle: 'It got so that the trainer wouldn't come on when I got injured!' he

joked. Supporter Brian Calvert recalls: 'I have memories of Frank clutch-
ing a sponge to his head, refusing to leave the pitch.' Mountford admits
that his apparent bravery had a rather more prosaic motivation: 'I didn't
want to ever come off as I might lose my place. I'd play anywhere to get a
game.' In an era when the alternative to a football career usually meant
shift-work at the local colliery, players fought tooth and nail to hold on to
their cherished first-team shirts and a decent pay-packet.

McGrory had already lost Matthews for half of City's matches. At 31,
Matthews' injuries might be getting the better of him and if Stoke were to
make anything of their season McGrory needed another way to feed
Freddie Steele. He restored George Mountford, who slotted neatly back
into Stoke's attack as City outclassed Preston 3-1 to extend their winning
run to five. That same day Neil Franklin was selected for England duty
and, defying the vagaries of the FA's international selection committee,
began a run of 27 consecutive full internationals – a new England record
– although if wartime internationals were included Franklin's record would
be 39 in a row.

England defeated Northern Ireland 7-2 in front of 60,000 in Belfast,
with Middlesbrough's Wilf Mannion bagging a 'debut' hat-trick. Attention
focused on England's right wing, where a precocious talent from Preston,
Tom Finney, also won his first England cap and scored a goal to boot.
Thus began the great football debate of the next decade – Matthews or
Finney, who should play at outside-right? For the moment, with Matthews
indisposed, England retained the same team, defeating Eire in Dublin 1-0
with another Finney goal.

Stoke's winning ways thrust them among the contenders for the league
title. The early leaders were Matt Busby's Manchester United, featuring
Jack Crompton in goal, Johnny Carey, Jimmy Delaney, and 45-goal partnership Jack Rowley and Stan Pearson. Busby's was an outstanding team
that would transform United from the music-hall joke of pre-war football
to post-war giants. United began the 1946-47 season with five victories,
including a 5-0 drubbing of mighty Liverpool. George Kay's Reds, stung
by that heavy defeat, had invested wisely. They splashed a club record
£13,000 on Albert Stubbins, who had been a major figure in wartime soccer, as Stoke had discovered to their cost the previous season. Bizarrely,
with both Merseyside clubs coveting his signature from Newcastle,
Stubbins tossed a coin and plumped for Liverpool. His 48-goal partnership
with former Stoke forward Jack Balmer – who became the first man to
score hat-tricks in three consecutive league games – kept the Anfield club
in the hunt. Most provocatively for Stoke fans, and particularly Bob
McGrory, Stan Matthews' wartime side Blackpool, under manager Joe
Smith, led the way for much of the campaign, with Stan Mortensen having a belter of a season, scoring 28 goals. The other main title contenders

were Ted Vizard's Wolves who, like Stoke, based their side on youth. An opening day 6-1 thrashing of Arsenal had laid out Wanderers' stall.

Stoke travelled to London to face Chelsea with the weekend's football under a cloud of industrial action. The Football Players' Union, the forerunner of the PFA, at loggerheads with the Football League for eighteen months, announced a strike the following Tuesday over its demands to have the maximum wage – unchanged since 1939 – upped. Neil Franklin recalls: 'this time it was serious. The players wanted to share in the post-war boom. They wanted some security for the future ... we were all wondering whether this would be our last game for some time. In case it was like that, we decided to celebrate, and we entertained the crowd to a scorching match.'

Stamford Bridge's biggest gate of the season saw George Mountford run riot, his pace and skill befuddling Chelsea's left-back White. Robertson touched Mountford's shot onto the bar and Steele banged in the rebound. Chelsea got back into the game controversially with Tommy Lawton, England's centre-forward, later admitting that he handled the ball, scrambling in from close range. Shortly after half-time Chelsea took the lead, a rip-roaring Lawton shot giving Jepson no chance. The lead was shortlived as the Blues' defence allowed Ormston to race in from the wing and stroke the ball inside Robertson's far post unchallenged. That goal inspired Stoke to rampage through the remainder of the game. Ormston completed a scintillating hat-trick and Kirton hammered home a long-range special. It was his first ever League goal, one of just two in 249 games for Stoke. Afterwards, the press corps dug deep for pottery superlatives: 'this scintillating side of eight locally produced players provided a Wedgwood pattern of football which made the home side look like a piece of clumsily produced utility china.' More palatable were compliments such as: 'what gives a relish to watching Stoke just now is the feeling that almost at any moment goals might turn up,' and 'a display of classical football the like of which has not been seen in the London area since well before the war. Top-speed play, keen tackling, crisp passing and splendid interchanging of positions, coupled with an almost uncanny sense of anticipation, delivered a lesson in how the game should be played.' Radio commentator Raymond Glendenning dubbed Stoke 'this wonderful football machine'. But interest in English football was global. The headline in the *Singapore Free Press* described Stoke as 'The Perfect XI'. Perhaps Stoke's dreams about winning something for the first time in the club's history could turn to reality.

In the event, the feud between Players' Union and Football League was averted by the Government, desperate to avoid a strike that might spark others. They brokered a tentative peace between the two sides.

One interesting side-show which illustrates the problems professional footballers faced surrounded Stoke's club captain, Jock Kirton. On 2nd

April 1946 Kirton had submitted a written transfer request to the board. Unusually, his reason was not specifically about money, rather his 'housing trouble' – Kirton could not find suitable accommodation for his wife and two young children and had become fed up 'camping' at his in-laws. The board agreed to 'do everything possible to get him a house to overcome this difficulty' and publicised Kirton's plight. No house materialised and Kirton, now shorn of the captaincy, issued a 'No house, no play' demand. With the deadlock dragging on through the autumn, 'even the Lord Mayor of Stoke has given personal attention to the ultimatum.'

Fan Rex Audley remembers: 'As Kirton ran through Leeds' defence to lay on a goal, one middle-aged, shabbily raincoated gent standing near us in the paddock, all the emotions of the past week induced by Jock's plight seemed to well up ... then spill over. He shouldered his way forward down the paddock steps to get closer to his hero. "Good old Jock", he shouted in a voice that could be heard over the din. "Thee canst coom an live wi' me!" Finally a suitable house was found and Stoke bore the cost of a month's rent plus a year's rates which softened Jock's animosity towards the club and he agreed to stay. Jock, you see, was never really happy anyway.' The next snatch of Kirton's domestic life we have is another complaint to the club that he was struggling to control his wild garden at this new house.

As his nickname suggests, John 'Jock' Kirton was a card-carrying Scot – unlike teammate Jock McCue. Kirton had arrived at Stoke from the Banks o'Dee club in Aberdeen, where he had won Scottish schoolboy caps, via Bob McGrory's Scottish scouting network as a nineteen-year-old in 1935. Kirton made a number of appearances as cover for Frank Soo over the following two seasons, before establishing himself when Soo moved to right-half to cover Arthur Tutin's retirement. Kirton's role was to win the ball and give it to the playmakers. A chunky 5ft 9½in and 11 stone, Kirton had a distinctive, bulbous nose and wiry, wavy thick black hair. He habitually wore his long baggy shorts rolled tightly up to his waist, exposing his muscular thighs to intimidate opponents and reflect his unceasing thirst for Stoke's cause. Kirton's passion could boil over, at times. Stoke youth player Don Whiston remembered: 'in a practice match once, he scissor-kicked George Mountford to the ground after they had an argument.'

Another experienced player aggrieved at his lot was centre-half Billy Mould. The war had cost Mould dear. From being mentioned as a potential England centre-half, his military service had opened the door for Neil Franklin to steal both his club and international place. On Monday, 16th September, Mould handed in a written transfer request. It was refused. But Mould's mind was set, and he repeated his demand on 25th October, citing a need, at 27, for first-team football.

Stoke's reserve games were soon populated with interested managers – including Derby's George Jobey and Portsmouth boss Jack Tinn – keeping tabs on Mould as well as young Johnny Sellars and Bobby Windsor. But in Mould's case, McGrory hit upon an inspirational solution to revive the player's Stoke career. Dissatisfied with the form of his regular right-back, Harry Brigham, particularly during the 0-3 home defeat by Wolves, McGrory chose to try Mould in his place. Mould adapted brilliantly and Stoke's defence tightened, conceding only six goals in the next nine games. Brigham responded by asking for a transfer himself. McGrory obliged and sold him to Nottingham Forest for £3,580, before travelling to Glasgow to clinch the signature of seventeen-year-old Scottish full-back John Kirkby of King Street FC of Aberdeen for £70.

Mould had joined Stoke from the local Summerbank club, along with Alec Ormston, in 1936. His style conformed to that of the classic physical stopper of the 1930s. At 5ft 9½in and 11st, Mould had an identical physique to Jock Kirton. In Mould's case, his sheepish smile under a high balding forehead, topped with dark curly hair, belied a tenacious tackling ability. Frank Mountford remembers: 'Billy was quiet and a bit dour, although he was a fine defender who read the game brilliantly.' Stanley Matthews described Mould as 'a class player, compact and muscular, a great club man who possessed a sharp and impish wit'. In February 1947, when Stoke thrashed Preston 5-0, Mould enjoyed an outstanding game against North End's left-winger Wharton. For much of the second half Wharton simply stood on the touchline watching the game passing by as Mould starved him of the ball. The Preston trainer bawled at Wharton, exhorting him to more strenuous efforts, encouraging him to 'turn on his party pieces'. On leaving the pitch, Mould passed the Preston dug-out and seeing the trainer enquired: 'Party pieces? You'd have been better sending out a search party for him!' In switching Mould to right-back, McGrory had managed to satisfy two great talents. Could he pull off the same trick with his twin right-wingers?

Having been injured for over a month, Stan Matthews was not selected for England's 3-0 win over Wales at Maine Road on 19th October. Not only that, his very *raison d'être* within the new all-action style was being questioned in the press. Neither club nor country missed him, as his replacements – Tom Finney and George Mountford – exhibited 'new and devastating directness'. Could Matthews' genius have become outmoded? Stoke's directors, prompted by McGrory, took the opportunity to lay down the law. The minutes of earlier board meetings show the directors becoming increasingly concerned about Matthews' lack of commitment to the club. Stan had not been seen at the Victoria Ground since picking up an injury against Manchester United, and the board had lost patience with their star's persistent refusal to dedicate what they considered to be enough time to the club. They attempted to force Matthews to train at Stoke. Matthews' injury, however, prevented him from driving, so he remained up in Blackpool, where, of course, he had a family and business to take care of. Matthews trained there, either alone or with his wartime teammates at Blackpool FC.

Now, however, Matthews' agenda changed. Clearly keen to impress the England selectors, and fearing that Tom Finney might present a major threat to his international place, Matthews declared himself fit and travelled to Stoke for a practice match on Tuesday, 15th October. Feeling no repercussions from his work-out, Stan declared himself available for Stoke's pending trip to Highbury. This left manager Bob McGrory with a quandary. Should he change his winning team, or reinstate the 'supreme virtuoso among footballers?'

When Stan told McGrory of his fitness, the manager's reaction was to stutter the word 'good'. McGrory took Matthews aside and asked him to 'have a run out in the reserves this Saturday' instead. Matthews was stunned and when McGrory told him that it was only a suggestion, Stan did not know how to take it. It wasn't an order, merely a suggestion. What kind of man-management was this? Matthews was not one to spout off lightly: for years he had played out his frustrations on the pitch, but on this occasion he flipped, retorting: 'You're the manager of this club, so manage it.' McGrory refused to turn his suggestion into an order, but told Matthews he would not be in the team to play Arsenal. Matthews, in turn, refused to turn out for the reserves against Aston Villa, arguing: 'I am perfectly fit to play and if they think I am not, I will stand down from football totally for a fortnight.' He then stalked off back to Blackpool.

The minutes of that Tuesday's board meeting show that the directors backed McGrory insistence that Matthews 'have a run in the second team to make sure he was 100 per cent fit before playing in the first team'. Matthews, however, was perhaps influenced by the ongoing dispute between Union and authorities. In his previous weekend's column in the *Sunday Express*, Matthews had declared: 'I agree with the Union.' Now, he put forward a financial reason for his difficulties: 'My value would be wrecked all round. I have many business activities that depend on my football and I cannot afford to see my prestige upset. Even now I am considering a stage contract that might easily double my income and no footballer is getting so much money from the game that he can ignore such offers. If I were looked on as a reserve, well, I could say goodbye to all that.'

Neil Franklin, more concerned with the footballing aspect of the dispute, expressed his feelings in his autobiography: 'Frankly I didn't blame him. If he said he was fit, he was fit, because Matthews will never lay claims to fitness unless he is absolutely 100 per cent fit. So a fit Matthews is a first-team player.' This was an understandable attitude, but one that comes from a fellow star player. Either way, the dispute had escalated into something more than whether or not Matthews was fit. It was manager versus star.

Matthews wrote in his autobiography that he 'never felt McGrory batted for me at the club. After a good performance he would bull up other players but seldom mention me. Perhaps he was a little envious of what I had achieved in the game. Whatever the reason I felt there had been an undercurrent between us since I had replaced his close pal Bobby Liddle in the Stoke team when Tom Mather was manager.'

But one must remember that we only have Matthews' side of this tale. After all, who *was* picking the team? The manager, or his star who wanted to pick and choose when to play? McGrory remained tight-lipped about the affair until his early death in 1954. As a simple managerial decision, one can understand why McGrory did not want to change a side that had thrashed Chelsea 5-2 in its last game – but that was not the explanation he gave to Matthews. Suffice it to say that the gruff Scot handled his star badly. Whether or not that was intentional is a matter for debate, which still continues to this day. And things were to get worse, not better, in the aftermath of the altercation. McGrory's approach merely served to add fuel to a fire which had been smouldering for years. Now he fanned its flames into a full-blown dispute which would hit the headlines and ultimately affect Stoke's destiny.

With no solution in sight, the next morning the story was splashed across every newspaper in the land: 'Matthews to all intents and purposes has left Stoke,' and 'Matthews wants to leave – will not play in reserve team.' Contradictory reports of stormy telephone conversations between manager and player followed as football fans across the country digested the revelations. To make matters worse, one paper claimed a deputation of Stoke players had asked McGrory not to change Stoke's winning team. Matthews retorted: 'it has been very badly handled by manager McGrory,' and that he 'had been dissatisfied for some time'.

From his home in Blackpool, Matthews felt isolated. Speculation was rife that Stan would soon join Blackpool, or Newcastle, Chelsea, Arsenal or Aston Villa, with Stoke having set a £20,000 fee that would smash the transfer record of £14,000 paid by Arsenal to Wolves for Bryn Jones. Could a 31-year-old, for whom 'obviously the best part of his playing career is over', as one paper believed, be worth that astronomical sum?

Stoke fans now had their own localised version of the Nuremberg trials, which had begun to dispense justice on captured Nazis. Neil Franklin recalls: 'the Potteries were wild with rumour at this time. There were the pro-Matthews group and the anti-Matthews group, and there were those people who spent their time inventing bigger and better stories.'

With the good folk of Stoke-on-Trent having abided by the government missive not to gossip during the war, they gave vent to their pent-up
tongues over 'The Matthews Affair'. Denials, unofficial statements, hearsay
and innuendo flowed thick and fast. Stoke Chairman Alderman Booth
denied that Matthews had requested a move. McGrory aired the dilemma
of changing a winning side or freezing out his star player. By the time the
saga had done a few rounds of the Stoke-on-Trent rumour mill, the most
commonly held verdict was that the rest of the team *had* demanded of
McGrory that Matthews earn his right to play. While opinions on the rights
and wrongs were divided, some went too far. Poison pen letters and plagu-
ing telephone calls forced Stan out of his Blackpool hotel to take meals
and enjoy a round of golf at Lytham St Annes, significantly, for the con-
spiracy theorists, in company with his Blackpool training mates.

As soon as new club captain Neil Franklin heard these rumours of a
barrack room revolt, he took action: 'I called all the players together, told
them of the stories and pleaded with the players to own up and tell the
truth. Everyone present assured me he had nothing against Stan and that
he had never even thought of approaching the management. So I asked
the players if I could deny the stories that were now being spread by the
press across the country and they all agreed and I wrote to Stan to assure
him that every one of us would be only too pleased and proud to play with
him.' Franklin's press statement, issued at Highbury prior to the game with
Arsenal, led Matthews to suspect McGrory as the architect of the spiteful
rumours. And not without reason, as Dennis Herod believes: 'McGrory
was a crafty man. It would be just like him to do something like that, but
we didn't know for sure.'

At Highbury, the gates closed on a crowd of 62,000, with thousands
locked outside clamouring to see what all the fuss was about. A battery of
press photographers besieged George Mountford: it all proved too much
for the young pretender and Mountford sealed his personal nightmare that
day with an 'air shot' after being set up with an open goal by Freddie Steele.
Arsenal's Irish amateur winger, Dr Kevin O'Flanagan, secured his side's
first home win with an 'amazing screw shot' to clinch a 1-0 victory. Minus
Matthews, City had lacked a big-game temperament when all eyes were
upon them. It was a lesson to which McGrory paid no heed.

While Stoke were succumbing to Arsenal, the redundant and doubtless
inwardly-smiling Matthews posed provocatively for photographs on the
Bloomfield Road terraces as Blackpool defeated Manchester United 3-1 in
their top of the table clash. Matthews had struck a blow at the manager
who he held responsible for starting those scurrilous rumours. Could there
be an end to all this posturing?

On the Monday morning Matthews received Franklin's letter refuting
press suggestions that a delegation of players had asked McGrory to leave

Stan out. Matthews announced that he 'was glad to hear that. I have no quarrel with the City players and could not imagine them quarrelling with me.' Almost simultaneously, Stan received a summons to attend Stoke's regular Tuesday board meeting, convened at the North Stafford Hotel. Perhaps the board feared to take too strong a line. If they insisted that Matthews train with the club twice a week, he might follow his friend Jock Dodds – now with Shamrock Rovers – through the 'hole-in-the-wall' to play outside the Football League and the constraints of its maximum wage.

Whatever their reasons, the board opted to dampen the flames and ask Stan to let bygones be bygones. In return for permitting him to do most of his training at home – relying 'on him to train as conscientiously as at Stoke', and not have to play in the reserves – Matthews was required to travel to Stoke for 'any *special* training'. Stan agreed and a statement was prepared: 'The differences between the Board and Stanley Matthews have been amicably settled, but because of the publicity of the past few days, Matthews has asked the Board to grant him a week's holiday. The Board have agreed to this request and, following the period of recuperation, hope the Board, manager Bob McGrory, Matthews and the rest of the Stoke team can now concentrate in the job in hand of working together to bring success to Stoke City Football Club.' Stan declared himself: 'glad it's all over. The past week has been a nightmare for me and I am naturally very tired.'

In the cold light of day, Matthews had won. But the scandal had taken its toll, both on its two central protagonists and on Stoke's players. With Matthews lolling around his Blackpool hotel, Stoke suffered a 0-3 home defeat by high-flying Wolves, which gave a stark indication of how far Stoke had slipped. Now Blackie, the magical black cat, was suspected of blighting City's run: 'On Saturday my wife saw a woman in a fur coat, who had come in a car with some Wolverhampton supporters, stroking Blackie at the club entrance. It's my belief that luck went to Wolverhampton, like the points.' Fortunately for McGrory – if such can be deemed good fortune – George Mountford pulled a leg muscle in that defeat, so the fit and rested Stanley Matthews was drafted back into the side for Stoke's visit to Sunderland.

Everyone in Britain now knew the name of 'Stanley Matthews' amid this press furore. Stan became the focus of a Sunderland student prank to raise funds in their 'Rag Week' in aid of Monkwearmouth and Southwick Hospital. Their plan? To kidnap Britain's star footballer and hold him to ransom. The one problem? The students could not actually recognise Matthews. They resorted to skulking around the hotel lobby posing as autograph hunters, asking passers by to point him out. One unnamed Stoke player mischievously pointed out Neil Franklin, who found himself summoned to the telephone. As he approached the booth the students pounced, dragging him out of the hotel and onto a tram. Stoke's star centre-half had been abducted! Panic raced through the Stoke staff until an anonymous call to Bob McGrory demanded just £5 ransom for Franklin's safe return. Although relieved that this was not, after all, an underhand device by Rokerite fans to enhance their own team's chances, McGrory, not surprisingly, did not see the funny side and rang the police. Franklin, however, was having a ball. Assured by his captors that he would make it to Roker Park in time for kick-off, he paraded through the streets helping the students to raise more money towards their target of £400. Once a total of £450 had been gathered, the students and and their hostage retired to their dorm and Neil spent the rest of the morning avoiding the proffered pile of toasted buns before being taken back to the hotel by motor car and handed over.

To settle the nerves while Franklin was abducted, McGrory took Stoke 'with sandshoes under their arms ... and had an hour's frolic on the beach'. Then, replete with the abductee, on to business at Roker Park. A record crowd of 57,290 hoped to see Matthews humbled by their left-back Jones, but soon found themselves 'roaring with laughter at the ease with which Stan beat his man': 'I have never seen a player exercise so much influence on a game. The surprising fact was that he was only once really tackled throughout.' Stanley Matthews was back.

Baker's early goal seized a win, Stoke's first ever at Sunderland. Bob McGrory then travelled on to Scotland to visit family, but added a decoy: 'Don't say a word to anybody ... I'm after an outside right.' Matthews' return galvanised Stoke to another winning run, just as Mountford's had done two months earlier. At Fratton Park, 'slippery Stanley danced and jigged' to another away win, before another huge crowd. Everton were Stoke's next victims in a bumptious game at the Vic. Antonio's disputed last-minute winner in fading light prompted the Toffees' livid players to swarm around the referee. The goal stood, although Antonio later admitted handling the ball into the net. McGrory sensed the omens had swung back in Stoke's favour and praised City's fans: 'there's no doubt that terrific roar won us the match. Wouldn't it be a strange thing if that late goal won us the championship.'

Confidence was high. By mid-November Stoke were the heaviest scorers in the top division but, worryingly, only three teams had conceded more. Things were shaping up so well that the board granted McGrory a £150 pay rise, upping his annual salary to £1,000. The only blip in City's run came, with two minutes remaining, at Huddersfield. Franklin trapped a clearance and attempted to ease past home winger Metcalfe, but was dispossessed. Metcalfe ran on to lash in the only goal of the game. That result negated the good fortune of the Everton win. Stoke were still fifth, but points dropped like that were not the hallmark of champions.

Franklin was not the type to worry about such blunders, as he proved in subduing hot-shot Stan Mortensen when fourth-placed Blackpool visited the Vic. Usually Stoke's opponents left the field dazed. In Blackpool's case that was how they entered it, after a lorry hit one of the taxis taking their players on a tour of pottery factories that morning. With six men shaken up, the Tangerines floundered in Matthews' wake on a soggy pitch. Stoke cruised to a 4-1 win with Stan netting a rare, but sensational goal. The *Sentinel* glowed: 'Matthews' goal will be talked about for years, and those who saw it will describe how he progressed by acute zigzags half the length of the field, with four or five Blackpool players trotting at his heel like a pack of dogs, until finally he made even the goalkeeper go the wrong way and tapped the ball into the net.'

In the final minute Blackpool's Kennedy took matters into his own hands, scything down Matthews to receive his marching orders. Stan simply picked himself up, smoothed down his muddied shorts, and got on with the game. At the final whistle both sets of players applauded Matthews off the pitch. After all, these were his two teams, the players he played with on Saturdays and trained with during the week. Bob McGrory's reaction is not recorded.

With injury-free Matthews back in the side, West Ham, Blackburn, Everton and Portsmouth made offers for George Mountford, while George Antonio – kept out by the consistency of Syd Peppitt – also attracted attention. Blackpool's chairman, Sir Lindsay Parkinson, cheekily enquired about the availability of both Matthews and George Mountford, but McGrory and the board curtly turned down all offers. In other times, players would be sold to keep the club afloat, but with gates booming and a serious title challenge unfolding – following a 4-1 win over lowly Brentford, which pushed Stoke into the top four – McGrory was even more determined to keep his players together.

The secret to City's run was the half-back line. Kirton and Frank Mountford tackled hard, winning back the ball and prompting Stoke forward insistently. Neil Franklin strode imperiously around the field, intercepting, anticipating and initiating attacks with swift passes to the wings or inside-forwards. Kirton often brought Matthews into play with long diagonal passes.

Frank Mountford, who had begun the war as a goalscoring centre-forward, was now pushing for England selection, challenging Wolves' Billy Wright for the No 4 shirt. Mountford loved his creature comforts and was rarely to be seen without his pet dog, seventeen-year-old Billy. Frank's mother, who had prevented him being seduced by Wolves before his seventeenth birthday, and insisted he sign for Stoke, attended every home match and became his biggest critic: 'Frank at one time did not tackle well enough, but he has improved a lot since then. Wright will have his work cut out now!' Frank was now employed at the fitting shop at Norton Colliery from 7am to 4pm, and married Marjorie Bailey in 1946, although they had to share his parents' home in Bradeley.

In mid-December the weather took an icy grip, causing problems in North Staffordshire including intermittent power cuts, not to mention widespread colds and flu. Stan Matthews, Jock Kirton, Freddie Steele, Frank Mountford and Billy Mould all caught chills which impaired their play over the Christmas period. The Victoria Ground pitch, normally a sea of grassless mud, became a veritable ice-rink. For the visit of Blackburn on the Saturday before Christmas, Stoke initiated an 'all-in thawing-out offensive;' '25 braziers, five tons of sand, and the prodigious exertions of a steam roller.' The match went ahead despite a pitch 'with frozen pot-holes the size of pint mugs. But even the most skilful player could not control the ball: 'a capricious object which periodically went into a freakish spell against which even the magic of Matthews could not prevail.' The nation's food misery worsened when the bacon ration was cut from two to three ounces. There was barely a cheer at New Year either, as the Government refused to extend licences beyond 11pm on New Year's Eve and a deepening fuel crisis restricted supplies. It looked set to be a long hard winter.

With the title race hotting up, Stoke faced a double-header against leaders Liverpool over Christmas. At the Victoria Ground on Christmas Day, with goalkeeper Sidlow ill in bed, deputy Ray Minshull earned applause for his display. But he could not keep out Freddie Steele's brace which won Stoke the game. On Boxing Day at Anfield, Liverpool played 'neat and lively but unproductive football,' until a Nieuwenhuys goal against both the run of play and a strong wind swung the game. Albert Stubbins found the back of Stoke's net once again, this time with his left foot to round off Liverpool's win.

That defeat inflicted extra misery on one group of Stoke supporters. Two fans, Peter Sherratt and Frank Cartlidge, hit upon a scheme to earn some cash. Their plan was to take ten supporters to Liverpool, charging sixpence each, in the back of Peter's father's greengrocer's van. But an eagle-eyed constable spotted the men clambering into the van early in the morning and stopped it. Not only did the PC's intervention ensure the supporters missed the game, but his evidence ensured a successful prosecution. The crime? – permitting a van to be used as an express carriage without a public vehicle licence, driving whilst uninsured, plus out of date road tax. Somewhat harshly, Sam Sherratt, the van's owner received a ten-shilling fine along with the two young men.

New Year brought the FA Cup back onto the agenda for the first time since Stoke's fateful visit to Bolton's Burnden Park the previous March. Two-leg ties from the previous season were abandoned, and the format reverted to its familiar shape. The club's elevated league position excited the board to the extent that they sanctioned spending on special training designed to spur the players all the way to Wembley. McGrory's training regimen included taking brine baths at Stafford, country walks and golf, the manager's favourite pastime.

A favourable Cup draw paired Stoke with Second Division Spurs. McGrory prepared by taking his men to Blackpool, possibly swayed by the close proximity of Lytham St Annes. The break allowed his players to shake off their coughs and colds, and cope better with the stresses and strains of four games in eight days over Christmas. Curiously, the fourteen-strong Stoke party stayed at Stanley Matthews' hotel, took in a couple of shows, and trained in the Revell Gymnasium which Matthews had placed at the club's disposal without charge. Snow, however, kept them from the golf course, much to McGrory's chagrin. Back in Stoke, at a public meeting, Chairman Booth attributed City's success to 'McGrory's wartime policy and to the wonderful team spirit which prevails throughout the club'. Stoke's ability to produce its own players from local leagues had led to the club becoming known as the 'Bob McGrory School'.

Stoke's players departed for London, suitably refreshed, on the Friday afternoon, following their usual routine for matches in the capital. Habitually, Stoke stayed in the Grand Hotel on Southampton Row in Bloomsbury. Unfortunately, the Grand was plush and warm, whereas Stoke's players lived in terraced houses that were cold and damp, which meant that they could not sleep before the game. This had led to a poor run of results in the capital.

The players did not always help themselves either, as Dennis Herod remembers with a wink: 'We'd be sent out for a walk, to keep us busy and wear us out a bit so we'd go to sleep, with staff members keeping tabs on us. But when we got to Ludgate Circus we'd all split up and find bars to have a drink in.'.

The night before this particular game, Stoke's players met up with their Spurs counterparts – who were also in a hotel on Southampton Row fresh from their own special training in Brighton – to exchange good luck greetings. Another huge crowd clamoured for Matthews and he did not disappoint. City took a two-goal lead at half-time, but took their foot off the pedal and allowed Spurs to force a draw. For the first time in seven years, midweek football returned in the shape of Cup replays with afternoon kick-offs. Thomas Taw notes its effects: 'On Wednesday morning early, 7,000 tickets went on sale at the Victoria Ground, attracting queues of 20,000. In the recently nationalised Staffordshire coalfields absenteeism that day was up to 42 per cent higher than normal; and there was "permitted absenteeism" in the pottery factories, i.e. the workers worked through lunchtime and returned afterwards.'

The 38,639 crowd saw Spurs goalkeeper Ted Ditchburn keep City at bay almost single-handedly until the intervention of Stan: 'Matthews beat almost as many opponents as he liked with his usual bewildering ease ... One Spurs player, so deceived that he could not keep his feet, resorted to grabbing the Stoke player by the ankle with both hands ... When the referee on another occasion adjudged Matthews to have committed a foul [the second against him in the memory of this writer who saw him on his first game for Stoke] the crowd showed its disbelief by a roar of laughter.' Stan struck the solitary goal with his left foot.

Matthews' genius attracted not only crowds of admirers, but villains. Liverpool's safe had been blown after Stoke's visit there, but the receipts had already been banked. Now, after 11pm on the evening of the Cup replay, an 'expert gang of safe breakers' burgled Stoke's club offices, blowing the door off McGrory's office, seeking the day's receipts. The thieves nicked £884, including £440 worth of tickets sold for Preston's forthcoming visit, £250 of McGrory's own money, and a sum set aside for tax. Fortunately, £3,000 of the gate money had already been deposited with the police for safe keeping. McGrory discovered the theft when he arrived for work the next morning. To his annoyance the thieves also helped themselves to a large slab of cake, gifted to him by well-wishing supporters, which he had left in his office. Mercifully they ignored his beloved cigarettes and whisky! The theft caused Stoke to invest in the club's first ever proper safe, while the thieves escaped without a trace.

While Stoke repeated their 'lucky' Blackpool routine before the next round, opponents Chester trained on sherry, eggs and milk whilst on their own special week's retreat at Abergele. Come the day, Stoke struggled to beat lower division opposition again. Third Division (North) Chester considered themselves unfortunate not have beaten Stoke in the first tie, with Jackie Arthur missing a late chance to make a name for himself.

Before the replay, heavy snowstorms blighted the country once again. Twenty-two foot drifts blocked the Great North Road and the RAF dropped ration packs into remote villages. With fuel stocks low, even Buckingham Palace had to resort to candles. On the morning of the game, groundsman Harry Loffill arrived at the Victoria Ground to discover thick snow, frozen to the pitch by 13 degrees of frost. Loffill improvised by using a blue wash to mark out the lines and the game went ahead. It proved a classic. Stoke cruised into a three-goal lead before a leg injury to Frank Mountford forced him off. With Mountford, the regular taker out of commission, Matthews saw his penalty saved by Scales, with Stan also putting the rebound wide. Chester capitalised and scored twice following Jepson errors – the second a bad punch which saw the ball fall at the feet of Yates. In the last minutes Stoke had to weather intense pressure. Mould headed Astbury's shot off the line. Chester claimed a goal, but referee

Martin asserted: 'I was right up with play. I don't care whether Mould was over the line or not. The ball certainly was not.' City were through, but McGrory was beginning to tire of his goalkeeper's handling errors.

When the great freeze descended in late January, Wolverhampton led the table with 37 points; followed by Preston 34; Manchester United, Middlesbrough and Blackpool 31; and Liverpool, Aston Villa and Stoke 30. The leaders' chances actually improved during a month in which they never played but their rivals did – and lost. In between the Cup-ties, Stoke dealt a blow to one of their title rivals by hammering second-placed Preston 5-0. The match was especially satisfying for Matthews, who saw his England rival Tom Finney subdued by Jock McCue, while he himself produced yet another: 'classic exhibition of wing play more fit for skates than football boots ... never once on that surface did Matthews soil his pants.'

The game also provides insight into how Matthews' mere status could delude full-backs. Preston's Bill Scott opted to play Matthews by refusing to tackle. He simply let Matthews run at him whilst Scott backed off in a crouching position, attempting to jockey Stan to the touchline. This encouraged Matthews to show off his full range of skills. Time and again he jinked slowly forward, grinding his marker back from the halfway line to the edge of the penalty area before setting up a yet another goalscoring opportunity. Scott's mood cannot have been helped by Stoke's fans in the Butler Street paddock chortling at his hapless efforts. He eventually snapped with five minutes to go, and caught Stan so badly that Matthews struggled for weeks afterwards with a groin injury. He missed Stoke's mid-week visit to Maine Road to play Manchester United, which turned into a tale of three penalties. United's Buckle missed in the twentieth minute, but then scored a second in the 45th. Ormston equalised from the spot early in the second half to keep Stoke in the title hunt.

But, even though the league chase continued to go well for Stoke, the distractions of the Cup, then perceived as football's Holy Grail, preoccupied the minds of Potteries football-lovers. Interest was so great in the fifth-round tie against Sheffield United that the Chief of Police ordered it to be made Stoke's first ever all-ticket match. In unprecedented scenes, thousands queued from 6am to get their hands on one of 50,000 tickets.

Sheffield sought revenge for defeat by Stoke in the fourth round of the previous season's Cup. By coincidence the clubs had been due to play in the league on the same day at Bramall Lane. That match was inevitably postponed, but more of that later.

The worst blizzards for seven years enveloped North Staffordshire under a deep white blanket. That ensured Stoke could not decamp to Blackpool for more 'lucky' special training. There was no golf either, so the players had to be satisfied with brine baths at Stafford and bitterly cold walks. The weather affected the match in many ways – 250 tons of snow was removed from the pitch by over 100 men. They worked by the head-lights of the twenty lorries used to cart the snow away. Fifteen tons of sand and several more of salt were dumped on the pitch in an attempt to melt the ice beneath. Ten thousand Blades fans did not make it to the Vic, foiled by cancellations of trains – due to the lack of fuel – and coaches – due to the icy roads.

Despite all the effort that had gone in, the Victoria Ground was 'the most dangerous playing pitch I have ever seen … The players who stood out were those prepared to take the biggest risk of broken bones.' The Blades set their stall out early on, with red-haired Scot Alex Forbes aiming 'wild kicks' at Stan Matthews: 'the crowd would have buried Forbes if he'd connected.' He soon did: 'Matthews lay on the floor and the referee raised a beckoning finger to Forbes, red-haired Sheffield left half. Many thought the finger was already pointing to the dressing room. There was a hush after Forbes walked slowly to the referee and then a storm of booing when it was seen that he was not going off.' The catcalls quickly turned into a blizzard of snowballs.

Stoke had all the play, hailing in shots, with Baker hitting the bar, Peppitt the post, Ormston nodding teasingly just wide, and Baker's shot striking a teammate on the line and rebounding to safety. Sheffield seemed pleased with a likely replay, but with 90 seconds left on the clock United's inside-right Harold Brook tried his luck from an 'impossible … freak … acute angle', the ball hitting the net to a stunned silence of disbelief.

Afterwards, McGrory dabbled in a bit of amateur psychology, taking his players out to view the spot from which Brook had loosed his 'bomb-shell' to impress upon them the freakishness of the goal. Any of them would have missed from that position, 'five times out of six … with no goalkeeper in.'

1946 had ended with professional footballers offered a new wage struc-ture – £11 per week maximum and £6 minimum in the winter; £9 maxi-mum and £4 minimum in the summer. The decision was ratified at a spe-cial League meeting on 24th February 1947. It constituted a small, but important victory for the players, who now at least felt they shared in the enormous profits of their clubs, even if in truth they were still little more than the performing monkeys to their employers organ-grinders. One player who had drawn his last Stoke pay packet was veteran striker Tommy Sale, who joined his former teammate, Harry Ware – the new manager of Northwich Victoria – on a free transfer.

Forgotten man George Mountford helped Stoke bounce back from their Cup exit when he replaced Matthews, absent with a nasty boil on his leg. Mountford returned against Chelsea in a sensational Stoke perform-ance. City were 6-1 ahead before half an hour had been played. Some

Chelsea supporters coaches were only just arriving, and the late-comers could not believe the score.

Afterwards, Bob McGrory invited sympathy for his revived selection problem: 'how would you like to be in my shoes when picking the side for next week.' Fortunately, or unfortunately, depending on one's point of view, Mountford injured a foot in training and Matthews was back for Saturday's 3-1 victory over Arsenal, which moved Stoke into third place, just three points adrift of leaders Wolves.

McGrory's luck in juggling his wingers in this way could not continue indefinitely. When push came to shove, with both of them fit, McGrory put his faith in the proven class of Matthews. Almost immediately, a trans-fer demand from Mountford landed on his desk. Arsenal's George Allison trumpeted his interest in whichever of the two wingers Stoke wanted to offload and made a formal offer for Mountford.

Coincidentally, the Football League council met in Manchester that week. McGrory was present and received a deluge of enquiries. Figures up to the magical £20,000 were bandied about as Blackpool, Sunderland, Spurs, Chelsea and Liverpool all tried to outbid each other for whichever of the pair McGrory chose to discard. Stoke's board, however, still had their eyes set on the championship, and in these circumstances decided they did not wish to part with either player.

Mountford was disappointed: 'I'll have to think over what I've been told. At any rate it looks as if I'm a Stoke player for the time being.' The next blow was a transfer demand from that disillusioned enigma George Antonio, who had lost his place to Syd Peppitt. West Brom, Spurs, Derby, Leeds, Burnley, Plymouth and Portsmouth wanted him, and within a fort-night he had joined Stuart McMillan's Rams for a fee of £4,000.

Stoke's local derby against Wolves was a massive match for both clubs. Over 55,000 packed Molineux to see top play third. Stoke began badly. Jepson all but threw Mullen's shot into his own net in the first minute, with Westcott getting the final touch. And things just got worse. Stoke could not cope with Wolves' directness, and the usually calm Franklin played his part in Wolves' second and third goals. The final score was 3-0, and the dif-ference was in the finishing. Wolves scored from three of their six chances, while Stoke wasted all of their multitude, with players leaving the ball to each other rather than take responsibility for a shot. City even missed their second successive penalty, when Williams saved Ormston's kick. By the close, Wolves had extended the gap over Stoke to five points, with City having played two games more. Despite McGrory's insistence that Stoke's chances were brighter than they appeared, it would surely take a superhu-man effort to win the League from here.

The night of 4th March witnessed the worst blizzard of the winter. Some 260 roads were blocked and the railways paralysed. For the first time this season, Stoke's pitch was unplayable and the visit of Sunderland on 8th March was postponed. A slight thaw followed, causing flooding, burst pipes and consequent chaos.

That same week the FA announced a voluntary ban on midweek football in order to assist industrial production, which had been hit hard by the weather and continuing fuel crisis. Factory owners resented the pull football exerted on its workforce. Race meetings and rugby also agreed to confine events to weekends. The Football League though, counting the weeks left and the mounting list of postponements – which already exceeded those of any previous season – knew that without midweek games the season could not be completed on schedule. In Stoke's case, they still had eleven games to play, but only eight Saturdays remained. Other clubs were in a worse position, but the ban on midweek games stood. Tight-lipped Stoke cancelled a planned summer tour of France, once they learned that they would play at Sheffield United on the last day of the extended season – on 14th June!

Matthews and Franklin appeared in the last midweek game, between the Scottish and English Leagues in front of 80,000 at Hampden on Wednesday 12th March. The Football League defeated their Scottish counterparts 3-1, but that night blizzards engulfed Scotland, severing Glasgow from the outside world. With Stoke due to play Aston Villa in Birmingham that Saturday, Franklin telephoned the club to say that he and Matthews were marooned, with road and rail travel impossible. The club told them to make every effort to reach Villa Park. The pair tried Renfrew airfield but all the available seats south had been commandeered by FA officials. The duo returned to Glasgow, where word reached them that the tracks had been cleared sufficiently for a train to depart for London at 10am the following day, Friday.

After spending another 24 hours twiddling their thumbs, Stan and Neil, accompanied by Harry Johnston and Stan Mortensen of Blackpool, Joe Smith, the Blackpool manager, Derby's Raich Carter and Peter Kippax of Burnley, made a beeline for the dining car to begin their long, slow journey south. The train ploughed its way through Arctic drifts, taking fifteen hours just to reach Preston! As Neil Franklin put it: 'I've never been so pleased to see Preston in all my life!' There a fateful decision was made. Instead of accompanying Franklin, who changed to a newspaper train bound for Stoke, Stan Matthews chose to head home with the other Blackpool-bound members of the group. Franklin pitched up in Stoke at 6am on Saturday morning. After a couple of hours' sleep in front of the fire in his favourite chair, he joined the Stoke squad headed to Villa Park through yet another snowfall.

Jock McCue also faced problems getting to Villa Park on time. He had been over in Paris playing for a British Army XI against the French Army, and afterwards braved heavy seas in the Channel to make it back to the Potteries at 3am on the morning of the game. Stan Matthews, however, despite a decent night's sleep, failed to make the train from Blackpool to Birmingham and also failed with a subsequent attempt to reach Villa Park by motor car. With McCue and Franklin having surmounted every hurdle thrust in their path, Matthews' failure to show up incensed his manager. The following week Frank Mountford remembers hearing the pair crossing swords in the tunnel of the Victoria Ground: 'they were going at it hammer and tongs. McGrory didn't like Matthews. He really thought Stan felt he was bigger than the club.'

The irony of the situation was that the race for Villa Park was in vain. Despite the pitch being free of snow at kick-off, a blizzard then engulfed Villa Park. The snowfall was so heavy that the pitch was white within 25 minutes and referee Todds abandoned the match midway through the second half with the score at 2-2.

The only good news that day was hearing that George Antonio kicked off his Derby career with a goal after just nine minutes, which put the Rams on the way to a 4-3 win over title-challengers Manchester United. The following day, Sunday 16th March, was transfer deadline day. A national newspaper chose the occasion to stir up the Matthews-McGrory saga, predicting the imminent sale of the player. Matthews telephoned his manager to learn the basis of the story and was told that McGrory knew nothing about it. Despite having several bids to contemplate, Stoke's board issued a statement: 'After careful consideration the Board have unanimously decided not to entertain the transfer of any players at the present time.'

Successive draws against Portsmouth and Everton – with late equalisers conceded in both games – seemed to have put the mockers on Stoke's title challenge. But while City were treading water, Wolverhampton were sinking. They went down 0-2 at Sheffield United to spark a run of three defeats in four. Suddenly, City had the leading pack within range. Blackpool only led the table by dint of having played more games, while Liverpool also lost form, going three games without a win. Manchester United emerged as the new favourites, winning four out of their next five matches.

The Easter holiday brought glowering skies, bleak and blustery weather with buckets of rain that drenched spectators at each of Stoke's three games crammed into four days. Nevertheless, Matthews' hotel in Blackpool experienced a rush of bookings. He contacted Stoke on Maundy Thursday to inform McGrory that, 'due to pressure of business' he would find it hard to get away to travel to Grimsby on Good Friday, but would be happy to play at Stoke on the Saturday. The internecine warfare, which had bubbled ever closer to the surface over the past decade, finally exploded into open hostility. Matthews thought he had only three or four seasons left in him, and wanted to get his hotel up and running. In short, he had chosen to put his business and family security above the interests of his club. McGrory, who now referred to Stan as 'Big 'Ed', found Matthews' attitude intolerable. No player could pick and choose when he played. That was the manager's job. Matthews chose not to travel to Grimsby and paid for his insubordination when he arrived at the Victoria Ground the following day. Stan had been dropped from the team to face Huddersfield.

Matthews later re-wrote this particular part of the story in his autobiography, claiming that his request not to play at Grimsby was for footballing reasons: 'England v Scotland was taking place on 12th April, the weekend after Easter. I had a word with Bob McGrory and asked if he would rest me for the Good Friday match away at Grimsby Town. Four big games in eight days would be too much, even for someone of my level of fitness. Bob agreed but said he would play me on the Saturday at home to Huddersfield Town. Stoke won comfortably at Grimsby and I drove down to Stoke half-expecting McGrory to inform me he wanted to keep the same team and I wouldn't have blamed him if he had. The next morning, however, I called into the manager's office at around 10.30 and was told by Bob that he had picked me. As I started to get changed, McGrory popped his head around the door and asked me to step into the corridor. Once outside he told me that he had changed his mind and was going to stick to the same team that had won at Grimsby, muttering a few words about it being a manager's prerogative to change his mind. McGrory's behaviour not only galled me, it started to eat away at what remaining respect I had for him as a manager.'

But look at it from McGrory's point of view. Neil Franklin faced the same schedule and didn't need a rest. Here was a star player, who put his outside business interests before his club, dashed off to his wife directly after games rather than socialising with his teammates, and seemed to want to dictate selection decisions to his manager. With Real Madrid not an option in 1947, the less exotic location of Blackpool seemed the obvious destination for this footballing megastar.

McGrory also took decisions on the fate of other players. Jepson's error-strewn performance at Molineux prompted the manager to hand back the No 1 jersey to the now fully recuperated Dennis Herod. Not the least of McGrory's concerns was that Jepson had to honour his contract with Nottinghamshire County Cricket Club. Now that Stoke's season would extend to mid-June, Jepson would be unavailable in any case.

Despite having Frank Mountford on the mend, McGrory stayed true to young Johnny Sellars – a whippet-like player with a knack of scoring goals in the reserves at centre-forward – at right-half. That prompted Mountford to mutter threats about leaving, but deadline day had passed. He would remain a Stoke player for the rest of the season at least.

Even with the benefit of hindsight, it is difficult to fault McGrory's tough decisions. Stoke's Easter programme could not have gone better. Following a 5-2 win at Grimsby on Good Friday, City travelled back to the Potteries that night and the next day beat Huddersfield 3-0. On Easter Monday Stoke coasted to another 3-0 win in the return with Grimsby. McGrory's side was on a roll.

For Stoke's next game – a win over relegation-haunted Brentford – Matthews' name was back on the teamsheet. McGrory told Stan: 'you can't have a player of your calibre, an England international, kicking his heels up in the stand,' only for Matthews to shortly learn the humiliating truth. He was only playing because of injury to inside-right Bert Mitchell; otherwise McGrory would have stuck with his winning team. The irate Matthews demanded a showdown with the directors, which McGrory did not attend.

Stan laid his cards down. He needed a change, 'to rekindle his fires', otherwise he might have to consider premature retirement. At first the board refused, but on 23rd April the minutes reveal the momentous decision had been taken: 'We accede to the request of S Matthews to be placed on the transfer list.' He would, moreover, be allowed to sign for his club of choice, Blackpool – but only in July. The transfer deadline had passed, and in any case, Stoke would not countenance Matthews assisting City's rivals at such a critical time in the title race.

The board minutes show an acerbic side-swipe: 'he [Matthews] had become a blessed nuisance to the Board.' They had realised that if he simply retired, they would not get a bean. But more antagonism followed. The discussions between board and player had been deemed 'secret', yet somehow the next morning the papers were full of it. Matthews was to depart for the Seaside. As Matthews later put it, 'Six men can keep a secret in football; if five of them are dead.'

On the pitch, all Stoke's rivals dropped points over Easter. Wolves lost 1-3 to Manchester United on Easter Saturday, while Blackpool drew 2-2 at Liverpool, who were now fifth on 42 points, but trailed Stoke and Manchester United on goal-average. This antiquated method of separating teams on the same points looked increasingly likely to play a part in the title run in. Stoke now had the best goal-average, but others made efforts to improve theirs. On Easter Monday, Wolves hammered Derby 7-2 to go back to the summit. Stoke's superior goal-average was now dictated by the need to keep a tight rein in defence, rather than scoring heavily. As goal-average was calculated by goals scored divided by goals conceded, the fewer a team concede, the lower their denominator. Although they were amongst the division's top scorers, City had also tightened up at the back and now boasted one of the best defences. Consequently, goal-average could prove to be Stoke's trump card. The team embarked upon a run of seven successive wins – the first four without Matthews – which thrust them into the heart of the title race.

Matthews' insistence on signing for Blackpool denied Stoke the benefits of an auction, which might have hiked up the asking price. Nevertheless, Stoke demanded a world record £20,000, which Blackpool's chairman, Colonel Lindsay Parkinson, rejected as 'ridiculous'. No 32-year-old could be worth so much. A stand-off over the size of the fee ensued.

Matthews' selection for England's draw with Scotland on 12th April conveniently removed him from the firing line when Stoke raided Bloomfield Road, won the game, and left Blackpool's title aspirations in tatters. The two points enabled Stoke to set a new club-record points tally in the First Division. Just to rub the Seasiders' face in it, Stan's replacement, George Mountford, scored the clinching second goal in a 2-0 win. Matthews, clearly affected by the hoo-hah, had a poor game for England and was omitted for the next international, against France on 3rd May, in favour of Tom Finney. But Stan was one of six Englishmen chosen for a Great Britain representative XI to face the Rest of Europe at Hampden on 10th May, in a game to celebrate the readmission of the four Home Associations to FIFA. The rift had lasted eighteen years, and had been sparked by disagreement over the definition of 'amateurism'.

Matthews actually scored in two of his last three Stoke games, against Brentford and Blackburn, where his 'variety of ruse, and his body swerve, wielded a mesmeric influence … left Bell in a sitting position, with a piece of close jugglery, and centred perfectly for Ormston to score.' His last appearance in red and white stripes was at already relegated Leeds, in what should have been Stoke's final game of the season. Matthews supplied the corner-kick from which Freddie Steele headed Stoke's equaliser in a 2-1 win. That marked City's seventh successive victory, a club record yet to be broken.

Stoke still had three more fixtures to play, but Stan was due to travel with an FA touring side to the Continent, thereby missing the first two of those. As Blackpool had already completed their fixtures, McGrory took the decision to allow Stan to depart forthwith. After all, trading Matthews' availability for one remaining match against Sheffield United, for his supposed disrupting effect on team-spirit, seemed a fair deal. The night after Great Britain had crushed the Rest of the World 6-1, the two chairmen and two managers assembled with the player in Stan's Glasgow hotel room to conclude the transfer. Strangely, Stoke's board minutes reveal a private acceptance of Blackpool's proffered £11,000. Before this was conveyed to Blackpool Chairman Parkinson, he upped his offer to £11,500. The cheque was written there and then. Stan Matthews had left Stoke City FC and was now a Blackpool player.

So, if Stoke were to win the League they would have to do it without their star, their talisman, their touchstone – Matthews. But things weren't as bleak as some would have us believe. Although Matthews' sale caused a storm of protest, many supporters accepted it as inevitable – it was only the timing that seemed crazy. Others considered George Mountford to be a more than adequate replacement; he chimed well with the rest of the forward line. After all, Stoke's winning run had largely been achieved without Matthews.

In fact, the shining stars of Stoke's season were to be found on the left wing, in the form of Alec Ormston and Frank Baker. Ormston, a devastating left-winger, with 'more trickery than the Magic circle', had an individual style which contrasted markedly with the power of Mountford and the guile of Matthews. Ormston would crouch over the ball with his body leaning forwards at a seemingly impossible angle. He hardly looked like an athlete, with shoulders hunched into an almost Quasimodo-like stance. Supporter Chris Lowe remembers: 'It was incredible. You would just see this pair of shoulders coming towards you.' The 5ft 6in winger's strengths were speed and accurate crossing. However, he could also tackle back, unusual for a winger in those days, and possessed a cannonball left-foot shot. This brought him twenty goals over the season, making him Stoke's second top scorer.

Inside Ormston, Frank Baker provided craft, dovetailing perfectly with his left-wing partner. The former laundry van driver had originally vied with Ormston for the outside-left position, but had gravitated inside under McGrory's watchful eye. Like Ormston, Baker could score his share of goals, often arriving late on the edge of the penalty area to lash in a rebound. Unlike Ormston, Baker's slender 5ft 7in frame remained classically erect. His boyish good looks were set off by brown, brooding eyes, and he kept his dark, wiry hair cut very short.

Noticeably, every contemporary commentator referred to Baker and Ormston as 'a pair'. Over the course of the season they earned many admirers and both came close to earning England honours, as McGrory had predicted. The selectors, however, preferred the genius of Preston's Tom Finney on England's left wing, in order to accommodate both Finney and Matthews, and few could argue with that. Off the pitch Baker and Ormston gelled as friends as well as colleagues. 'They drank like fish – most of the time together,' recalls Dennis Herod. They were the hub of the players' social life and, where Baker and Ormston led, the likes of the younger Franklin and Herod were sure to follow.

But Baker had a cruel run of injuries and Peter Cotton, a young supporter back in 1947, remembers why Baker earned the unwanted tag of 'most injured man in football'. One Saturday afternoon Peter broke his ankle whilst playing local football and was taken by his father to North

Staffordshire Royal Infirmary. Whilst they waited in casualty, a man joined them. Peter's father recognised the newcomer as Stoke's inside-left. He had been rushed from the Victoria Ground after sustaining the latest of his long line of damaged limbs. One of the nursing staff confirmed Baker's identity: 'He's in here every week!' she said. Unlike the superannuated stars of today, Baker had to wait his turn as Peter was plastered up first.

Of the other championship contenders, Blackpool had fallen by the wayside. Liverpool had lost their FA Cup semi-final 0-1 to Second Division Burnley, but beaten Manchester United 1-0 on 3rd May, holing United's championship hopes irreparably. Wolves now seemed to have the edge, but they promptly blew it with a 2-3 home defeat by Everton. Before Stoke's home game with Sunderland on 17th May, the table read:

		P	W	D	L	F	A	(GA)	Pts
1	Wolves	39	24	5	10	93	51	(1.82)	53
2	Stoke	39	23	6	10	88	51	(1.73)	52
3	Manchester U	40	20	12	8	86	52	(1.65)	52
4	Liverpool	39	23	6	10	79	49	(1.61)	52

But the overriding factor in high-pressure title run-ins is confidence, and Matthews' departure had dealt a crucial blow to Stoke's. Irrespective of his teammates' personal feelings about Stan's conduct, and his urge to leave them, they knew better than anyone how he could inspire simply through his near-mystical presence, never mind his ability to turn a game on one magical moment. This was something that McGrory subjugated to his own need to exert authority. In the process, he was culpable of destroying the team's aura of indefatigability. McGrory's ego had dictated that he sell Matthews. He wanted *his* team to win the title, in order to prove he did not need 'Big 'Ed'. This miscalculation had precisely the opposite effect to that intended. Instead of bolstering confidence, he undermined it.

Without Matthews, Stoke failed to score at home to Sunderland, a side he had personally humiliated at Roker earlier in the season. The Rokerites were buoyed by his absence, with Stoke's players looking correspondingly subdued. Indeed, Herod needed to be 'cat-like in his saves' to rescue even a point. The players trudged off at the end believing they had blown their chance. Instead, they returned to the changing rooms to hear encouraging results: Brentford 1 Liverpool 1, and Wolves 3 Blackburn 3.

		P	W	D	L	F	A	(GA)	Pts
1	Liverpool	41	24	7	10	82	51	(1.61)	55
2	Wolves	40	24	6	10	96	54	(1.78)	54
3	Manchester U	41	21	12	8	89	52	(1.71)	54
4	Stoke	40	23	7	10	88	51	(1.73)	53

Stanley Matthews took the field for England's next international, in Zurich, Switzerland, on 18th May, as a Blackpool player. The match proved memorable for Neil Franklin. Four minutes from the end, Stoke's centre-half tackled Hiegenthaler roughly, but fairly, according to the referee. The crowd thought otherwise and invaded the pitch 'thirsting for blood', and hurling beer bottles and an umbrella. England's reception in Portugal on 27th May was equally hot. Their hosts fancied their chances of a first victory over England, but the visitors fielded Matthews and Finney in the same team – Finney on the left – and crushed Portugal 10-0. Matthews rounded off the scoring with a sensational individual goal, bamboozling the entire Portuguese defence before tapping the ball over the line. Neil Franklin remembers: 'It was a massacre more than a football match. It was the easiest walkover in which I ever played.'

In their penultimate game, Stoke nervily won 1-0 at Aston Villa, spending the majority of the game clinging onto George Mountford's early goal. In doing so, they registered only their second win ever at Villa Park, and their first in peacetime. City had now captured 21 of 24 points in a run of twelve games without defeat. Indeed, Stoke had lost just twice in the League since Christmas, to Wolves and Derby. Elsewhere, a 1-0 win for Wolves at Huddersfield rendered Manchester United's 6-2 demolition of Sheffield United meaningless. Despite United having struck 95 goals and boasted fewer defeats than anyone else, they were out of the running for the title. They had run out of games and could not finish top. Now there were three.

		P	W	D	L	F	A	(GA)	Pts
1	Wolves	41	25	6	10	97	54	(1.80)	56
2	Manchester U	42	22	12	8	95	54	(1.76)	56
3	Stoke	41	24	7	10	89	51	(1.75)	55
4	Liverpool	41	24	7	10	82	51	(1.61)	55

This was the first and last occasion in which four clubs could have won the English crown with one match remaining, which made it the most exciting title race ever. But now it boiled down to the last two games. On 31st May, Liverpool would visit Wolves in a head-to-head decider. Stoke's fate hinged on the outcome. Wolves would secure the championship if they won. But if Wolves did not win, City would be champions if they won at Bramall Lane on 14th June.

The weather had turned turtle. On 30th May it hit 90 degrees in Stoke-on-Trent, the hottest day for twelve years. That night thunder storms deluged the region, and rain fell relentlessly for weeks. As Stoke's final opponents, Sheffield United, still had two other games to squeeze in, City faced a wait of more than a fortnight.

To keep his players match fit, McGrory took them on a tour of Ireland. But from the start, the trip turned into a disaster. The club considered flying to Ireland, but instead chose the Holyhead to Dun Laoghaire ferry. On arrival at the Welsh port on 31st May, Neil Franklin discovered he had forgotten his passport. He had to return to Stoke to fetch it, which meant missing the ferry. Being as parsimonious as any other football club at that time, Stoke's directors paid for the players to travel 'steerage' – the lowest class of travel. The Irish Sea was at its roughest, imposing dreadful torments on players meant to be preparing for what might be the most important game of their lives. The worst afflicted took days to recover.

The party bussed into Northern Ireland for a tour of the glens of Antrim. This preceded a benefit game for Belfast Distillery's Eddie Lonsdale, in which Distillery included several internationals as guests. A record Grosvenor Park crowd of 22,000 saw Stoke win 4-1. The following night, back in Dublin, saw a second benefit game, this time against Drumcondra. Stoke lacked form and appetite for the contest, and lost 0-3. Worse, Alec Ormston strained a ligament.

Whilst in Ireland, news arrived of the tumultuous match between Wolves and Liverpool, which would affect Stoke's fate. Before kick-off, Wanderers' captain and centre-half, Stan Cullis, announced his imminent retirement, but he was unable to spur his side to their first League title. In sweltering heat, Liverpool's Balmer and Stubbins scored first-half goals. Dunn pulled one back, but Liverpool hung on.

Stoke's players cheered the news lustily. Victory at Sheffield United would put them on top of the table for the first time all season, at the most opportune time. It would clinch the championship and earn the first piece of silverware in the club's history. Anything less than a Stoke win would hand Liverpool the first post-war title, and leave City in fourth place.

		P	W	D	L	F	A	(GA)	Pts
1	Liverpool	42	25	7	10	84	52	(1.62)	57
2	Manchester U	42	22	12	8	95	54	(1.76)	56
3	Wolves	42	25	6	11	98	56	(1.75)	56
4	Stoke	41	24	7	10	89	51	(1.75)	55

The Stoke players returned to England on 4th June, still with ten days to wait for their Waterloo. The seemingly endless wait dragged by interminably and took its toll on nerves. In such situations, footballers and supporters look to pretty much anything to predict the outcome. Some omens boded well, however, as the Blades were in wretched form. Despite having finished the previous season as League North champions, and were guaranteed to finish sixth this time whatever the result, they were still widely thought to be beatable.

Even better news for Stoke was that United would need to field three reserves. Star inside-forward Jimmy Hagan was injured. To replace him, the Blades manager Ted Davison – down to the bare bones – called up 38-year-old former England international Jack Pickering, who had not played all season.

But other omens were grim. Stoke's players could hardly rid their minds of Sheffield's recent last-gasp winner in the FA Cup, and the previous season the Blades had thrashed City home and away in the League. Having wrecked City's Cup dreams, they now had the chance to wreck their League dreams too.

Stoke supporters spent the long days calculating the ifs and buts, together with the various goal-average permutations. In practice, any win would do. True, a 14-13 (or greater) victory would mean Stoke losing out to Liverpool on goal-average, but such a score was, to say the least, unlikely. Former full-back Harry Brigham telephoned the Victoria Ground to wish his former teammates well, while Neil Franklin received Good Luck messages from as far afield as The Gold Coast (what is now Ghana) and Singapore.

Stoke's board announced record profits for their most successful ever season. £32,207 15s gross set a new record for any English football club. The club boasted £29,000 in the bank and had completed the purchase of the ground and an adjacent fourteen acres for future development. As the end of the accounting year was 30th April, the balance sheet did not even include the sale of Matthews.

With so much time to kill, McGrory tried to make the Sheffield United game feel just like any other. The daily training routine was broken by afternoon games of bowls or golf. When McGrory announced his team, on Tuesday 10th June, the only change was Neil Franklin, in for Frank Mountford. Frank had deputised at centre-half at Villa Park while Franklin was on the England tour. Mountford was shattered by being first reserve on this, of all occasions, and the following day handed in a transfer request. Stoke's boat was rocked once again. Despite this, McGrory remained confident: 'The players know they have a particularly hard task in front of them, but are hopeful that they will pull off the much coveted championship. It would certainly be a fitting result in view of the grand football they have played this season.'

Jock Kirton, restored to the captaincy during Franklin's England absence, reflected his team's determination: 'Supporters can rest assured that the boys will do their utmost to win this most vital match. They are fit and well and keen to gain a victory which will mean a distinction not only for the club but for the City of Stoke-on-Trent itself. The players are looking forward to hearing the encouragement of those many supporters they know are making the journey.'

The players' bus departed the Vic at 10.30am on matchday morning, besieged by photographers and autograph hunters. Not wanting to tempt fate, no special arrangements had been made to cater for a Stoke win. Either way, the players would return straight after the match. Whatever its destiny, the Championship trophy would be presented at a meeting of the Football League in London on 30th June. Stoke, at least, had already qualified for 'talent money' for the first time since its introduction. The sum ranged from £275 if Stoke finished as champions, £220 for second, £165 third and £110 fourth. Thirteen Championship medals had been struck. If the winning club needed more, they would have to apply to the League. If successful, Stoke would surely present medals to Frank Mountford and Arthur Jepson – big-part players not selected at Bramall Lane – but what about Stanley Matthews?

Over 10,000 Stoke supporters invaded Sheffield. Extra carriages were put on trains from Stoke to Derby, and thence to Sheffield. Bus companies did not have enough vehicles to satisfy demand. *En route*, the drizzle of the Potteries turned into a South Yorkshire deluge. Stoke's team coach arrived at Sheffield shortly after midday and, after a light luncheon, the players relaxed for an hour at a hotel before travelling to the ground, where they were met by great cheers from assembled Stoke fans.

The modern mind has to question whether there were any suspicious circumstances surrounding the match. This, after all, was a one-off game to win the League title. It was wide open to undesirable elements to try to influence the result, whether they might come from outside or within the competing teams. Dennis Herod believes: 'I'm sure Liverpool offered Sheffield a considerable bonus for beating us. When we got to the ground the Sheffield players had locked themselves in their own dressing room. We knew something was going on, as that was so unusual. It was quite unsettling.'

But if that is the case, one has to ask why Stoke had not tried the same ruse themselves? Sheffield, after all, had nothing ostensibly to play for, nothing to lose. But the thought appears never to have crossed their minds. Instead, Stoke were more concerned by the Matthews factor. Herod again: 'Because Stan had gone we felt a bit down. And none of us were quite the same after Stan went. Sheffield knew that. You could tell they were buoyed by it.'

Stoke knew that Sheffield United were a quality side who were only two places below them in the table. Guaranteed to finish sixth, despite their recent run of horrible results, the Blades had won the 1945-46 War League with something to spare. All this played on Stoke's players' minds as they readied themselves for their date with destiny.

Under a steady downpour, Stoke took the field for the most important game in the club's history. As both teams wore red and white stripes, City

were kitted in a new change strip of white shirts and black shorts, replacing the traditional away kit of blue and white stripes. Stoke supporters gen-
erated a Cup-tie atmosphere with an orchestra of rattles. The puddles
which littered the pitch during the kick-about merely disguised the bath of
mud which lay beneath.

By a twist of fortune, on this one game would Stoke's long-term policy of team-building through the war years be judged. It was all or nothing.
Referee Mr W H Dixon of Lincoln got the game under way and the match
began in a whirlwind. United's Jack Pickering, unmarked, hit a bobbling
cross-shot which Herod misjudged. The keeper appeared to dive in slow
motion over the ball, which bounced into the net off a post. Dennis
remembers the moment vividly: 'I was slow to get down to it and it has
given me nightmares ever since, because winning the Championship of the
First Division is the highlight of any professional footballer's career.' The
Liverpool Echo's reporter gleefully described it as, 'as soft a goal as you could
wish to see.' After just two minutes and 25 seconds, Stoke were a goal
down and had a mountain to climb.

City hurled themselves into the attack and, within two minutes fash-
ioned a classic equaliser. Steele sent George Mountford away down the
right and then raced into the box to nod down for Ormston to shoot past
United's keeper Smith. McGrory's faith in Mountford began to look justified. Five minutes gone, 1-1. The title was back within touching distance.
Then, controversy. Latham toppled Steele for what looked a cast-iron
penalty, but the referee waved away Stoke's appeals. As the playing conditions deteriorated, chances fell at both ends. Ormston shot across the face
of goal, while Herod made a last-ditch save from Collindridge's header.
Smith punched Baker's cross against Steele, but the ball flipped up and
wide. Half-time was reached with the game locked at 1-1.

It should be appreciated that the two-week wait was as agonising for
Liverpool as it was for Stoke. Worse really, because their fate was out of
their hands. Everyone would have preferred to be in Stoke's position. They,
at least, were masters of their destiny. Liverpool were helpless bystanders.
But they were in action too. On the same day, full-strength Liverpool and
Everton teams contested the Liverpool Senior Cup final in front of a
packed Anfield. The kick-off time was put back so, as the *Liverpool Echo*
reported, 'the news and result at Sheffield could be known ... for good or
ill. If Sheffield win, Duggie Livingstone, the [Blades] trainer, has promised
to "snaffle"' the ball for Reds chairman Bill McConnell. If Stoke win, no
one in Liverpool will want so much as the lace.'

The Bramall Lane pitch turned the second half into a 'mudlark', with
the rain growing ever heavier. The pitch would play its part in the title's
outcome. Four minutes after the break, John McCue, Stoke's Mr Reliable,
lost his footing while trying to intercept Pickering's crossfield aerial pass.

United's Walter Rickett was left with a clear run on Herod's goal and he restored Sheffield's lead with aplomb. Back at Anfield, 'the biggest cheer of all rent the skies when the scoreboard was changed to show Sheffield United beating Stoke 2-1.'

Stoke still had plenty of time to get the two goals they needed, but United's rearguard stood firm. Smith tipped Mountford's shot onto the bar. A goalmouth scramble ensued, in which Peppitt and Mountford impeded each other in their eagerness to put the ball into the gaping net. Liverpool's scribe described it as the 'miss of the match'. At the other end, Stoke's goal had an escape as Rickett hit the outside of the post. Then Steele's header stuck in the mud near Sheffield's goal-line, with Cox clearing desperately as Mountford closed in.

Both sides picked up casualties in this war of attrition – McCue for Stoke, and Cox, hurt attempting to tackle Baker, for United. In such a no-quarter-asked encounter on such a strength-sapping pitch, the players tired towards the end. With the minutes ticking away and Stoke needing two goals, the game subsided into a June mudbath. The Sheffield wall held firm and Stoke ran themselves to a standstill. The *Sentinel*'s verdict: 'It was no ordinary game, just as it had not been an ordinary season.'

Back at Anfield, however: 'All interest went in this match [the Merseyside derby] five minutes before the finish when Mr George Richards the Liverpool director announced over the loud-speaker that Sheffield United had beaten Stoke and that Liverpool were therefore League Champions.' The roar which greeted this made Hampden's sound like a whimper. At the final whistle the Kop invaded the pitch to celebrate Liverpool's fifth championship, and their first since 1923, lifting their heroes shoulder-high.

In contrast, the scenes in Stoke's dressing room after the players had trudged dejectedly off the pitch were sombre in the extreme. Dennis Herod recalls the players' emotions all too vividly: 'The atmosphere was dreadful. I can't tell you how depressing it was. Actually it took me six months to get over it.' The players hurt to the core and it still cuts deep to this day. When your author asked him how he personally felt, Dennis simply replied: 'That's a stupid question.' He then paused for a long time before continuing: 'I can tell you that it was the longest and quietest bus journey home that night.'

Stoke have never come so close to winning the Championship again.

		P	W	D	L	F	A	(GA)	Pts
1	Liverpool	42	25	7	10	84	52	(1.62)	57
2	Manchester U	42	22	12	8	95	54	(1.76)	56
3	Wolves	42	25	6	11	98	56	(1.75)	56
4	Stoke	42	24	7	12	90	53	(1.70)	55

At the end of any such mind-numbing campaign, players and supporters look back and relive all those 'What might have been' moments. In a footballing sense, accusing fingers pointed to conceding that last-minute equaliser at Everton, the late defeat at Huddersfield Town, and the goalless draw with Sunderland. But inevitably the inquests focused on Stoke's preparation for that final, crucial game itself. Neil Franklin says: 'The trouble was, of course, nerves. We soon had to forget the mud because Pickering scored in the third minute. That was a shock.' Dennis Herod has a different slant: 'I mean, how could he sell Matthews? I am not taking away anything from McGrory who did a great deal for Stoke City, but he wanted the limelight himself and was jealous of players like Stan and Neil Franklin. To sell the best forward in the world to Blackpool was sheer stupidity. What a tragedy.'

So, would Stan's presence on that gluepot pitch at Bramall Lane have made a difference? No one can ever tell. But suffice to say that big-game players – and there was no bigger-game player than Stan Matthews – exist specifically for the purpose of winning vital games. Without Stan, the team lacked the inner belief which all champions need.

That rain-drenched afternoon in Sheffield marked the high-point of Stoke City's fortunes under Bob McGrory. Almost at once the team began to break up. So many players' careers had been lost to the war that, almost without noticing, McGrory's 'Babes' were past their prime and on a slippery downward slope. In the immediate aftermath of the defeat at Sheffield, McGrory was linked to the post of manager of Portsmouth, following the resignation of Jack Tinn. McGrory politely declined: 'I have no intention of leaving Stoke City and in any case my present contract has another three years to run.'

But despite McGrory's pursuit of England's centre-forward Tommy Lawton and inside-forward Wilf Mannion, and his breaking of the club transfer record twice in September 1947, Stoke struggled to recapture their form which had taken them so close to the championship. Early in the 1947-48 season Freddie Steele damaged his knee cartilage against Charlton. It was ten years to the month since a similar injury had occurred against the same goalkeeper, Sam Bartram. Steele would never be the same player again. Both Stoke's club record signings, Tom Kiernan and Jimmy McAlinden, suffered debilitating injuries within weeks of arriving at the Victoria Ground. Stoke finished fifteenth.

By 1950, Neil Franklin and George Mountford had flown the Stoke nest to try their luck as footballing outlaws in Colombia. McGrory resigned in May 1952 and Stoke were relegated to the Second Division a year later.

With hindsight, it can be seen that the club's relentless downturn in fortunes can be traced directly to the sale of Stanley Matthews and Stoke's failure to win that fateful match at Bramall Lane. This was the legacy of the decade-long spat between manager and star.

Dennis Herod has had over 50 years to ponder what Matthews' departure meant to his team: 'It's quite straightforward really. McGrory's jealousy of Stan Matthews' fame cost Stoke their best chance of the First Division title. After he left the magic was gone, the spell was broken.'

~ Guide to Seasonal Summaries ~

Col 1: Match number (for league fixtures); Round (for cup-ties).
e.g. 4R means 'Fourth round replay.'

Col 2: Date of the fixture and whether Home (H), Away (A), or Neutral (N).

Col 3: Opposition.

Col 4: Attendances. Home gates appear in roman; Away gates in *italics*.
Figures in **bold** indicate the largest and smallest gates, at home and away.
Average home and away attendances appear after the final league match.

Col 5: Respective league positions of Stoke and opponents after the game.
Stoke's position appears on the top line in roman.
Their opponents' position appears on the second line in *italics*.
For cup-ties, the division and position of opponents is provided.
e.g. 2:12 means the opposition are twelfth in Division 2.

Col 6: The top line shows the result: W(in), D(raw), or L(ose).
The second line shows Stoke's cumulative points total.

Col 7: The match score, Stoke's given first.
Scores in **bold** show Stoke's biggest league win and heaviest defeat.

Col 8: The half-time score, Stoke's given first.

Col 9: The top line shows Stoke's scorers and times of goals in roman.
The second line shows opponents' scorers and times of goals in *italics*.
A 'p' after the time of a goal denotes a penalty; 'og' an own-goal.
The third line gives the name of the match referee.

Team line-ups: Stoke line-ups appear on top line, irrespective of whether
they are home or away. Opposition teams are on the second line in *italics*.
Players of either side who are sent off are marked 'l'
Stoke players making their league debuts are displayed in **bold**.

NB: Where players or referees are unknown, these are marked 'unknown'.
Unknown goalscorers or goal-times are left blank.

LEAGUE DIVISION 1

Manager: Bob McGrory

SEASON 1939-40

No	Date	Att	Pos	Pt	F-A	H-T	Scorers, Times, and Referees	1	2	3	4	5	6	7	8	9	10	11
1	H CHARLTON 26/8	16,268		W 2	4-0	2-0	Soo 12, Smith 31, 84, Sale 75	McMahon	Brigham	Tennant	Massey	Mould	Soo	Matthews	Smith	Sale	Gallacher	Baker
							Ref: G Dutton	Bartram	Turner	Oakes James	Green	Oakes John	Wright	Wilkinson	Brown	Tadman	Welsh	Hobbis
2	H BOLTON 28/8	13,067		L 2	1-2	0-1	Gallacher 65	McMahon	Brigham	Tennant	Massey	Mould	Soo	Matthews	Smith	Sale	Gallacher	Baker
							Hunt 35, Rothwell 53	Hanson	Winter	Hubbick	Goslin	Hurst	Taylor	Geldard	Howe	Hunt	Westwood	Rothwell
							Ref: H Hartles											
3	A MIDDLESBROUGH 2/9	12,088	9 / 21	D 3	2-2	0-1	Sale 56, 65	McMahon	Brigham	Tennant	Tutin	Massey	Soo	Matthews	Smith	Sale	Gallacher	Baker
							Fenton 42, 48	Cumming	Laking	Stuart	McKenzie	Baxter	Murphy D	Chadwick	Mannion	Fenton	Yorston	Milne
							Ref: J Greenan											

A sedate opening livens up when Bartram tips Sale's header over. Soo rifles in off the bar from 20 yards as Jimmy Seed's men back off. Don Welsh limps off (16). Hobbis hits a post. Smith twice profits as Bartram pushes out fierce Baker and Sale drives. Sale nods in Matthews' cross.

City are slip-shod. Two defensive errors gift goals to Charles Foweraker's side. Hunt nets calmly and Rothwell slots after McMahon drops the ball. Gallacher heads a corker, but Stoke fail to get going. Sale hits Hanson's legs. Massey picks up a leg injury. First home loss for 10 months.

Fenton has a goal disallowed for offside before rattling in a 20-yarder. Yorston misses a penalty after Fenton is fouled (20). Fenton nods home Chadwick's cross. Sale drops deeper to run onto the ball. He beats two to round Cumming. Matthews dummies a corner and Sale's shot rips in.

Football League suspended owing to outbreak of World War II

WAR LEAGUE WESTERN DIVISION

Each match is shown on two lines: the upper line is the club's line-up and scorers; the lower (italic) line is the opponents' line-up and scorers. Positions run 1–11 (GK, RB, LB, RH, CH, LH, OR, IR, CF, IL, OL).

#	Vn	Opponent	Att	Date	Res	HT	1	2	3	4	5	6	7	8	9	10	11	Scorers
1	A	EVERTON	3,998	21/10	D 4-4	1-2	Jones	Brigham	Griffiths J	Tutin	Soo	Mould	Smith	Peppitt	Sale	Liddle	Ormston	Sale 34, 53p, 90, Liddle 80
							Sagar	*Jackson*	*Greenhalgh*	*Lidley*	*Watson*	*Jones TG*	*Gillick*	*Bentham*	*Lawton*	*Stevenson*	*Boyes*	*Stev' 7, Boyes 15, Law' 46, Jones 50*
2	H	STOCKPORT	2,100	28/10	W 4-2	1-1	Jones	Brigham	Griffiths J	Tutin	Soo	Mould	Smith	Peppitt	Sale	Liddle	Ormston	Matthews 43, Soo 54, Sale 61, Orm' 80
							Hall	*Topping*	*Owens*	*Reid*	*Lumby*	*Titterington*	*Bagley*	*Grove*	*Catterick*	*Howe*	*Sullivan L*	*Catterick 34, Howe 58*
3	A	WREXHAM	3,935	4/11	D 4-4	2-1	Jones	Brigham	Griffiths J	Tutin	Soo	Mould	Smith	Peppitt	Sale	Liddle	Ormston	Peppitt 1, 7, Ormston 68, Smith 86
							McMahon	*Cooper*	*Screen*	*Tunney*	*Briggs*	*Snow*	*Hughes*	*Rogers*	*Roberts*	*Redfern*	*Brown*	*Roberts 5, 50, 54, Redfern 90*
4	H	NEW BRIGHTON	2,420	11/11	W 4-1	1-0	Wilkinson	Brigham	Griffiths J	Soo	Kirton	Mould	Smith	Matthews	Sale	Liddle	Ormston	Sale 21, 55, Ormston 81, 89
							Hawthorne	*Ratcliffe*	*Buxton*	*Murphy*	*Davis*	*Hughes S*	*Small*	*Waring*	*Frost*	*Rawcliffe*	*Hanson*	*Frost 85*
5	A	MANCHESTER C	8,038	18/11	D 1-1	1-1	Jones	Brigham	Griffiths J	Tutin	Soo	Mould	Smith	Peppitt	Sale	Liddle	Ormston	Sale 35p
							Robinson	*Barkas*	*Westwood*	*Percival*	*Bray*	*Cardwell*	*Blackshaw*	*Herd*	*Heale*	*Doherty*	*Walsh*	*Percival 25p*
6	H	CHESTER	1,425	25/11	W 2-0	0-0	Jones	Brigham	Griffiths J	Massey	Soo	Mould	Peppitt	Matthews	Sale	Liddle	Ormston	Sale 78, Peppitt 86
							Shortt	*Brown*	*Common*	*Howarth*	*Cole*	*Walters*	*Horsman*	*McGough*	*McMahon*	*Leyfield*	*Sanders*	
7	A	CREWE	3,403	2/12	L 2-4	1-1	Jones	Brigham	Griffiths J	Massey	Soo	Mould	Peppitt	Liddle	Sale	Ormston	Baker	Sale 11p, 88
							Gilchrist	*Brown*	*Dyer*	*Cooper*	*Still*	*Cope*	*Waring*	*Rice*	*Stevens*	*Cobourne*	*Foreman*	*Rice 30, Stevens 75, Cob' 76, Waring 89*
8	H	LIVERPOOL	1,269	9/12	W 3-1	2-0	Jones	Brigham	Griffiths J	Hampson	Soo	Mould	Matthews	Peppitt	Sale	Liddle	Ormston	Liddle 22, Matthews 40, Sale 75
							Riley	*Cooper*	*Tennant*	*Bushby*	*McInnes*	*Bush*	*Nieuwenhuys*	*Taylor*	*Fagan*	*Paterson G*	*Van den Berg*	*Unknown*
9	H	TRANMERE	714	6/1	W 1-0	0-0	Jones	Brigham	Griffiths J	Massey	Soo	Mould	Matthews	Peppitt	Sale	Antonio	Ormston	Peppitt 75
							Daniels	*Anderson*	*Owen*	*Davies*	*Byrom*	*Price WB*	*Oldham*	*Bellis*	*Sloan*	*Bridges*	*Bellis*	
10	A	MANCHESTER U	2,884	20/1	L 3-4	2-0	Westland D	Brigham	Soo	Massey	Liddle	Mould	Bowyer	Peppitt	Sale	Baker	Ormston	Peppitt 40, Sale 45, Bowyer 46
							Breedon	*Redwood*	*Roughton*	*Warner*	*Carey*	*McKay*	*Kilshaw*	*Butt*	*Jones*	*Pearson*	*Mitten*	*Jones 48, 87, Butt 50, Pearson 60*
11	H	EVERTON	3,910	10/2	W 1-0	1-0	Jones	Brigham	Griffiths J	Soo	Kirton	Mould	Matthews	Peppitt	Sale	Bell	Ormston	Sale 28
							Wilkinson	*Jackson*	*Greenhalgh*	*Lindley*	*Watson*	*Bentham*	*Gillick*	*Sweeny*	*Pearson*	*Stevenson*	*Boyes*	
12	A	STOCKPORT	2,037	24/2	W 5-1	1-0	Jones	Brigham	Scrimshaw	Massey	Soo	Mould	Matthews	Peppitt	Sale	Liddle	Ormston	Soo 5, Peppitt 49, 67, 69, 87
							McDonough	*Topping*	*Owens*	*Read*	*Titterington*	*Toseland*	*Owens*	*Essex*	*Catterick*	*Bagley*	*Howe*	*Bagley 55*
13	H	WREXHAM	2,974	2/3	W 3-1	2-0	Westland D	Brigham	Scrimshaw	Massey	Kirton	Mould	Liddle	Bellis	Steele	Soo	Ormston	Ormston 35, 37, Steele 54
							Jones	*Tunney*	*Cook*	*Read*	*Kirton*	*Snow*	*Hughes*	*Williams*	*Coen*	*Rogers*	*Brown*	*Rogers 86*
14	A	NEW BRIGHTON	1,357	9/3	L 1-3	0-2	Westland D	Brigham	Scrimshaw	Massey	Soo	Mould	Matthews	Liddle	Sale	Baker	Ormston	Baker 62
							Hawthorn	*Ratcliffe*	*Buxton*	*Davis*	*Murphy*	*Hughes S*	*Davis*	*Malam*	*Fost*	*Waring*	*Hanson*	*Waring 30, 60, Westland D (og) 32*
15	H	MANCHESTER C	3,520	16/3	W 2-1	1-1	Jones	Clark	Scrimshaw	Liddle	Soo	Mould	Peppitt	Matthews	Sale	Westland J	Smith	Smith 10, Sale 86
							Swift	*Clark*	*Westwood*	*Percival*	*Walsh*	*Cardwell*	*Blackshaw*	*Herd*	*Heale*	*Emptage*	*Rudd*	*Herd 44p*
16	A	CHESTER	4,116	23/3	D 3-3	1-1	Jones	Brigham	Scrimshaw	Massey	Soo	Mould	Peppitt	Matthews	Sale	Emptage	Ormston	Peppitt 15, 61, Ormston 52
							Shortt	*Hollis H*	*Brown*	*Brown*	*Butcher*	*Walters*	*Horsman*	*Astbury*	*Yates*	*Pendergast*	*Sanders*	*Yates 38, Horsman 58, Sanders 85*
17	H	PORT VALE	9,450	25/3	W 5-1	3-0	Jones	Brigham	Scrimshaw	Massey	Cumberlidge	Mould	Liddle	Peppitt	Sale	Steele	Ormston	Orm' 30, 70, Grif' H 39, 45 (ogs), Sale 80
							Jepson	*Rowe*	*Griffiths J*	*Griffiths J*	*Cumberlidge*	*Griffiths H*	*Butcher*	*Higgins*	*Pursell*	*Griffiths P*	*Tunnicliffe*	*Roberts 57*
18	H	CREWE	2,460	30/3	D 1-1	1-1	Jones	Brigham	Scrimshaw	Tutin	Liddle	Mould	Matthews	Peppitt	Sale	Steele	Ormston	Sale 1
							Poskett	*Dyer*	*Scrimshaw*	*Kneale*	*Still*	*Turner*	*Still*	*Steele*	*Baker*	*Griffiths P*	*Johnson*	*Stevens 17*
19	A	LIVERPOOL	8,130	6/4	W 2-1	1-1	Jones	Brigham	Scrimshaw	Soo	Kirton	Mould	Matthews	Peppitt	Sale	Steele	Ormston	Steele 44, Peppitt 80
							Dyer	*Riley*	*Scrimshaw*	*Ramsden*	*McInnes*	*Brown*	*Soo*	*Rice*	*Fagan*	*Cobourne*	*Liddell*	*Balmer 8*
20	A	PORT VALE	3,053	6/5	W 2-1	1-1	Jones	Brigham	Scrimshaw	Tutin	Soo	Mould	Matthews	Steele	Sale	Sale	Ormston	Sale 33, Steele 50
							Jepson	*Pursell*	*Scrimshaw*	*Scrimshaw*	*Brown*	*Ware*	*Soo*	*Balmer*	*Blunt*	*Carney L*	*Bellis*	*Roberts 42*
21	A	TRANMERE	2,434	13/5	L 1-5	1-4	Jones	Brigham	Oakes	Tutin	Hodgson	Mould	Smith	Peppitt	Mountford	Sale	Mitton	Mountford 6 [Yates 44]
							Anderson	*Teasdale*	*Oakes*	*Howarth*	*Hodgson*	*Walters*	*Owen*	*Jones B*	*Yates*	*Griffiths*	*Mitton*	*Jones B 15, Griffiths 27, 70, Mitton 36, Teasdale 45*
22	H	MANCHESTER U	3,227	25/5	W 3-2	2-1	Brigham	Brigham	Oakes	Massey	Soo	Mould	Matthews	Peppitt	Sale	Liddle	Ormston	Peppitt 36, 61, Ormston 45
							Goodall	*Redwood*	*Gemmell*	*Anderson*	*Manley*	*Briggs*	*Oakes*	*Dougal*	*Burdett*	*Pearson*	*Mitten*	*Burdett 25, 85*

WAR LEAGUE CUP

Manager: Bob McGrory **SEASON 1939-40**

War League Cup

No	V	Date	Opposition	Result (HT)	Scorers	Att	1	2	3	4	5	6	7	8	9	10	11
1:1	A	20/4	NEW BRIGHTON	W 4-1 (0-0)	Steele 54, 59, 68, Sale 83 / *Frost 86p*	5,289	Wilkinson / *Hawthorn*	Brigham / *Ratcliffe*	Mould / *Hughes S*	Tennant / *Buxton*	Soo / *Anderson*	Kirton / *Davis*	Matthews / *Main*	Peppitt / *Malam*	Steele / *Frost*	Sale / *Waring*	Ormston / *Small*
1:2	H	27/4	NEW BRIGHTON	W 2-1 (1-0)	Sale 12, Steele 86 / *Frost 48*	3,654	Wilkinson / *Hawthorn*	Brigham / *Ratcliffe*	Mould / *Hughes S*	Tennant / *Buxton*	Soo / *Davies*	Kirton / *Davis*	Matthews / *Small*	Peppitt / *Malam*	Steele / *Frost*	Sale / *Waring*	Ormston / *Tomkin*
2:1	A	4/5	BARROW	W 2-0 (1-0)	Steele 37, 62	11,870	Jones / *Phillipson*	Brigham / *Hollingsworth*	Mould / *Hall*	Oakes / *Simpson*	Soo / *Hartley*	Kirton / *Davies*	Matthews / *Samuel*	Peppitt / *Cargill*	Steele / *Harris*	Sale / *McCormick*	Ormston / *Hamilton*
2:2	H	11/5	BARROW	W 6-1 (2-0)	Sale 9, 30, Ormston 46, Steele 51, Harris 70 / *[Peppitt 86, Liddle 88]*	2,898	Wilkinson / *Phillipson*	Brigham / *Hollingsworth*	Mould / *Hall*	Tennant / *Simpson*	Soo / *Hartley*	Kirton / *Alcock*	Liddle / *Samuel*	Peppitt / *Cargill*	Steele / *Harris*	Sale / *Davies*	Ormston / *McCormick*
3	A	18/5	EVERTON	L 0-1 (0-0)	*Lawton 85p*	3,557	Jones / *Sagar*	Brigham / *Jackson*	Mould / *Jones*	Oakes / *Greenhalgh*	Franklin / *Mercer*	Soo / *Watson*	Matthews / *Caskie*	Peppitt / *Bentham*	Sale / *Lawton*	Liddle / *Stevenson*	Ormston / *Boyes*

Friendlies

V	Date	Opposition	Result (HT)	Scorers	Att	1	2	3	4	5	6	7	8	9	10	11
H	19/8	WOLVES	L 2-4 (0-2)	Sale 68, 82 / *Dorsett 10, 15, 57, Galley 54*	6,440	Westland D / *Scott*	Brigham / *Morris*	Mould / *Rooney*	Tennant / *Taylor*	Soo / *Gardiner*	Kirton / *Galley*	Matthews / *Maguire*	Smith / *McIntosh*	Sale / *Westcott*	Gallacher / *Dorsett*	Ormston / *Mullen*
H	16/9	COVENTRY	W 3-1 (1-1)	Baker 19, Peppitt 53, Sale 89 / *Lowrie 31*	4,647	McMahon / *Morgan*	Brigham / *Tooze*	Mould / *Mason*	Tennant / *Elliott*	Tutin / *Frith*	Soo / *Bolleau*	Matthews / *Ashall*	Peppitt / *Lowrie*	Sale / *Crawley*	Baker / *Davidson*	Ormston / *Coen*
H	23/9	PORT VALE	W 3-2 (2-0)	Sale 1, Ormston 36, Baker 63 / *Jones 60, Beresford 88*	4,512	Martin / *Jepson*	Brigham / *Rowe*	Mould / *Griffiths*	Oldham / *Cumberlidge*	Massey / *Hannah*	Soo / *Smith*	Matthews / *Triner*	Peppitt / *Roberts*	Sale / *Jones*	Ormston / *Nolan*	Baker / *Beresford R*
A	30/9	WEST BROM	L 0-6 (0-2)	*Jones E 8, 52, Jones HJ 40, 81, 89, [Johnson 71]*	1,516	Martin / *Saunders*	Brigham / *White*	Mould / *Gripton*	Oldham / *Shaw*	Massey / *Sankey*	Soo / *McNab*	Peppitt / *Jones E*	Antonio / *Banks*	Sale / *Jones HJ*	Ormston / *Connolly*	Baker / *Johnson*
H	7/10	MANCHESTER U	D 2-2 (1-1)	Antonio 27, Warner (og) 49 / *Pearson 2, Hanlon 55*	3,148	Wilkinson / *Breedon*	Brigham / *Redwood*	Mould / *Voce*	Oldham / *Roughton*	Massey / *Warner*	Kirton / *McKay*	Matthews / *Bryant*	Smith / *Carey*	Sale / *Hanlon*	Antonio / *Pearson*	Baker / *Wrigglesw'th*
H	14/10	BIRMINGHAM	W 3-2 (2-0)	Westland J 17, 60, Smith 28 / *Jones 65, Batty 68*	2,171	Wilkinson / *Wheeler*	Brigham / *Quinton*	Mould / *Turner*	Griffiths J / *Jennings*	Soo / *Bye*	Kirton / *Devey*	Matthews / *Edwards*	Smith / *Duckhouse*	Westland J / *Jones*	Sale / *Craven*	Ormston / *Batty*
H	16/12	SHEFFIELD WED	W 2-1 (1-0)	Liddle 10, Sale 58 / *Ward 63*	2,035	Jones / *Smith*	Brigham / *Ashley*	Mould / *Hanford*	Griffiths J / *Lester*	Hampson / *Russell*	Soo / *Walker*	Matthews / *Massarella*	Peppitt / *Robinson*	Sale / *Hunt*	Liddle / *Millership*	Ormston / *Ward*
A	25/12	BOLTON	L 0-3 (0-1)	*Cunliffe 25, Sidebottom 70, Hunt 85*	1,707	Jones / *Goodall*	Brigham / *Eastwood*	Mould / *Atkinson*	Griffiths J / *Hubbick*	Hampson / *Whalley*	Soo / *Taylor*	Matthews / *Jones E*	Peppitt / *Cunliffe*	Sale / *Hurst*	Liddle / *Sidebottom*	Ormston / *Connor*
H	26/12	BOLTON	L 1-5 (0-0)	Ormston 47	2,234	Jones / *Goodall*	Brigham / *Eastwood*	Mould / *Atkinson*	Glover / *Hubbick*	Franklin / *Whalley*	Soo / *Connor*	Peppitt / *Jones WE*	Liddle / *Cunliffe*	Ormston / *Hurst*	Baker / *Sidebottom*	McCue / *Jones S*
A	30/12	BURY	L 6-7 (1-1)	Sale 42, 59, 62, Bak' 72, Mat' 75, Pep' 78 / *Burd' 16, 68, 89, Dou' 57, 61, 70, Jones 69*	700	Jones / *Bradshaw*	Brigham / *Robinson*	Mould / *McGowan*	Glover / *Gemmell*	Hampson / *Livingstone*	Soo / *Halton*	Matthews / *Jones*	Peppitt / *Davies*	Sale / *Burdett*	Ormston / *Dougal*	Baker / *Hulbert*
A	13/1	PRESTON	L 1-2 (1-1)	Sale 26p / *O'Donnell H 2, Beattie R 82*	956	Jones / *Holdcroft*	Brigham / *Gallimore*	Mould / *Smith*	Griffiths J / *Williams*	Massey / *Shankly*	Soo / *Batey*	Matthews / *Dougal*	Peppitt / *Mutch*	Sale / *O'Donnell F*	Liddle / *Beattie R*	Ormston / *O'Donnell H*
A	22/3	CHESTERFIELD	L 1-3 (1-0)	Peppitt 17 / *Jones 50p, 60p, Milligan 74*	4,525	Westland D / *Middleton*	Brigham / *Watson*	Mould / *Booker*	Oldham / *Kidd*	Tutin / *Brindle*	Massey / *Sutherland*	Peppitt / *Garrett*	Liddle / *Hartley*	Sale / *Milligan*	Ormston / *Jones*	Baker / *Sinclair*
A	13/4	NOTT'M FOREST	W 3-2 (2-2)	Sale 20, 37, 55 / *Trim 25, Drury 44*	2,224	Wilkinson / *Westland D*	Brigham / *Challinor*	Mould / *Graham*	McCue / *Brawley*	Soo / *Barks*	Kirton / *Smith*	Peppitt / *Nixon G*	Liddle / *Hinchcliffe*	Steele / *Starling*	Sale / *Drury*	Ormston / *Trim*
A	8/6	ROCHDALE	W 3-2 (1-1)	Mountford 15, Basnett 50, Sale 78 / *Colquhoun 40, Richardson 54*	2,224	Bridges / *Carey*	Glover / *Smith*	Franklin / *Brown*	McCue / *Byron*	Hampson / *Eastwood*	Soo / *Warburton*	Basnett / *Colquhoun*	Bowyer / *Hunt*	Mountford / *Richardson*	Sale / *Duff*	Longland / *Hornby*

Division 1 on outbreak of war

		P	W	D	L	F	A	Pts
1	Blackpool	3	3	0	0	5	2	6
2	Sheffield Utd	3	2	1	0	3	1	5
3	Arsenal	3	2	1	0	8	4	5
4	Liverpool	3	2	0	1	6	3	4
5	Everton	3	1	2	0	5	4	4
6	Bolton	3	2	0	1	6	5	4
7	Derby	3	2	0	1	3	3	4
8	Charlton	3	2	0	1	4	4	4
9	STOKE	3	1	1	1	7	4	3
10	Manchester U	3	1	1	1	5	3	3
11	Brentford	3	1	1	1	3	3	3
12	Chelsea	3	1	1	1	4	4	3
13	Grimsby	3	1	1	1	2	4	3
14	Aston Villa	3	1	0	2	3	3	2
15	Sunderland	3	1	0	2	6	7	2
16	Wolves	3	0	2	1	3	4	2
17	Huddersfield	3	1	0	2	2	3	2
18	Portsmouth	3	1	0	2	3	5	2
19	Preston	3	0	2	1	0	2	2
20	Blackburn	3	0	1	2	3	5	1
21	Middlesbrough	3	0	1	2	3	8	1
22	Leeds	3	0	1	2	0	2	1

War League Western Division

		P	W	D	L	F	A	Pts
1	STOKE	22	13	5	4	57	41	31
2	Liverpool	22	12	5	5	66	40	29
3	Everton	22	12	4	6	64	33	28
4	Manchester U	22	14	0	8	74	41	28
5	Manchester C	22	12	4	6	73	41	28
6	Wrexham	22	10	5	7	45	50	25
7	New Brighton	22	10	3	9	55	52	23
8	Port Vale	22	10	2	10	52	56	22
9	Chester	22	7	5	10	40	51	19
10	Crewe	22	6	1	15	44	79	13
11	Stockport	22	4	3	15	45	79	11
12	Tranmere	22	2	3	17	41	93	7

Appearances and Goals

Player	Appearances Lge	WL	WC	Frie	Goals Lge	WL	WC	Frie	Tot
Antonio, George								1	1
Baker, Frank	3	4		6		1		3	4
Basnett, Fred (A)		1		1				1	1
Bowyer, Frank		1		1					
Bridges, Pat		1		1					
Brigham, Harry	3	22	5	13		2			2
Franklin, Neil		1		2					
Gallagher, Patsy		3		3					
Glover, Stanley		1				1			1
Griffiths, Jack*		8		3					
Hampson, Eric				4					
Jones, Doug*		15	2	5					
Kirton, Jock		4	4	4					
Liddle, Bobby		20	2	7		2	1	1	4
Longland, Eric*		1							
McCue, Jock		1		3					
McMahon, Patrick	3		1						
Martin, John				2					
Massey, Alf		10		4					
Matthews, Stan	3	12	4	9		2		1	3
Mould, Billy	2	22	5	13					
Mountford, Frank		1	1	1					2
Oakes, John*		2		4					
Oldham, George				1					
Ormston, Alec		21	5	12		10	1	2	13
Peppitt, Syd		20	5	10		14	1	3	18
Sale, Tommy	3	20	5	14	3	17	4	13	37
Scrimshaw, Charlie*		10							
Smith, Clem	3	7		3		2	2	1	5
Soo, Frank	3	20	5	12		1		2	3
Steele, Freddie		5	4	1		3	7		10
Tennant, Jack		3	3	2					
Tutin, Arthur	1	7		2					
Westland, Doug		4		2					
Westland, Jim		1		1					
Wilkinson, Norman		2	3	3				2	2
(own-goals)									3
37 players used	**33**	**242**	**55**	**154**	**7**	**57**	**14**	**30**	**108**

* guest players

SOUTHERN REGIONAL LEAGUE — Manager: Bob McGrory — SEASON 1940-41

No	Date	Venue	Team	Att Pos	Pt	F-A	H-T	1	2	3	4	5	6	7	8	9	10	11	Scorers, Times, and Referees
1	31/8	H	NOTTS CO	2,421	W	4-1	3-0	Bridges	Brigham	Griffiths J	Hampson	Franklin	Soo	Matthews	Peppitt	Mountford	Sale	Liddle	Mountford 17, 43, 73, Sale 42
								Sidlow	*Nicholas*	*Beattie A*	*Massie*	*Iverson*	*Keen*	*Crooks*	*Edwards*	*Broome*	*Fenton*	*Duncan*	*Crooks 53*
2	7/9	A	NOTTS CO	3,000	L	2-3	2-1	Bridges	Brigham	Griffiths J	Hampson	Mould	Kirton	Matthews	Bowyer	Steele	Sale	Liddle	Sale 7, Bowyer 20
								Sidlow	*Sneddon*	*Beattie A*	*Corkhill*	*Nicholas*	*Keen*	*Crooks*	*Fenton*	*McEwan*	*Beattie R*	*Duncan*	*Duncan 40, Fenton 47, McEwan 81*
3	14/9	A	MANSFIELD	3,120	W	3-2	2-2	Bridges	Brigham	Griffiths J	Hampson	Franklin	Soo	Matthews	Peppitt	Mountford	Sale	Liddle	Mountford 25, Bowyer 31, Liddle 80
								Downham	*Stimpson*	*Barke*	*Corkhill*	*McCall*	*Simms*	*Hillard*	*Egan*	*Hubbard*	*Flowers*	*Beaumont*	*Egan 16, 20*
4	21/9	H	MANSFIELD	2,000	W	5-0	0-0	Bridges	Brigham	McCue	Hampson	Franklin	Soo	Matthews	Peppitt	Mountford	Sale	Liddle	Mountford 57, 77 Bowyer 60, 72 [Liddle 75]
								Hubbard	*Stimpson*	*McCall*	*Corkhill*	*Barke*	*Mills*	*Harkin*	*Simms*	*Egan*	*Flower*	*Beaumont*	
5	28/9	A	LEICESTER	3,213	L	0-1	0-0	Bridges	Glover	McCue	Hampson	Franklin	Soo	Matthews	Peppitt	Mountford	Sale	Liddle	
								Calvert	*Frame*	*Jones*	*Sharman*	*Heywood*	*Howe*	*Wright*	*Smith J*	*Dewis*	*Liddle D*	*Mullen*	*Liddle D 52*
6	5/10	H	LEICESTER	2,814	D	3-3	3-2	Bridges	Glover	McCue	Hampson	Franklin	Soo	Matthews	Peppitt	Mountford	Sale	Liddle	Mountford 21, 24, Sale 35
								Calvert	*Frame*	*Howe*	*Sharman*	*Heywood*	*Johnston*	*Wright*	*Smith J*	*Dewis*	*Liddle D*	*Mullen*	*Dewis 5, Liddle D 44, Heywood 85p*
7	12/10	A	WEST BROM	4,091	W	1-0	0-0	Bridges	Brigham	McCue	Hampson	Franklin	Soo	Matthews	Peppitt	Mountford	Sale	Liddle	Bowyer 69
								Adams	*Bassett*	*Shaw*	*Sankey*	*Gripton*	*Edwards*	*Newsome*	*Clarke*	*Richardson*	*Connelly*	*Johnson*	
8	19/10	H	WEST BROM	3,441	L	1-3	1-1	Bridges	Brigham	McCue	Hampson	Franklin	Soo	Matthews	Peppitt	Mountford	Sale	Liddle	Soo 45
								Adams	*Kinsell*	*Shaw*	*Sankey*	*Gripton*	*Edwards*	*Heaslegrave*	*Clarke*	*Richardson*	*Connelly*	*Johnson*	*Richardson 10, 70, Johnson 72*
9	26/10	A	NOTT'M FOR	1,500	D	3-3	2-2	Bridges	Brigham	McCue	Hampson	Franklin	Soo	Liddle	Peppitt	Mountford	Sale	Longland	Mountford 15, 62, Bowyer 41
								Rutherford	*Brook*	*Challinor*	*Barks*	*Rawson*	*Kirton*	*Wood*	*Crisp*	*Smith*	*Antonio*	*Langton*	*Langton 30, Wood 36, Antonio 80*
10	2/11	H	NOTT'M FOR	714	W	5-0	1-0	Bridges	Brigham	McCue	Hampson	Franklin	Soo	Liddle	Peppitt	Mountford	Sale	Smith	Soo 42p, 68 Mountford 65, Bowyer 72, [Sale 88]
								Rutherford	*Brook*	*Challinor*	*Barks*	*Rawson*	*Kirton*	*Hunter*	*Crisp*	*Smith*	*Antonio*	*Langton*	
11	9/11	H	BIRMINGHAM	4,980	W	5-0	5-0	Bridges	Brigham	McCue	Hampson	Franklin	Soo	Ormston	Peppitt	Mountford	Sale	Smith	Mountford 10, 15, 25 Ormston 20, 41
								Wheeler	*Quinton*	*Hughes*	*Bye*	*Turner*	*Harris*	*Brown*	*Gardner*	*Trigg*	*Jones*	*Craven*	
12	16/11	A	BIRMINGHAM	1,462	L	2-6	0-4	Bridges	Brigham	McCue	Hampson	Franklin	Soo	Liddle	Peppitt	Mountford	Sale	Smith	Liddle 50, Smith 54
								Merrick	*Quinton*	*Hughes*	*Devey*	*Turner*	*Harris*	*Brown*	*Jennings*	*Trigg*	*Jones*	*Craven*	*Trigg 15, 20, 26, 41, 48, Craven 51*
13	7/12	H	CARDIFF	2,000	W	5-1	2-1	Bridges	Brigham	McCue	Hampson	Franklin	Soo	Matthews	Bowyer	Mountford	Steele	Sale	Mountford 14, Sale 44, 60, Steele 85, [Bowyer 87]
								Pritchard	*Pugh R*	*Springthorpe*	*Baker*	*Pugh J*	*Allen*	*Steggles*	*James*	*Parker*	*Wood*	*Moore*	*Steggles 17*
14	14/12	A	CARDIFF	800	L	0-4	0-1	Bridges	Brigham	McCue	Hampson	Franklin	Soo	Liddle	Bowyer	Sale	Wordley	Mitchell	
								Pritchard	*Burns*	*Granville*	*Baker*	*Pugh*	*Steggles*	*Parker*	*James*	*Morris*	*Tovin*	*Moore*	*Morris 12, James 60, 75, 82*
15	21/12	H	WALSALL	540	D	2-2	1-1	Bridges	Brigham	McCue	Hampson	Franklin	Soo	Matthews	Peppitt	Mountford	Liddle	Sale	Soo 43, Liddle 65
								Biddlestone	*Shelton*	*Male*	*Richsrds*	*Morgan*	*Godfrey*	*Hanckocks*	*Brown*	*Vinall*	*Starling*	*Rowley*	*Starling 2, Rowley 60*
16	25/12	A	MANSFIELD	3,450	L	2-7	2-4	Bridges	Brigham	McCue	Hampson	Franklin	Liddle	Smith	Bowyer	Mountford	Sale	Longland	Mountford 18, Smith 22, [Robertson]
								Rigby	*Johnstone*	*Poyser*	*McCall*	*Barke*	*Harkin*	*Unknown*	*Robertson*	*Rickards*	*Hubbard*	*Egan*	*Ric' 3, Harkin 7, Hubbard, Egan, McCall*

No.	V	Opponent	Date	Att	Res	Score	HT	Scorers (team / opponents)
17	A	WALSALL	28/12	3,518	L	1-5	1-1	Steele 18 / *Vinall 43, 70, 88, Rowley 49, 72*
18	H	NOTTS CO	25/1	300	D	2-2	0-1	Sale 59, Dunkley / *Broome 40,*
19	A	NOTTS CO	1/2	1,000	L	1-2	0-1	Steele 65 / *Broome 43, Duncan 68*
20	H	WALSALL	1/3	1,045	D	1-1	1-0	Sale 15p / *Broom 48*
21	A	WALSALL	8/3	1,616	L	3-7	1-2	Liddle 31, Longland, Bowyer (Vinall 59) / *Brown 7, 90, Starling 12, Dryden 52,*
22	A	WEST BROM	15/3	2,086	D	2-2	0-2	Liddle 64, Franklin 79 / *Sankey 19, Richardson 44*
23	H	WEST BROM	22/3	794	L	0-2	0-1	/ *Elliott 42, 48*
24	H	NOTT'M FOR	29/3	500	W	4-0	1-0	Sale 26, Mountford
25	A	NOTT'M FOR	5/4	300	L	2-3	0-2	Basnett 57, Mitchell 87 / *Collins 15, Norris 20, Wood 80*
26	A	NORTHAMPTON	14/4	3,000	L	0-7	0-1	[Alsop, Smalley 80p] / *Beattie R 37, Curtis, King,*
27	A	WREXHAM	14/4	3,370	L	2-5	1-1	Sale 45, Mitchell 64 [Steen 89] / *Redfern 36, Redfern 51, Park 60, 77,*
28	H	NORTHAMPTON	10/5	400	W	2-1	1-1	Bowyer 8, Brigham 74p / *Basnett 35*
29	A	WREXHAM	2/6	1,898	D	3-3	0-3	Basnett 55, Steele 68, Sale 84 / *Harrison 5 (og), Steen 14, Yates 18*
30	A	LEICESTER	7/6	1,500	L	1-2	1-1	Brigham 35p / *Dewis 12, Smith 65*

Lineups (team / opponent)

No.	1	2	3	4	5	6	7	8	9	10	11
17	Herod / *Biddlestone*	Glover / *Shelton*	Soo / *Male*	Hampson / *Richards*	Franklin / *Morgan*	Liddle / *Godfrey*	Matthews / *Hancocks*	Smith / *Brown*	Mountford / *Vinall*	Steele / *Starling*	Sale / *Rowley*
18	Herod / *Stretton*	Brigham / *Griffiths*	Glover / *Elliott*	Harrison / *Vallance*	Franklin / *Nicholas*	Sale / *Baileau*	Liddle / *Taylor*	Bowyer / *Crooks*	Mountford / *Broome*	Sale / *Green*	Dunkley / *Duncan*
19	Bridges / *Stretton*	Brigham / *Griffiths*	Glover / *Elliott*	Hampson / *Kinsley*	Franklin / *Nicholas*	Sale / *Baileau*	Liddle / *Taylor*	Bowyer / *Crooks*	Mountford / *Broome*	Steele / *Green*	Dunkley / *Duncan*
20	Herod / *Biddlestone*	Brigham / *Shelton*	Glover / *Male*	Franklin / *Wood*	Turner / *Morgan*	Harrison / *Godfrey*	Liddle / *Hancocks*	Steele / *Brown*	Mountford / *Vinall*	Steele / *Brown*	Longland / *Dryden*
21	Herod / *Biddlestone*	Brigham / *Shelton*	Glover / *Male*	Franklin / *Wood*	Turner / *Morgan*	Harrison / *Godfrey*	Liddle / *Hancocks*	Bowyer / *Brown*	Mountford / *Vinall*	Sale / *Starling*	Longland / *Dryden*
22	Wilkinson / *Adams*	Brigham / *Bassett*	Glover / *Kinsell*	Franklin / *Sankey*	Franklin / *Lowery*	Hampson / *Edwards*	Liddle / *Elliott*	Bowyer / *Heaselgrave*	Mountford / *Richardson*	Sale / *Jones*	Longland / *Johnson*
23	Herod / *Adams*	Brigham / *Bassett*	Glover / *Kinsell*	Franklin / *Sankey*	Turner / *Lowery*	Massey / *Edwards*	Peppitt / *Elliott*	Bowyer / *Heaselgrave*	Mountford / *Richardson*	Steele / *Chapman*	Sale / *Johnson*
24	Holden / *Morgan*	Glover / *Metcalfe*	McCue / *Kirton*	Franklin / *Barks*	Turner / *Ware*	Harrison / *Antonio*	Liddle / *Wood*	Steele / *Curtis*	Bowyer / *Crawley*	Bowyer / *Finch*	Sale / *Walker*
25	Holden / *Morgan*	Glover / *Elliott*	Challinor / *Metcalfe*	Franklin / *Barks*	Turner / *Mason*	Kirton / *Iverson*	Liddle / *Wood*	Steele / *Norris*	Sale / *Collins*	Basnett / *Jones*	Mitchell / *Moon*
26	Wilkinson / *Wood*	Brigham / *Smalley*	Challinor / *Beattie A*	Kinson / *Hunter*	Turner / *Bedford*	Kirton / *Dennison*	Liddle / *Curtis*	Steele / *King*	Mountford / *Alsop*	Westland J / *Beattie R*	Curtis / *Ashall*
27	Herod / *Jones*	Glover / *Cope*	McCue / *Bellamy*	Harrison / *Kelsall*	Franklin / *Hayward*	Wordley / *Blunt*	Gould / *Steen*	Bowyer / *Morris*	Sale / *Park*	Antonio / *Redfern*	Mitchell / *Smallwood*
28	Herod / *Wood*	Brigham / *Smalley*	Glover / *Dennison*	Franklin / *Hunter*	Turner / *Bedford*	Harrison / *Fagan*	Peppitt / *Basnett*	Peppitt / *Billingham*	Mountford / *Alsop*	Jackson / *Curtis*	Mitchell / *King*
29	Herod / *Jones*	Brigham / *Anderson*	Glover / *Owen*	Liddle / *Howarth*	Franklin / *Hayward*	Harrison / *Blunt*	Basnett / *Park*	Bowyer / *Waring*	Steele / *Yates*	Sale / *Redfern*	Ormston / *Steen*
30	Hayward L / *Calvert*	Brigham / *Frame*	Hayward LE / *Howe*	Ware / *Frith*	Mould / *Sheard*	Thompson / *Patterson*	Liddle / *Sanderson*	Blunt / *Smith*	Steele / *Dewis*	Steele / *Liddle*	Sale / *Adam*

Inter-League Matches

No.	V	Opponent	Date	Att	Res	Score	HT	Scorers (team / opponents)
1	A	TRANMERE	30/11	1,000	D	2-2	1-0	Mountford 17, 52 / *Smith 56 (og), Jones 70*
2	H	CHESTER	26/4	400	L	1-2	0-1	Sale 85 / *Yates 43, 83*
3	H	CHESTER	3/5	1,200	L	0-1	0-0	/ *Roberts 63*
4	H	CHESTERFIELD	17/5	500	D	2-2	2-1	Steele 27, Brigham 50p / *Milligan 8, 75*
5	A	CHESTERFIELD	24/5	1,000	L	1-5	0-1	Sale 77 / *Milligan 20, 71, 88, 90, Crooks 85*

No.	1	2	3	4	5	6	7	8	9	10	11
1	Bridges / *Teasdale*	Brigham / *Anderson*	Glover / *Wishart*	Hampson / *Gibbons*	Franklin / *Price*	Soo / *Hodgson*	Matthews / *Ashcroft*	Liddle / *Davies*	Mountford / *King*	Sale / *Paterson*	Smith / *Jones*
2	Holden / *Shortt*	Brigham / *Turnbull*	Glover / *McNeil*	Franklin / *Cole*	Turner / *Williams*	Kinson / *Howarth*	Basnett / *Roberts*	Bowyer / *Astbury*	Sale / *Yates*	Jackson / *Pendergast*	Mitchell / *Bremner*
3	Herod / *Shortt*	Brigham / *Hollis*	Challinor / *McNeil*	Thompson / *Cole*	Turner / *Williams*	Howell / *Howarth*	Liddle / *Roberts*	Steele / *Astbury*	Stevens / *Yates*	Steele / *Pendergast*	Longland / *Lanceley*
4	Herod / *Middleton*	Brigham / *Milburn*	Glover / *Kidd*	Franklin / *Hartley*	Turner / *Whittaker*	Harrison / *Pringle*	Basnett / *Crooks*	Bowyer / *Hunt*	Steele / *Milligan*	Sale / *Regan*	Mitchell / *White*
5	Herod / *Middleton*	Brigham / *Milburn*	Glover / *Kidd*	Harrison / *Hartley*	Franklin / *Pringle*	Hampson / *Sutherland*	Basnett / *Crooks*	Bowyer / *Hunt*	Sale / *Milligan*	Liddle / *Jones*	Mitchell / *Lynam*

WAR LEAGUE CUP   Manager: Bob McGrory   SEASON 1940-41

War League Cup

				Res		Scorers / Lineup											
1:1	A	MANSFIELD 15/2	2,000	L	1-6	1-3	Mountford 43 [Beaumont 52, Egan 87] Rickards 5, 75, Robertson 7, 35,	Jones *Ashton*	Brigham *McCall*	Glover *Johnstone*	Harrison *Harkin*	Griffiths H *Barke*	Sale *Marshall*	Liddle *Hubbard*	Steele *Robertson*	Mountford *Rickards*	Bowyer *Egan*	Ormston *Beaumont*
1:2	H	MANSFIELD 22/2	1,000	W	2-0	1-0	Sale 30p, Longland 57	Herod *Ashton*	Brigham *McCall*	Glover *Johnstone*	Franklin *Harkin*	Mould *Barke*	Harrison *Marshall*	Liddle *Hubbard*	Bowyer *Robertson*	Mountford *Rickards*	Sale *Egan*	Longland *Beaumont*

Midland Cup

				Res		Scorers / Lineup											
1:1	A	LEICESTER 4/1	2,224	L	2-6	1-1	Mountford 40, Sale 85 [Mullen 78] Smith 43, 65, Dewis 50, Wright 55, 86,	Herod *Calvert*	Brigham *Frame*	Challinor *Howe*	Soo *Rocester*	Franklin *Frith*	Kirton *Liddle*	Liddle *Wright*	Bowyer *Dewis*	Mountford *Lee*	Steele *Smith*	Sale *Mullen*
1:2	H	LEICESTER 11/1	2,000	L	3-5	2-3	Mountford 15, 40, Sale 59 [Smith 85] Cha'r 20(og), Dew' 33, Mul' 35, Lee 77, Calvert	Herod *Calvert*	Glover *Frame*	Challinor *Howe*	Massey *Frith*	Franklin *Heywood*	Soo *Liddle*	Liddle *Wright*	Steele *Dewis*	Mountford *Lee*	Sale *Smith*	Dunkley *Mullen*

Friendlies

				Res		Scorers / Lineup											
1	H	RAF XI 23/11	825	W	3-2	2-2	Sale 26, 41, Smith 84 Acquroff 24, Parr 43	Bridges *Arthur*	Brigham *Markham*	McCue *Dutton*	Hampson *Herford*	Franklin *Lindley*	Soo *Cutting*	Matthews *Eden*	Peppitt *Parr*	Mountford *Acquroff*	Sale *Warren*	Smith *Bulger*
2	H	RAF XI 8/2	300	W	9-1	5-1	Mount' 2, 5, 20, 32, Steele 43, 47, 75,85, Herod [Sale 67] Arthur Thursby 30	Herod *Arthur*	Brigham *Garnham*	Glover *Rooney*	Harrison *Cutting*	Franklin *Lindley*	Soo *Davids*	Liddle *Bulger*	Steele *Carr*	Mountford *Thursby*	Sale *Warren*	Mitchell *Houghton*
3	H	ARMY XI 12/4	400	W	7-2	4-0	Mitchell 2, 15, 40, 72, Liddle 31, Kirton 60, Steele 62 [Mount' 65, 78] Wilkinson	Sherratt *Wilkinson*	Glover *Challinor*	McCue *Goodhead*	Franklin *Steele*	Turner *Betmead*	Harrison *Kirton*	Liddle *Weaver*	Bowyer *Antonio*	Mountford *Williams*	Sale *Westland J*	Mitchell *Cooper*

Southern Regional League

		P	W	D	L	F	A	G Ave^
1	Crystal Palace	27	16	4	7	86	44	1.954
2	West Ham	25	14	6	5	70	39	1.794
3	Coventry	10	5	3	2	28	16	1.750
4	Arsenal	19	10	5	4	66	38	1.736
5	Cardiff	24	12	5	7	75	50	1.500
6	Reading	26	14	5	7	73	51	1.431
7	Norwich	19	9	2	8	73	55	1.327
8	Watford	35	15	6	14	96	73	1.315
9	Portsmouth	31	16	2	13	93	71	1.296
10	Tottenham	23	9	5	9	53	41	1.292
11	Millwall	31	16	5	10	73	57	1.280
12	Walsall	32	14	7	11	100	80	1.250
13	West Brom	28	13	5	10	83	69	1.202
14	Leicester	33	17	5	11	87	73	1.191
15	Northampton	30	14	3	13	84	71	1.183
16	Bristol City	20	10	2	8	55	48	1.145
17	Mansfield	29	12	6	11	77	68	1.132
18	Charlton	19	7	4	8	37	34	1.088
19	Aldershot	24	14	2	8	73	68	1.073
20	Brentford	23	9	3	11	51	51	1.000
21	Chelsea	23	10	4	9	57	58	0.981
22	Birmingham	16	7	1	8	38	43	0.883
23	Fulham	30	10	7	13	62	73	0.849
24	Luton	35	11	7	17	82	100	0.820
25	**STOKE**	36	9	9	18	76	96	0.791
26	QP Rangers	23	8	3	12	47	60	0.783
27	Brighton	25	8	7	10	51	75	0.680
28	Nott'm For	25	7	3	15	50	77	0.649
29	Bournemouth	27	9	3	15	59	92	0.641
30	Notts Co	21	8	4	10	42	66	0.636
31	Southend	29	12	4	13	64	101	0.633
32	Southampton	31	4	4	23	53	111	0.477
33	Swansea	10	2	1	7	12	33	0.363
34	Clapton Orient	15	1	3	11	19	66	0.287

^ Positions were decided by goal-average (goals scored divided by goals conceded). The table also took into account the cup competitions and Inter-League matches.

	Appearances					Goals				
	Lge	IL	WC	MC	Frie	Lge	WC	MC	Frie	Tot
Antonio, George	5	3			1					
Basnett, Fred (A)						2				2
Blunt, Edwin*	1									
Bowyer, Frank	16	3	2	1	2	10				10
Bridges, Pat	18	1			1					
Brigham, Harry	29	5	2	1	2	3				3
Challinor, Jack	3	1		2						
Curtis, C	1									
Dunkley, Robert	2			1		1				1
Franklin, Neil	30	4		2	4	1				1
Glover, Stanley	17	4	2	1	3					
Gould, Wally					1					
Griffiths, Harry*	3		1							
Griffiths, Jack*	20	2	1		1					
Hampson Eric	8	2	1		3					
Harrison, Stanley	1									
Hayward, Lionel*	1									
Hayward, Eric*	10	3	1	2	2					
Herod, Dennis	3	1								
Holden, Tom	3	1								
Howell, Len	1	1								
Jackson, John	2	1								
Jones, Doug*	1		1							
Kinson, Bill	2	1								
Kirton, Jock	3			1	1					
Liddle, Bobby	27	3	2	2	2	6	1			7
Longland, Eric*	6	1	1		3	1	1			2
McCue, Jock	14				3					
Massey, Alf	1			1						
Matthews, Stan	12	1			1					
Mitchell, Bert	6	3			3					
Mould, Billy	6	1								
Mountford, Frank	25	1	2	2	3	1			5	6
Ormston, Alec	2	1			1	19	1	3	6	29
Peppitt, Syd	14					2				2
Sale, Tommy	32	5	2	2	4	14	1	2	4	21
Sherratt, Fred		1			1					
Smith, Clem	6	1		2	2	2			1	3
Soo, Frank	18	1	2	2	1	4				4
Steele, Freddie	13	2	1	2	1	5			4	9
Stevens, George*	1	1								
Thompson, M	2	1								
Turner, Arthur*	11	3			1					
Ware, Harry*	1									
Westland, Jim	1									
Wilkinson, Norman	2									
Wordley, Ted	2	1			1					
47 players used	**374**	**55**	**22**	**22**	**44**	**71**	**3**	**5**	**21**	**100**

* guest players

LEAGUE NORTH 1st PHASE   Manager: Bob McGrory   SEASON 1941-42

No	Date	Att	Pos	Pt	F-A	H-T	Scorers, Times, and Referees	1	2	3	4	5	6	7	8	9	10	11
1	H EVERTON 30/8	4,000	W	2	8-3	4-1	Sale 7,37, Brig' 10p, Lid' 40, Bas'63, [Blunt]	Herod	Brigham	Glover	Hamlett	Mould	Caton	Liddle	Bowyer	Sale	Blunt	Basnett F
							Cat' 41, Boyes 61, Cook p	*Lovett*	*Cook*	*Greenhalgh*	*Mercer*	*Hill*	*Jones JE*	*Barber*	*Bentham*	*Catterick*	*Boyes*	*Lyon*
2	H EVERTON 6/9	6,000	L	2	1-3	0-1	Brigham 65p	Herod	Brigham	Glover	Hamlett	Mould	Caton	Liddle	Bowyer	Sale	Blunt	Basnett F
							Cook 37, Cunliffe 46, 89	*Sagar*	*Cook*	*Greenhalgh*	*Bentham*	*Jones TG*	*Mercer*	*Hill*	*Cunliffe*	*Jackson*	*Stevenson*	*Lyon*
3	A WREXHAM 13/9	4,500	W	4	7-1	1-0	Blunt 38, Bas' 49, Sale62,88, Bow'72,74, [Brigham 79p]	Herod	Brigham	Glover	Hamlett	Mould	Caton	Liddle	Bowyer	Sale	Blunt	Basnett F
							Redfern 61	*Jones*	*Roberts*	*Wallbank*	*Tutin*	*Turner*	*Carver*	*Horsman*	*Brenner*	*Park*	*Redfern*	*Steen*
4	H WREXHAM 20/9	3,000	W	6	5-2	2-0	Sale 33, 47, 68, Blunt 39, Bowyer 79	Herod	Brigham	Glover	Hamlett	Griffiths	Caton	Peppitt	Bowyer	Sale	Blunt	Basnett F
							Horsman 56, 86	*Sidlow*	*Milburn*	*Wallbank*	*Tutin*	*Turner*	*Roberts*	*Horsman*	*Bremner*	*Stevens*	*Redfern*	*Steen*
5	H CHESTER 27/9	4,000	L	6	2-5	1-2	Bowyer 30, Blunt 49	Herod	Brigham	Glover	Hamlett	Mould	Caton	Peppitt	Bowyer	Sale	Blunt	Basnett F
							Leyfield 6, Roberts 25, Yates 80, 83, 85	*Shortt*	*Turnbull*	*McNeil*	*Cole*	*Williams*	*Howarth*	*Roberts*	*Astbury*	*Yates*	*Pendergast*	*Ormston*
6	A CHESTER 4/10	4,000	W	8	4-3	2-0	Bowyer 19, 85, Sale 35, Basnett F 62	Herod	Brigham	Glover	Hamlett	Mould	Soo	Peppitt	Bowyer	Sale	Blunt	Basnett F
							Yates 49, Glaister 50, 51	*Shortt*	*Turnbull*	*McNeil*	*Cole*	*Williams*	*Howarth*	*Roberts*	*Astbury*	*Yates*	*Leyfield*	*Glaister*
7	A MANCHESTER C 11/10	5,150	L	8	3-4	2-3	Sale 8, 9, 60	Herod	Brigham	Glover	Soo	Franklin	Kirton	Liddle	Bowyer	Soo	Sale	Basnett F
								Swift	*Clark*	*Walker*	*Robinson*	*Eastwood*	*Bray*	*Kirton*	*Currier*	*Boothway*	*Barkas*	*Wild*
8	H MANCHESTER C 18/10	3,000	W	10	5-0	2-0	Sale 25, 55, 63, Basnett F 31, Peppitt 75	Herod	Brigham	Glover	Franklin	Mould	Soo	Peppitt	Bowyer	Soo	Blunt	Basnett F
							Barkas 18, 26, 86p, Boothway 19	*Swift*	*Clark*	*Walker*	*Walsh*	*Eastwood*	*Bray*	*Kirton*	*Currier*	*Boothway*	*Davenport*	*Wild*
9	H MANCHESTER U 25/10	4,520	D	11	1-1	1-0	Liddle 38	Herod	Hamlett	Glover	Glover	Mould	Soo	Liddle	Bowyer	Sale	Blunt	Basnett F
							Carey 65	*Breedon*	*Roughton*	*Redwood*	*Warner*	*Porter*	*Whalley*	*Bryant*	*Smith*	*Rowley*	*Carey*	*Mitten*
10	A MANCHESTER U 1/11	4,000	L	11	0-3	0-2			Brigham	Glover	Hamlett	Franklin	Caton	Liddle	Bowyer	Sale	Blunt	Basnett F
							Whalley 1, Rowley 21, Carey 53	*Breedon*	*Roughton*	*Redwood*	*Warner*	*Porter*	*Whalley*	*Bryant*	*Smith*	*Rowley*	*Carey*	*Mitten*
11	A NEW BRIGHTON 8/11	2,000	W	13	5-3	3-2	Bas' 23, Mount'd F 31, 69, Haml't 43,	Herod	Brigham	Glover	Hamlett	Franklin	Caton	Mountford F	Bowyer	Steele	Blunt	Basnett F
							Waring 6, 65, Frost 30 [Steele 75]	*Adams*	*Parker*	*Lowe*	*Hill*	*Chedgzoy*	*Pilling*	*Dellow*	*Waring*	*Frost*	*Mallam*	*Brand*
12	H NEW BRIGHTON 15/11	2,094	W	15	4-0	2-0	Sale 12, 25, 55, Hamlett 53	Herod	Brigham	Glover	Hamlett	Franklin	Kirton	Liddle	Bowyer	Sale	Soo	Basnett F
								Adams	*Parker*	*Lowe*	*Hill*	*Chedgzoy*	*Pilling*	*Dellow*	*Waring*	*Frost*	*Mallam*	*Eden*
13	H TRANMERE 22/11	1,500	W	17	9-0	3-0	Sale 9p, 23, 47, 82, 89, Basnett 35, 61, [Bowyer 55, Mountford F 63]	Herod	Brigham	Glover	Hamlett	Franklin	Blunt	Liddle	Bowyer	Sale	Mountford F	Basnett F
								Lovett	*Price JT*	*Owen*	*Wishart*	*Price WB*	*Cartwright*	*Caffrey*	*Aldis*	*Climo*	*McPeake*	*Cooper*
14	A TRANMERE 29/11	2,000	W	19	7-2	2-2	Lid' 16, Sale 26, 51, 80, Bas' F 47, 62, 82	Herod	Brigham	Glover	Hamlett	Mould	Franklin	Liddle	Bowyer	Sale	Soo	Basnett F
							Rosenthal 22, Climo 39	*Lovett*	*Wishart*	*Owen*	*Anderson*	*Price WB*	*Ferguson*	*Jones TB*	*Rosenthal*	*Climo*	*McPeake*	*Cooper*
15	A STOCKPORT 6/12	500	W	21	6-1	2-0	Sale 1, 58, 65, Soo 5, 62, Basnett 55	Herod	Brigham	Glover	Hamlett	Mould	Franklin	Liddle	Bowyer	Sale	Soo	Basnett F
							Catterick 85	*Fallows*	*Topping T*	*Topping A*	*Cutting*	*Steele*	*Chappel*	*Toseland*	*Watson*	*Catterick*	*Lawrence*	*Ridgeway*
16	H STOCKPORT 13/12	2,000	W	23	3-1	1-1	Sale 30, Mountford F 60, Basnett F 76	Herod	Brigham	Glover	Hamlett	Franklin	Blunt	Liddle	Bowyer	Sale	Mountford F	Basnett F
							Howe 18	*Rigby*	*Topping T*	*Topping A*	*Cutting*	*Steele*	*Titterington*	*Toseland*	*Watson*	*Catterick*	*Howe*	*Noble*
17	A LIVERPOOL 20/12	4,000	D	24	1-1	0-1	Bowyer	Herod	Brigham	Glover	Hamlett	Franklin	Harrison	Mountford F	Bowyer	Sale	Blunt	Basnett F
							Liddell 20	*Hobson*	*Gutteridge*	*Lambert*	*Eastham*	*Cook*	*Kaye*	*Liddell*	*Ainsley*	*McIntosh*	*Carney*	*Polk*
18	H LIVERPOOL 25/12	8,000	W	26	4-3	0-2	Sale, 84p, Liddle, Basnett F	Herod	Brigham	Glover	Hamlett	Franklin	Harrison	Liddle	Bowyer	Sale	Blunt	Basnett F
							Nieuwenhuys, Polk, Liddell	*Hobson*	*Gutteridge*	*Young*	*Lambert*	*Cook*	*Spicer*	*Liddell*	*Polk*	*Nieuwenhuys*	*Paterson*	*Holligan*

LEAGUE NORTH 2nd PHASE

#	V	Opponent	Date	Res	FT	HT	Pos	Att	1	2	3	4	5	6	7	8	9	10	11
1	A	BLACKPOOL	28/3	L	0-4	0-2	0	4,000	Herod / *Roxburgh*	Brigham / *Cope*	Glover / *Williams*	Hamlett / *Powell*	Franklin / *Whittaker*	Hayward / *Johnson*	Liddle / *Matthews*	Bowyer / *Mortensen*	Sale / *Dodds*	Soo / *Finan*	Basnett F / *O'Donnell*
2	A	WALSALL	11/4	L	0-1	0-0	0	1,047	Herod / *Roxburgh*	Brigham / *Shelton*	Glover / *Tranter*	Hamlett / *Lewis*	Franklin / *Mould*	Franklin / *Jarvis*	Liddle / *Newsome*	Bowyer / *Wood*	Sale / *Vinall*	Mountford F / *Dudley*	Basnett F / *Beasley*
3	H	WALSALL	18/4	L	2-3	1-2	0	1,500	Herod / *Biddlestone*	Glover / *Shelton*	McCue / *Tranter*	Hamlett / *Lewis*	Franklin / *Morgan*	Harrison / *Jarvis*	Liddle / *Newsome*	Bowyer / *Wood*	Sale / *Vinall*	Mountford F / *Ashley*	Basnett F / *Dudley*
4	A	CHESTER	25/4	W	4-2	4-1	2	1,500	Herod / *Rigby*	Glover / *Bates*	Williams / *McNeil*	Hamlett / *Howarth !*	Franklin / *Griffiths*	Harrison / *Armeson*	Mountford F / *Yates*	Bowyer / *Iddon*	Sale / *Guest*	Liddle / *Astbury*	Basnett F / *Polk*
5	H	CHESTER	2/5	D	2-2	0-2	3	2,000	Herod / *Shortt*	Williams / *Bates*	McCue / *McNeil*	Hamlett / *Howarth*	Franklin / *Williams*	Kirton / *Cole*	Mountford F / *Payne*	Bowyer / *Astbury*	Sale / *Yates*	Soo / *Iddon*	Basnett F / *Piercy*
6	A	PRESTON	9/5	W	2-1	1-0	5	2,500	Herod / *Fairbrother*	Brigham / *Mansley*	Williams / *Bradford*	Hamlett / *Shankly*	Franklin / *Smith*	Caton / *Mutch*	Liddle / *Horton*	Bowyer / *McLaren*	Steele / *Dougal*	Steele / *Bremner*	Clewlow / *Wharton*
7	A	NORTHAMPTON	23/5	L	0-10	0-3	5	3,000	Herod / *Wood*	Brigham / *Smalley*	Glover / *Dennison*	Brown / *Harris*	Franklin / *Shepherdson*	Kirton / *Woodburn*	Liddle / *Pritchard*	Bowyer / *Dearson*	Sale / *Ware*	Steele / *Fagan*	Longland / *Alsop*
8	H	NORTHAMPTON	30/5	W	3-2	2-1	7	1,500	Herod / *Wood*	Brigham / *Smalley*	Griffiths / *Dennison*	Hamlett / *Harris*	Franklin / *Shepherdson*	Brown / *Ware*	Liddle / *Pritchard*	Mountford F / *Fagan*	Sellars / *Alsop*	Blunt / *Johnston*	Basnett F / *Lyman*

Scorers:
1. Dodds 30, 32, 66, O'Donnell 62
2. Vinall 49
3. Liddle 26, Sale 46 / Dudley 18, Newsome 45, Ashley 49
4. Bowyer 7, 31, Basnett F 21, Sale 44p / Astbury 4
5. Liddle 60, Bowyer / Piercy 10, Yates 12
6. Liddle 35, McLaren
7. Ware 50, 87, Har' 57, Fag' 60, Pritch' 75 / Dear' 15, 42, 65, Als' 22, Glov' 48(og), Wood
8. Sale 15, Liddle 18, Blunt 53 / Alsop 5, 66

LEAGUE CUP Qualifying

#	V	Opponent	Date	Res	FT	HT	Att	1	2	3	4	5	6	7	8	9	10	11
1	A	WALSALL	27/12	W	4-1	3-0	3,000	Herod / *Biddlestone*	Brigham / *Shelton*	Glover / *Male*	Hamlett / *Ashley*	Franklin / *Morgan*	Blunt / *Batty*	Liddle / *Bulger*	Bowyer / *Wood*	Sale / *Vinall*	Steele / *Starling*	Clewlow / *Beasley*
2	H	WALSALL	3/1	W	8-0	2-0	3,000	Herod / *Biddlestone*	Brigham / *Shelton*	Glover / *Male*	Hamlett / *Lewis*	Franklin / *Morgan*	Soo / *Batty*	Liddle / *Hancocks*	Bowyer / *Wood*	Sale / *Vinall*	Blunt / *Starling*	Basnett F / *Beasley*
3	A	WEST BROM	10/1	L	0-4	0-3	7,320	Herod / *Biddlestone*	Brigham / *Bassett*	Glover / *Shaw*	Hamlett / *Sankey*	Franklin / *Edwards*	Soo / *McNab*	Liddle / *Elliott*	Bowyer / *McKennon*	Sale / *Richardson*	Blunt / *Evans*	Basnett F / *Johnson*
4	H	WEST BROM	17/1	W	2-1	0-0	4,758	Herod / *Merrick*	Brigham / *Bassett*	McCue / *Shaw*	Hamlett / *Sankey*	Franklin / *Edwards*	Kirton / *McNab*	Liddle / *Elliott*	Bowyer / *McKennon*	Sale / *Richardson*	Steele / *Evans*	Mitchell / *Johnson*
5	H	CHESTERFIELD	31/1	W	2-1	2-0	1,500	Herod / *Middleton*	Brigham / *Milburn*	Glover / *Alderson*	Hamlett / *Hartley*	Franklin / *Whittaker*	Soo / *Sutherland*	Liddle / *Hunt*	Bowyer / *Jones*	Sale / *Lyman*	Steele / *Hulme*	Basnett F / *Miller*
6	H	BOLTON	14/2	W	3-1	3-0	2,000	Herod / *Grimsditch*	Brigham / *Banks*	Glover / *Hubbick*	Hamlett / *McCormick*	Franklin / *Connor*	Caton / *Johnson WH*	Liddle / *Steen*	Bowyer / *Johnson JW*	Sale / *Hunt*	Steele / *Boulter*	Basnett F / *Chadwick*
7	A	NOTT'M FOR	21/2	L	0-1	0-0	1,000	Herod / *Rutherford*	Brigham / *Astley*	Glover / *Metcalfe*	Hamlett / *McCall*	Franklin / *Shaw*	Caton / *Burgess*	Liddle / *Crooks*	Bowyer / *Starling*	Sale / *Vause*	Mitchell / *Beaumont*	Basnett F / *Duncan*
8	H	NOTT'M FOR	28/2	L	1-3	1-1	3,480	Herod / *Rutherford*	Brigham / *Astley*	Glover / *Metcalfe*	Hamlett / *McCall*	Franklin / *Vause*	Caton / *Burgess*	Liddle / *Crooks*	Bowyer / *Starling*	Sale / *Bowers*	Steele / *Beaumont*	Basnett F / *Duncan*
9	A	CHESTERFIELD	14/3	L	1-2	0-1	2,500	Herod / *Middleton*	Hamlett / *Milburn*	Glover / *Alderson*	Blunt / *Hartley*	Franklin / *Whittaker*	Soo / *Devine*	Liddle / *Steele*	Bowyer / *Collins*	Sale / *Linacre*	Steele / *Lyman*	Basnett F / *Miller*
10	A	BOLTON	21/3	D	1-1	1-1	4,320	Herod / *Grimsditch*	Brigham / *Haslam*	Glover / *Hubbick*	Hamlett / *Goslin*	Franklin / *Atkinson*	Hayward / *Johnson WH*	Liddle / *Morris*	Bowyer / *Hunt*	Sale / *Lofthouse*	Ormston / *Knight*	Basnett F / *Chadwick*

Scorers:
1. Clewlow 5, Sale 20, 25, 80 / Vinall 71
2. Sale 15, 21, 46, 53, Soo 61, Blunt
3. Elliott 6, Richardson 40, McKennan 45, Merrick [Johnson 50]
4. Mitchell 60, Sale 75 / Elliott 85
5. Sale 1, 41 / Miller 88
6. Sale 25, 38, 44 / Franklin 78 (og)
7. Beaumont 90
8. Sale 43p / Duncan 30, Bowers
9. Sale 72p / Blunt 43 (og), Hartley 47
10. Basnett F 43 / Morris 8

LEAGUE CUP Proper

#	V	Opponent	Date	Res	FT	HT	Att	1	2	3	4	5	6	7	8	9	10	11
1:1	A	WEST BROM	4/4	W	5-3	3-0	5,000	Herod / *Adams*	Brigham / *Bassett*	Glover / *Shaw*	Hamlett / *Ashley*	Franklin / *Edwards*	Hayward / *McNab*	Liddle / *Elliott*	Bowyer / *Heaselgrave*	Sale / *Richardson*	Westland J / *Evans*	Basnett F / *Johnson*
1:2	H	WEST BROM	6/4	L	1-6	1-1	13,864	Herod / *Adams*	Brigham / *Bassett*	Glover / *Shaw*	Hamlett / *Sankey*	Franklin / *Gripton*	Kirton / *McNab*	Liddle / *Elliott*	Bowyer / *McKennon*	Sale / *Richardson*	Westland J / *Evans*	Basnett F / *Edwards*

Scorers:
1:1. Sale 25, 30, 72p, Basnett F 40, 55 / Johnson 78, Elliott 83p, Evans 89
1:2. Sale 42 / McKen' 60p, 67, Sankey 80, Elliott 58, Richardson 22, 75

FRIENDLY

#	V	Opponent	Date	Res	FT	HT	Att	1	2	3	4	5	6	7	8	9	10	11
1	A	DERBY	25/5	L	1-2	1-1	1,000	Herod / *Prince*	Brigham / *Carr*	Williams / *Pallett*	Hamlett / *Hibbs*	Franklin / *Nicholas*	Brown / *Hann*	Liddle / *Crooks*	Bowyer / *Powell*	Sellars / *Bowers*	Sale / *Ramage*	Basnett F / *Duncan*

Scorers:
1. Sellars 5 / Duncan 15, Powell 70

LEAGUE TABLES

Ended 25 December 1941

		P	W	D	L	F	A	Pts
1	Blackpool	18	14	1	3	75	19	29
2	Lincoln	18	13	3	2	54	28	29
3	Preston	18	13	1	4	58	18	27
4	Manchester U	18	10	6	2	79	27	26
5	STOKE	18	12	2	4	75	36	26
6	Everton	18	12	2	4	61	31	26
7	Blackburn	18	10	6	2	40	24	26
8	Liverpool	18	11	4	3	66	44	26
9	Gateshead	18	9	5	4	39	35	23
10	Sunderland	18	9	4	5	50	30	22
11	Huddersfield	18	10	1	7	48	33	21
12	Bradford	18	8	5	5	33	28	21
13	Grimsby	18	7	6	5	41	31	20
14	Barnsley	18	8	4	6	39	31	20
15	Newcastle	18	7	5	6	46	39	20
16	Sheffield Wed	18	7	5	6	33	37	19
17	Manchester C	18	8	3	7	48	54	19
18	Sheffield Utd	18	7	4	7	39	38	18
19	Burnley	18	6	6	6	36	40	18
20	Halifax	18	7	3	8	29	41	17
21	Oldham	18	6	4	8	40	49	16
22	Rochdale	18	6	4	8	28	52	16
23	Chesterfield	18	5	5	8	27	31	15
24	Chester	18	6	3	9	45	53	15
25	Middlesbrough	18	6	3	9	44	56	15
26	Leeds	18	7	1	10	36	46	15
27	Doncaster	18	6	2	10	39	46	14
28	Rotherham	18	5	4	9	32	42	14
29	Rotherham	18	6	2	10	33	47	14
30	New Brighton	18	4	6	8	39	75	14
31	Tranmere	18	5	3	10	35	60	13
32	York	18	4	4	10	41	55	12
33	Mansfield	18	6	0	12	29	50	12
34	Bolton	18	3	5	10	35	48	11
35	Southport	18	5	1	12	33	61	11
36	Bury	18	3	3	12	37	59	9
37	Wrexham	18	2	5	11	40	69	9
38	Stockport	18	2	2	14	34	73	6
		684	275	134	275	1636	1636	684

SEASON 1941-42

	Appearances			Goals			
	Lge	WC	Frie	Lge	WC	Frie	Tot
Basnett, Fred (A)	23	10	1	15	3		18
Blunt, Edwin*	16	4		5	1		6
Bowyer, Frank	25	12	1	10			10
Brigham, Harry	22	11	1	3			3
Brown, Roy	2						
Caton, Bill	8	3					
Clewlow, Stan	1	1			1		1
Franklin, Neil	20	12	1				
Glover, Stanley	23	11					
Griffiths, Harry*	3						
Hamlett, Lol*	23	12	1	2			2
Harrison, Stanley	3						
Hayward, Eric*	1	2					
Herod, Denis	26	12	1				
Kirton, Jock	4	3					
Liddle, Bobby	19	12	1	10			10
Longland, Eric*	1						
McCue, Jock	2	1					
Mitchell, Bert	2					1	1
Mould, Billy	10						
Mountford, Frank	9			4			4
Ormston, Alec	1	1					
Peppitt, Syd	4	1		1			1
Sale, Tommy	24	12	1	35	21		56
Sellars, Johnny	1	1					1
Soo, Frank	9	3		2	1		3
Steele, Freddie	3	5		1			1
Westland, Jim	2						
Williams, Emlyn*	3		1				
29 players used	286	132	11	88	28	1	117

* guest players

North 2nd League (27/12/41 to 8/3/42)

	Team							Pts	Avg
1	Manchester U	19	12	4	3	44	25	33.89	
2	Blackpool	22	14	4	4	108	34	33.45	
3	Northampton	21	14	2	5	70	31	32.85	
4	Liverpool	21	14	2	5	57	39	32.85	
5	Wolves	20	13	1	6	52	29	31.05	
6	Huddersfield	20	9	6	5	42	33	27.60	
7	Blackburn	22	10	6	6	40	31	27.18	
8	West Brom	18	9	3	6	53	43	26.83	
9	Grimsby	18	8	5	5	31	22	26.83	
10	Sunderland	22	9	7	6	53	42	26.13	
11	Cardiff	20	9	4	7	59	38	25.30	
12	Preston	19	6	7	6	41	30	23.00	
13	Chesterfield	18	8	2	8	32	31	23.00	
14	Middlesbrough	18	7	4	7	37	36	23.00	
15	Everton	23	9	5	9	37	41	23.00	
16	**STOKE**	20	9	2	9	41	49	23.00	
17	Leicester	18	6	4	8	39	38	20.44	
18	Bradford PA	19	5	6	8	35	40	19.36	
19	Halifax	19	4	7	8	30	40	18.15	
20	Burnley	19	7	1	11	29	53	18.15	
21	Chester	20	6	3	11	34	41	17.25	
22	Oldham	18	4	3	11	30	43	14.05	

Only those playing 18 or more games qualified for the Championship.

Points average calculated on 23 games.

Stoke's 20 games (8 League North 2nd phase; 10 League Cup qualifiers; 2 League Cup proper)

LEAGUE NORTH 1st PHASE — Manager: Bob McGrory — SEASON 1942-43

No	Date	Att	Pos	Pt	F-A	H-T	Scorers, Times, and Referees	1	2	3	4	5	6	7	8	9	10	11
1	H CREWE 29/8	3,000		W	4-1	4-1	Sale 12, 30, 35, Peppitt 28 / Ibbs 36	Herod	Brigham	McCue	Hamlett	Franklin	Soo	Liddle	Bowyer	Sale	Peppitt	Basnett F
								Poskett	*Tagg*	*Bateman*	*Tutin*	*Williams*	*Still*	*Aldersea*	*Essex*	*Dickinson*	*Ibbs*	*Trentham*
2	A CREWE 5/9	2,204		W	2-1	2:1	Liddle 1, Sale 7 / Chandler 18	Sherratt	Brigham	McCue	Tutin	Caton	Soo	Liddle	Bowyer	Sale	Mountford F	Basnett F
								Poskett	*Tagg*	*Bateman*	*Still*	*Williams*	*Cope*	*Eden*	*Chandler*	*Ibbs*	*Kinneard*	*Trentham*
3	A WOLVES 12/9	7,251		L	2-3	0-2	Bowyer 50, Mountford F 62 / Westcott 23, 28, 80	Sherratt	Brigham	McCue	Soo	Franklin	Caton	Liddle	Bowyer	Sale	Blunt	Mountford F
								Sidlow	*Taylor*	*Ashton*	*Wright*	*Galley*	*Gardiner*	*Jackson*	*Crook*	*Westcott*	*Alderson*	*Clarke*
4	H WOLVES 19/9	4,640		W	1-0	1-0	Soo 42	Sherratt	Brigham	McCue	Hamlett	Franklin	Caton	Basnett F	Bowyer	Sale	Soo	Mountford F
								Sidlow	*Dowen*	*Taylor*	*Wright*	*Ashton*	*Alderton*	*Pritchard*	*Crook*	*Westcott*	*Ball*	*Roberts*
5	H DERBY 26/9	5,855		W	5-2	1-0	Mountford F 24, Bowyer, Soo 86, 89p / Challenger 50, Duncan	Sherratt	Brigham	McCue	Hamlett	Franklin	Caton	Liddle	Bowyer	Sale	Soo	Mountford F
								Townsend	*Nicholas*	*Parr*	*Challenger*	*Bailey*	*Hann*	*Smith*	*Powell*	*Lyman*	*Ramage*	*Duncan*
6	A DERBY 3/10	11,500		W	1-0	1-0	Sale 8	Bates	Brigham	McCue	Hamlett	Franklin	Soo	Liddle	Bowyer	Sale	Ormston	Baker
								Townsend	*Wilcox*	*Beattie*	*Hann*	*Nicholas*	*Ward*	*Crooks*	*Powell*	*Lyman*	*Ramage*	*Duncan*
7	A BIRMINGHAM 10/10	2,500		L	0-1	0-0	Acquroff 87	Bates	Brigham	McCue	Hamlett	Franklin	Caton	Liddle	Bowyer	Sale	Soo	Mountford F
								Merrick	*Quinton*	*Jennings*	*Shaw*	*Turner*	*Mitchell*	*McCormick*	*Acquroff*	*Dearson*	*Ottewell*	*Pearson*
8	H BIRMINGHAM 17/10	3,758		L	1-3	1-1	Sale 22 / Bate 31, Craven 55, Gill 84	Bates	Brigham	McCue	Hamlett	Franklin	Caton	Liddle	Bowyer	Sale	Soo	Mountford F
								Merrick	*Quinton*	*Jennings*	*Bate*	*Turner*	*Shaw*	*McCormick*	*Gill*	*Ottewell*	*Craven*	*Pearson*
9	A ASTON VILLA 24/10	10,000		L	0-4	0-4	Haycock 10, 20, Parkes 30, Edwards 38 Wakeman	Bates	Brigham	McCue	Hamlett	Franklin	Caton	Liddle	Bowyer	Sale	Jackson	Mountford F
								Wakeman	*Potts*	*Cummings*	*Starling*	*Massie*	*Iverson*	*Edwards*	*Broome*	*Haycock*	*Parkes*	*Houghton*
10	H ASTON VILLA 31/10	5,563		W	1-0	1-0	Sale 5p	Bates	Brigham	McCue	Hamlett	Mould	Soo	Liddle	Bowyer	Sale	Mountford F	Mitchell
								Wakeman	*Potts*	*Cummings*	*Starling*	*Massie*	*Iverson*	*Edwards*	*Broome*	*Haycock*	*Parkes*	*Houghton*
11	A WEST BROM 7/11	6,564		D	0-0	0-0		Bates	Brigham	McCue	Hamlett	Franklin	Soo	Liddle	Bowyer	Sale	Mountford F	Mitchell
								Adams	*Bassett*	*Smith*	*Sankey*	*Gripton*	*Millard*	*Newsome*	*Heaselgrave*	*Simms*	*Evans C*	*Finch*
12	H WEST BROM 14/11	3,331		W	5-1	2-0	Basnett AE 37, 78, Bowyer 39, 48, Evans C 59 [Basnett F 61]	Bates	Brigham	McCue	Hamlett	Franklin	Soo	Basnett AE	Bowyer	Sale	Mountford F	Basnett F
								Adams	*Bassett*	*Kinsell*	*Sankey*	*Gripton*	*Evans J*	*Newsome*	*Clarke*	*Butler*	*Evans C*	*Finch*
13	A WREXHAM 21/11	3,500		W	4-2	3-1	Caton 11, Basnett F 15, Mountford F 17, Gray [Liddle 53, Mountford F] Muir 1, Blunt 81 [Liddle 76]	Herod	Brigham	McCue	Hamlett	Franklin	Caton	Basnett AE	Bowyer	Sale	Mountford F	Basnett F
								Reeder	*Hughes*	*Jones JE*	*Stuttard*	*Stuttard*	*Hill F*	*Muir*	*Blunt*	*Moore*	*Bremner*	*McNee*
14	H WREXHAM 28/11	2,478		W	2-0	1-0	Mountford F 14, 75	Bates	Glover	McCue	Hamlett	Franklin	Soo	Liddle	Bowyer	Peppitt	Mountford F	Basnett F
								Clegg	*Jones C*	*Lloyd*	*Dolby*	*Stuttard*	*Hill F*	*Muir*	*Blunt*	*Jones D*	*Kirton*	*Hill J*
15	H CREWE 5/12	2,858		D	3-3	1-2	Liddle 14, Mountford F 24, Sale 62 Chandler 43, Waring 55, Malam 90	Bates	Brigham	McCue	Hamlett	Franklin	Sale	Liddle	Bowyer	Mountford G	Mountford F	Basnett F
								Poskett	*Glover*	*Bateman*	*Tagg*	*Williams*	*Still*	*Essex*	*Malam*	*Waring*	*Chandler*	*Lewis*
16	H CREWE 12/12	2,000		W	6-1	2-0	Basnett F 37, Mountford G 42, 55, Gray [Liddle 53, Mountford G F]	Bates	Brigham	McCue	Hamlett	Franklin	Sale	Liddle	Bowyer	Mountford G	Mountford F	Basnett F
								Poskett	*Glover*	*Bateman*	*Tagg*	*Williams*	*Still*	*Gray*	*Waring*	*Boothway*	*Chandler*	*Lewis*
17	H WALSALL 19/12	5,100		W	7-1	2-1	Mount' F 23, 38, Bas' 48, Mount' G 55, Nich' 10 [Sale 62, Lid' 76, Male 80 (og)]	Bates	Brigham	McCue	Hamlett	Massey	Sale	Liddle	Bowyer	Peppitt	Mountford F	Basnett F
								Hind	*Shelton*	*Male*	*Lewis*	*Morgan*	*Tranter*	*Newsome*	*Lindley*	*Nicholls*	*Kirton*	*Ireland*
18	A WALSALL 25/12	2,229		D	2-2	1-0	Basnett F 43, Bowyer 50 / Tranter 75, 82	Herod	Brigham	McCue	Hamlett	Franklin	Sale	Mountford G	Bowyer	Mountford F	Basnett F	Liddle
								Hind	*Shelton*	*Male*	*Lewis*	*Morgan*	*Tranter*	*Newsome*	*Lindley*	*Nicholls*	*Emmanuel*	*Ireland*

LEAGUE NORTH 2nd PHASE

No	Date	Att	Pos	Pt	F-A	H-T	Scorers, Times, and Referees	1	2	3	4	5	6	7	8	9	10	11
1	A NOTTS CO 3/4	4,180		D	1-1	1-1	Bowyer 16 / Rawcliffe 20	Bilton	Brigham	McCue	Hamlett	Franklin	Sale	Mountford G	Bowyer	Mountford F	Liddle	Basnett F
								Wilkinson	*Corkhill*	*Benner*	*Barke*	*Leuty*	*Kirton*	*Dunns*	*Jones L*	*Bowers*	*Rawcliffe*	*Towler*
2	H NOTTS CO 10/4	2,080		D	1-1	0-1	Liddle 75 / Rickard 30	Foster	Brigham	McCue	Howell	Hamlett	Sale	Liddle	Bowyer	Mountford F	Jackson	Clewlow
								Ashton	*Corkhill*	*Barke*	*Clarke*	*Leuty*	*Hughes*	*Duns*	*Jones*	*Rickard*	*Rawcliffe*	*Liddle*
3	A DERBY 17/4	4,250		L	1-2	0-0	Hamlett 47 / Lyman 66, 90	Foster	Brigham	McCue	Hamlett	Franklin	Sale	Sellars	Bowyer	Mountford F	Liddle	Basnett F
								Townsend	*Parr*	*Butler*	*Nicholas*	*Vose*	*Pithie*	*Crooks*	*Powell*	*Lyman*	*Tunstall*	*Bivens*

#		Opponent	Date	Res	Score	HT	Att	1	2	3	4	5	6	7	8	9	10	11	Scorers
4	H	WOLVES	24/4	L	1-4	1-3	2,677	Foster *Sidlow*	Brigham *Kelly*	McCue *Crook*	Brown *McLean*	Franklin *Ashton*	Sale *Wright*	Mountford G *Jackman*	Bowyer *Dunn*	Mountford F *Westcott*	Liddle *Dorsett*	Basnett F *Crowe*	Mountford F 45 / *Westcott 6, 35, Dorsett 43, 66*
5	A	LEICESTER	26/4	W	2-1	2-1	2,424	Foster *Grant*	Kinson *Walton*	McCue *Wyles*	Hamlett *Johnston*	Franklin *Gemmell*	Kirton *Howe*	Mountford G *Hughes*	Sellars *Phillips*	Mountford F *Sharman*	Sale *Browne*	Jackson *Liddle*	Liddle 10
6	H	LEICESTER	1/5	W	3-0	1-0	1,500	Herod *Grant*	Kinson *Walton*	McCue *Gemmell*	Cowden *Smith*	Hamlett *Burdett*	Sale *Johnston*	Mountford G *Birks*	Bowyer *Staples*	Mountford F *Harrison*	Jackson *Dunkley*	Vallance *Longland*	Bowyer 24, Vallance 53, Mountford G 75

FRIENDLY

#		Opponent	Date	Res	Score	HT	Att	1	2	3	4	5	6	7	8	9	10	11	Scorers
1	A	WREXHAM	15/5	W	2-1	2-0	2,650	Podmore *Smith*	Kinson *Jones*	Vallance *Owen*	Edwards *Livingstone*	Hamlett *Stuttard*	Sale *Hill*	Mountford G *Ashcroft*	Bowyer *MacKillop*	Mountford F *Mead*	Jackson *Baines*	Basnett F *Hewitt*	Jackson 17, Mountford F 29 / *Baines 76*

LEAGUE CUP Qualifying

#		Opponent	Date	Res	Score	HT	Att	1	2	3	4	5	6	7	8	9	10	11	Scorers
1	H	CREWE	26/12	W	6-1	5-1	5,685	Bates *Poskett*	Brigham *Tagg*	McCue *Bateman*	Hamlett *Chandler*	Franklin *Glover*	Sale *Still*	Mountford G *Caffrey*	Bowyer *Waring*	Mountford F *Boothway*	Liddle *Malam*	Basnett F *Bartholemew*	Mountford F 3, 15, 66, Mountford G 8, Bates / *Still 38* [Basnett F 24, Bowyer 43]
2	A	CREWE	2/1	W	3-1	0-0	2,500	Herod *Poskett*	Kinson *Tagg*	McCue *Bateman*	Soo *Chandler*	Hamlett *Glover*	Sale *Baker*	Mountford G *Aldersea*	Bowyer *Merry*	Mountford F *Boothway*	Liddle *Malam*	Basnett F *Bartholemew*	Basnett F 48, 78, Mountford G 53 / *Waring 55*
3	H	ASTON VILLA	9/1	W	1-0	1-0	4,040	Herod *Wakeman*	Kinson *Potts*	McCue *Cummings*	Hamlett *Massie*	Franklin *Callaghan*	Sale *Iverson*	Mountford G *Broome*	Bowyer *Starling*	Mountford F *Bate*	Liddle *Parkes*	Basnett F *Houghton*	Bowyer 39
4	A	ASTON VILLA	16/1	L	0-3	0-2	10,000	Bates *Wakeman*	Brigham *Potts*	McCue *Cummings*	Hamlett *Massie*	Franklin *Callaghan*	Sale *Iverson*	Mountford G *Broome*	Bowyer *Starling*	Mountford F *Edwards*	Liddle *Parkes*	Basnett F *Houghton*	Edwards 33, 40, Broome 61
5	A	WOLVES	23/1	D	4-4	2-2	6,226	Sidlow *Wakeman*	Kinson *Dowen*	McCue *Ashton*	Hamlett *McLean*	Franklin *Galley*	Sale *Burden*	Mountford G *Buchanan*	Bowyer *Dunn*	Mountford F *Wright*	Liddle *Pritchard*	Basnett F *Mynard*	Basnett F 3, 40, Bowyer 52, 89 / *Wright 2, 45, 90, Pritchard 62*
6	H	WOLVES	30/1	D	2-2	1-1	4,250	Bates *Sidlow*	Brigham *Dowen*	McCue *Kirkham*	Hamlett *McLean*	Franklin *Mould*	Sale *Thornhill*	Mountford G *Wright*	Bowyer *Dunn*	Mountford F *Somerfield*	Liddle *McIntosh*	Basnett F *Rowley*	Bowyer 16, Mountford F 60 / *McIntosh 30, Wright 76*
7	H	WALSALL	6/2	W	2-1	1-1	4,000	Bates *Williams*	Brigham *Shelton*	McCue *Male*	Hamlett *Lewis*	Franklin *Morgan*	Sale *Harper*	Mountford G *Dunkley*	Bowyer *Newsome*	Mountford F *Ashley*	Liddle *Emmanuel*	Clewlow *Batty*	Bowyer 37, 75p / *Ashley 16*
8	A	WALSALL	13/2	L	1-4	1-1	3,000	Bates *Williams*	Brigham *Shelton*	McCue *Male*	Hamlett *Lewis*	Franklin *Harper*	Micklewright *Vause*	Mountford F *Dunkley*	Bowyer *Newsome*	Mountford F *Ashley*	Sale *Nicholls*	Basnett F *Batty*	Bowyer 9p / *Nicholls 26, 55, 88, Newsome 84*
9	H	DERBY	20/2	W	4-0	2-0	5,080	Bilton *Townsend*	Brigham *Parr*	McCue *Trim*	Hamlett *Hibbs*	Franklin *Vose*	Sale *Hann*	Mountford G *Crooks*	Bowyer *Powell*	Mountford F *Lyman*	Liddle *Weaver*	Basnett F *Duncan*	Basnett F 29, 33, Soo 51, Bowyer 57
10	A	DERBY	27/2	W	1-0	0-0	8,900	Bilton *Townsend*	Brigham *Delaney*	McCue *Beattie*	Hamlett *Corkill*	Franklin *Smith T*	Sale *Weaver*	Mountford G *Rickards*	Bowyer *Crooks*	Mountford F *McCulloch*	Liddle *Lyman*	Basnett F *Duncan*	Bowyer 77

LEAGUE CUP Proper

#		Opponent	Date	Res	Score	HT	Att	1	2	3	4	5	6	7	8	9	10	11	Scorers
1:1	A	CHESTER	6/3	W	3-2	2-0	6,500	Bilton *Fairbrother*	Brigham *Hughes*	McCue *McNeill*	Hamlett *Harris*	Franklin *Williams*	Sale *Welsh*	Mountford G *Collins*	Bowyer *Asthury*	Mountford F *Compton*	Liddle *Sharp*	Basnett F *McIntosh*	Mountford F 11, 85, Mountford G 38 / *Harris 65, Compton 78*
1:2	H	CHESTER	13/3	W	5-2	3-1	7,232	Bilton *Shortt*	Brigham *Hughes*	McCue *McNeill*	Hamlett *Clarke*	Franklin *Williams*	Sale *Booth*	Mountford G *Bremner*	Bowyer *Iddon*	Mountford F *Compton*	Liddle *Sharp*	Basnett F *McIntosh*	Bas 7, Liddle 9, Sale 45, Bow 48, 49 / *Brenner 35, Compton 62*
2:1	H	ASTON VILLA	20/3	L	1-3	0-1	18,000	Bilton *Wakeman*	Brigham *Potts*	McCue *Gutteridge*	Hamlett *Massie*	Franklin *Callaghan*	Sale *Starling*	Mountford G *Edwards*	Bowyer *Haycock*	Mountford F *Davis*	Liddle *Parkes*	Brown *Houghton*	Bowyer 85 / *Davis 36, 78, Houghton 67p*
2:2	A	ASTON VILLA	27/3	L	0-2	0-1	22,921	Bilton *Wakeman*	Brigham *Potts*	McCue *Gutteridge*	Caton *Massie*	Hamlett *Callaghan*	Sale *Starling*	Mountford G *Broome*	Bowyer *Edwards*	Mountford F *Davis*	Liddle *Haycock*	Basnett F *Houghton*	*Edwards 21, Houghton 55*

LEAGUE TABLES

SEASON 1942-43

War League North (ended 25/12/1942)	P	W	D	L	F	A	Pts
1 Blackpool	18	16	1	1	93	28	33
2 Liverpool	18	14	1	3	70	34	29
3 Sheffield Wed	18	12	3	3	61	26	27
4 Manchester U	18	12	2	4	58	26	26
5 Huddersfield	18	10	6	2	52	32	26
6 STOKE	18	11	4	3	46	25	26
7 Coventry	18	10	5	3	28	16	25
8 Southport	18	11	3	4	64	42	25
9 Derby	18	11	3	4	51	37	25
10 Bradford PA	18	8	7	3	46	21	23
11 Lincoln	18	9	5	4	58	36	23
12 Halifax	18	10	3	5	39	27	23
13 Gateshead	18	10	3	5	52	45	23
14 Aston Villa	18	10	2	4	47	33	22
15 Everton	18	10	2	5	52	41	22
16 Grimsby	17	8	5	5	42	31	21
17 York	18	9	3	6	47	36	21
18 Blackburn	18	9	3	6	56	43	21
19 Barnsley	18	8	5	5	39	30	21
20 Sheffield Utd	18	7	6	5	45	35	20
21 Birmingham	18	9	2	7	27	30	20
22 Sunderland	18	8	3	7	46	40	19
23 Chester	18	7	4	7	43	40	18
24 Walsall	18	6	5	7	33	31	17
25 Northampton	18	8	1	9	38	44	17
26 Newcastle	18	6	4	8	51	52	16
27 Chesterfield	18	5	6	7	30	34	16
28 West Brom	18	6	4	8	35	43	16
29 Notts Co	18	7	2	9	34	57	16
30 Manchester C	18	7	1	10	46	47	15
31 Nott'm For	18	6	3	9	38	39	15
32 Burnley	18	5	5	8	35	45	15
33 Leicester	18	5	4	9	53	37	14
34 Bury	18	6	2	10	53	81	14
35 Stockport	18	5	3	10	34	55	13
36 Rotherham	18	4	5	9	30	48	13
37 Tranmere	18	5	3	10	36	63	13
38 Wolves	18	5	2	11	26	41	12
39 Crewe	18	5	2	11	43	64	12
40 Middlesbrough	18	4	4	10	30	50	12
41 Rochdale	18	5	2	11	34	57	12
42 Wrexham	18	5	1	12	43	67	11
43 Leeds	18	3	4	11	28	45	10
44 Oldham	18	4	2	12	29	54	10
45 Bradford C	18	4	2	12	31	63	10
46 Bolton	18	3	3	12	31	52	9
47 Doncaster	17	3	3	11	23	41	9
48 Mansfield	18	2	4	12	25	65	8

	Appearances			Goals			
	Lge	Cup	Fri	Lge	Cup	Fri	Tot
Basnett, Albert (AE)	2			2			2
Basnett, Fred (A)	10	12	1	6	8		14
Baker, Frank	4						
Bates, Philip	11	6					
Bilton, Donald*	1	6					
Blunt, Edwin*	1						
Bowyer, Frank	23	14	1	7	12		19
Brigham, Harry	21	11					
Brown, Roy	1	1					
Caton, Bill	8	1		1			1
Clewlow, Stan	1	1					
Cowden, Stuart	1						
Edwards, Joe			1			1	1
Foster, Manny	4						
Franklin, Neil	19	12					
Glover, Stanley	1						
Hamlett, Lol*	21	13	1	1			1
Herod, Dennis	4	2					
Howell, Len	1		1				
Jackson, John	4		1				
Kinson, Bill	2	3					
Kirton, Jock	1						
Liddle, Bobby	19	13		6	1		7
McCue, Jock	24	14					
Massey, Alf	1						
Mitchell, Bert	2	1					
Micklewright, R		1					
Mountford, Frank	22	14	1	13	6	1	20
Mountford, George	8	13	1	4	4		8
Mould, Billy	1	1					
Ormston, Alec	2						
Peppitt, Sid	2			1			1
Podmore, Edgar		1	1				
Sale, Tommy	23	14	1	9	1		10
Sellars, Johnny	2						
Sherratt, Fred	4						
Soo, Frank	12	1		3	1		4
Tutin, Arthur	1						
Vallance, Tommy	1		1	1			1
Ware, Harry*	1						
(own-goals)				1			1
38 players used	264	154	11	55	33	2	90
*guest players							

North 2nd Phase (26/12/41 to 1/5/43)

	P	W	D	L	F	A	Pts
1 Liverpool	20	15	2	3	64	32	32
2 Lovell's Athletic	20	11	5	4	63	32	27
3 Manchester C	19	11	5	3	43	24	27
4 Aston Villa	20	13	1	6	44	30	27
5 Sheffield Wed	20	9	8	3	43	26	26
6 Manchester U	19	11	3	5	52	26	25
7 York	18	11	3	4	52	30	25
8 Huddersfield	19	11	3	5	48	28	25
9 Coventry	20	11	3	6	33	21	25
10 STOKE	20	10	4	6	42	34	24
11 West Brom	20	11	2	7	49	40	24
12 Notts Co	18	9	6	5	37	34	24
13 Blackpool	19	8	7	4	49	31	23
14 Newcastle	19	10	3	6	62	42	23
15 Blackburn	18	9	4	5	45	35	22
16 Bristol City	19	8	6	5	41	33	22
17 Chesterfield	20	9	4	7	35	30	22
18 Derby	20	8	5	7	41	34	21
19 Aberaman	18	10	1	7	39	41	21
20 Sunderland	19	8	4	7	58	40	20
21 Rochdale	16	9	2	5	39	26	20
22 Leicester	20	9	2	9	40	37	20
23 Sheffield Utd	19	8	4	7	43	42	20
24 Bradford PA	19	7	5	7	35	31	19
25 Everton	19	9	1	9	51	46	19
26 Bath	18	7	4	7	49	46	18
27 Birmingham	20	8	2	10	32	29	18
28 Barnsley	17	8	2	7	34	37	18
29 Nott'm For	18	7	4	7	30	34	18
30 Crewe	20	7	4	9	44	57	18
31 Bradford C	16	7	2	7	29	29	16
32 Wrexham	17	7	3	7	36	37	17
33 Bolton	17	7	2	8	34	42	16
34 Tranmere	20	6	4	10	37	48	16
35 Halifax	18	7	2	9	30	39	16
36 Chester	20	6	3	11	40	49	15
37 Northampton	17	6	2	9	30	37	14
38 Wolves	17	5	4	8	38	45	14
39 Swansea	18	4	6	8	36	52	14
40 Grimsby	13	4	5	4	30	27	13
41 Bury	16	5	3	8	44	42	13
42 Doncaster	17	5	3	9	27	41	13
43 Rotherham	18	4	5	9	28	43	13
44 Gateshead	13	6	0	7	29	36	12
45 Stockport	19	4	4	11	37	76	12
46 Southport	18	4	3	11	38	58	11
47 Leeds	16	5	1	10	32	50	11
48 Oldham	18	4	3	11	28	47	11
49 Middlesbrough	18	5	0	13	31	69	10
50 Lincoln	10	4	1	5	23	18	9
51 Burnley	14	3	3	8	17	31	9
52 Walsall	16	3	2	11	22	35	8
53 Cardiff	17	2	3	12	22	47	7
54 Mansfield	10	1	1	8	12	41	3

Stoke's 20 games (6 League North 2nd phase; 10 League Cup qualifiers; 4 League Cup proper)

LEAGUE NORTH 1st PHASE — Manager: Bob McGrory — SEASON 1943-44

No	H/A	Date	Team	Att	Pos	Pt	F-A	H-T	Scorers, Times, and Referees	1	2	3	4	5	6	7	8	9	10	11
1	H	28/8	ASTON VILLA	6,000	L	0	0-2	0-1	*Broome 25, Edwards 52*	Podmore / *Wakeman*	Brigham / *Potts*	McCue / *Gutteridge*	Hamlett / *Massie*	Franklin / *Callaghan*	Sale / *Iverson*	Mountford G / *Edwards*	Bowyer / *Haycock*	Mountford F / *Broome*	Liddle / *Starling*	Basnett F / *Houghton*
2	A	4/9	ASTON VILLA	12,000	L	0	1-2	0-1	Sale 88 / *Houghton 35p, Broome 62*	Podmore / *Wakeman*	Brigham / *Potts*	McCue / *Cummings*	Hamlett / *Massie*	Simpson / *Morby*	Soo / *Iverson*	Mountford G / *Edwards*	Bowyer / *Haycock*	Sale / *Broome*	Sale / *Starling*	Mountford F / *Houghton*
3	H	11/9	CREWE	4,905	L	0	1-2	1-2	Mountford F 14 / *Anderson 6, Inskip 20*	Podmore / *Paskett*	Brigham / *Parker*	McCue / *Scott*	Hamlett / *Chandler*	Simpson / *Slater*	Sale / *Glover*	Mountford G / *Anderson*	Bowyer / *Malam*	Mountford F / *Black*	Liddle / *Blunt*	Basnett F / *Inskip*
4	H	18/9	CREWE	3,950	W	2	4-2	2-1	Sale 24, Bowyer 28, 85, Mountford G 88 / *Blunt 7, Mould 50 (og)*	Podmore / *Paskett*	Brigham / *Parker*	McCue / *Glover*	Hamlett / *Chandler*	Mould / *Slater*	Franklin / *Gregory*	Mountford G / *Aldersey*	Bowyer / *Malam*	Sale / *Black*	Liddle / *Blunt*	Basnett F / *Inskip*
5	H	25/9	DERBY	4,000	W	4	5-1	1-1	Leuty 16 (og), Peppitt 62, 88, Crooks 17 [Mountford G 65, Franklin 78] *Townsend*	Podmore / *Townsend*	Brigham / *Parr*	McCue / *Firth*	Hamlett / *Hibbs*	Mould / *Leuty*	Franklin / *Musson*	Mountford G / *Crooks*	Bowyer / *Powell*	Sale / *Challenger*	Peppitt / *Hinchcliffe*	Crossley / *Duncan*
6	A	2/10	DERBY	6,287	D	5	2-2	2-2	Bowyer 1, Liddle 44 / *Nicholas 16, Duncan 20*	Podmore / *Boulton*	Hamlett / *Parr*	McCue / *Howe*	Harrison / *Nicholas*	Franklin / *Leuty*	Sale / *Hann*	Mountford G / *Jones*	Bowyer / *Powell*	Mountford F / *Thompson*	Liddle / *Crooks*	Basnett F / *Duncan*
7	H	9/10	WOLVES	5,119	W	7	5-0	4-0	Basnett F 2, 43, Bowyer 29, [Mountford G 37, 75] *Prince*	Podmore / *Prince*	Kinson / *Kelly*	McCue / *Taylor*	Hamlett / *McLean*	Franklin / *Shorthouse*	Sale / *Crook A*	Mountford G / *Wagg*	Bowyer / *Dunn*	Mountford F / *Wishaw*	Liddle / *Crooks*	Basnett F / *Aldecoa*
8	A	16/10	WOLVES	6,221	W	9	2-1	0-1	Basnett F 8, 53 / *Isherwood 88*	Podmore / *Sidlow*	Kinson / *Kelly*	McCue / *Taylor*	Hamlett / *McLean*	Mould / *Ashton*	Sale / *Morgan*	Mountford G / *Stephens*	Bowyer / *Isherwood*	Sale / *Dorsett*	Liddle / *Crook W*	Basnett F / *Aldecoa*
9	A	23/10	BIRMINGHAM	4,085	D	10	1-1	1-1	Mountford G 16 / *Dearson 28*	Podmore / *Merrick*	Kinson / *Turner H*	McCue / *Quinton*	Franklin / *Accuroff*	Wright / *Turner A*	Sale / *Bye*	Mountford G / *Mulraney*	Bowyer / *Dearson*	Jackson / *Trigg*	Ormston / *Shaw*	Basnett F / *Bright*
10	H	30/10	BIRMINGHAM	3,900	L	10	0-1	0-1	*Trigg 24, Mulraney 68*	Podmore / *Merrick*	Kinson / *Turner H*	McCue / *Quinton*	Franklin / *Shaw*	Turner A / *Turner A*	Sale / *Mitchell*	Mountford G / *Mulraney*	Bowyer / *Dearson*	Jackson / *Trigg*	Liddle / *Jennings*	Basnett F / *Sibley*
11	A	6/11	WEST BROM	3,520	D	11	3-3	1-1	Sale 25, 56, Liddle 53 / *Elliott 37, Richardson 68, Hodgetts 71*	Podmore / *Heath*	Kinson / *Bassett*	McCue / *Southam*	Kinson / *Sankey*	Mould / *Gripton*	Kirton / *Millard*	Liddle / *Elliott*	Bowyer / *Armstrong*	Sale / *Richardson*	Mountford F / *Evans A*	Basnett F / *Hodgetts*
12	H	13/11	WEST BROM	6,912	D	11	0-3	0-3	*Evans C 5, Richardson 30, 37*	Podmore / *Heath*	Brigham / *Bassett*	McCue / *Southam*	Edwards / *Whitcombe*	Shufflebotham / *Gripton*	Kinson / *Millard*	Mountford G / *Hodgetts*	Mountford G / *Evans C*	Sale / *Richardson*	Mountford F / *Evans A*	Basnett F / *Russell*
13	A	20/11	WREXHAM	3,850	L	11	1-4	1-1	Sale 15 [Livingstone 90] / *Horsman 17, 46, Malam 49p*	Podmore / *Smith*	Jones / *Smith*	McCue / *Stuttard*	Franklin / *Savage*	Tudor / *Tudor*	Sale / *Hill*	Mountford G / *Simms*	Bowyer / *Bremner*	Mountford F / *Horsman*	Liddle / *Livingstone*	Basnett F / *Malam*
14	A	27/11	WREXHAM	3,000	W	13	7-3	3-2	Sale 14, 56p, Bas' 16, 85, Steele 28, 80, Horsman 23, 47, Livingstone 25, Liddle 86	Foster / *Whitelaw*	Kinson / *Jones*	McCue / *Stuttard*	Franklin / *Savage*	Mould / *Hayward*	Franklin / *Livingstone*	Liddle / *Smith*	Bowyer / *Bremner*	Steele / *Horsman*	Sale / *Malam*	Basnett F / *Hill*
15	H	4/12	CREWE	3,521	W	15	5-0	2-0	Sale 6, 82, Peppitt 40, 70, Basnett 51	Foster / *Paskett*	Kinson / *Parker*	McCue / *Bateman*	Franklin / *Jones*	Mould / *Hayward*	Wordley / *Livingstone*	Basnett F / *Inskip*	Bowyer / *McCormick*	Peppitt / *Cochrane*	Sale / *Blunt*	Ormston / *Hepley*
16	A	11/12	CREWE	3,000	L	15	1-2	1-0	Franklin 37 / *Roberts 46, Blunt 88*	Foster / *Paskett*	Kinson / *Parker*	McCue / *Bateman*	Franklin / *Jones*	Mould / *Cope*	Mountford F / *Still*	Liddle / *Inskip*	Bowyer / *McCormick*	Peppitt / *Roberts*	Sale / *Blunt*	Ormston / *Hepley*
17	A	18/12	WALSALL	1,116	L	15	2-4	0-1	Clewlow 68, Rist 83 (og) / *Batty 44, Roberts 48, Brown 71, 80*	Foster / *Williams*	Hamlett / *Shelton*	Glover / *Male*	Hamlett / *Lewis*	Mould / *Rist*	Mountford F / *Emanuel*	Liddle / *Roberts*	Bowyer / *Hinsley*	Sale / *Tranter*	Clewlow / *Brown*	Basnett F / *Batty*
18	H	25/12	WALSALL	6,022	L	15	0-1	0-1	*Unknown*	Foster / *Williams*	Dunn / *Shelton*	Valance / *Male*	Hamlett / *Lewis*	Franklin / *Rist*	Mountford F / *Emanuel*	Liddle / *Roberts*	Windsor / *Cooper*	Sale / *Richman*	West / *Brown*	Basnett F / *Batty*

LEAGUE NORTH 2nd PHASE

No	H/A	Date	Team	Att	Pos	Pt	F-A	H-T	Scorers, Times, and Referees	1	2	3	4	5	6	7	8	9	10	11
19	H	18/3	LEICESTER	3,279	L	15	2-5	1-3	Mountford F 40, Sellars / *Knott 2, 20, 90, Smith A 45, Little*	Foster / *Bradley*	Kinson / *Frame*	McCue / *Howe*	Franklin / *Smith B*	Hayward / *Gemmell*	Liddle / *Dickie*	Mountford G / *Little*	Sellars / *Smith A*	Sale / *Knott*	Bowyer / *Jones*	Mountford F / *Crossland*
20	A	25/3	LEICESTER	7,000	D	16	2-2	1-0	Dewis 82, 88	Foster / *Bradley*	Kinson / *Frame*	McCue / *Howe*	Franklin / *Sparrow*	Mould / *Gemmell*	Mountford F / *Sheard*	Basnett F / *King*	Bowyer / *Smith S*	Sale / *Dewis*	Liddle / *Dickis*	Mountford F / *Ormston*
21	H	10/4	CREWE	4,350	W	18	6-1	3-0	Bowyer 8, Mountf'd F 25, Pointon 30, Sale / *Jones*	Wilkinson / *French*	Brigham / *Glover*	McCue / *Bateman*	Kinson / *Jones*	Franklin / *Hughes*	Mountford F / *Hill*	Liddle / *Inskip*	Bowyer / *Blunt*	Pointon / *Bailey*	Sale / *Roberts*	Harrison / *Aldersey*
22	H	29/4	WOLVES	1,422	D	19	2-2	0-0	Jackson 80, Sale 86 / *Aldecoa 50, Wishaw 55*	Herod / *Billingsley*	Brigham / *Ashton*	McCue / *Owens*	Edwards / *Alderton*	Franklin / *McLean*	Franklin / *Crook*	Mountford F / *Stephens*	Sellars / *Dunn*	Sale / *Wishaw*	Bowyer / *Wood*	Jackson / *Aldecoa*
23	A	6/5	WOLVES	1,997	L	19	1-2	1-2	Watkin 26 / *McLean 16, Aldecoa 24*	Foster / *Billingsley*	Kinson / *Kelly*	McCue / *Ashton*	Franklin / *McLean*			Basnett F / *Stephens*			Bowyer / *Liddle*	

LEAGUE CUP Qualifying

#		Date	Opponent		Res	FT	HT	Att	Scorers
1	A	27/12	WOLVES		D	1-1	0-0	19,951	Sale 76 / *Aldecoa 86*
2	H	1/1	WOLVES		W	9-3	6-1	5,671	St' 7,32,36,49,57,68, Sa' 25p,29, Lid' 38 / *Wright 4, Griffiths 48 (og), Westcott 86*
3	H	8/1	ASTON VILLA		W	6-3	4-0	16,492	Peppitt 14, 20, 75, Sale 33, 35p, 78 / *O'Donnell 51, Haycock 53, Houghton 84*
4	A	15/1	ASTON VILLA		W	2-0	1-0	32,000	Kirton 4, Ormston 81
5	A	22/1	BIRMINGHAM		L	1-4	0-2	10,000	Basnett F 48 [Bright 77] / *Mitchell 24, Acquroff 30, Mulraney 55, Merrick 55*
6	H	29/1	BIRMINGHAM		W	4-1	2-0	19,558	Steele 20, 56, 80p, Sale 43 / *Trigg 88*
7	H	5/2	WALSALL		W	5-1	2-1	3,962	Sale 5, 16, Shelton 75 (og), Peppitt 82, / *Brown 25 [Ormston 88]*
8	A	12/2	WALSALL		W	2-0	0-0	3,127	Sale 47, Mountford F 80
9	A	19/2	WEST BROM		W	8-2	2-0	5,000	Sale 5, 55, 62, Steele 32, Bowyer / *Duns, Elliott p*
10	H	26/2	WEST BROM		W	5-4	3-1	8,030	Sale 22, 88, Steele 24, 25, Mountf'd G 48 / *Elliott 15, 50, 77, Duns 84*

Line-ups (bold = team; *italic = opponents*)

#	Foster	Griffiths	Hayward	Massey	Franklin	Cowden	Liddle	Bowyer	Sale	Mountford F	Basnett F
	Sidlow	*Kelly*	*Dowen*	*Crook*	*Ashton*	*Gardner*	*Stephens*	*Hazelton*	*McLean*	*Dunn*	*Aldecoa*
1	Foster	Griffiths	Hayward	Massey	Franklin	Cowden	Liddle	Bowyer	Sale	Mountford F	Basnett F
	Sidlow	*Kelly*	*Dowen*	*Crook*	*Ashton*	*Gardner*	*Stephens*	*Hazelton*	*McLean*	*Dunn*	*Aldecoa*
2	Foster	Griffiths	Hayward	Soo	Franklin	Kirton	Liddle	Bowyer	Steele	Sale	Mountford F
	Sidlow	*Kelly*	*Kirkham*	*Crook*	*Ashton*	*McLean*	*Jackman*	*Wright*	*Westcott*	*Alderton*	*Aldecoa*
3	Foster	Brigham	McCue	Franklin	Mould	Franklin	Matthews	Bowyer	Peppitt	Peppitt	Basnett F
	Wakeman	*Potts*	*Cummings*	*Starling*	*Marby*	*Iverson*	*Broome*	*Parkes*	*O'Donnell*	*Haycock*	*Houghton*
4	Foster	Hayward	McCue	Franklin	Mould	Kirton	Matthews	Peppitt	Steele	Sale	Ormston
	Wakeman	*Potts*	*Cummings*	*Massie*	*Callaghan*	*Iverson*	*Broome*	*Starling*	*Davies*	*Haycock*	*Houghton*
5	Wilkinson	Brigham	McCue	Mountford F	Franklin	Kirton	Basnett F	Bowyer	Steele	Sale	Ormston
	Merrick	*Turner H*	*Jennings*	*Dearson*	*Turner A*	*Mitchell*	*Mulraney*	*Roberts*	*Acquroff*	*Shaw*	*Bright*
6	Wilkinson	Griffiths	Hayward	Franklin	Mould	Kirton	Matthews	Peppitt	Steele	Sale	Ormston
	Merrick	*Turner H*	*Jennings*	*Dearson*	*Turner A*	*Shaw*	*Mulraney*	*Quinton*	*Trigg*	*Roberts*	*Bright*
7	Foster	Griffiths	McCue	Franklin	Hayward	Mountford F	Mountford G	Liddle	Peppitt	Sale	Ormston
	Williams	*Shelton*	*Batty*	*Dougal*	*Lewis*	*Emanuel*	*Mullen*	*Hinsley*	*Welsh*	*Brown*	*Dudley*
8	Wilkinson	Kinson	McCue	Franklin	Mould	Kirton	Mountford G	Mountford F	Peppitt	Sale	Ormston
	Williams	*Shelton*	*Batty*	*Lowrie*	*Lewis*	*Emanuel*	*Mullen*	*Hinsley*	*Dougal*	*Brown*	*Dudley*
9	Wilkinson	Kinson	McCue	Franklin	Mould	Mountford F	Mountford G	Bowyer	Steele	Sale	Liddle
	Heath	*Southam*	*Smith*	*Millard*	*Gripton*	*McNab*	*Elliott*	*Jones E*	*Duns*	*Evans C*	*Hodgetts*
10	Wilkinson	Kinson	McCue	Franklin	Mould	Kirton	Mountford G	Bowyer	Steele	Sale	Liddle
	Heath	*Southam*	*Smith*	*Millard*	*Gripton*	*Williams*	*Duns*	*McNab*	*Elliott*	*Evans C*	*Hodgetts*

LEAGUE CUP Proper

#		Date	Opponent		Res	FT	HT	Att	Scorers
1:1	H	4/3	ASTON VILLA		L	4-5	4-3	11,050	Steele 15, 39, Sale 34p, 45p / *Martin 10, Broome 21,62, Hough' 26, 50*
1:2	A	11/3	ASTON VILLA		L	0-3	0-0	23,500	/ *Houghton 46, 50p, Broome*

#	Foster	Griffiths	Hayward	Massey	Franklin	Cowden	Liddle	Bowyer	Sale	Mountford F	Basnett F
1:1	Foster	Brigham	McCue	Franklin	Mould	Kirton	Mountford G	Peppitt	Steele	Mountford F	Liddle
	Wakeman	*Potts*	*Cummings*	*Massie*	*Callaghan*	*Iverson*	*Broome*	*Martin*	*O'Donnell*	*Starling*	*Houghton*
1:2	Foster	Brigham	McCue	Massey	Franklin	Kirton	Mountford G	Bowyer	Mountford F	Sale	Basnett F
	Wakeman	*Potts*	*Cummings*	*Massie*	*Callaghan*	*Iverson*	*Broome*	*Starling*	*O'Donnell*	*Parkes*	*Houghton*

MIDLAND CUP

#		Date	Opponent		Res	FT	HT	Att	Scorers
1:1	H	1/4	DERBY		W	3-1	2-1	7,000	Peppitt 38, Steele 40, Bowyer 57 / *Harrison 23*
1:2	H	8/4	DERBY		D	1-1	0-0	5,788	Basnett F 66 / *Grace 54*
SF 1	H	15/4	WEST BROM		D	1-1	1-1	3,434	Sale 15 / *Elliott 18*
SF 2	A	22/4	WEST BROM		L	1-3	1-1	7,030	Southam 12 (og) / *Elliott 18, Heaselgr' 59, Richardson 65*

#	Foster	Griffiths	Hayward	Massey	Franklin	Cowden	Liddle	Bowyer	Sale	Mountford F	Basnett F
1:1	Wilkinson	Brigham	McCue	Franklin	Mould	Mountford F	Peppitt	Bowyer	Steele	Sale	Ormston
	Swindin	*Griffiths*	*Trim*	*Nicholas*	*Leury*	*Hann*	*Crooks*	*Harrison*	*McCulloch*	*Grace*	*Duncan*
1:2	Wilkinson	Brigham	McCue	Mountford F	Franklin	Cowden	Liddle	Windsor	Sale	Bowyer	Basnett F
	Swindin	*Parr*	*Trim*	*Lambert*	*Leury*	*Musson*	*Jones T*	*Crooks*	*Knight*	*Grace*	*Duncan*
SF 1	Foster	Brigham	McCue	Mountford F	Franklin	Cowden	Sellars	Bowyer	Sale	Pointon	Basnett F
	Heath	*Millard*	*Smith*	*Williams*	*Gripton*	*McNab*	*Elliott*	*Heaselgrave*	*Acquroff*	*Evans C*	*Hodgetts*
SF 2	Foster	Kinson	McCue	Franklin	Mould	Mountford F	Liddle	Blunt	Peppitt	Sale	Clewlow
	Heath	*Southam*	*Smith*	*Millard*	*Gripton*	*McNab*	*Elliott*	*Heaselgrave*	*Richardson*	*Evans C*	*Hodgetts*

LEAGUE TABLES

SEASON 1943-44

War League North (Ending 25/12/1943)

		P	W	D	L	F	A	Pts
1	Blackpool	18	12	4	2	56	20	28
2	Manchester U	18	13	2	3	56	30	28
3	Liverpool	18	13	1	4	72	26	27
4	Doncaster	18	11	5	2	45	25	27
5	Bradford PA	18	11	4	3	65	28	26
6	Huddersfield	18	12	2	4	48	25	26
7	Northampton	18	10	5	3	43	25	25
8	Aston Villa	18	11	3	4	43	27	25
9	Sunderland	18	10	3	5	46	30	23
10	Hartlepool	18	10	3	5	44	31	23
11	Everton	18	9	4	5	60	34	22
12	Blackburn	18	10	2	6	47	32	22
13	Rochdale	18	10	2	6	43	41	22
14	Sheffield Utd	18	8	5	5	30	26	21
15	Lincoln	18	8	4	6	51	40	20
16	Birmingham	18	8	4	6	38	31	20
17	Manchester C	18	9	2	7	38	35	20
18	Mansfield	18	9	2	7	32	33	20
19	Derby	18	8	4	6	43	45	20
20	Chester	18	9	2	7	40	43	20
21	Grimsby	18	8	3	7	32	36	19
22	West Brom	18	8	3	7	42	44	19
23	Gateshead	18	8	2	8	40	51	18
24	Burnley	18	5	7	6	24	22	17
25	Walsall	18	5	7	6	27	31	17
26	Nott'm For	18	6	5	7	33	39	17
27	Leeds	18	6	5	7	38	50	17
28	Leicester	18	6	4	8	30	30	16
29	Darlington	18	6	4	8	49	48	16
30	Rotherham	18	7	2	9	38	42	16
31	York	18	7	2	9	35	40	16
32	Halifax	18	6	4	8	27	36	16
33	Southport	18	6	4	8	33	51	16
34	STOKE	18	6	3	9	40	35	15
35	Chesterfield	18	7	1	10	29	31	15
36	Oldham	18	7	1	10	30	44	15
37	Stockport	18	5	5	8	24	43	15
38	Coventry	18	4	6	8	25	23	14
39	Newcastle	18	5	4	9	32	37	14
40	Sheffield Wed	18	5	4	9	34	34	14
41	Middlesbrough	18	4	6	8	35	52	14
42	Wolves	18	5	3	10	30	42	13
43	Bury	18	6	1	11	31	44	13
44	Barnsley	18	5	2	11	32	42	12
45	Bradford C	18	4	3	11	27	47	11
46	Wrexham	18	5	1	12	24	63	11
47	Notts Co	18	4	3	11	26	53	11
48	Bolton	18	3	4	11	24	46	10
49	Tranmere	18	4	1	13	39	71	9
50	Crewe	18	4	1	13	29	82	9

	Appearances		Goals		
	Lge	Cup	Lge	Cup	Tot
Basnett, Fred (A)	16	1	6	2	8
Blunt, Edwin*		1			
Bowyer, Frank	22	15	7	2	9
Brigham, Harry	9	7			
Caton, Bill	2	1			
Clewlow, Stan	1		1		1
Cowden, Stuart	1	3			
Crossley, Roy	2				
Dunn, Douglas		1			
Edwards, Joe	3				
Foster, Manny	8	9	2		2
Franklin, Neil	18	16			
Glover, Stanley	1				
Griffiths, Jack*		4			
Hamlett, Lol*	9	1			
Harrison, Stanley	2				
Hayward, Eric*		5			
Herod, Dennis	1				
Jackson, John	3		1		1
Kinson, Bill	14	4			
Kirton, Jock	7	7		1	1
Liddle, Billy	19	8	3	1	4
McCue, Jock	21	13			
Matthews, Stan		3			
Massey, Alf		2			
Mould, Billy	11	9			
Mountford, Frank	17	12	3	1	4
Mountford, George	13	6	5	1	6
Ormston, Alec	4	6	1	2	3
Pappitt, Sid	3	8	4	5	9
Podmore, Edgar	13				
Pointon, Arthur*	1	1			
Sale, Tommy	23	16	12	18	30
Sellars, Johnny	2	1	1		1
Shufflebotham, Roy	1				
Simpson, Jock*	2				
Soo, Frank	1	1			
Steele, Freddie	1	8	2	18	20
Vallance, Tommy	1				
Watkin, Cyril	1		1		1
West, Ken	1				
Wilkinson, Norman	1	7			
Windsor, Bobby	1	1			
Wordley, Ted	1				
Wright, George*	1				
(own-goals)			2	2	4
45 players used	253	176	52	53	105

* guest players

Stoke lost to the eventual League North Cup winners Aston Villa, who beat the holders, Stan Matthews' Blackpool, 5-4 on aggregate in the final.

		P	W	D	L	F	A	Pts
1	Bath	21	16	2	3	78	26	34
2	Wrexham	21	15	4	2	62	29	34
3	Liverpool	21	14	2	5	71	38	30
4	Birmingham	20	12	5	3	47	19	29
5	Rotherham	21	12	5	4	54	30	29
6	Aston Villa	21	13	3	5	50	34	29
7	Blackpool	20	12	3	5	53	27	27
8	Cardiff	21	13	1	7	53	28	27
9	Manchester U	21	10	7	4	53	28	27
10	Bradford PA	20	11	4	5	55	38	26
11	Newcastle	20	13	0	7	50	30	26
12	Everton	21	12	1	8	47	36	25
13	STOKE	21	10	5	6	73	39	25
14	Leicester	21	10	5	6	66	45	25
15	Darlington	21	11	2	8	40	32	24
16	Nottingham F	20	9	6	5	50	30	24
17	Sheffield U	21	11	2	8	32	20	24
18	Coventry	21	10	4	7	53	35	24
19	Manchester C	21	9	6	6	48	37	24
20	Lovell's	20	10	2	8	48	30	22
21	Gateshead	21	9	4	8	45	53	22
22	Doncaster	17	9	3	5	42	33	21
23	Derby	21	8	5	8	33	28	21
24	Rochdale	20	8	5	7	40	36	21
25	Barnsley	17	8	4	5	34	30	20

		P	W	D	L	F	A	Pts
26	Halifax	20	8	4	8	44	42	20
27	Chester	20	9	2	9	65	63	20
28	Hartlepool	20	8	4	8	49	50	20
29	Stockport	19	10	0	9	44	49	20
30	Sheffield W	20	8	4	8	32	36	20
31	Blackburn	16	8	3	5	30	27	19
32	Huddersfield	21	8	3	10	41	40	19
33	WBA	21	8	3	9	46	48	19
34	Bolton	21	8	3	10	42	49	19
35	Leeds	18	8	3	7	34	40	19
36	Northampton	19	9	0	10	37	39	18
37	Burnley	18	6	6	6	39	42	18
38	Bristol C	18	6	5	9	38	42	17
39	York	20	7	2	11	37	40	16
40	Middlesbrough	21	6	4	11	41	51	16
41	Swansea	20	7	2	11	42	67	16
42	Grimsby	15	6	3	6	23	28	15
43	Bury	20	6	3	11	38	55	15
44	Oldham	18	5	4	9	36	36	14
45	Sunderland	19	6	2	11	44	58	14
46	Chesterfield	19	5	4	10	31	41	14
47	Mansfield	14	6	1	7	23	25	13
48	Wolves	20	3	6	11	28	56	12
49	Walsall	17	3	6	8	17	35	12
50	Tranmere	20	6	0	14	29	62	12

Stoke's 21 games (5 League North 2nd phase; 10 League Cup qualifiers; 2 League Cup proper; 4 Midland Cup)

LEAGUE NORTH 1st PHASE — Manager: Bob McGrory — SEASON 1944-45

No	Date	Att	Pos	Pt	F-A	H-T	Scorers, Times, and Referees	1	2	3	4	5	6	7	8	9	10	11
1	A ASTON VILLA 26/8	18,000		0	0-4	0-1	*Parkes 40, 85, Iverson 49, Edwards 70*	Podmore / *Wakeman*	Brigham / *Potts*	McCue / *Cummings*	Mountford F / *Massie*	Franklin / *Callaghan*	Cowden / *Starling*	Mountford G / *Goffin*	Bowyer / *Edwards*	Steele / *Parkes*	Sale / *Iverson*	Poulton / *Houghton*
2	H ASTON VILLA 2/9	9,022	W	2	3-1	0-0	Poulton 63, Sale 88, 73p / *Parkes 80*	Podmore / *Wakeman*	Brigham / *Potts*	McCue / *Cummings*	Mountford F / *Massie*	Franklin / *Callaghan*	Cowden / *Starling*	Liddle / *Goffin*	Bowyer / *Edwards*	Steele / *Parkes*	Sale / *Haycock*	Poulton / *Houghton*
3	H NORTHAMPTON 9/9	6,311	W	4	5-0	4-0	Bowyer 15, Steele 22, 27, 79, Poulton 25	Podmore / *Lee*	Brigham / *Smalley*	McCue / *Welsh*	Mountford F / *Harris*	Franklin / *Shepherdson*	Cowden / *Coley*	Mountford G / *Roberts*	Bowyer / *O'Neill*	Steele / *Perry*	Sale / *Greenway*	Poulton / *Pritchard*
4	A NORTHAMPTON 16/9	3,972	D	5	1-1	1-1	Bowyer 6 / *Perry 4*	Podmore / *Lee*	Brigham / *Smalley*	McCue / *Dennison*	Mountford F / *Harris*	Franklin / *Shepherdson*	Cowden / *Coley*	Mountford G / *Pritchard*	Bowyer / *Billingham*	Steele / *Perry*	Sale / *Welsh*	Poulton / *Harrell*
5	H WOLVES 23/9	16,669	W	7	2-0	0-0	Poulton 52, 69	Podmore / *Scott*	Brigham / *Morris*	McCue / *Smith*	Mountford F / *McLean*	Franklin / *Ashton*	Cowden / *Patterson*	Matthews / *Roberts*	Bowyer / *Finch*	Steele / *Acquroff*	Sale / *Dorsett*	Poulton / *Mullen*
6	A WOLVES 30/9	12,134	L	7	1-4	0-1	Sale 68 / *Wright 15, Acquroff 60, Alderton 67, [Finch 84]*	Podmore / *Scott*	Brigham / *Morris*	McCue / *Smith*	Mountford F / *Wharton*	Franklin / *McLean*	Cowden / *Crook*	Liddle / *Roberts*	Bowyer / *Alderton*	Steele / *Acquroff*	Sale / *Wright*	Poulton / *Finch*
7	A WALSALL 7/10	4,269	D	8	1-1	1-0	Sale 4 / *Vinall 87*	Marks / *Williams*	Brigham / *Shelton*	McCue / *Male*	Mountford F / *Lewis*	Franklin / *Rist*	Cowden / *Lowery*	Mountford G / *White*	Bowyer / *Hinsley*	Sale / *Vinall*	Steele / *Vinall*	Poulton / *Hobbis*
8	H WALSALL 14/10	4,126	L	8	0-2	0-1	*Vinall 33, Hobbis 55*	Marks / *Williams*	Brigham / *Shelton*	McCue / *Male*	Mountford F / *Lewis*	Franklin / *Rist*	Cowden / *Vinall*	Mountford G / *White*	Bowyer / *Hinsley*	Sale / *Armstrong*	Steele / *Peace*	Jackson / *Hobbis*
9	H BIRMINGHAM 21/10	4,962	D	9	0-0	0-0		Herod / *Merrick*	Kinson / *Jennings*	McCue / *Craven*	Brown / *Shaw*	Franklin / *Turner*	Cowden / *Stanton*	Mountford G / *Mulraney*	Sellars / *Faulkener*	Mountford F / *Dearson*	Steele / *Barrett*	Poulton / *Bright*
10	A BIRMINGHAM 28/10	7,988	D	10	1-1	1-1	Steele 11 / *Bright 25*	Herod / *Merrick*	Kinson / *Jennings*	McCue / *Jenks*	Brown / *Small*	Franklin / *Turner*	Mountford F / *Hickin*	Sellars / *Faulkener*	Sellars / *Mulraney*	Sellars / *Dearson*	Bowyer / *Shaw*	Bright
11	A WEST BROM 4/11	18,656	W	12	3-2	2-1	Sale 35, 47, Matthews 65 / *Elliott 12, Evans 33*	Foster / *Lewis*	Kinson / *Tranter*	McCue / *Millard*	Mountford F / *Williams*	Franklin / *Gripton*	Cowden / *McNab*	Matthews / *Elliott*	Sellars / *Heaselgrave*	Steele / *Clarke*	Bowyer / *Evans*	Sale / *Hodgetts*
12	H WEST BROM 11/11	7,664	L	12	2-3	2-3	Steele 10, Sale 14p / *Clarke 7, 36, 44*	Foster / *Lewis*	Kinson / *Tranter*	McCue / *Millard*	Mountford F / *Williams*	Franklin / *Gripton*	Cowden / *McNab*	Matthews / *Elliott*	Matthews / *Heaselgrave*	Bowyer / *Clarke*	Sale / *Evans*	Mannion / *Hodgetts*
13	H PORT VALE 18/11	16,163	W	14	2-0	0-0	Bowyer 56, 70	Foster / *Prince H*	Watkin / *Griffiths J*	McCue / *Sproson*	Mountford F / *Smith*	Franklin / *Griffiths H*	Jackson / *Wright*	Matthews / *Prince E*	Bowyer / *Lane*	Bowyer / *Pursell*	Sale / *Bellis*	Mannion / *Painton*
14	A PORT VALE 25/11	9,618	L	14	0-3	0-2	*McDowall 24, Bellis 35, Griffiths P 71*	Foster / *Prince H*	Brigham / *Griffiths J*	McCue / *Sproson*	Mountford F / *Martin*	Franklin / *Griffiths H*	Jackson / *Sproson*	Mountford G / *Lane*	Bowyer / *McDowall*	Basnett F / *Griffiths P*	Sale / *Bellis*	Mannion / *Maudesley*
15	A COVENTRY 2/12	6,405	W	16	1-0	0-0	Sale 61	Herod / *Bowles*	Brigham / *Brown*	McCue / *Elliott*	Mountford F / *O'Brien*	Mountford F / *Mason*	Jackson / *Crawley*	Mountford G / *McKeown A*	Bowyer / *Frith*	Bowyer / *Paul*	Liddle / *McKeown J*	Sellars / *Edwards*
16	H COVENTRY 9/12	3,584	W	18	5-0	1-0	Sale 37p, 55, 61, Bowyer, Mannion	Foster / *Bowles*	Brigham / *Douglas F*	McCue / *Elliott*	Sellars / *Frith*	Mountford F / *Mason*	Jackson / *O'Brien*	Basnett F / *Simpson*	Bowyer / *Crawley*	Sale / *Robinson*	Liddle / *Kerry*	Edwards / *Edwards*
17	H LEICESTER 16/12	4,120	W	20	5-2	1-2	Frame 5 (og), Matthews 56, 77, [Sale 58, 85] / *Iddon 16, Cheney 35*	Herod / *Major*	Brigham / *Frame*	McCue / *Howe*	Mountford F / *Towers*	Franklin / *Moody*	Jackson / *Sheard*	Matthews / *Dunkley*	Bowyer / *Smith B*	Sale / *Sanderson*	Liddle / *Iddon*	Mannion / *Cheney*
18	A LEICESTER 23/12	8,000	W	22	5-1	3-0	Sale 4, 36, Matthews 30, Bowyer 50, [Mountford G 79] / *Rickards 46*	Herod / *Bradley*	Brigham / *Frame*	McCue / *Howe*	Mountford F / *Towers*	Franklin / *Smith S*	Jackson / *Sheard*	Matthews / *Dunkley*	Bowyer / *Rickards*	Sale / *Sanderson*	Liddle / *Iddon*	Mountford G / *Buckley*

LEAGUE NORTH 2nd PHASE

No	Date	Att	Pos	Pt	F-A	H-T	Scorers, Times, and Referees	1	2	3	4	5	6	7	8	9	10	11
19	H DERBY 26/12	5,600	W	24	4-2	2-0	Sale 25, 36, 84p, Basnett F 71 / *Carter 49, 55*	Herod / *Savage*	Brigham / *Nicholas*	McCue / *Parr*	Mountford F / *Bullions*	Franklin / *Leuty*	Jackson / *Musson*	Basnett F / *Smith*	Bowyer / *Carter*	Sale / *Lyman*	Soo / *Morrison*	Ormston / *Duncan*
20	A DERBY 2/4	21,791	L	24	1-2	0-1	Sellars 71 / *Lyman 13, Doherty 85*	Herod / *Eccles*	Brigham / *Nicholas*	McCue / *Parr*	Mountford F / *Bullions*	Franklin / *Leuty*	Kirton / *Musson*	Sellars / *Jones*	Windsor / *Carter*	Sale / *Lyman*	Soo / *Doherty*	Mountford G / *Duncan*
21	H PORT VALE 5/5	800	W	26	6-0	3-0	Mountford G 20, 32, 44, Sellars, Sale	Herod / *Prince H*	Brigham / *Bateman*	McCue / *Watkin*	Mountford G / *Painton F*	Cowden / *Griffiths H*	Kirton / *Cooper*	Mountford G / *Birks*	Sellars / *Roden*	Sale / *Wilshaw*	Jackson / *Bailey*	Basnett F / *Clunn*
22	A PORT VALE 9/5	5,550	W	28	4-2	0-0	Sellars 48, 55, Kirton 62, Jackson 75 / *Isherwood 84, Griffiths H 89*	Herod / *Prince H*	Brigham / *Bateman*	McCue / *Sproson*	Mountford F / *McKay*	Cowden / *Hughes*	Kirton / *Bray*	Windsor / *Roden*	Sellars / *Griffiths H*	Sale / *Isherwood*	Jackson / *Cooper*	Basnett F / *Allen*

LEAGUE NORTH 2nd PHASE (Continued)

Match details

No	Venue	Opponent	Date	Att	Res	Score	HT	Scorers	Opp scorers (italic)
23	H	EVERTON	19/5	2,500	W	5-1	2-1	Mountford G 30, Jackson 36, Sale 51, [Bayford 56, Sellars 85]	Catterick 43
24	A	CREWE	21/5	4,000	L	2-3	1-0	Jackson 20, 50	Hancock 58, Boothway 60, 84
25	A	EVERTON	26/5	8,000	L	2-3	1-1	Bowyer 31, Sale 86	Wyles 5, 75, Bentham 50

LEAGUE CUP Qualifying

No	Venue	Opponent	Date	Att	Res	Score	HT	Scorers	Opp scorers (italic)
1	H	WOLVES	30/12	8,542	W	2-0	0-0	Jackson 80, Bowyer 85	
2	A	WREXHAM	6/1	10,400	D	2-2	1-1	Sale 44,	Baines 19, Watson
3	A	WREXHAM	13/1	8,100	L	1-2	0-1	Mountford G 82	Baines 2, Dix 75
4	A	CHESTER	3/2	3,396	W	3-2	1-2	Mountford G 34, Sale 75, Basnett F 79	Armstrong 9, 15
5	H	CHESTER	10/2	10,843	W	7-0	3-0	Basnett F 11, 20, Sale 31, Mountford F	King
6	H	PORT VALE	17/2	13,000	W	8-1	5-1	Bas' 14, Mount' G 23, 42, 47, 63, 80, [Soo 24, 30]	Cardwell 35
7	A	PORT VALE	24/2	17,040	W	6-2	3-1	Sale 1, 47, Steele 35, 43, 85, Soo 63	McShane 28, Pointon W 55
8	A	WOLVES	3/3	17,784	W	3-1	0-1	Sale 51, 75, Mountford G 61	Buchanan 5
9	H	CREWE	10/3	8,525	L	1-2	0-2	Liddle 69	Boothway 22, 33
10	A	CREWE	17/3	12,649	D	2-2	1-2	Sale 1, 76	Sellars 18p, Bridges 43

LEAGUE CUP Proper

No	Venue	Opponent	Date	Att	Res	Score	HT	Scorers	Opp scorers (italic)
1:1	A	BURY	24/3	11,692	L	2-3	1-3	Steele 33, 46	Carter 6, Griffiths W 11, 20p
1:2	H	BURY	31/3	18,000	W	3-0	1-0	Sale 25, Basnett F 68, Mountford G 80	
2:1	A	MANCHESTER U (Maine Rd)	7/4	45,616	L	1-6	0-2	Chilton (og) [Smith 52, Rowley,]	Bryant 36, Wrigglesworth 41
2:2	H	MANCHESTER U	14/4	5,906	L	1-4	1-1	Whalley 9 (og) [Brigham (og)]	McCulloch 45, Bryant

MIDLAND CUP

No	Venue	Opponent	Date	Att	Res	Score	HT	Scorers	Opp scorers (italic)
1:1	H	ASTON VILLA	21/4	5,227	W	1-0	1-0	Jackson 30	
1:2	A	ASTON VILLA	28/4	16,200	L	0-2	0-1		Edwards 34, Goffin 65

Line-ups (Team = regular; Opp = italic)

Match	Side	1	2	3	4	5	6	7	8	9	10	11
23	Team	Leigh	Brigham	Watkin	Mountford F	Cowden	Kirton	Mountford G	Sellars	Sale	Jackson	Bayford
23	Opp	Burnett	Jackson	Greenhalgh	Grant	Humphreys	Watson	Makin	Ashley	Catterick	Bentham	Bayes
24	Team	Leigh	Brigham	Watkin	Mountford F	Cowden	Kirton	Matthews	Sellars	Sale	Jackson	Bayford
24	Opp	Haining	Tagg	Bateman	Miller	Hughes	Still	Hancock	Basnett	Boothway	Chandler	Hanson
25	Team	Leigh	Brigham	McCue	Mountford F	Cowden	Kirton	Mountford G	Sellars	Sale	Bowyer	Basnett F
25	Opp	Burnett	Jackson	Greenhalgh	Grant	Humphreys	Watson	Heath	Ashley	Wyles	Bentham	Makin
1	Team	Foster	Brigham	McCue	Mountford F	Franklin	Jackson	Matthews	Bowyer	Sale	Liddle	Ormston
1	Opp	Scott	Morris	Ashton	Alderton	McLean	Green	Davies	Dunn	Acquroff	Finch	Mullen
2	Team	Herod	Brigham	McCue	Mountford F	Franklin	Jackson	Matthews	Bowyer	Sale	Liddle	Ormston
2	Opp	Whitelaw	Jones	Jefferson	Franklin	Tudor	Bellis	Hancocks	Dix	Baines	Bremner	Watson
3	Team	Herod	Brigham	McCue	Mountford F	Franklin	Jackson	Mountford G	Bowyer	Sale	Liddle	Ormston
3	Opp	Whitelaw	Jones	Jefferson	Hughes	Tudor	Bellis	Isherwood	Dix	Baines	Bremner	Duns
4	Team	Herod	Brigham	McCue	Sellars	Mountford F	Jackson	Mountford G	Basnett F	Sale	Liddle	Howshall
4	Opp	King	Dyer	McNeil	Corkill	Stuart	Harris	Sanbridge	Astbury	Armstrong	eott	Newsome
5	Team	Herod	Brigham	McCue	Mountford F	Franklin	Jackson	Matthews	Peppitt	Sale	Liddle	Pearson
5	Opp	King	Tucker	McNeil	Hatton	Pincott	Williams	Heary	Astbury	Armstrong	Bett	Howshall
6	Team	Herod	Brigham	McCue	Mountford F	Franklin	Jackson	Mountford G	Peppitt	Sale	Soo	Basnett F
6	Opp	King	Griffiths H	Bateman	Hannah	Cardwell	Lane	McDowall	McDowall	Booth	Sproson	McShane
7	Team	Herod	Brigham	McCue	Mountford F	Franklin	Soo	Matthews	Peppitt	Sale	Steele	Basnett F
7	Opp	Prince H	Lane	Sproson	Pointon F	Cardwell	Cooper	Clough	McDowall	Pointon W	Bellis	McShane
8	Team	Herod	Brigham	McCue	Mountford F	Franklin	Jackson	Matthews	Mountford G	Sale	Soo	Basnett F
8	Opp	Scott	Morris	Kirkham	McLean	Ashton	Alderton	Buchanan	Dunn	Acquroff	Dorsett	Finch
9	Team	Herod	Brigham	McCue	Sellars	Mountford F	Jackson	Mountford G	Liddle	Sale	Steele	Basnett F
9	Opp	Graham	Tagg	Still	Hill	Hughes	Bray	Jones	Liddle	Boothway	Chandler	Makin
10	Team	Herod	Brigham	McCue	Franklin	Mountford F	Soo	Matthews	Mountford G	Sale	Steele	Basnett F
10	Opp	Graham	Tagg	Still	Hill	Hughes	Bray	Jones	McCormick	Boothway	Chandler	Makin
1:1	Team	Herod	Brigham	McCue	Mountford F	Mould	Soo	Mountford G	Bowyer	Sale	Steele	Sellars
1:1	Opp	Bradshaw	Hart	Gorman	Jones	Griffiths W	Halton	Worsley	Blunt	Berry	Drury	Carter
1:2	Team	Herod	Brigham	McCue	Mountford F	Franklin	Kirton	Mountford G	Basnett F	Sale	Soo	Sellars
1:2	Opp	Bradshaw	Hart	Gorman	Jones	Griffiths W	Hamilton	Worsley	Blunt	Berry	Drury	Halton
2:1	Team	Herod	Brigham	Watkin	Mountford F	Franklin	Kirton	Matthews	Sellars	Mountford F	Sale	Basnett F
2:1	Opp	Crompton	Walton	Roughton	Warner	Whalley	Chilton	Chadwick	Smith	Bryant	Rowley	Wrigglesworth
2:2	Team	Herod	Brigham	Watkin	Mountford F	Jackson	Kirton	Basnett AE	Basnett F	Sellars	Sale	Williams
2:2	Opp	Crompton	Walton	Roughton	McCulloch	Whalley	Chilton	Chadwick	Smith	Bryant	McKay	Wrigglesworth
MC 1:1	Team	Herod	Brigham	Watkin	Mountford F	Franklin	Kirton	Basnett F	Sale	Sellars	Jackson	Williams
MC 1:1	Opp	Wakeman	Potts	Cummings	Massie	Morby	Starling	Broome	Berry	Edwards	Iverson	Houghton
MC 1:2	Team	Herod	Brigham	Watkin	Mountford F	Franklin	Kirton	Matthews	Sale	Steele	Jackson	Williams
MC 1:2	Opp	Wakeman	Potts	Cummings	Massie	Callaghan	Starling	Goffin	Berry	Edwards	Parkes	Houghton

SEASON 1944-45

War League North (ended 23/12/1944)	P	W	D	L	F	A	Pts
1 Huddersfield	18	14	1	3	50	22	29
2 Derby	18	14	–	4	54	19	28
3 Sunderland	18	12	4	2	52	25	28
4 Aston Villa	18	12	3	3	54	19	27
5 Everton	18	12	2	4	58	25	26
6 Wrexham	18	11	3	4	40	25	25
7 Doncaster	18	12	0	6	48	27	24
8 Bradford PA	18	10	4	4	45	31	24
9 Bolton	18	9	6	3	34	22	24
10 Manchester C	18	9	4	5	53	31	22
11 STOKE	18	9	4	5	37	25	22
12 Birmingham	18	8	6	4	30	21	22
13 Barnsley	18	10	2	6	42	32	22
14 Rotherham	18	9	4	5	30	25	22
15 West Brom	18	9	4	5	36	30	22
16 Liverpool	18	9	3	6	41	30	21
17 Grimsby	18	9	3	6	37	29	21
18 Halifax	18	8	5	5	30	29	21
19 Chester	18	9	3	6	45	45	21
20 Blackpool	18	9	2	7	53	38	20
21 Burnley	18	8	4	6	39	27	20
22 Leeds	18	9	2	7	53	42	20
23 Sheffield Wed	18	9	2	7	34	30	20
24 Chesterfield	18	8	3	7	30	30	19
25 Darlington	18	9	1	8	19	19	19
26 Wolves	18	7	5	6	52	45	19
27 Rochdale	18	7	5	6	31	27	19
28 Crewe	18	9	1	8	35	33	19
29 Blackburn	18	7	4	7	43	41	18
30 Manchester U	18	7	4	7	40	29	18
31 Preston	18	8	2	8	40	40	18
32 Walsall	18	7	4	7	26	28	18
33 Gateshead	18	5	6	7	27	29	16
34 Northampton	18	7	2	9	45	53	16
35 Newcastle	18	5	6	7	51	38	16
36 Sheffield Utd	18	7	1	10	27	38	15
37 Hartlepool	18	6	3	9	41	25	15
38 Oldham	18	7	1	10	28	47	15
39 Mansfield	18	6	3	9	31	36	15
40 Nott'm For	18	5	5	8	22	40	15
41 Coventry	18	6	2	10	22	34	14
42 York	18	6	1	11	49	42	13
43 Middlesbrough	18	6	1	11	34	52	13
44 Bradford C	18	6	1	11	35	57	13
45 Accrington	18	5	3	10	29	60	13
46 Port Vale	18	5	2	11	29	46	12
47 Bury	18	5	2	11	28	36	12
48 Stockport	18	5	1	12	33	48	11
49 Hull	18	4	3	11	23	70	11
50 Southport	18	3	4	11	32	60	10
51 Lincoln	18	3	4	11	32	55	10
52 Leicester	18	4	2	12	32	56	10
53 Tranmere	18	3	4	11	23	46	10
54 Notts Co	18	2	1	15	20	53	5

	Appearances		Goals		
	Lge	Cup	Lge	Cup	Tot
Basnett, Albert (AE)	1				
Basnett, Fred (A)	8	9	1	6	7
Bayford, Eric	2		1		1
Bowyer, Frank	20	4	7	1	8
Brigham, Harry	22	14			
Brown, Roy	2				
Cowden, Stuart	15				
Cunliffe, James *	1				
Foster, Manny	5	1			
Franklin, Neil	21	11			
Herod, Dennis	12	13			
Howshall, Thomas		1			
Jackson, John	13	10	4	2	6
Kinson, Bill	4				
Kirton, Jock	8	3	1		1
Leigh, William	2				
Liddle, Bobby	6	5		1	1
Mannion, John	5		1		1
Marks, George *	2				
Matthews, Stan	8	7	4		4
McCue, Jock	21	12			
Mould, Billy		2			
Mountford, Frank	26	14		1	1
Mountford, George	14	9	6	9	15
Ormston, Alec	1	3			
Pearson, Tommy *		1			
Peppitt, Syd		2			
Podmore, Edgar	6				
Poulton, Wallace	8		4		4
Sale, Tommy	27	13	21	13	34
Sellars, Johnny	12	6	5		5
Soo, Frank	2	6		3	3
Steele, Freddie	13	4	5	5	10
Watkin, Cyril	7	2			
Williams, S *	1	2			
Windsor, Bobby	2				
35 players used	297	154	63	41	104
(own-goals)			3		3

* guest players

Stoke lost to the eventual League North Cup runners-up, Manchester United, who lost the final 2-3 on aggregate to Bolton Wanderers.

North 2nd League (25/12/44-to 26/5/45)

	P	W	D	L	F	A	Pts
1 Derby	26	19	3	4	78	28	41
2 Everton	27	17	3	7	79	43	37
3 Liverpool	24	16	3	5	67	26	35
4 Burnley	26	15	3	8	56	36	33
5 Newcastle	23	15	1	7	71	38	31
6 Aston Villa	25	14	2	9	70	45	30
7 Chesterfield	24	10	9	5	40	24	29
8 Wolves	24	11	7	6	45	31	29
9 Manchester U	22	13	3	6	47	33	29
10 Darlington	24	13	3	8	61	45	29
11 Bristol C	24	13	2	9	55	33	28
12 Blackburn	24	13	2	9	62	51	28
13 Huddersfield	27	12	4	11	52	49	28
14 Wrexham	22	10	7	5	55	36	27
15 Bolton	23	11	5	7	52	35	27
16 Blackpool	24	12	3	9	58	42	27
17 STOKE	23	12	2	9	67	42	26
18 Lovell's	19	12	2	5	44	27	26
19 Cardiff	20	12	2	6	41	27	26
20 Grimsby	21	10	6	5	51	37	26
21 Birmingham	24	9	7	8	38	34	25
22 Crewe	23	11	3	9	50	50	25
23 Doncaster	20	11	2	7	44	26	24
24 Bradford PA	22	10	4	8	49	39	24
25 Accrington	24	9	6	9	39	41	24
26 Barnsley	24	11	2	11	39	42	24
27 Rotherham	20	10	3	7	41	37	23
28 Gateshead	21	9	5	7	46	42	23
29 Preston	25	9	4	12	41	56	22
30 Sheffield Utd	24	9	3	12	56	48	21
31 Sunderland	25	9	3	13	53	54	21
32 Leeds	22	9	3	10	53	55	21
33 Sheffield Wed	25	8	5	12	53	56	21
34 Leicester	21	7	6	8	40	38	20
35 Bath	20	10	0	10	50	48	20
36 Bury	20	8	4	8	38	43	20
37 York	22	8	4	10	48	56	20
38 Chester	22	9	2	11	49	61	20
39 Bradford C	20	8	3	9	43	46	19
40 West Brom	22	6	7	9	39	44	19
41 Hartlepool	21	8	3	10	34	54	19
42 Coventry	21	6	6	9	36	53	18
43 Nottingham F	17	5	7	5	23	25	17
44 Tranmere	23	8	1	14	40	56	17
45 Halifax	18	6	5	7	22	35	17
46 Lincoln	17	6	4	7	42	51	16
47 Manchester C	19	7	2	10	32	43	16
48 Northampton	14	6	3	5	23	30	15
49 Oldham	21	7	1	13	39	56	15
50 Stockport	19	7	0	12	31	50	14
51 Middlesbrough	24	6	2	16	40	73	14
52 Walsall	18	5	3	10	24	33	13
53 Port Vale	21	5	2	14	27	60	12

Stoke's 23 games (7 League North 2nd phase; 10 League Cup qualifiers; 4 League Cup proper; 2 Midland Cup)

FOOTBALL LEAGUE NORTH

Manager: Bob McGrory

SEASON 1945-46

No		Opponent	Date	Att	Pos	Pt	F-A	H-T	Scorers, Times, and Referees	1	2	3	4	5	6	7	8	9	10	11
1	A	BRADFORD PA	25/8	15,725		0	0-1	0-1	*Walker 60*	Herod	Brigham	Topham	Mountford F	Franklin	Kirton	Mountford G	Sellars	Steele	Sale	Basnett F
										Farr	*Stephen*	*Farrell*	*Stabb*	*Danskin*	*Greenwood*	*Smith*	*Shackleton*	*Hepworth*	*Downie*	*Walker*
2	H	BRADFORD PA	1/9	13,498		2	3-0	2-0	Steele 11, Sale 18, Basnett F 69	Herod	Brigham	Topham	Mountford F	Franklin	Kirton	Matthews	Sellars	Steele	Sale	Basnett F
										Farr	*Stephen*	*Farrell*	*Stabb*	*Greenwood*	*Dobson GA*	*Smith*	*Shackleton*	*Hepworth*	*Hawksworth*	*Walker*
3	H	MANCHESTER C	8/9	15,784		4	2-0	1-0	Mountford F 25, Mountford G 75	Herod	Brigham	Topham	Harrison	Franklin	Kirton	Mountford G	Sellars	Mountford F	Sale	Basnett F
										Swift	*Sproston*	*Clark*	*Walsh*	*Eastwood*	*McDowall*	*Bootle*	*Herd*	*Plimbley*	*Smith*	*Hilton*
4	H	LEEDS	13/9	6,594		6	2-1	1-0	Steele 33, 85 / *Hindle 86*	Herod	Brigham	Topham	Mountford F	Cowden	Kirton	Mountford G	Sellars	Steele	Sale	Basnett F
										Hodgson	*Hodson*	*Jones*	*Duffy*	*Butterworth*	*Coyne*	*Grainger*	*Stephens*	*Iceton*	*Hindle*	*Jones EW*
5	H	MANCHESTER C	15/9	12,882		8	2-0	1-0	Steele 10, 78	Herod	Brigham	Topham	Mountford F	Cowden	Kirton	Mountford G	Bowyer	Steele	Sale	Basnett F
										Daniels	*Clark*	*Barkas*	*Welsh*	*Eastwood*	*Brown*	*Linaker*	*Sproston*	*Smith*	*McDowall*	*Campbell*
6	H	MANCHESTER U	20/9	16,917		8	1-2	0-0	Mountford G 85 / *Reid 50, Hullett 80*	Herod	Brigham	McCue	Mountford F	Franklin	Kirton	Mountford G	Bowyer	Steele	Sale	Basnett F
										Crompton	*Walton*	*Roach*	*Warner*	*Whalley*	*Cockburn*	*Bryam*	*Reid*	*Hullett*	*Keeley*	*Wrigglesworth*
7	A	NEWCASTLE	22/9	46,349		8	1-9	1-3	Steele 35 / *[Hair 84, Wayman 86]* *Stub' 10, 27, 29, 55, 75, Clift 57, 65, Swinburne*	Herod	Brigham	Topham	Mountford F	Cowden	Kirton	Matthews	Sellars	Steele	Bowyer	Basnett F
										Hair	*Cowell*	*Corbett*	*Gordon*	*Smith*	*Crowe*	*Milburn*	*Clifton*	*Stubbins*	*Wayman*	*Hair*
8	H	NEWCASTLE	29/9	20,229		10	3-1	1-1	Mountford G 36, Basnett F 52, 54 / *Stubbins 45*	Herod	Brigham	Topham	Mountford F	Franklin	Cowden	Matthews	Mountford G	Steele	Sale	Basnett F
										Wood	*Cowell*	*Corbett*	*Gordon*	*Smith*	*Crowe*	*Milburn*	*Clifton*	*Stubbins*	*Wayman*	*Hair*
9	H	SHEFFIELD WED	6/10	21,451		12	3-0	2-0	Steele 3, 41, Basnett F 86	Herod	Brigham	Topham	Mountford F	Franklin	Cowden	Matthews	Mountford G	Steele	Sale	Basnett F
										Morton	*Swift*	*Pickering*	*Turton*	*Gale*	*Cockroft*	*Rogers*	*Thompson*	*Lindsay*	*Frogatt*	*Tomlinson*
10	A	SHEFFIELD WED	13/10	33,387		12	0-1	0-1	*Lindsay 13*	Herod	Brigham	Topham	Mountford F	Franklin	Cowden	Sellars	Mountford G	Steele	Sale	Basnett F
										Morton	*Swift*	*Pickering*	*Turton*	*Gale*	*Cockroft*	*Rogers*	*Robinson*	*Lindsay*	*Frogatt*	*Tomlinson*
11	A	SUNDERLAND	17/10	10,000		12	2-4	0-2	*[Brown]* Sale 48, Steele 60 / *Spuhler 12, Cairns 23, Whitelum,*	Herod	Brigham	Topham	Jackson	Mountford F	Kirton	Sellars	Mountford G	Steele	Sale	Basnett F
										Bircham	*Stelling*	*Ford*	*Waler*	*Howson*	*Wharton*	*Spuhler*	*Brown*	*Whitelum*	*Cairns*	*Burbanks*
12	H	HUDDERSFIELD	20/10	11,493		12	1-3	0-1	Steele 53 / *Glazzard 8, Rodgers 73, 75*	Herod	Brigham	Topham	Brown	Cowden	Jackson	Sellars	Antonio	Steele	Sale	Craddock
										Hestord	*Bailey*	*Barker*	*Willingham*	*Brown*	*Best*	*Bateman*	*Glazzard*	*Rodgers*	*Carr*	*Poole*
13	H	HUDDERSFIELD	27/10	18,831		14	6-2	2-1	Sale 5, Steele 29, 75, 78, Mount' G 50, Basnett F 55] / *Price 24, 89*	Herod	Brigham	Topham	Mountford F	Franklin	Cowden	Matthews	Mountford G	Steele	Sale	Basnett F
										McManus	*Bailey*	*Barker*	*Willingham*	*Brown*	*Best*	*Bateman*	*Glazzard*	*Price*	*Carr*	*Watson*
14	A	CHESTERFIELD	3/11	28,387		16	6-1	4-0	Matthews 8p, Sale 32, Basnett F 35, Davies 50 *[Steele 42, 47, 63]*	Herod	Brigham	Kinson	Mountford F	Franklin	Cowden	Matthews	Mountford G	Steele	Sale	Basnett F
										Middleton	*Milburn*	*Kidd*	*Binney*	*Whittaker*	*Hobson*	*Linacre*	*Glazzard*	*Davie*	*Carr*	*Collins*
15	A	CHESTERFIELD	10/11	26,301		17	1-1	0-0	Basnett F 70 / *Davie 83*	Herod	Brigham	Kinson	Mountford F	Franklin	Cowden	Matthews	Mountford G	Steele	Sale	Basnett F
										Middleton	*Milburn*	*Kidd*	*Binney*	*Whitaker*	*Hobson*	*Linacre*	*Pringle*	*Davie*	*Dooley*	*Collins*
16	A	BARNSLEY	17/11	25,000		18	2-2	2-2	Steele 19, 22, Basnett F 55 / *Asquith 35p, Smith 37, 90*	Herod	Brigham	Kinson	Mountford F	Franklin	Kirton	Matthews	Mountford G	Steele	Sale	Basnett F
										Holdcroft	*Harston*	*Ferrier*	*Mansley*	*Logan*	*Asquith*	*Smith*	*Pringle*	*Davie*	*Dooley*	*Collins*
17	H	BARNSLEY	24/11	18,707		20	4-0	1-0	Antonio 8, Matthews 48p, Steele 66, 71	Herod	Brigham	Kinson	Mountford F	Franklin	Cowden	Matthews	Mountford G	Steele	Antonio	Craddock
										Holdcroft	*Cunningham*	*Ferrier*	*Mansley*	*Logan*	*Asquith*	*Smith*	*Cooling*	*Fisher*	*Baxter*	*McGarry*
18	H	EVERTON	1/12	20,743		20	2-3	0-1	Sellars 68, Mountford G 75 / *Rawlings 32, Catterick 49, 78*	Herod	Brigham	Kinson	Mountford F	Franklin	Cowden	Matthews	Mountford G	Steele	Sale	Basnett F
										Burnett	*Jackson*	*Greenhalgh*	*Cookson*	*Jones*	*Bentham*	*Rawlings*	*Elliott*	*Catterick*	*Fielding*	*Boyes*
19	A	EVERTON	8/12	28,066		20	1-6	1-4	Steele 45 *[Wainwright 37, 70, 80]* *Catterick 25, 43, Rawlings 35,*	Herod	Brigham	Challinor	Mountford F	Cowden	Sale	Matthews	Mountford G	Steele	Antonio	Sellars
										Burnett	*Jackson*	*Greenhalgh*	*Mercer*	*Humphreys*	*Bentham*	*Rawlings*	*Wainwright*	*Catterick*	*Fielding*	*Boyes*
20	A	BOLTON	15/12	22,402		21	2-2	2-1	Peppit 11, Mountford G 20 / *Westwood 40, Hamlett 67*	Herod	Brigham	Challinor	Mountford F	Franklin	Cowden	Mountford G	Peppit	Steele	Westwood	Valiance
										Hanson	*Threlfall*	*Hubbick*	*Hurst*	*Hamlett*	*Murphy*	*Geldard*		*Lofthouse*	*Westwood*	*Woodward*
21	H	BOLTON	22/12	13,000		23	4-1	1-0	Antonio 38, Steele 60, 70, 72 / *Barass 47*	Herod	Brigham	McCue	Mountford F	Franklin	Cowden	Matthews	Mountford G	Steele	Antonio	Sellars
										Hanson	*Threlfall*	*Hubbick*	*Taylor*	*Hamlett*	*Murphy*	*Geldard*	*Hunt*	*Lofthouse*	*Westwood*	*Barnes*

No	V	Opponent	Date	Att.	Res	Score	HT	Scorers	1	2	3	4	5	6	7	8	9	10	11
22	H	PRESTON	25/12	18,603	W	6-0	3-0	Antonio, Steele, Sellars, Mountford G	Herod / *Fairbrother*	Brigham / *Beattie*	McCue / *Summerbee*	Mountford F / *Simpson*	Franklin / *Batey*	Cowden / *Anders*	Matthews / *Dougal*	Mountford G / *Horton*	Steele / *Iddon*	Antonio / *Mutch*	Sellars / *McIntosh*
23	A	PRESTON	26/12	26,784	W	4-2	2-1	Sellars, Dodd, Steele / Mutch, Iddon	Herod / *Fairbrother*	Brigham / *Beattie*	McCue / *Summerbee*	Mountford F / *Simpson*	Franklin / *Batey*	Cowden / *Anders*	Matthews / *Dougal*	Mountford G / *Horton*	Steele / *Iddon*	Dodd / *Mutch*	Sellars / *McIntosh*
24	A	LEEDS	29/12	22,000	D	0-0	0-0		Herod / *Hodgson*	Brigham / *Duthalt*	McCue / *Laking*	Mountford F / *Butterworth*	Franklin / *Holley*	Cowden / *Coyne*	Matthews / *Powell*	Mountford G / *Short*	Steele / *Ainsley*	Antonio / *Hindle*	Sellars / *Heaton*
25	H	SUNDERLAND	19/1	8,593	D	0-0	0-0		Herod / *Mapson*	Brigham / *Stelling*	McCue / *Jones*	Mountford F / *Willingham*	Franklin / *Lockie*	Cowden / *Houson*	Windsor / *Whitelum*	Bowyer / *White*	Steele / *Brown*	Antonio / *Davey*	Ormston / *Burbanks*
26	A	SHEFFIELD UTD	2/2	16,608	L	0-4	0-3	Collinridge 5, 44 Nightingale 16, [Rickett 63]	Herod / *Smith*	Brigham / *Furniss*	Challinor / *Shimwell*	Mountford F / *Machant*	Cowden / *Latham*	Hampson / *Forbes*	Mountford G / *Spuhler*	Peppitt / *Nightingale*	Steele / *Collinridge*	Antonio / *Brook*	Baker / *Rickett*
27	H	MIDDLESBROUGH	16/2	9,123	L	1-4	1-3	Murphy 26, 35 Spuhler 33, Stobbart 47	Herod / *Cumming*	Brigham / *Laking*	Challinor / *Stuart*	Mountford F / *Bell*	Cowden / *Shepherdson*	Hampson / *Gordon*	Peppitt / *Murphy*	Peppitt / *Stobbart*	Steele / *Stobbart*	Antonio / *Dows*	Ormston / *Douglas*
28	H	BURNLEY	23/2	11,689	D	0-0	0-0		Herod / *Strang*	Brigham / *Woodruff*	McCue / *Mather*	Mountford F / *Attwell*	Franklin / *Johnson*	Cowden / *Bray*	Matthews / *Chew*	Mountford G / *Morris*	Steele / *Jackson*	Antonio / *Haigh*	Basnett F / *Kippax*
29	A	GRIMSBY	16/3	15,000	W	2-0	1-0	Sale 27, Steele 86	Herod / *Moulson*	Brigham / *Vincent*	Challinor / *Hodgson JV*	Mountford F / *Hadson S*	Franklin / *Charlesworth*	Kirton / *Buck*	Matthews / *Crack*	Steele / *Moore N*	Steele / *Howe*	Sale / *Jones TW*	Baker / *Wardle*
30	H	BLACKPOOL	23/3	16,416	W	6-3	2-1	Steele 12, 75, 78, 88, Sale 17, 80 / Blair 20, Mortensen 48, 65	Herod / *Roxburgh*	Brigham / *Burke*	Kinson / *Lewis*	Mountford F / *Kelly*	Mould / *Stuart*	Kirton / *Johnston*	Matthews / *Hobson*	Peppitt / *Buchan*	Steele / *Mortensen*	Sale / *Blair*	Baker / *O'Donnell H*
31	A	BLACKPOOL	30/3	13,006	L	1-2	1-0	Sale 30 / Mortensen 80, O'Donnell H 84	Herod / *Thorpe*	Brigham / *Burke*	McCue / *Lewis*	Mountford F / *Kelly*	Mould / *Stuart*	Kirton / *Johnston*	Windsor / *Hobson*	Peppitt / *Mortensen*	Steele / *Dodds*	Sale / *Buchan*	Baker / *O'Donnell H*
32	H	BURNLEY	1/4	10,607	L	0-1	0-0	/ Morris	Herod / *Strong*	Brigham / *Woodruff*	McCue / *Mather*	Mountford F / *Loughran*	Mould / *Johnson*	Kirton / *Bray*	Basnett F / *Milner*	Peppitt / *Murray*	Steele / *Jackson*	Sale / *Burns*	Ormston / *Kippax*
33	H	LIVERPOOL	6/4	11,000	L	0-1	0-1	/ Done 24	Herod / *Sidlow*	Brigham / *Harley*	McCue / *Ramsden*	Mountford F / *Lambert*	Brown / *Hughes*	Kirton / *Paisley*	Mountford G / *Niewenhuys*	Peppitt / *Balmer*	Sellars / *Done*	Sale / *Fagan*	Ormston / *Priday*
34	H	SHEFFIELD UTD	8/4	9,000	L	0-3	0-2	/ Thompson 6, Hagan 37, Nightingale 89	Herod / *Smith*	Brigham / *Furniss*	McCue / *Hooper*	Mountford F / *Brook*	Brown / *Latham*	Kirton / *Forbes*	Peppitt / *Rickett*	Antonio / *Nightingale*	Sale / *Thompson*	Ormston / *Hagan*	Baker / *Reid*
35	A	LIVERPOOL	13/4	23,880	L	1-4	0-3	Peppitt 80 / Priday 29, 37, Fagan 44, Balmer 46	Herod / *Sidlow*	Brigham / *Westby*	McCue / *Ramsden*	Mountford F / *Taylor*	Mould / *Hughes*	Kirton / *Spicer*	Sellars / *Niewenhuys*	Sellars / *Balmer*	Peppitt / *Done*	Steele / *Fagan*	Baker / *Priday*
36	H	GRIMSBY	15/4	7,000	W	4-2	4-0	Boothway 10, Sellars 12, Peppitt 19, Vincent 48p, Lewis 63 / Ormston 21	Herod / *Tweedy*	Brigham / *Vincent*	Meakin / *Hodgson J*	Mountford F / *Hadson S*	Franklin / *Charlesworth*	Kirton / *Buck*	Sellars / *Lewis*	Mountford G / *Clifton*	Boothway / *Howe*	Mountford G / *Jones*	Ormston / *Wardle*
37	A	BURY	19/4	12,000	W	4-2		Sellars, Mountford G, Steele	Herod / *Unknown*	Brigham / *Unknown*	Meakin / *Unknown*	Mountford F / *Unknown*	Franklin / *Unknown*	Kirton / *Unknown*	Sellars / *Unknown*	Mountford G / *Unknown*	Steele / *Unknown*	Peppitt / *Unknown*	Ormston / *Unknown*
38	A	BLACKBURN	20/4	9,000	L	1-5	0-0	Peppitt 89 / Smith 53, 81, 83, Campbell 67, 88	Herod / *Patterson*	Brigham / *Wightman*	McCue / *Cook*	Mountford F / *Whiteside*	Franklin / *Pryde*	Kirton / *Bell*	Sellars / *Godwin*	Mountford G / *Campbell*	Steele / *Smith*	Peppitt / *Stephen*	Ormston / *Langton*
39	H	BURY	22/4	12,206	W	2-0	2-0	Steele 36, Antonio 45	Herod / *Bradshaw*	Brigham / *Griffiths G*	McCue / *Quigley*	Sellars / *Griffiths W*	Mountford F / *Hart*	Kirton / *Halton*	Matthews / *Kishaw*	Antonio / *Herbert*	Steele / *Livingstone*	Baker / *Black*	Ormston / *Moss*
40	H	BLACKBURN	27/4	5,000	W	5-0	0-0	Antonio 48, 90, Steele 51, Ormston 70, 80	Herod / *Patterson*	Brigham / *Wightman*	Meakin / *Cook*	Mountford F / *Whiteside*	Brown / *Boydell*	Kirton / *Bell*	Mountford G / *Godwin*	Antonio / *Godwin*	Steele / *Smith*	Antonio / *Stephen*	Ormston / *Langton*
41	A	MIDDLESBROUGH	1/5	25,000	L	1-3	0-1	Steele 48 / Fenton 10, Dews	Herod / *Unknown*	Brigham / *Unknown*	McCue / *Unknown*	Mountford F / *Unknown*	Brown / *Unknown*	Kirton / *Unknown*	Mountford G / *Unknown*	Antonio / *Unknown*	Steele / *Unknown*	Baker / *Unknown*	Ormston / *Stephen*
42	A	MANCHESTER U	4/5	37,773	L	1-2	0-0	Peppitt 61 / Pearson 66, Buckle 85	Herod / *Crompton*	Brigham / *Hamlett*	Hampson / *Chilton*	Mountford F / *Aston*	Brown / *Whalley*	Kirton / *Cockburn*	Matthews / *Delaney*	Antonio / *Pearson*	Peppitt / *Rowley*	Sellars / *Buckle*	Ormston / *Wrigglesworth*

FA CUP

Manager: Bob McGrory

SEASON 1945-46

FA Cup

3:1 H BURNLEY 5/1 — W 3-1 — 21,776
Steele 20, 27, 78 / Morris 84 / Ref: J Briggs

Herod	Brigham	McCue	Mountford F	Franklin	Cowden	Matthews	Mountford G	Steele	Antonio	Basnett F
Foxcroft	*Woodruff*	*Mather*	*Martindale*	*Johnson*	*Loughran*	*Hayes*	*Morris*	*Jackson*	*Haigh*	*Kippax*

On a tricky pitch Steele nods in Basnett's cross. Morris is felled. Herod flings himself to save Jackson's pen. Kippax puts the rebound over (25). Steele volleys in Johnson's mistimed clearance and rounds off a five-man move with a grand low drive. Morris taps in from close range.

3:2 A BURNLEY 7/1 — L 1-2 — 18,403
Antonio 85 / Jackson 38, Kippax 56p / Ref: J Briggs
(Stoke win 4-3 on aggregate)

Herod	Brigham	McCue	Mountford F	Franklin	Kirton	Matthews	Mountford G	Steele	Antonio	Ormston
Breedon	*Woodruff*	*Mather*	*Wilson*	*Johnson*	*Loughran*	*Hayes*	*Morris*	*Jackson*	*Haigh*	*Kippax*

Cliff Britton's Clarets exert immense pressure. Brigham and Franklin clear off the line. Jackson's shot bobbles past the unsighted Herod. He is then fouled for the pen. Johnson denies Antonio on the line. Steele and Ormston both miss. Antonio dashes through to convert Matthews' pass.

4:1 H SHEFFIELD UTD 26/1 — W 2-0 — 35,306
Mountford G 13, Steele 75 / Ref: W Rothwell

Herod	Brigham	McCue	Mountford F	Franklin	Kirton	Matthews	Mountford G	Steele	Antonio	Ormston
Smith	*Furniss*	*Shimwell*	*Machant*	*Latham*	*Forbes*	*Jones*	*Nightingale*	*Collindridge*	*Brook*	*Rickett*

In steady rain, G Mountford swaps passes with Antonio to crack into the corner. Antonio's fierce shot knocks out Hooper. Ormston hits the post twice. Steele nets but the ball was out before Matthews' cross. Steele heads in Kirton's free-kick. Smith turns Steele's header onto the bar.

4:2 A SHEFFIELD UTD 28/1 — L 2-3 — 50,649
Antonio 30, Steele 31 / Collindridge 40, 51, 88 / Ref: W Rothwell
(Stoke win 4-3 on aggregate)

Herod	Brigham	McCue	Mountford F	Franklin	Kirton	Matthews	Mountford G	Steele	Antonio	Ormston
Smith	*Hooper*	*Shimwell*	*Machant*	*Latham*	*Forbes*	*Jones*	*Nightingale*	*Collindridge*	*Hutchinson*	*Rickett*

About 6,000 storm the cricket side of the pitch. Both teams have two goals ruled out. Smith fumbles G Mountford's shot. Antonio nets. Steele converts Antonio's pass. Collindridge's hat-trick comes far too late. He scores from close range, on the run and a header from Rickett's corner.

5:1 H SHEFFIELD WED 9/2 — W 2-0 — 40,452
Steele 22, 72 / Ref: J Williams

Herod	Brigham	McCue	Mountford F	Franklin	Kirton	Matthews	Mountford G	Steele	Antonio	Ormston
Goodfellow	*Swift*	*Pickering*	*Cockroft*	*Gale*	*Wands*	*Driver*	*Thompson*	*Aveyard*	*Froggatt*	*Tomlinson*

The rain keeps many fans away. Franklin plays on his chipped ankle but struggles. The rampant Steele heads two stunning goals from corners. Antonio fires wide. Brigham nearly deflects past Herod. Franklin nods Thompson's header off the line. Goodfellow denies Steele and Antonio.

5:2 A SHEFFIELD WED 11/2 — D 0-0 — 62,728
Ref: J Williams
(Stoke win 2-0 on aggregate)

Herod	Brigham	McCue	Mountford F	Franklin	Kirton	Matthews	Peppitt	Steele	Antonio	Baker
Goodfellow	*Swift*	*Pickering*	*Cockroft*	*Gale*	*Wands*	*Driver*	*Robinson*	*Aveyard*	*Froggatt*	*Tomlinson*

Skipper Robinson returns but Owls fail to find a way through. McCue and Franklin star. The gusty wind makes for a bitty game. Herod denies Tomlinson. Aveyard hits the bar. Steele fails to score when clear. McCue clears off the line from Aveyard. Biggest crowd of the season so far.

QF 1 H BOLTON 2/3 — L 0-2 — 50,735
Westwood 35, 71 / Ref: G Dutton

Herod	Brigham	McCue	Mountford F	Franklin	Kirton	Matthews	Peppitt	Steele	Antonio	Basnett F
Hanson	*Threlfall*	*Hubbick*	*Hurst*	*Hamlett*	*Murphy*	*Woodward*	*Howe*	*Lofthouse*	*Westwood*	*Moir*

On a frosty pitch Stoke's defence are pulled out of position. F Mountford deflects Westwood's shot wide, who then forces in Woodward's corner. Threlfall blocks a Steele thunderbolt. Moir sets Westwood up to tap in. Matthews replaces torn shorts with a PC shielding his modesty.

QF 2 A BOLTON 9/3 — D 0-0 — 65,419
Ref: G Dutton
(Stoke lose 0-2 on aggregate)

Herod	Brigham	McCue	Mountford F	Franklin	Kirton	Matthews	Peppitt	Steele	Sale	Baker
Hanson	*Threlfall*	*Hubbick*	*Hurst*	*Hamlett*	*Murphy*	*Geldard*	*Howe*	*Lofthouse*	*Westwood*	*Woodward*

Burnden Park Disaster. 33 killed as huge numbers cram into a small section of terracing. Stoke have the better of a subdued game on a surface chewed up by the crowd spilling onto it. Baker wallops the bar. Steele and Sale waste good chances. Woodward fires over Bolton's best effort.

VJ Day Friendly

H PORT VALE 17/8 — W 6-0 — 2,900
Basnett F 3, Steele, Sellars, Sale

Leigh	Brigham	Topham	Mountford F	Cowden	Kirton	Matthews	Sellars	Steele	Sale	Basnett F
Prince	*Bateman*	*Potts*	*Pointon F*	*Turner*	*Cooper*	*Clunn*	*Birks*	*Green*	*Johnson H*	*Allen*

Football League North

		P	W	D	L	F	A	Pts
1	Sheffield Utd	42	27	6	9	112	62	60
2	Everton	42	23	9	10	88	54	55
3	Bolton	42	20	11	11	67	45	51
4	Manchester U	42	19	11	12	98	62	49
5	Sheffield Wed	42	20	8	14	67	60	48
6	Newcastle	42	21	5	16	106	70	47
7	Chesterfield	42	17	12	13	68	49	46
8	Barnsley	42	17	11	14	76	68	45
9	Blackpool	42	18	9	15	94	92	45
10	Manchester C	42	20	4	18	78	75	44
11	Liverpool	42	17	9	16	80	70	43
12	Middlesbrough	42	17	9	16	75	87	43
13	**STOKE**	42	18	6	18	88	79	42
14	Bradford PA	42	17	6	19	71	84	40
15	Huddersfield	42	17	4	21	90	89	38
16	Burnley	42	13	10	19	63	84	36
17	Grimsby	42	13	9	20	61	89	35
18	Sunderland	42	15	5	22	55	83	35
19	Preston	42	14	6	22	70	77	34
20	Bury	42	12	10	20	60	85	34
21	Blackburn	42	11	7	24	60	111	29
22	Leeds	42	9	7	26	66	118	25
		924	375	174	375	1693	1693	924

	Appearances		Goals		
	Lge	FAC	Lge	FAC	Tot
Antonio, George	16	7	7	2	9
Baker, Frank	9	2			
Basnett, Fred (A)	18	2	8		8
Boothway, John	1		1		1
Bowyer, Frank	4				
Brigham, Harry	42	8	1		1
Brown, Roy	8				
Challinor, Jack	4				
Cowden, Stuart	21	1			
Craddock, Harry	2				
Dodd, John	1				
Franklin, Neil	23	8	1		1
Hampson, Eric	2				
Harrison, Stanley	1				
Herod, Dennis	42	8			
Jackson, John	2				
Kinson, Bill	5				
Kirton, Jock	25	7			
Matthews, Stan	20	8	2		2
McCue, Jock	15	8			
Meakin, Harry	3				
Mould, Billy	4				
Mountford, Frank	40	8	1		1
Mountford, George	32	6	8	1	9
Ormston, Alec	11	4	3		3
Peppitt, Syd	13	2	5		5
Sale, Tommy	23	1	8		8
Sellars, Johnny	21		7		7
Steele, Freddie	36	8	36	7	43
Topham, Cyril	12				
Vallance, Tommy					
Windsor, Bobby	3				
32 players used	460	88	88	10	98

LEAGUE DIVISION 1 — Manager: Bob McGrory — SEASON 1946-47

---

1. H CHARLTON — 31/8
Att 32,335 | D | Pt 1 | F-A 2-2 | H-T 1-1
Scorers: Ormston 21, Steele 50 / *Duffy 30, Welsh 63* — Ref: G Iliffe

1	2	3	4	5	6	7	8	9	10	11
Herod	Brigham	Meakin	Mountford F	Franklin	Kirton	Matthews	Antonio	Steele	Baker	Ormston
Bartram	*Turner*	*Shreeve*	*Dawson*	*Oakes*	*Johnson*	*Tadman*	*Revell*	*Robinson*	*Welsh*	*Duffy*

Former guest John Oakes clears Steele's shot off the line. Franklin dribbles out of defence to tee up Ormston. Duffy and Welsh net courtesy of Robinson's passes against the run of play. Matthews' dummy run draws three players and Steele fires in. Antonio stutters when clean through.

---

2. H BOLTON — 2/9
Att 23,214 | L | Pt 1 | F-A 1-2 | H-T 0-1
Scorers: Steele 75 / *Westwood 16, Woodward 55* — Ref: G Fletcher

1	2	3	4	5	6	7	8	9	10	11
Herod	Brigham	Meakin	Mountford F	Franklin	Kirton	Matthews	Antonio	Steele	Baker	Ormston
Hanson	*Threlfall*	*Hubbick*	*Howe*	*Hamlett*	*Forrest*	*Woodward*	*Moir*	*Lofthouse*	*Westwood*	*Rothwell*

6pm kick-off. Bolton's artistry opens up Stoke time and again. Woodward sets up Westwood to slam in. Westwood returns the compliment for Woodward to skip round Herod. Ormston's drive rattles the bar. Steele's header prompts City to wake up. Matthews fires over from five yards.

---

3. A MIDDLESBROUGH — 7/9
Att 43,685 | L | Pt 1 | F-A 4-5 | H-T 3-3
Scorers: Mountford G 27, Steele 34, 44, 81 / *Fenton 10, 29, 42, 90, Mannion 65* — Ref: R Mortimer

1	2	3	4	5	6	7	8	9	10	11
Herod	Brigham	Meakin	Mountford F	Franklin	Kirton	Mountford G	Peppitt	Steele	Baker	Ormston
Cummins	*Robinson*	*Hardwick*	*Bell*	*Shepherdson*	*Gordon*	*Spuhler*	*Mannion*	*Fenton*	*Dowes*	*Walker*

Micky Fenton's treble arrives from a tap in, a fierce shot and a back-heel. Mountford scores via a post. Steele beats two to fire home, crashes in from close range and nods in Ormston's cross. Mannion's shot flies in off the post. Ormston's bounces clear. Fenton rounds Herod to clinch it.

---

4. A BOLTON — 11/9
Att 24,616 | Pos 20 (opp 4) | L | Pt 1 | F-A 2-3 | H-T 1-1
Scorers: Ormston 28, Mountford G 80 / *Barrass 25, 62, Roberts 70* — Ref: C Fletcher

1	2	3	4	5	6	7	8	9	10	11
Foster	Brigham	Meakin	Mountford F	Franklin	Kirton	Mountford G	Antonio	Steele	Baker	Ormston
Hanson	*Hamlett*	*Hubbick*	*Howe*	*Atkinson*	*Forrest*	*Woodward*	*Roberts*	*Lofthouse*	*Barrass*	*Moir*

Walter Rowley's men shoot on sight. Barrass shoots off a post. Ormston's rocket is so fast Hanson fails to move. After pulling off a wonder save from Lofthouse, Foster allows Roberts' effort to slip in and misses a corner that Barrass heads home. Ormston sets up Mountford's tap in.

---

5. H DERBY — 14/9
Att 35,218 | Pos 16 (opp 20) | W | Pt 3 | F-A 3-2 | H-T 1-1
Scorers: Steele 15, Mount' G 65, Ormston 86 / *Carter 31, Doherty 55p* — Ref: H Hartley

1	2	3	4	5	6	7	8	9	10	11
Jepson	Brigham	McCue	Mountford F	Franklin	Kirton	Mountford G	Antonio	Steele	Baker	Ormston
Woodley	*Parr*	*Howe*	*Ward*	*Leuty*	*Musson*	*Broome*	*Carter*	*Doherty*		*Morrison*

Honeymooning McCue returns. Steele looks offside as he scores. Stuart McMillan's FA Cup holders field new man Frank Broome. At last a win. for Carter to nod in. Doherty is upended by Jepson for the pen. Mountford nets Steele's cross. Ormston converts Antonio's pass.

---

6. H LEEDS — 16/9
Att 22,315 | Pos 14 (opp 22) | W | Pt 5 | F-A 5-2 | H-T 2-1
Scorers: Steele 28, 88, Antonio 29, 80, / *Ainsley 25, 75 [Ormston 74]* — Ref: J Williams

1	2	3	4	5	6	7	8	9	10	11
Jepson	Brigham	McCue	Mountford F	Franklin	Kirton	Mountford G	Antonio	Steele	Baker	Ormston
Hodgson	*Bannister*	*Milburn*	*Price*	*Kane*	*Batey*	*Cochrane*	*Powell*	*Ainsley*	*Hindle*	*Grainer*

Jepson misses Cochrane's cross. Ainsley nods in. City stung into life. Steele nets a trademark header and Antonio races clear to beat Hodgson. Ormston tricks two defenders to crash in. Ainsley beats Franklin to drive home. Antonio slots Mountford G's centre. Steele heads in a corner.

---

7. H MANCHESTER U — 21/9
Att 41,699 | Pos 8 (opp 1) | W | Pt 7 | F-A 3-2 | H-T 1-0
Scorers: Antonio 19, Steele 58, 59 / *Hanlon 73, Delaney 78* — Ref: R Greenwood

1	2	3	4	5	6	7	8	9	10	11
Jepson	Brigham	McCue	Mountford F	Franklin	Kirton	Matthews	Antonio	Steele	Baker	Ormston
Crompton	*Carey*	*McGlen*	*Warner*	*Chilton*	*Cockburn*	*Delaney*	*Pearson*	*Hanlon*	*Rowley*	*Mitten*

A fit again Stan runs rings round Matt Busby's league leaders, dragging McGlenn about the pitch to create huge holes. Antonio smashes in off the bar. Steele beats Chilton for pace to hammer home and nods in Kirton's centre. Hanlon scores in a scrimmage. Delaney from a tight angle.

---

8. A PRESTON — 28/9
Att 22,787 | Pos 6 (opp 16) | W | Pt 9 | F-A 3-1 | H-T 2-0
Scorers: Steele 11, Ormston 15, Antonio 55 / *Shankly 63p* — Ref: S Roberts

1	2	3	4	5	6	7	8	9	10	11
Jepson	Brigham	McCue	Mountford F	Brown	Kirton	Mountford G	Antonio	Steele	Baker	Ormston
Fairbrother	*Beattie*	*Scott*	*Shankly*	*Hamilton*	*Watson*	*Dougal*	*Mutch*	*McIntosh*	*Wharton*	*Jessop*

Franklin and Tom Finney star for England in Belfast. Fairbrother performs heroics. Baker crosses for Steele to bullet a header in. Ormston taps in. Steele nods down a corner. Antonio nets. Frank Mountford trips Wharton for the pen. Jepson traps McIntosh's header between fist and post.

---

9. H SHEFFIELD UTD — 5/10
Att 29,146 | Pos 6 (opp 10) | W | Pt 11 | F-A 3-0 | H-T 1-0
Scorers: Steele 18, 85, 86 — Ref: W Dixon

1	2	3	4	5	6	7	8	9	10	11
Jepson	Brigham	McCue	Mountford F	Franklin	Kirton	Mountford G	Antonio	Steele	Baker	Ormston
Smith	*Shimwell*	*Cox*	*Machent*	*Latham*	*Forbes*	*Thompson D*	*Nightingale*	*Thompson C*	*Hagan*	*Rickett*

City outplay Ted Davison's League North Champions. Antonio splits open the defence for Steele to flick in. Steele screws in off a post from an acute angle to bring up his century in League football. Fred's hat-trick arrives with a header from Baker's cross. First clean sheet of the season.

---

10. A CHELSEA — 12/10
Att 68,189 | Pos 6 (opp 13) | W | Pt 13 | F-A 5-2 | H-T 1-1
Scorers: Steele 35, Ormston 50, 58, 78, / *Lawton 39, 46 [Kirton 74]* — Ref: C Barrick

1	2	3	4	5	6	7	8	9	10	11
Jepson	Brigham	McCue	Mountford F	Franklin	Kirton	Mountford G	Antonio	Steele	Baker	Ormston
Robertson	*Winter*	*White*	*Goddard*	*Harris*	*Foss*	*Spence*	*Walker*	*Lawton*	*Machin*	*Dolding*

George Mountford outpaces White. His shot hits the bar. Steele nods in. Lawton hooks in, later admitting he handled, and blazes in on the run. Ormston curls home, slots cutely and hammers in off the post. Kirton's 35-yarder makes the crowd gasp. Steele hits crossbar, post and keeper.

11 · A ARSENAL 19/10 — 60,266 · 7 · 18 · 13 · L 0-1

O'Flanagan 38
Ref: H Pearce

Stoke	Jepson	Brigham	McCue	Mountford F	Brown	Kirton	Mountford G	Antonio	Steele	Baker	Ormston
Arsenal	Swindin	Scott	Joy	Male	Compton	Waller	McPherson	Gudmundsson	Lewis	Curtis	O'Flanagan

The trauma of the Matthews saga take its toll. George Allison's struggling Gunners secure victory thanks to Dr Kevin O'Flanagan, an amateur outside-left, who cuts inside to net with a screw shot. Steele whacks the bar with a header. The game turns scrappy as Stoke shoot profligately.

12 · H WOLVES 26/10 — 37,881 · 9 · 2 · 13 · L 0-3

Mullen 25, Pye 29, 65
Ref: W Prescott

Stoke	Jepson	Brigham	McCue	Mountford F	Brown	Kirton	Mountford G	Antonio	Steele	Baker	Ormston
Wolves	Williams	McLean	Creek	Galley	Cullis	Wright	Hancocks	Alderton	Pye	Forbes	Mullen

Ted Vizard's in-form Wolves take control. Cullis wins the battle of the England centre-halves. He sets up Mullen who rounds two to net. Pye deftly fires home. Jepson misses a cross. Pye pounces. George Mountford is injured to nullify Stoke's attack. Steele has a goal disallowed for offside.

13 · A SUNDERLAND 2/11 — 57,290 · 7 · 6 · 15 · W 1-0

Baker 11
Ref: H Holt

Stoke	Jepson	Brigham	McCue	Mountford F	Franklin	Kirton	Matthews	Antonio	Steele	Baker	Ormston
Sunderland	Mapson	Stelling	Jones	Willingham	Hall	Housam	Duns	Lloyd	Whitelum	Watson	Burbanks

Baker latches onto a rebound to slot home. Franklin commands the centre of the field. Mapson denies Ormston at full stretch. Matthews shows neat footwork on a tricky surface. Mould lets in Burbanks but recovers to tackle. City are superior in all departments. A first ever win at Roker.

14 · H ASTON VILLA 9/11 — 38,919 · 9 · 10 · 16 · D 0-0

Ref: H Williams

Stoke	Jepson	Brigham	McCue	Mountford F	Franklin	Kirton	Matthews	Antonio	Steele	Baker	Ormston
Aston Villa	Rutherford	Petts	Cummings	Iverson	Moss	Lowe	Dixon	Martin	Edwards	Dorsett	Smith

City fail to break down Alex Massie's men who have only let in 13 goals this season. Villa's offside trap catches City out time and again. Potts heads Matthews' shot off the line. In steady drizzle the game degenerates into a roughhouse with the referee having to speak to several players.

15 · A PORTSMOUTH 16/11 — 37,999 · 6 · 20 · 18 · W 3-1

Steele 23, Ormston 38, Peppitt 66 / Reid 55
Ref: L Brown

Stoke	Jepson	Mould	McCue	Mountford F	Franklin	Kirton	Matthews	Antonio	Steele	Peppitt	Ormston
Portsmouth	Butler	Reekes	Ferrier	Wharton	Flewin	Dickinson	Barlow	Reid	Froggatt	McAlinden	Parker

Both sides probe. Steele heads in Peppitt's centre. Matthews shimmies clear but hits Butler. Ormston finishes a tidy move. Froggatt nods wide. Reid hammers home from 16 yards. Peppitt drives into the corner from Ormston's pass. Stoke sit back and soak up Pompey pressure with ease.

16 · H EVERTON 23/11 — 27,798 · 5 · 18 · 20 · W 2-1

Matthews 51, Antonio 88 / Dodds 32
Ref: H Moore

Stoke	Jepson	Mould	McCue	Mountford F	Franklin	Kirton	Matthews	Antonio	Steele	Peppitt	Ormston
Everton	Sagar	Jackson	Watson	Bentham	Jones	Farrell	McIlhatton	Wainwright	Dodds	Stevenson	Eglington

In driving rain Sagar touches over Antonio's header and Peppitt's shot. McCue blocks Wainwright's drive. Jock Dodds flicks McIlhatton's low corner home. Jackson deflects Matthews' effort into the net. In fading light the referee misses Antonio's handball as he stabs home in a melée.

17 · A HUDDERSFIELD 30/11 — 26,767 · 5 · 22 · 20 · L 0-1

Metcalfe 88
Ref: H Nattrass

Stoke	Jepson	Mould	McCue	Mountford F	Franklin	Kirton	Matthews	Peppitt	Steele	Baker	Ormston
Huddersfield	Hesford	Bailey	Beet	Smith	Briggs	Watson	Bateman	Glazzard	Brook	Thompson	Metcalfe

David Steele's bottom club struggle. Baker flashes wide. Hesford twists to save a Matthews free-kick and claws away Peppitt's header at full length. Frustration sets in. A dawdling Franklin loses the ball to Metcalfe who lashes in. Steele is felled, but no pen is given. McGrory is livid.

18 · H BLACKPOOL 7/12 — 28,728 · 5 · 4 · 22 · W 4-1

Steele 20, Peppitt 25, Baker 62, Dick 35, [Matthews 65]
Ref: H Holt

Stoke	Jepson	Mould	McCue	Mountford F	Franklin	Kirton	Matthews	Peppitt	Steele	Baker	Ormston
Blackpool	Wallace	Sibley	Kennedy !	Farrow	Hayward	Johnston	Munro	Dick	Mortensen	Blair	McIntosh

Joe Smith's long-time league leaders are slain. In difficult conditions Steele beats two to rifle home. Peppitt races through to net. Jepson denies McIntosh, but Dick nods in. Baker nets off both posts. Matthews beats five and flicks past Wallace. Kennedy departs for flattening Matthews.

19 · A BRENTFORD 14/12 — 29,172 · 4 · 21 · 24 · W 4-1

Peppitt 36, 80, Crozier 51 (og), Townsend 35, [Ormston 61]
Ref: P Stevens

Stoke	Jepson	Mould	McCue	Mountford F	Franklin	Kirton	Matthews	Peppitt	Steele	Baker	Ormston
Brentford	Crozier	Gorman	Munro	Toulouse	Smith G	Wilkins	Hopkins	Macauley	Townsend	MacDonald	Smith A

Stoke revel in the sticky conditions. Ormston twice fires wide. Townsend scores after Jepson's double save. Peppitt's neat footwork takes him clear to score. Crozier drops Peppitt's centre over the line. Ormston wins two tackles and cracks in. Peppitt slots Frank Mountford's free-kick.

20 · H BLACKBURN 21/12 — 23,518 · 4 · 5 · 25 · D 0-0

Ref: G Womersley

Stoke	Jepson	Mould	McCue	Mountford F	Franklin	Kirton	Matthews	Peppitt	Steele	Baker	Ormston
Blackburn	Hayhurst	Cook	Bell	Stephen	Pryde	Wightman	Rogers	Guest	Smith	Campbell	Langton

In Arctic snows Kirton blazes wide. Hayhurst saves Steele's header. Mould subdues England winger Langton. Rogers fails to net after nicking the ball past Jepson. Stoke press hard. Fog descends. Hayhurst touches Ormston's drive round. The ball bursts on a railing at the Boothen End.

21 · H LIVERPOOL 25/12 — 30,518 · 4 · 1 · 27 · W 2-1

Steele, Stubbins 82
(Ref: —)

Stoke	Jepson	Mould	McCue	Mountford F	Franklin	Kirton	Matthews	Peppitt	Steele	Baker	Ormston
Liverpool	Minshull	Lambert	Jones	Taylor	Easdale	Paisley	Nieuwenhuys	Balmer	Stubbins	Eastham	Liddell

A sell-out all-ticket crowd roars Stoke on. On a heavy pitch both sides pass well. Ormston injures his knee. City are quicker and more forceful. Minshull denies Steele and Matthews. Steele buries two bullet headers from Matthews' crosses. The score does not reflect Stoke's superiority.

LEAGUE DIVISION 1

Manager: Bob McGrory

SEASON 1946-47

No	Date	Att	Pos		Pt	F-A	H-T	Scorers, Times, and Referees	1	2	3	4	5	6	7	8	9	10	11
22	A LIVERPOOL 26/12	49,465	5	L 2	27	0-2	0-0	Nieuwenhuys 68, Stubbins 85	Jepson	Mould	McCue	Mountford F	Franklin	Kirton	Matthews	Peppitt	Steele	Baker	Ormston
									Minshull	Lambert	Jones	Taylor	Bush	Paisley	Nieuwenhuys	Balmer	Stubbins	Eastham	Liddell

The gates are closed with 20,000 locked outside. George Kay's Reds play neat football, but Stoke carry the greater threat. Pool's South African Nieuwenhuys whacks home a 25-yarder against the strong wind. Stubbins switches the ball from right to left foot before finishing with style.

No	Date	Att	Pos		Pt	F-A	H-T	Scorers	1	2	3	4	5	6	7	8	9	10	11
23	A CHARLTON 28/12	36,388	7	L 17	27	0-1	0-1	Purves	Jepson	Mould	McCue	Mountford F	Franklin	Kirton	Mountford G	Antonio	Steele	Peppitt	Baker
									Bartram	Croker	Shreeve	Dawson	Phipps	Revell	Hurst	Johnson	Robinson	Purves	Duffy

Stoke lack the injured Matthews and Ormston, and consequently their cutting edge. Charlton dominate territorially. Bartram denies Peppitt and Kirton. As Jimmy Seed's men pour forward, Mould and McCue tackle desperately. Jepson denies Johnson. Purves scores slots Duffy's cross.

No	Date	Att	Pos		Pt	F-A	H-T	Scorers	1	2	3	4	5	6	7	8	9	10	11
24	H MIDDLESBROUGH 4/1	33,986	7	W 3	29	3-1	1-1	Mitchell 33, 50, Peppitt 65 / Fenton 21 — Ref: R Mortimer	Jepson	Mould	McCue	Mountford F	Franklin	Kirton	Matthews	Peppitt	Steele	Baker	Mitchell
									Cumming	Robinson	Stuart	Bell	McCabe	Gordon	Spuhler	Dews	Fenton	Mannion	Walker

Fenton beats Franklin to daisy-cut home. Steele's injury restricts City but reserve left-winger Bert Mitchell stars. He slots after Steele's shot is blocked, then races on to convert Peppitt's pass. Matthews hits the bar, Peppitt follows up. Spuhler and Fenton fire wide for David Jack's men.

No	Date	Att	Pos		Pt	F-A	H-T	Scorers	1	2	3	4	5	6	7	8	9	10	11
25	A DERBY 18/1	31,156	8	L 10	29	0-3	0-1	Stamps 21, Carter 84, Harrison 85 — Ref: H Hartley	Jepson	Mould	McCue	Mountford F	Franklin	Kirton	Matthews	Mountford G	Peppitt	Baker	Ormston
									Grant	Mozley	Howe	Ward	Leuty	Musson	Harrison	Carter	Morrison	Stamps	Broome

City lack Steele (leg muscle). Derby's biggest crowd of the season see Stoke wilt. Slack marking allows Stamps to head in Broome's free-kick. Peppitt is denied a goal by the linesman's flag. Carter initiates and finishes a close passing move. Harrison wallops in a 20-yarder. Well beaten.

No	Date	Att	Pos		Pt	F-A	H-T	Scorers	1	2	3	4	5	6	7	8	9	10	11
26	H PRESTON 1/2	32,753	8	W 2	31	5-0	1-0	Peppitt 27, 55, Steele 54, 59 [Ormston 76] — Ref: S Roberts	Jepson	Mould	McCue	Sellars	Franklin	Wordley	Matthews	Peppitt	Steele	Baker	Ormston
									Fairbrother	Nuttall	Scott	Shankly	Williams	Hamilton	Finney	McLaren	McIntosh	Beattie	Wharton

Despite the changes Stoke run riot. Stan wins the battle of the England wingers as McCue snuffs out Finney. Peppitt converts Sellars' pass and Ormston's cross. Steele nets left-footed and buries Matthews' cross. Ormston's cross-shot ends the rout. Matthews is injured by Scott's lunge.

No	Date	Att	Pos		Pt	F-A	H-T	Scorers	1	2	3	4	5	6	7	8	9	10	11
27	A MANCHESTER U 5/2 (at Maine Road)	8,456	7	D 6	32	1-1	0-1	Ormston 48p / Buckle 45p — Ref: R Greenwood	Jepson	Mould	McCue	Sellars	Franklin	Wordley	Mountford G	Peppitt	Jackson	Mitchell	Ormston
									Fielding	Aston	Walton	Warner	Chilton	Cockburn	Delaney	Morris	Hanlon	Pearson	Buckle

In appalling weather Franklin slips but Hanlon muffs. Mould handles. Buckle puts the pen wide (20). Mould is penalised for hands again. This time Buckle scores. Aston scythes down Peppitt. Ormston fires in the pen. Franklin roams forwards. Cledan through Ormston lashes just wide.

No	Date	Att	Pos		Pt	F-A	H-T	Scorers	1	2	3	4	5	6	7	8	9	10	11
28	H CHELSEA 15/2	30,469	4	W 14	34	6-1	2-1	Sellars 2, Ormston 5, 12, Pep't 11, 27, Machin 17 [Baker 18] — Ref: C Barrick	Jepson	Mould	Meakin	Sellars	Franklin	Kirton	Mountford G	Peppitt	Steele	Baker	Ormston
									Medhurst	Winter	Steffan	Machin	Harris	Macauley	Spence	Walker	Lawton	Goulden	Paton

A light covering of snow doesn't stop Mountford running riot. His shot is saved but Sellars follows up. Ormston nets two drives. Peppitt scores from a tight angle and races clear to net. Machin lobs Jepson. Baker dips in a 20-yarder. Lawton muffs two sitters. Billy Birrel's men humbled.

No	Date	Att	Pos		Pt	F-A	H-T	Scorers	1	2	3	4	5	6	7	8	9	10	11
29	H ARSENAL 22/2	31,642	3	W 17	36	3-1	1-0	Baker 23, Jackson 64, Sellars 71 / Rooke 81 — Ref: H Pearce	Jepson	Mould	Meakin	Sellars	Franklin	Kirton	Matthews	Peppitt	Jackson	Baker	Ormston
									Swindin	Scott	Barnes	Sloan	Compton	Mercer	McPherson	Logie	Rooke	Jones	Rutkin

As snow falls heavily Swindin pushes Baker's shot against a post. Baker nods in Ormston's cross. A triangular movement sets Jackson clear to net. Sellars lashes home after Swindin's error. Kirton breasts Jones' drive off the line. Rooke taps in. Jepson denies McPherson at full stretch.

No	Date	Att	Pos		Pt	F-A	H-T	Scorers	1	2	3	4	5	6	7	8	9	10	11
30	A WOLVES 1/3	55,592	4	L 1	36	0-3	0-3	Westcott 1, Mullen 22, Forbes 40 — Ref: W Prescott	Jepson	Mould	McCue	Sellars	Franklin	Kirton	Matthews	Peppitt	Steele	Baker	Ormston
									Williams	McLean	Crook	Galley	Cullis	Wright	Hancocks	Ramscar	Westcott	Forbes	Mullen

City's visit to Ted Vizard's leaders starts badly as leading scorer Westcott taps in. Williams moves from Baker. Sellars fires over. Stoke pile on pressure. Mullen nets on the breakaway. Forbes hammers high into the net. Crook handles and Ormston takes the pen but Williams saves (75).

No	Date	Att	Pos		Pt	F-A	H-T	Scorers	1	2	3	4	5	6	7	8	9	10	11
31	H PORTSMOUTH 22/3	27,708	7	D 16	37	1-1	0-0	Steele 55 / Reid 78 — Ref: L Brown	Jepson	Mould	McCue	Sellars	Franklin	Kirton	Matthews	Peppitt	Steele	Baker	Ormston
									Butler	Reekes	Ferrier	Scoular	Flewin	Dickinson	Froggatt	McAlinden	Reid	Barlow	Parker

A quiet game is roused by Reid's 35-yard drive which grazes the bar. Kirton provokes Stoke into life. His pass sets Steele free, who drives low under Butler. Jepson saves one-handed and Pompey appeal for a goal. Reid dashes in to net Dickinson's cross. Another home point dropped.

No	Venue	Date	Opponent	Attendance	Pos	Res	FT		Pts
32	A	29/3	EVERTON	40,092	6	D	2-2	14	38
33	A	4/4	GRIMSBY	26,537	4	W	5-2	16	40
34	H	5/4	HUDDERSFIELD	28,966	3	W	3-0	20	42
35	H	7/4	GRIMSBY	34,269	3	W	3-0	17	44
36	A	12/4	BLACKPOOL	30,000	4	W	2-0	2	46
37	H	19/4	BRENTFORD	28,685	4	W	3-1	21	48
38	A	26/4	BLACKBURN	26,323	3	W	2-0	18	50
39	A	3/5	LEEDS	21,714	2	W	2-1	22	52
40	H	17/5	SUNDERLAND	32,000	3	D	0-0	10	53
41	A	26/5	ASTON VILLA	39,947	2	W	1-0	7	55
42	A	14/6	SHEFFIELD UTD	26,890	4	L	1-2	6	55

Home 30,870   Away 33,188   Average 33,188

---

32. A 29/3 EVERTON — 2-0 (HT 2-0)
Baker 27, Peppitt 30 / Eglington 66, Fielding 88

City	Everton
Herod	*Sagar*
Mould	*Jackson*
McCue	*Greenhalgh*
Sellars	*Bentham*
Franklin	*Jones TG*
Kirton	*Farrell*
Matthews	*McIlhatton*
Peppitt	*Stevenson*
Steele	*Wainwright*
Baker	*Fielding*
Ormston	*Eglington*

The Grand National delays kick-off till 5.45pm. Matthews sets up Baker to net. Peppitt races clear to nod past Jones and net. City let slip a first victory at Goodison since 1905-06. Everton's long ball pays off. Eglington heads in a right wing cross. Mould fails to clear and Fielding nets.

---

33. A 4/4 GRIMSBY — 3-1 (HT 3-1)
Peppitt 7, Steele 25, 44, 72 / Cairns 9, Wardle 48 [Ormston 85p]
Ref: S Fox

City	Grimsby
Herod	*Moulson*
Mould	*Mouncer*
McCue	*Fisher*
Sellars	*Taylor*
Franklin	*Betmead*
Kirton	*Reeve F*
Matthews	*Wallbanks*
Peppitt	*Clifton*
Steele	*Cairns*
Baker	*Blenkinsopp*
Ormston	*Wardle*

City tear Charles Spencer's Grimsby apart. Peppitt nods in Mountford's cross. Steele lashes in a hat-trick, breaking Charlie Wilson's club goal-scoring record. His second is the best - a hook shot. Franklin has stitches above his eye. City's last ever five-goal league haul away from home.

---

34. H 5/4 HUDDERSFIELD — 1-0 (HT 1-0)
Steele 42, Ormston 57p, Baker 64
Ref: F Wort

City	Huddersfield
Herod	*Hesford*
Mould	*Bailey*
McCue	*Boot*
Sellars	*Barker*
Franklin	*Hepplewhite*
Kirton	*Watson*
Matthews	*Whittingham*
Peppitt	*Thomson*
Steele	*Price*
Baker	*Doherty*
Ormston	*Bateman*

In driving rain Stoke open at top speed. Steele heads in Mountford's corner. Peppitt is fouled. Ormston nets the pen. Steele and Baker go close. Steele latches onto Steele's pass to flash home. Herod is a total spectator. Sellars subdues Peter Doherty.

---

35. H 7/4 GRIMSBY — 2-0 (HT 2-0)
Ormston 27, Jackson 37, 60
Ref: S Fox

City	Grimsby
Herod	*Chisholm*
Mould	*Mouncer*
McCue	*Fisher*
Sellars	*Hall*
Franklin	*Betmead*
Kirton	*Reeve F*
Matthews	*Johnson*
Peppitt	*Clifton*
Jackson	*Reeve K*
Baker	*Cairns*
Ormston	*Wardle*

Hepplewhite constantly fouls Steele. Baker latches onto Steele's pass to flash home. Herod is a total spectator. Sellars subdues Peter Doherty. Jackson in for Steele whose head has suffered from Hepplewhite's attentions. In new kit, City rip into Town. Jackson flicks on for Ormston to race clear and bury. Peppitt hits the post. Chisholm fails to hold Baker's shot. Jackson tucks away. Jackson beats Chisholm in the air to nod in.

---

36. A 12/4 BLACKPOOL — 1-0 (HT 1-0)
Ormston 22p, Mountford G 53
Ref: H Holt

City	Blackpool
Herod	*Wallace*
Mould	*Garrett*
McCue	*Stuart*
Sellars	*Farrow*
Brown	*Hayward*
Kirton	*Lewis*
Mountford G	*Munro*
Peppitt	*Dick*
Steele	*McKnight*
Baker	*Blair*
Ormston	*McIntosh*

Each side has two playing for England against Scotland. Mitchell is felled and Ormston slots coolly. McKnight departs after Brown sends him flying into the low wall surrounding the pitch. Mountford rounds off Baker and Ormston's brilliant move. Stuart handles, but no pen is given.

---

37. H 19/4 BRENTFORD — 0-1 (HT 0-1)
Steele 72, Mountford G 78, Naylor 5 [Matthews 83]
Ref: P Stevens

City	Brentford
Herod	*Crozier*
Mould	*Munro*
McCue	*Oliver*
Sellars	*Macauley*
Franklin	*Smith*
Kirton	*Paterson*
Matthews	*Hopkins*
Mountford G	*Stewart*
Steele	*Townsend*
Baker	*Naylor*
Ormston	*Girling*

In blinding sunshine a four-man move ends with Naylor tapping in. City build up a head of steam. Steele has three chances cleared off the line. Crozier denies Baker one-handed. Steele and Mountford nod in Ormston's crosses. Matthews scores left footed. New club Div 1 points record.

---

38. A 26/4 BLACKBURN — 1-0 (HT 1-0)
Ormston 22, Matthews 60
Ref: C Womersley

City	Blackburn
Herod	*Marks*
Mould	*Cook*
McCue	*Bell*
Sellars	*Whiteside*
Franklin	*Pryde*
Kirton	*Horton*
Matthews	*Oakes*
Peppitt	*Campbell*
Steele	*Weir*
Baker	*Venters*
Ormston	*Langton*

Ormston fires Matthews' cross high into the net. A passing move sets up Steele, but Marks smothers. Herod saves at Weir's feet but is laid out. Kirton deputises while he receives treatment and makes a dashing save. Matthews scores a deflected shot. Weir nets but handles in the process.

---

39. A 3/5 LEEDS — 0-0 (HT 0-0)
Steele 75, 86, Short 54
Ref: J Williams

City	Leeds
Herod	*Toomery*
Mould	*Milburn*
McCue	*Willingham*
Sellars	*Gadsby*
Brown	*Holley*
Kirton	*Henry*
Matthews	*Grainger*
Peppitt	*Powell*
Steele	*Clarke*
Baker	*Short*
Ormston	*Heston*

Willis Edwards' relegated Leeds start well. Powell and Short go close. Holley's mastery of Matthews earns applause. Short heads in Powell's corner. Baker wastes when sent clear. Steele heads in Matthews' cross. Mould handles but City escape. Steele dives to head in Kirton's cross.

---

40. H 17/5 SUNDERLAND — 0-0 (HT 0-0)
Ref: H Holt

City	Sunderland
Herod	*Mapson*
Mould	*Spelling*
McCue	*Hudgell*
Sellars	*Housam*
Brown	*Walsh*
Kirton	*McLean*
Matthews	*Duns*
Mountford G	*Robinson*
Steele	*Davis*
Baker	*Lloyd*
Ormston	*Burbanks*

City lack Franklin, with England, Matthews sold, Frank Mountford and Peppitt injured. A scrappy game sees Stoke frustrated by their inability to finish. Mountford muffs an easy chance. Baker and Kirton hit the bar. McCue's tackle denies Robinson. A point lost in the race for the title.

---

41. A 26/5 ASTON VILLA — 1-0 (HT 1-0)
Mountford G 3
Ref: H Williams

City	Aston Villa
Herod	*Rutherford*
Mould	*Potts*
McCue	*Gutteridge*
Sellars	*Iverson*
Mountford F	*Moss P*
Kirton	*Parkes*
Mountford G	*Edwards*
Peppitt	*Dixon*
Steele	*Evans*
Baker	*Dorsett*
Ormston	*Smith*

In Whit Monday sun City start tigerishly. George Mountford flicks home Ormston's corner. The hen hits the bar. A ferocious game sees Frank Mountford, Mould, McCue and Iverson all limping. Matters become tense as Stoke opt to defend. Herod's flying save denies Dorsett's rocket.

---

42. A 14/6 SHEFFIELD UTD — 1-2 (HT 1-1)
Ormston 4 / Pickering 3, Rickett 47
Ref: W Dixon

City	Sheffield Utd
Herod	*Smith*
Mould	*Young*
McCue	*Cox*
Sellars	*Jackson*
Franklin	*Latham*
Kirton	*Forbes*
Mountford G	*Rickett*
Peppitt	*Nightingale*
Steele	*Collinridge*
Baker	*Pickering*
Ormston	*Jones G*

Herod misjudges Pickering's weak shot, which bobbles in. Ormston rifles in Mountford's cross. McCue slips. Rickett dashes in to score. Smith tips Mountford's shot onto the bar. Steele's header sticks in mud on the line. City run themselves to a standstill but the Championship is gone.

FA CUP

Manager: Bob McGrory

SEASON 1946-47

No	Date	Att	Pos	Pt	F-A	H-T	Scorers, Times, and Referees	1	2	3	4	5	6	7	8	9	10	11
3	A TOTTENHAM 11/1	65,681	7 / 2:6	D	2-2	2-0	Ludford 40 (og), Mountford F 42 / *Bennett 78, Ludford 87* / Ref: G Iliffe	Herod / *Ditchburn*	Mould / *Willis*	McCue / *Buckingham*	Mountford F / *Ludford*	Franklin / *Nicholson*	Kirton / *Burgess*	Matthews / *Walters*	Peppitt / *Bennett*	Steele / *Foreman*	Baker / *Dix*	Ormston / *Stevens*
3R	H TOTTENHAM 15/1	38,639	7 / 2:6	W	1-0	1-0	Matthews 29 / Ref: G Iliffe	Jepson / *Ditchburn*	Mould / *Willis*	McCue / *Buckingham*	Mountford F / *Ludford*	Franklin / *Nicholson*	Kirton / *Burgess*	Matthews / *Walters*	Peppitt / *Bennett*	Steele / *Foreman*	Baker / *Dix*	Ormston / *Stevens*
4	A CHESTER 25/1	18,500	8 / 3W:3	D	0-0	0-0	Ref: W Martin	Jepson / *Scales*	Mould / *Butcher*	McCue / *McNeil*	Mountford F / *Marsh*	Franklin / *Walters*	Kirton / *Lee*	Matthews / *Arthur*	Peppitt / *Burden*	Steele / *Yates*	Baker / *Astbury*	Ormston / *Hamilton*
4R	H CHESTER 29/1	22,663	8 / 3W:3	W	3-2	1-0	Steele 23, 55, Ormston 66 / *Hamilton 72, Yates 75* / Ref: W Martin	Jepson / *Scales*	Mould / *Butcher*	McCue / *McNeil*	Mountford F / *Marsh*	Franklin / *Walters*	Kirton / *Lee*	Matthews / *Arthur*	Peppitt / *Burden*	Steele / *Yates*	Baker / *Astbury*	Ormston / *Hamilton*
5	H SHEFFIELD UTD 8/2	39,688	6 / 9	L	0-1	0-0	*Brook 90* / Ref: R Mortimer	Jepson / *Smith*	Mould / *Furniss*	McCue / *Cox*	Sellars / *Jackson*	Franklin / *Latham*	Kirton / *Forbes*	Matthews / *Rickett*	Peppitt / *Brook*	Steele / *Nightingale*	Baker / *Hagan*	Ormston / *Collindridge*

Match 3 (A Tottenham): Herod denies Foreman and Bennett. McCue subdues Walters. Ormston's shot is going wide before Ludford, in trying to clear, nets. Mountford unleashes a 30-yard screamer. Joe Hulme's men fight back. Herod saves Dix's shot. Bennett forces in after a melée. Ludford's low shot levels.

Match 3R (H Tottenham): Queues form three hours before the 2.15pm start. Stoke pen home Spurs back. Ted Ditchburn makes countless brilliant saves. Willis clears Peppitt's effort off the line. Matthews sweeps home Ormston's centre. Ormston races 40 yards to fire just wide. Baker hits a post. Jepson has little to do.

Match 4 (A Chester): Frank Brown's Chester press hard, but Stoke's defence is organised. Steele beats Scales but McNeil clears off the line. Scales denies Ormston and Baker. Matthews and Baker hit the post. Yates nods wide and sees a volley saved. Two minutes from time Arthur muffs a golden chance.

Match 4R (H Chester): Despite heavy frost, blue lines and posts mean the game is on. Steele pivots to flash into the corner, then lashes in. Injured Mountford departs. Ormston's miskick sails in. Hamilton and Yates latch onto Jepson errors to net. Scales saves Matthews' pen. Mould heads off the line late on.

Match 5 (H Sheffield Utd): Stoke's first all-ticket match remains on despite the snow. City dominate. Baker shoots straight at Smith and then hits the bar. Cox handles, but no pen is given. Peppitt hits the post. Cox blocks Steele's shot. Brook curls a shot wide of Jepson. The goal is greeted by a silence of disbelief.

	P	Home					Away					Pts
		W	D	L	F	A	W	D	L	F	A	
1 Liverpool	42	13	3	5	42	24	12	4	5	42	28	57
2 Manchester U	42	17	3	1	61	19	5	9	7	34	35	56
3 Wolves	42	15	1	5	66	31	10	5	6	32	25	56
4 STOKE	42	14	5	2	52	21	10	2	9	38	32	55
5 Blackpool	42	14	1	6	38	32	8	5	8	33	38	50
6 Sheffield Utd	42	12	4	5	51	32	9	3	9	38	43	49
7 Preston	42	10	7	4	45	27	8	4	9	31	47	47
8 Aston Villa	42	9	6	6	39	24	9	3	9	28	29	45
9 Sunderland	42	11	3	7	33	27	6	5	9	32	39	44
10 Everton	42	13	5	3	40	24	4	4	13	22	43	43
11 Middlesbro'	42	11	3	7	46	32	6	5	10	27	36	42
12 Portsmouth	42	11	1	7	42	27	5	6	10	24	33	41
13 Arsenal	42	9	5	7	43	33	7	4	10	29	37	41
14 Derby	42	13	2	6	44	28	5	3	13	29	51	41
15 Chelsea	42	9	3	9	33	39	7	4	10	36	45	39
16 Grimsby	42	9	4	8	37	35	4	6	11	22	47	38
17 Blackburn	42	6	5	10	23	27	8	3	10	22	26	36
18 Bolton	42	8	5	8	30	28	5	3	13	27	41	34
19 Charlton	42	8	6	7	34	32	6	1	14	23	39	34
20 Huddersfield	42	11	4	6	34	24	2	3	16	19	55	33
21 Brentford	42	5	5	11	19	35	4	2	15	26	53	25
22 Leeds	42	6	5	10	30	30	0	1	20	15	60	18
	924	232	90	140	882	631	140	90	232	631	882	924

Odds & ends

Double wins: (6) Blackpool, Brentford, Chelsea, Grimsby, Leeds, Preston.

Double losses: (2) Bolton, Wolves.

Won from behind: (8) Derby (h), Leeds (h), Chelsea (a), Everton (h), Brentford (a), Middlesbrough (h), Brentford (h), Leeds (a).

Lost from in front: (0).

High spots: 5-2 wins at Chelsea and Grimsby.

The seven straight wins from April, which took City close to the title.

Steele's 31 goals.

The Baker and Ormston left-wing combination.

A new club record average attendance – only exceeded once since.

Finishing with the second fewest goals-against total.

Low spots: Coming so close to winning a first ever League title.

Failure to win away between 14 December and 4 April.

The Matthews Controversy and his departure before the final game.

Ever-presents: (0).

Hat-tricks: (5) Steele 3, Ormston, Peppitt.

Leading Scorer: (31) Freddie Steele.

Player	Appearances		Goals		
	Lge	FAC	Lge	FAC	Tot
Antonio, George	16		5		5
Baker, Frank	39	5	6		6
Brigham, Harry	12				
Brown, Roy	4				
Franklin, Neil	37	5			
Foster, Manny	1				
Herod, Dennis	14	1			
Jackson, John	3				
Jepson, Arthur	27	4	3		3
Kirton, Jock	37	5		1	1
Matthews, Stan	23	5	4	1	5
McCue, John	36	5			
Meakin, Harry	6				
Mitchell, Bert	4		2		2
Mould, Billy	30	5			
Mountford, Frank	26	4			
Mountford, George	23		6		6
Ormston, Alec	40	5	20	1	21
Peppitt, Sid	24	5	12		12
Sellars, John	17	1	2		2
Steele, Freddie	38	5	29	2	31
Wordley, Ted	5		1		1
(own-goals)				1	1
22 players used	462	55	90	6	96

Subscriber	Scorer of Best Goal	Opponents	Season	Competition
Stephen Allen	Mark Stein	Manchester U	1993-94	League Cup
Brian Andrews				
Stephen Armitt	Nigel Gleghorn	Plymouth	1992-93	League
Frank Armitt	Stanley Matthews	Luton	1962-63	League
Rex Audley	Freddie Steele	Preston	1944-45	League
Dennis John Ayling	John Ritchie	Arsenal	1970-71	League
Owen Bennion	Freddie Steele	Wolves	1943-44	War Lg Cup
Julian Boodell	James O'Connor	Cardiff	2001-02	Play-off
David Bostock	Calvin Palmer	Manchester U	1966-67	League
I A Brown	Peter Beagrie	Bournemouth	1988-89	League
David C Brownsword	Johnny King	Aston Villa	1959-60	League
George W Burgess	Ade Akinbiyi	Reading	2002-03	League
Brian Calvert	Stanley Matthews	Blackpool	1946-47	League
M Cartwright	Terry Conroy	Arsenal	1970-71	League
Paul Cashman	George Eastham	Chelsea	1971-72	League Cup
Malcolm Clarke	George Eastham	Chelsea	1971-72	League Cup
Gordon Clowes	Peter Beagrie	Bournemouth	1988-89	League
Neil Cutcliffe	George Eastham	Chelsea	1971-72	League Cup
Tom Dodd	Mark Stein	Manchester U	1993-94	League Cup
Stephen Dray	Stefan Thordarson	Charlton	2000-01	League Cup
Ole Egeriis	Micky Adams	Bristol City	1993-94	League
John George Garner	Paul Richardson	Notts Co	1978-79	League
Mick Grayson				
Ben Hackney	Peter Hoekstra	Reading	2003-04	League
Stephen W J Heath	Terry Conroy	Arsenal	1970-71	League
Les Holloway	John Ritchie	Manchester U	1971-72	League Cup
Ian Howe	Mark Stein	Manchester U	1993-94	League Cup
Joyce, Kevin & Janette James	Mickey Thomas	Liverpool	1982-83	League
Robert James Keeling				
Peter Kirkham	Freddie Steele	Blackpool	1948-49	League
Neil Kirkham	George Eastham	Chelsea	1971-72	League Cup
Steve Knowles	Mark Stein	Manchester U	1993-94	League Cup
Keith Lawson	Peter Beagrie	Bournemouth	1988-89	League
Barry Leigh	George Eastham	Chelsea	1971-72	League Cup
Jonathan Lowe	Peter Hoekstra	Reading	2003-04	League
Chris Lowe	Terry Conroy	Chelsea	1971-72	League Cup

Subscriber	Scorer of Best Goal	Opponents	Season	Competition
Paul Andrew Lunt	Mark Chamberlain	Birmingham	1982-83	League
Keith Mackenzie-Ingle	Peter Beagrie	Bournemouth	1988-89	League
Paul Marriott	George Eastham	Chelsea	1971-72	League Cup
Roger Martin	Stanley Matthews	Luton	1962-63	League
Duncan & Pat Mason	Paul Richardson	Notts Co	1978-79	League
Ted McCoy	Mark Stein	Manchester U	1993-94	League Cup
Chris Mills	Terry Conroy	Arsenal	1970-71	League
Gordon Morse	Jimmy Greenhoff	Birmingham	1974-75	League
Rob Nicholls	Graham Kavanagh	Bristol City	1999-00	Auto-Wind'
Mick O'Rourke	Stefan Thordarson	Charlton	2000-01	League Cup
Dougie Old	Dave Watson	Southampton	1981-82	League
Mark Oliver	Terry Conroy	Arsenal	1970-71	League
Dennis Plant	Peter Hoekstra	Ipswich	2003-04	League
Mike Preston	Stanley Matthews	Luton	1962-63	League
Gary Rowland	Robbie James	Southampton	1983-84	League
Stuart Rowland	Robbie James	Southampton	1983-84	League
Carolyn & Paul Ruane	Souleyman Oulare	Cardiff	2001-02	Play-off
Nigel John Rushton	George Eastham	Chelsea	1971-72	League Cup
Phil Ryles	Stefan Thordarson	Charlton	2000-01	League Cup
David Salmon	Terry Conroy	Arsenal	1970-71	League
Liam J Sims	Kevin Keen	Wolves	1994-95	League
Gordon M Sims	Mark Stein	Manchester U	1993-94	League Cup
Michael J Sparkes				
Mark Stanley	Terry Conroy	Liverpool	1975-76	League
Jonathan Tindall	Peter Hoekstra	Watford	2002-03	League
Bill Townsend	Stanley Matthews	Luton	1962-63	League
A Tunnicliffe				
John Twigg	Freddie Steele	Aston Villa	1946-47	League
Philip John Unwin	Terry Conroy	Arsenal	1970-71	League
Graham Walker	Denis Smith	Leeds	1973-74	League
Sara Wardle				
Stan Whitmore	Peter Dobing	Leeds	1967-68	League
Gary P Wilcox	Mark Stein	Manchester U	1993-94	League Cup
Craig Williams	Peter Beagrie	Bournemouth	1988-89	League
Bernard John Wood	Peter Beagrie	Bournemouth	1988-89	League
Pete Wyatt	John Ritchie	Southampton	1973-74	League
Steve Yates	Jimmy Greenhoff	Birmingham	1974-75	League